TABLE OF CONTENTS

VAULT EDITIONS

Copyright

This book is a new work created by Vault Editions Ltd.

ISBN: 978-1-922966-76-6

ART SUPPLIES YOU'LL NEED

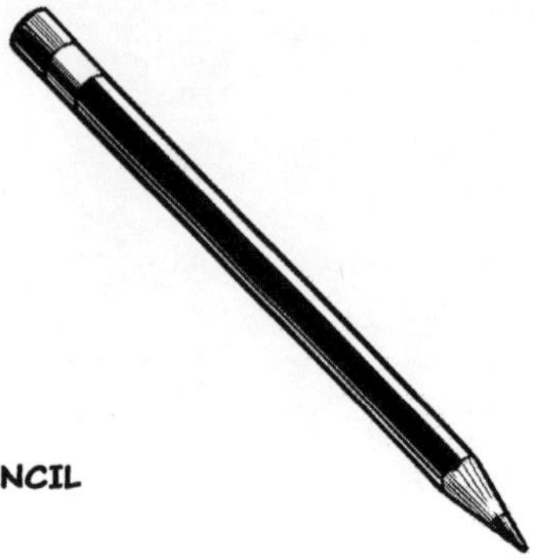

PENCIL

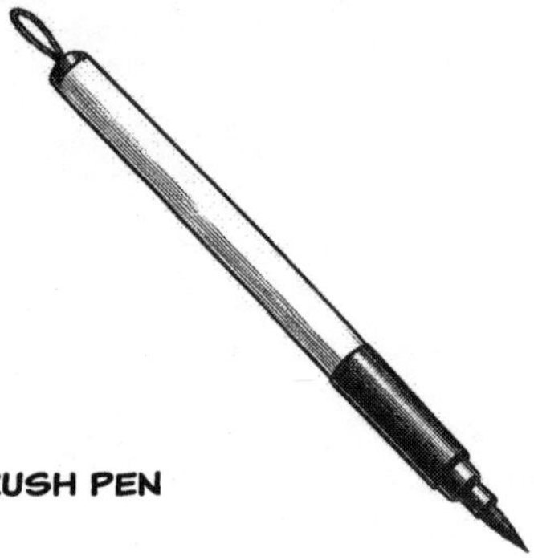

BRUSH PEN

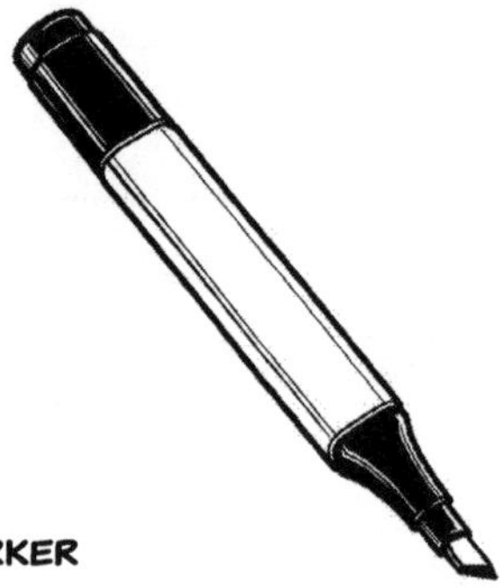

MARKER

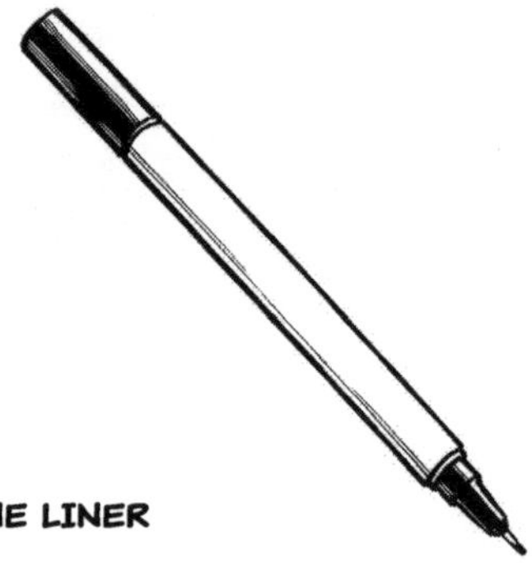

FINE LINER

Pro Tip: These tools are all helpful to have, but not all of them are essential. You don't need a full kit to begin your comic journey: a simple pencil or pen and a piece of paper are enough. Fancy materials can make the process smoother, but they won't replace the value of practice. What matters most is that you start drawing, experiment freely and build confidence through repetition. Everything else can be added later as your skills grow.

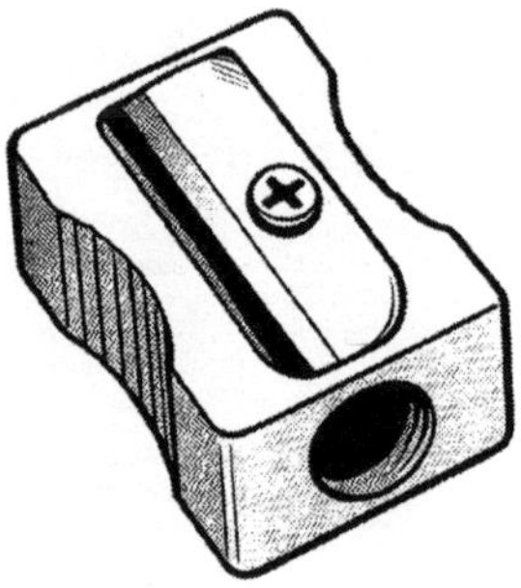

SHARPENER

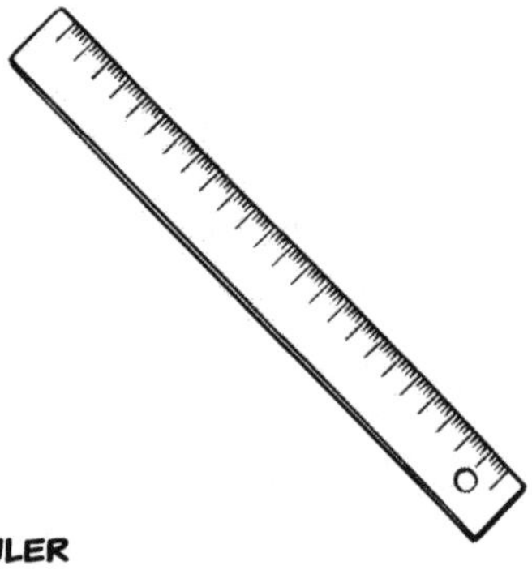

RULER

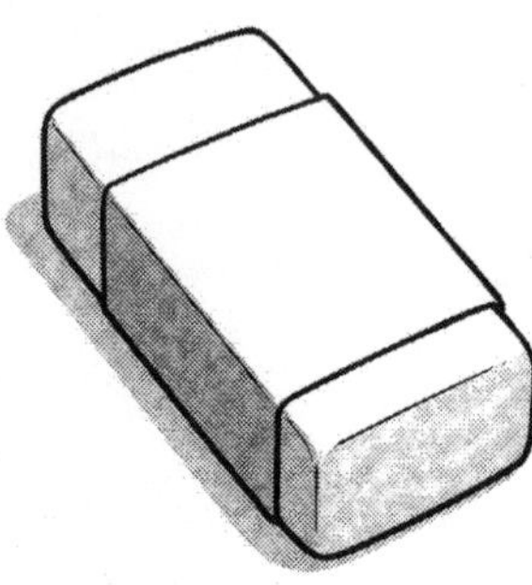

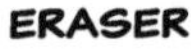

ERASER

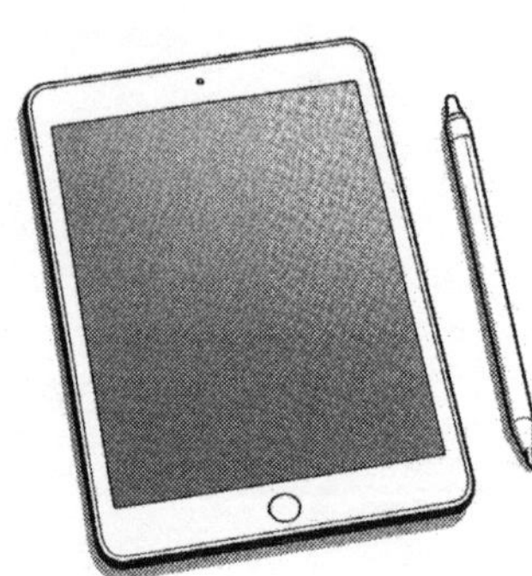

TABLET

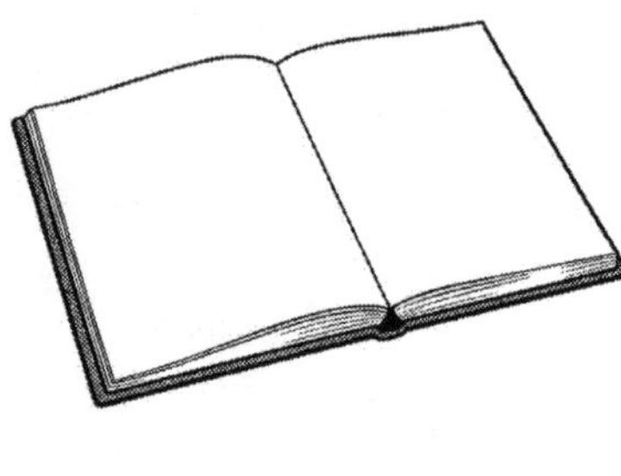

SKETCH BOOK

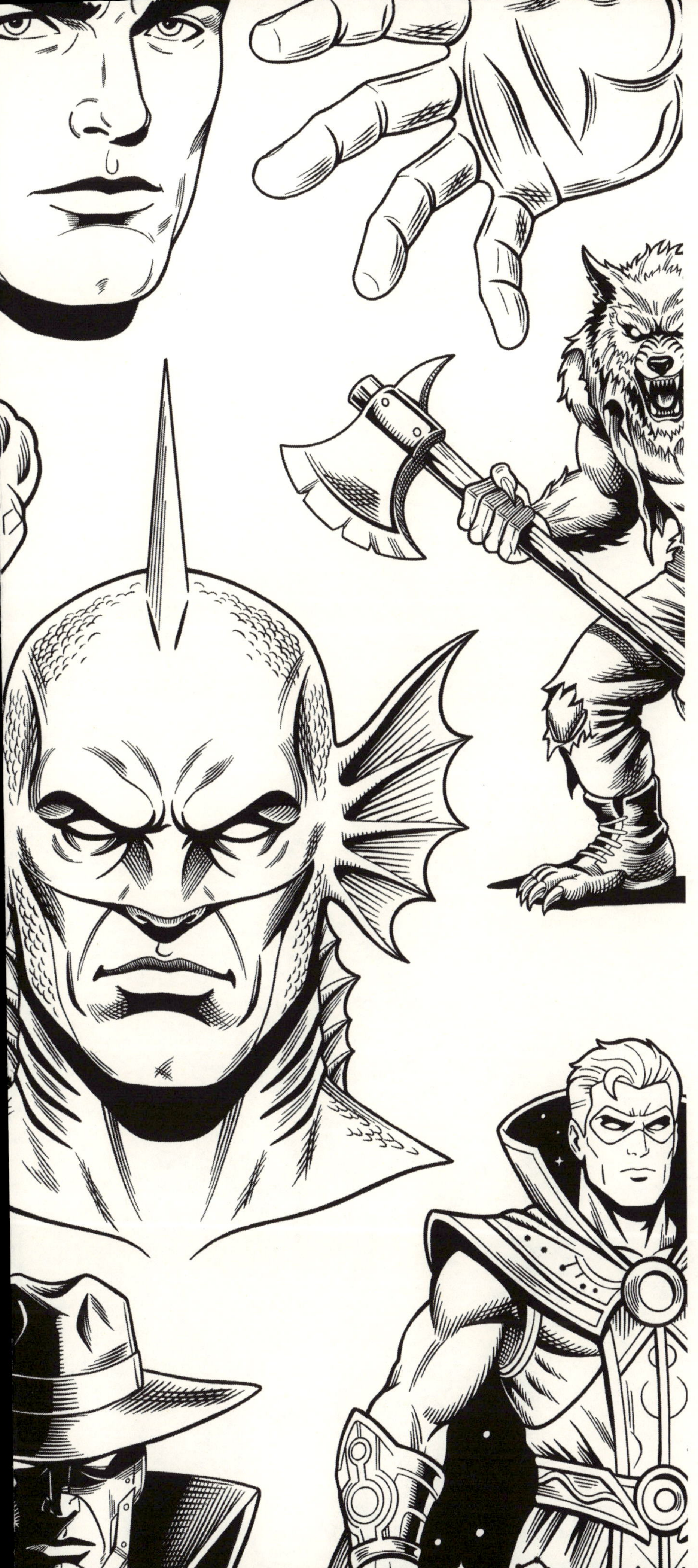

THE VAULT EDITIONS GUIDE TO
MASTERING
THE ART OF
DRAWING

HOW TO DRAW SUPERHEROES

A HELPFUL MANUAL FOR ARTISTS AND DESIGNERS

STEP BY STEP

HAND DRAWN
UNIQUE 48 DESIGNS
BEST QUALITY

Vault Editions

INTRODUCTION

Comics have become one of the most recognised and beloved visual storytelling traditions in the world, defined by expressive characters, dynamic panel layouts, and a visual language that spans countless genres and styles. Behind every compelling comic character are clear drawing principles: proportion, gesture, expression, and composition that artists have carefully developed over generations.

How to Draw Superheroes and Comic Characters for Beginners introduces these foundations through the Vault Editions 12-step drawing method. Each subject is broken into simple, guided stages that show you how to construct characters and scenes from basic shapes to finished drawings. This approach removes the guesswork and builds confidence as your skills develop with each exercise you complete.

Inside, you'll find essential lessons on faces, body types, expressions, and dynamic poses, along with popular character archetypes and impactful comic effects. Every design has been chosen for its relevance to the comic art style and its value to beginner artists.

Clear, intentional artwork makes each step easy to follow, helping you understand not just what to draw, but why it works. Whether you're new to drawing or exploring comics for the first time, this book provides a structured, accessible way to learn the fundamentals and begin creating your own characters and stories.

Download Your Files:

This book includes downloadable files to support your drawing practice. You'll find instructions on how to access them on the final pages of this book.

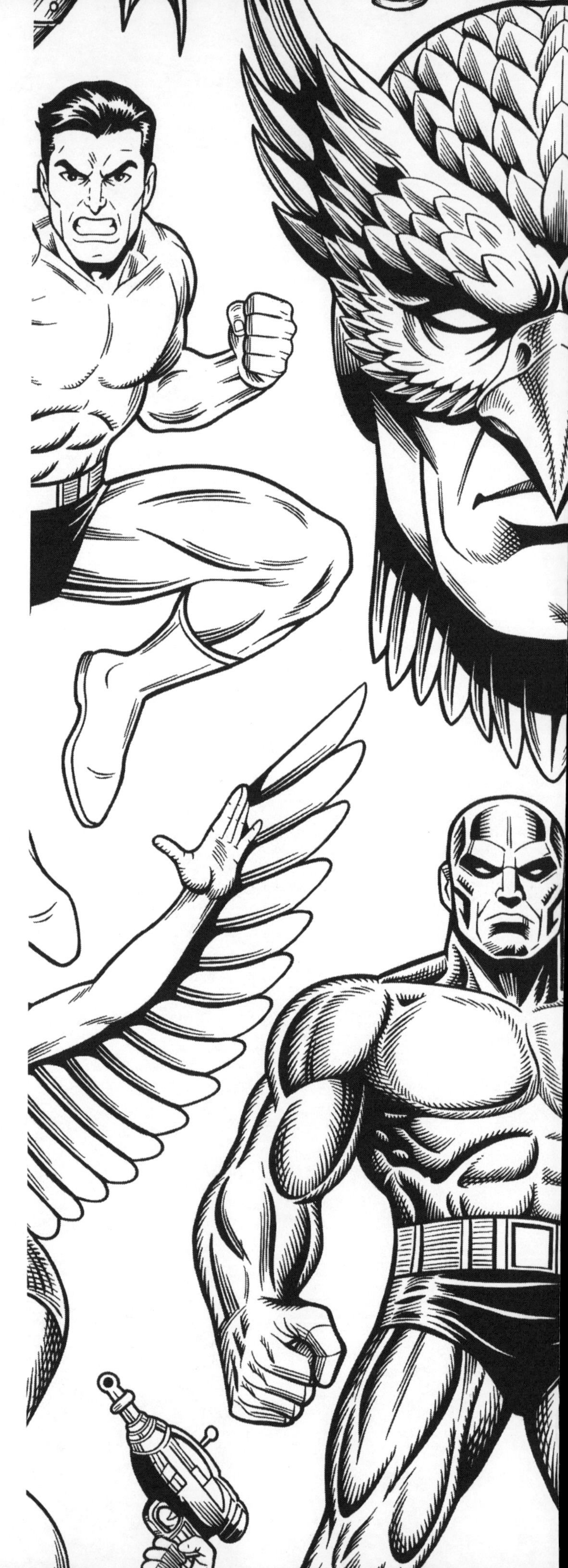

A MINDSET FOR SUCCESS

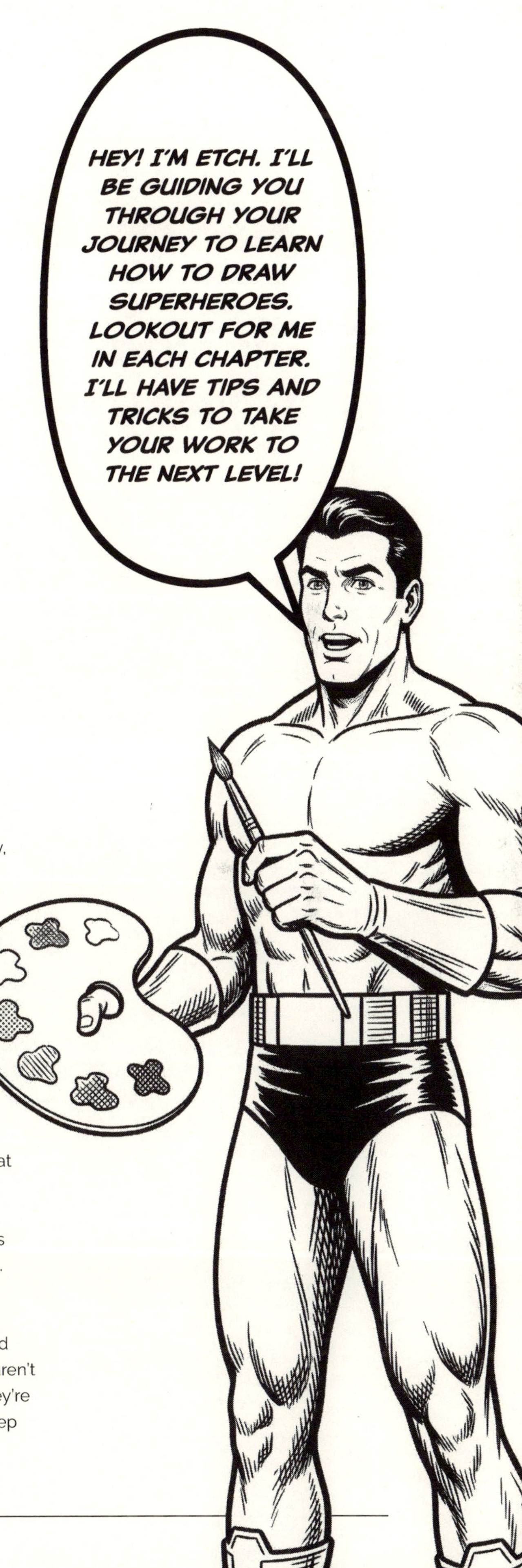

Pro Tip: Learning to draw comics is as much about mindset as it is about technique. When you start, it's easy to get caught up comparing your work to the artists you admire, but every one of them began exactly where you are, with clumsy lines and uncertain strokes. The key is to accept that progress in drawing isn't about perfection, it's about persistence. Your goal isn't to make a masterpiece every time you pick up a pencil; it's to build the habit of drawing, to show up each day and make something.

One of the most important skills you'll develop early on is resilience. You'll have days when your proportions feel wrong, when your characters look stiff, or when you can't capture the emotion you imagined. That's normal. Instead of judging those drawings harshly, use them as markers of growth. Every page you fill brings you closer to control, confidence, and understanding. Finishing a sketch, even one you don't love, is far more valuable than abandoning it in frustration.

Consistency is what transforms beginners into artists. Draw every day, even if it's just for ten minutes. Sketching a single head, hand, or expression builds your visual memory and strengthens your line control. Over time, these small efforts compound into noticeable improvement. Learn to celebrate incremental successes: a cleaner line, a better pose, a more expressive face. Each one is proof that your hard work is paying off.

Ultimately, learning to draw comics is about falling in love with the process. When you approach practice with patience and curiosity rather than expectation, you'll improve faster, and you'll enjoy it more. The best artists aren't those who never make mistakes. They're the ones who embrace them and keep drawing anyway.

01| THE HUMAN FIGURE

YOUR FOUNDATION FOR EVERY HERO

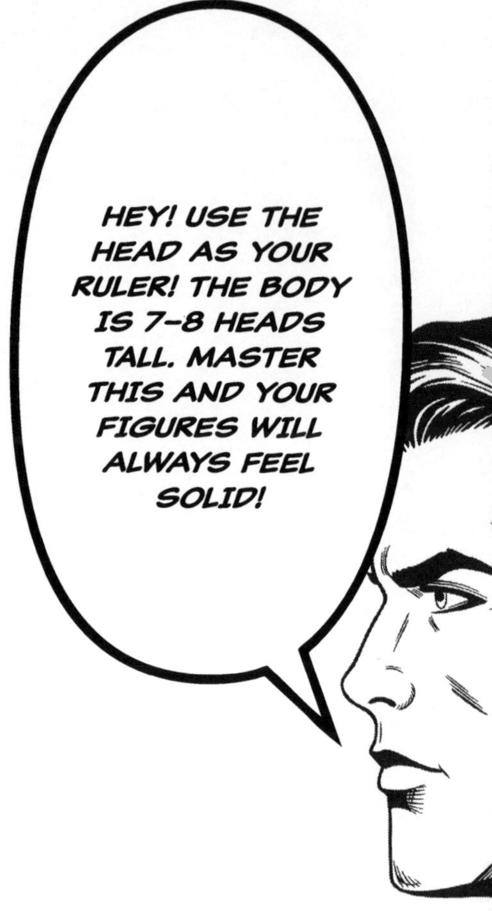

Before you can design a jaw-dropping superhero, a cunning villain, or a quirky sidekick, you need to master the most fundamental tool in your artistic arsenal: the human body.

Think of this chapter as your training ground. Every great comics artist built their iconic style on a rock-solid understanding of human anatomy. The exaggerated muscles, the dynamic poses, the expressive faces that leap off the page: none of that is possible without first learning the rules. And the good news? Once you know the rules, you'll know exactly how to break them.

The human body is both your greatest challenge and your greatest asset as a comics artist. It is something every single reader will instinctively respond to, because we all live in one. That means your audience will notice when something feels off, even if they can't quite put their finger on why. A figure that's slightly out of proportion, a hand that doesn't quite sit right, a face where the eyes are just a little too far apart: these are the things that pull a reader out of the story. But when you get it right, when your figures feel solid, believable and alive, readers stop noticing the art entirely and lose themselves in the world you've created. That's the goal.

The great secret that every experienced artist knows is that drawing convincing figures is not about raw talent. It's about understanding a set of principles that can be learned, practised and gradually made your own. Anatomy isn't a barrier to creativity, it's the foundation that makes creativity possible. Once your hand and eye understand how the body is put together, you'll find that dynamic poses, expressive characters and bold stylistic choices come far more naturally than you'd expect.

In this chapter, we'll tackle both the male and female figure, exploring how proportion, structure, and gesture work differently across body types. We'll break the body down into manageable building blocks, so no more staring at a blank page wondering where to start.
It's worth taking your time here. The artists who progress fastest are rarely the ones who rush through the fundamentals to get to the exciting stuff. They're the ones who put in the work early, build a strong foundation, and find that everything else follows naturally. Consider this chapter your investment in every drawing you'll ever make from this point forward.

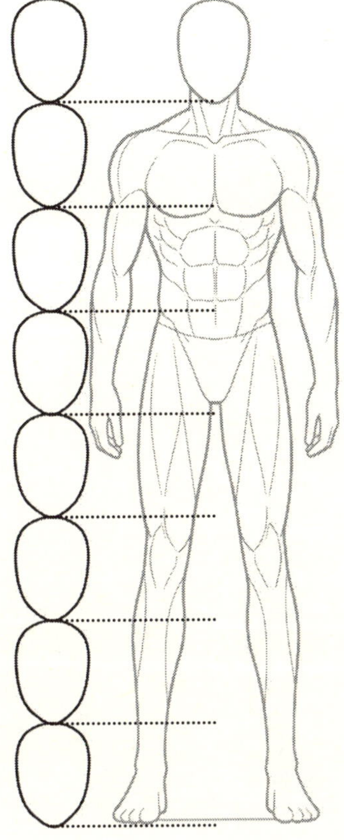

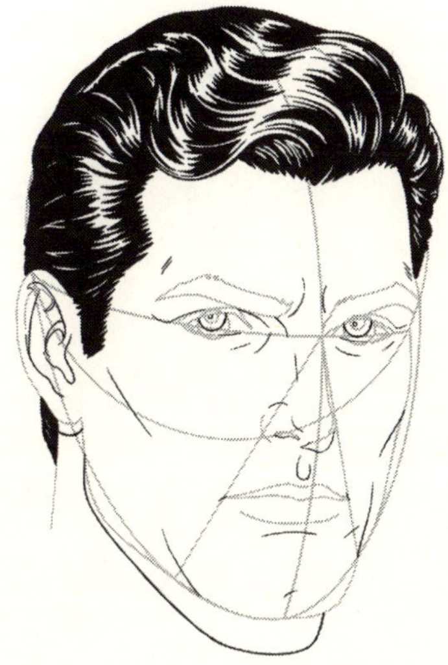

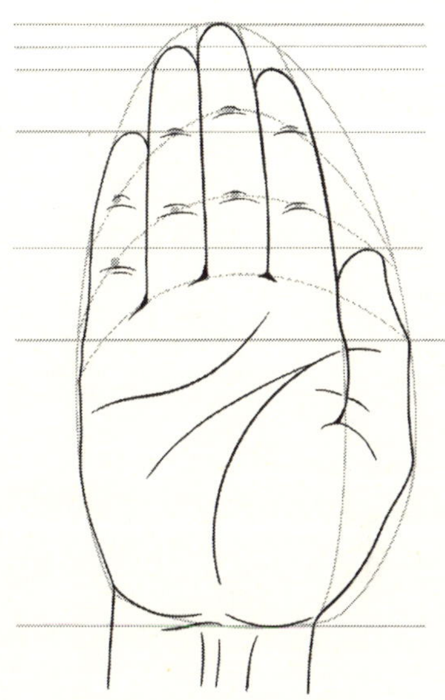

Proportions: One of the most liberating discoveries you'll make as a comics artist is that the human body isn't as unpredictable as it first appears. Beneath all the variety of different shapes, sizes and body types lies a set of reliable measurements that artists have used for centuries to construct convincing figures quickly and consistently. The most useful of these is the head-based system, where the height of the head is used as a unit of measurement for the entire body. In realistic figure drawing the body is roughly seven to eight heads tall. Once you understand this system you'll never have to guess again. You'll know instinctively where the shoulders fall, where the waist sits, where the knees land. It becomes a mental scaffold that you erect at the start of every drawing and build your character around.

Faces: The face is where your character lives. It's the first thing a reader looks at in any panel and the feature that makes one character instantly distinguishable from another. It is also, for many beginners, one of the most frustrating things to get right. A feature placed slightly too high or too wide can throw off an entire drawing, and without a reliable system to fall back on, every face can feel like starting from scratch. The good news is that the face, like the body, follows a consistent set of proportions that once learned, take the guesswork out of the process entirely. Our step-by-step system takes you from a simple circle all the way through to a fully structured, convincing face, using construction lines and geometric guides to establish the position of every feature before a single detail goes down on the page. It's a method you can return to again and again, for every character you create, and one that will give your faces a solidity and consistency that readers will feel even if they never quite know why.

Hands and Feet: Ask any group of beginner artists what they find hardest to draw and hands will come up every single time. Feet are a close second. Hands are remarkably complex structures full of joints, knuckles and subtle curves that shift depending on what the hand is doing. But they are also enormously expressive, and in action comics they carry a huge amount of storytelling weight. The key to unlocking them is learning to see hands not as a collection of fiddly details but as a set of simple shapes working together. We'll show you how to block out the basic form first and build detail on top. Feet follow a similar logic and are critical to grounding your figures convincingly.
A character whose feet don't connect properly with the surface they're standing on will always look slightly wrong. We'll cover the most common angles you'll encounter and give you a process that makes drawing both hands and feet feel as natural and manageable as any other part of the figure.

DRAWING THE MALE FACE

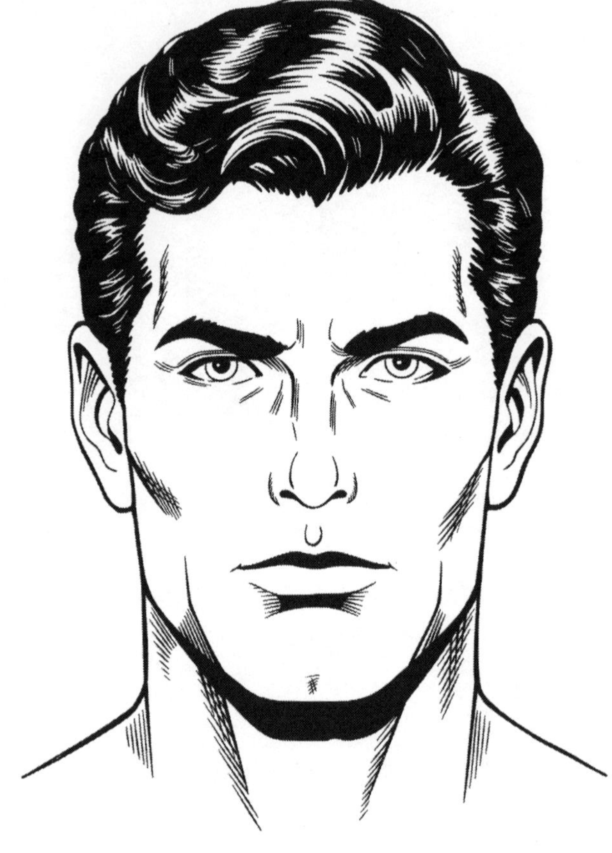

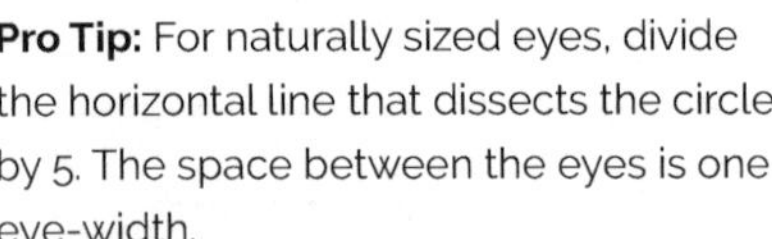

Pro Tip: For naturally sized eyes, divide the horizontal line that dissects the circle by 5. The space between the eyes is one eye-width.

01

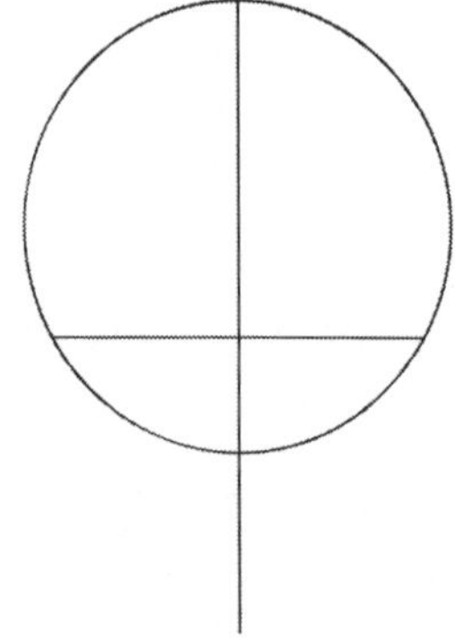

Start by drawing a circle. Divide it evenly into quarters, then extend a vertical line down from the bottom half of the circle. This will form the centre line of the face.

02

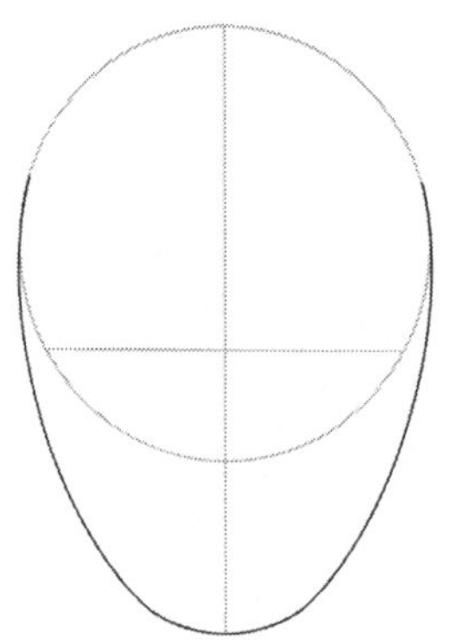

Sketch the jawline. Connect the left and right sides of the circle to the end of the vertical centre line to create the shape of the chin.

03

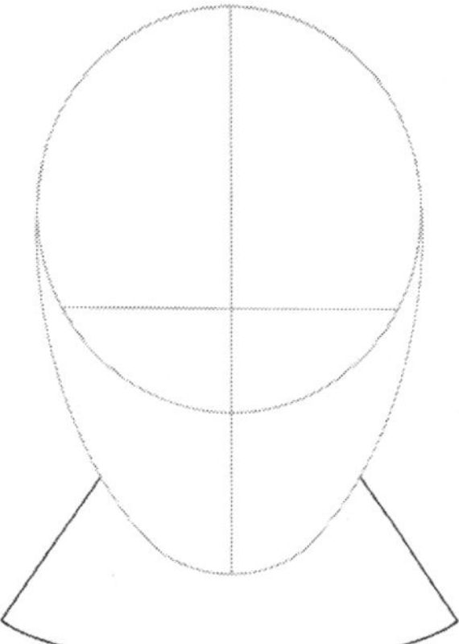

Sketch in two lines extending out from the jaw. Connect them with a slightly arced line. This will define the width of the upper shoulders.

04

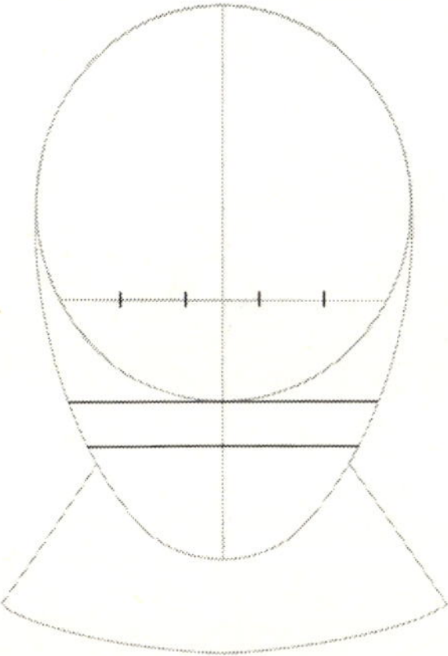

To determine the width of the eye, know that the head will be five eyes wide. The space between the eyes will measure one eye width.

05

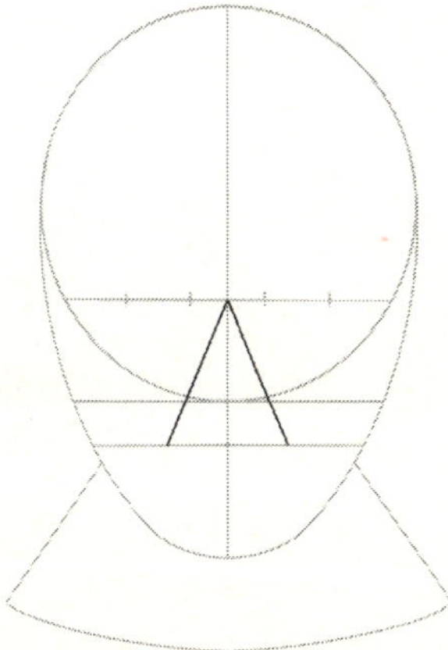

From the bridge of the nose, draw an equilateral triangle pointing downward. This defines the overall width of the nose and mouth.

06

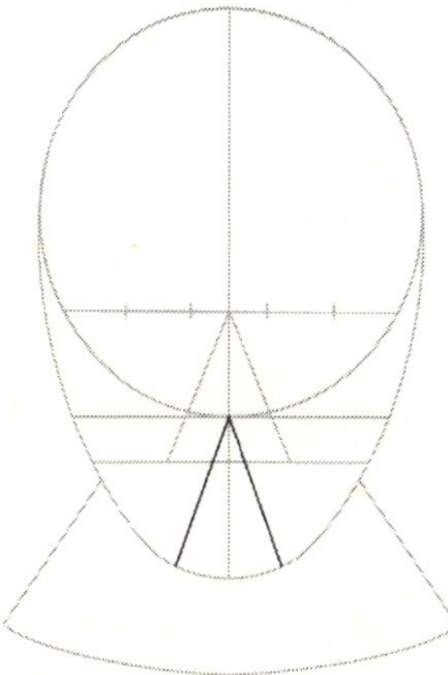

Add another equilateral triangle starting at the bottom of the circle. The base of the triangle will help you determine a natural width for the chin.

07

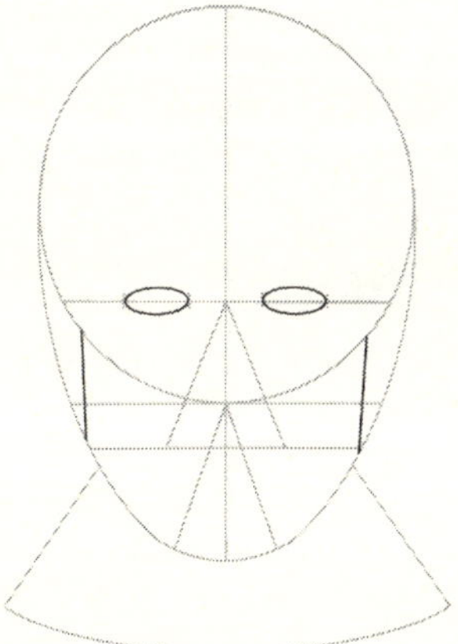

Sketch in basic oval shapes for the eyes and draw in two vertical lines, slightly angled inward, to define the jaw.

08

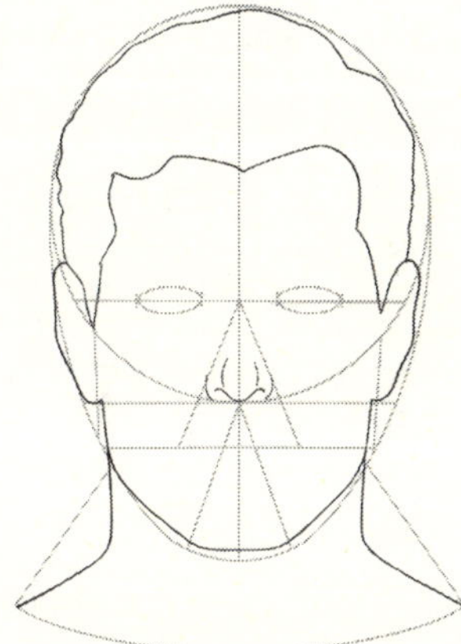

Sketch in the shape of the nose. The width of the nose should touch the outer edges of the top triangle, but not exceed them.

09

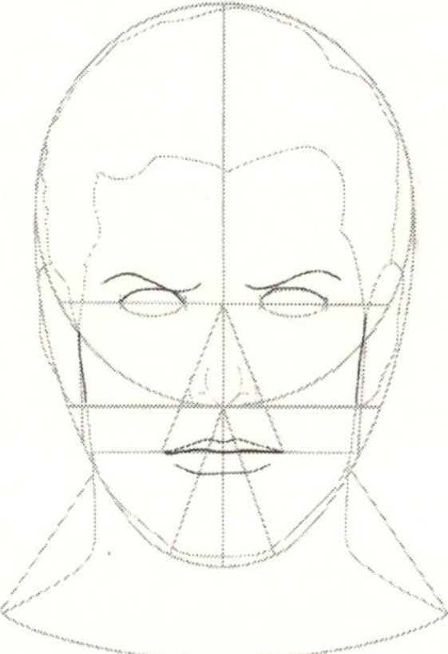

Sketch in the shape of the eyebrows and the mouth. The width of the mouth should be exactly the width of the base of the top triangle.

10

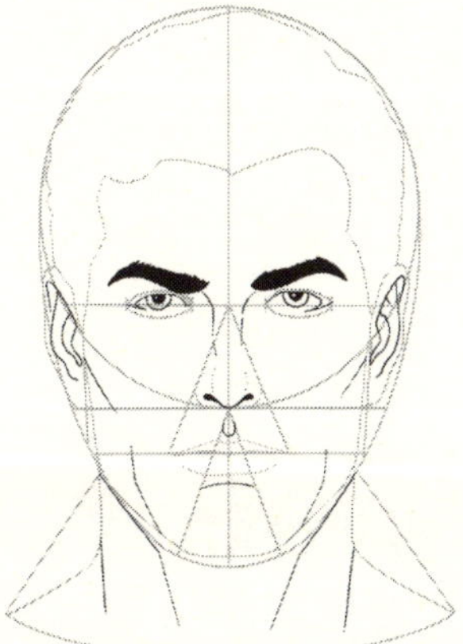

Using an inking pen, start adding in the details of the eyes and eyebrows.

11

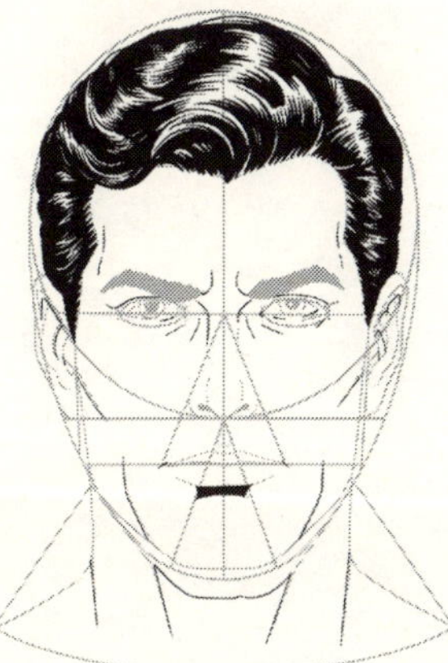

Continue adding details to the nose, mouth, ears and hair. Be sure to add in some additional skin fold lines around the eyes to help define the features and give the face a natural look.

12

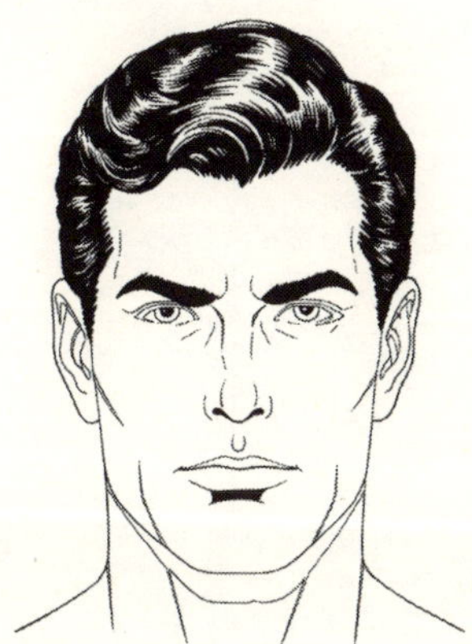

Draw in the outline of the face and erase any exisiting construction lines.

DRAWING THE MALE FACE IN PROFILE VIEW

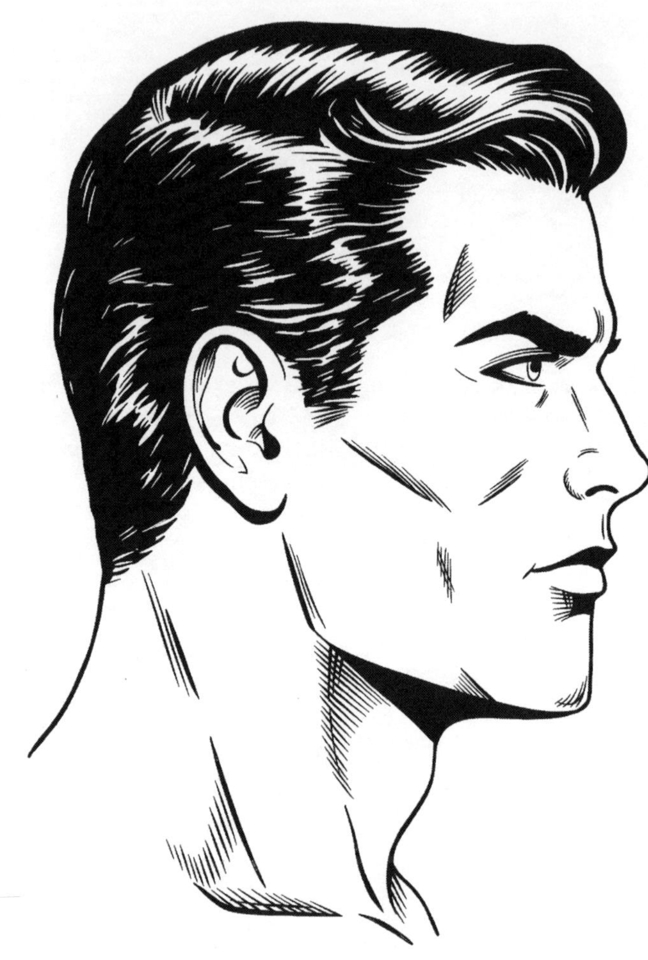

Pro Tip: When sketching in profile, focus on how each feature aligns along the vertical centre and horizontal lines. Visualising these relationships early helps maintain correct proportions.

01

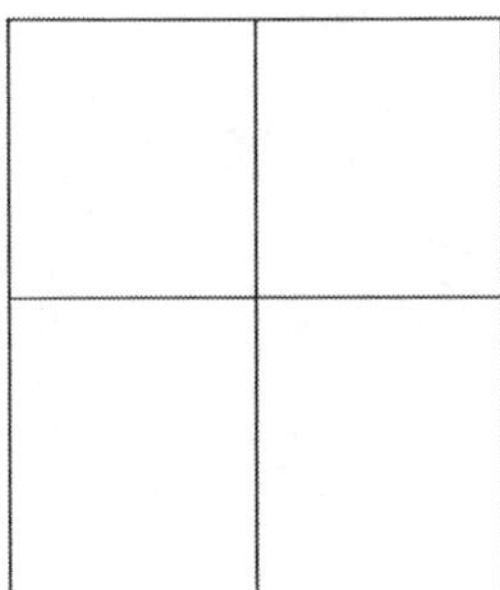

Start by drawing a rectangle. Imagine a square lightly stretched upwards. Now divide it into 4 quarters.

02

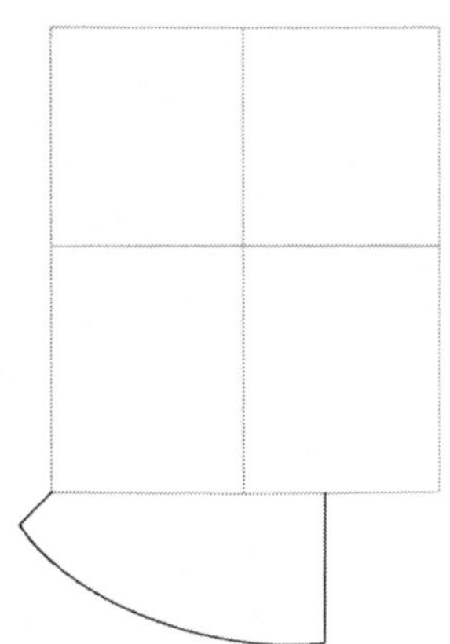

Sketch in a rough neck shape. Take notice of where the vertical line descends and replicate this.

03

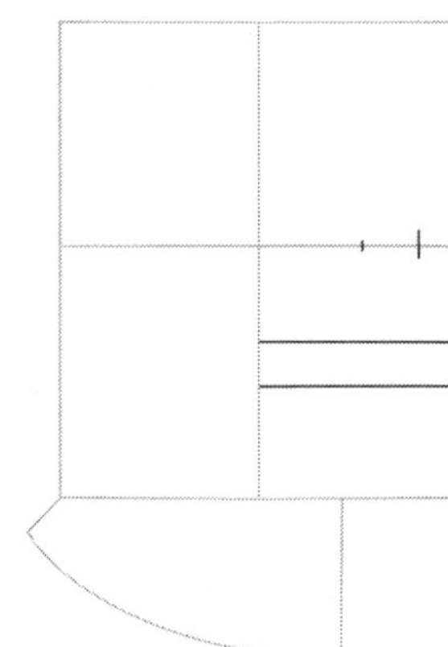

Define your horizontal feature guidelines within the front half of the square. These marks indicate where the brow, nose, and mouth will sit.

04

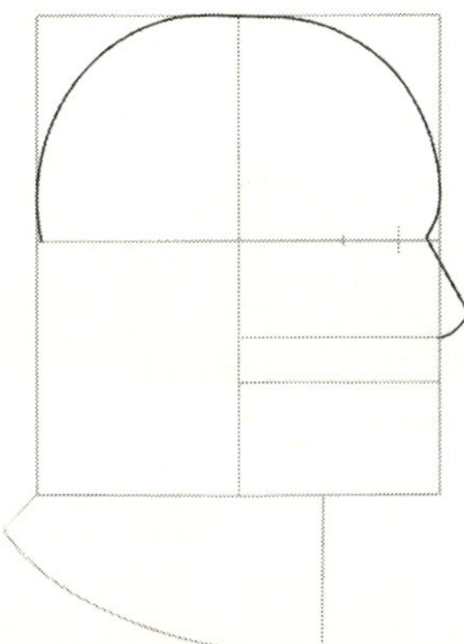

Sketch the cranial dome. It starts as a semi-circle at the top of the grid and slopes down to meet the brow line.

05

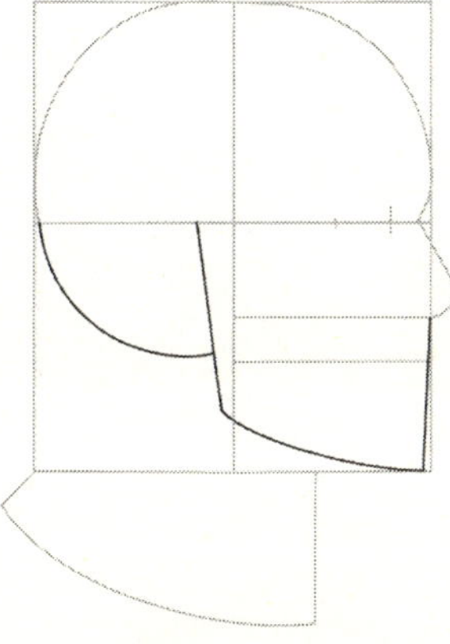

Connect the nose to the chin to create the facial plane. Notice the slight outward "V" angle of the jawline as it moves toward the neck.

06

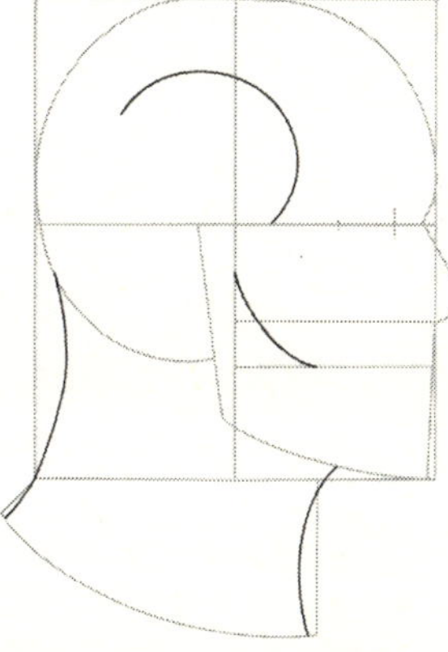

Mark the cheekbone on the front face plane. Begin sketching a rough neck shape below, paying close attention to where the vertical line descends.

07

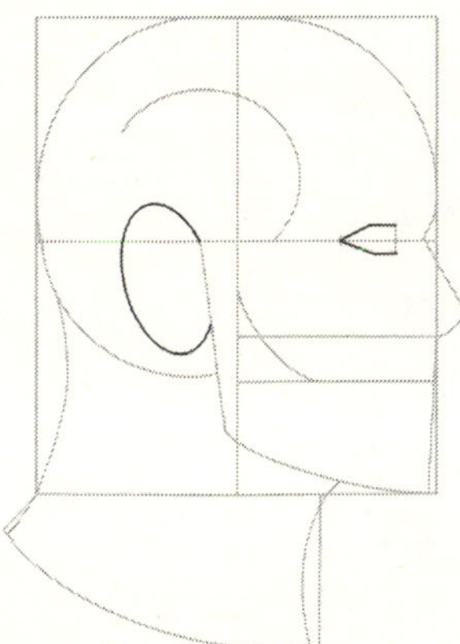

Mark the ear as an oval at the junction of the cranium and jaw, aligned with the horizontal eye line. Add a placeholder for the eye socket on the front face plane.

08

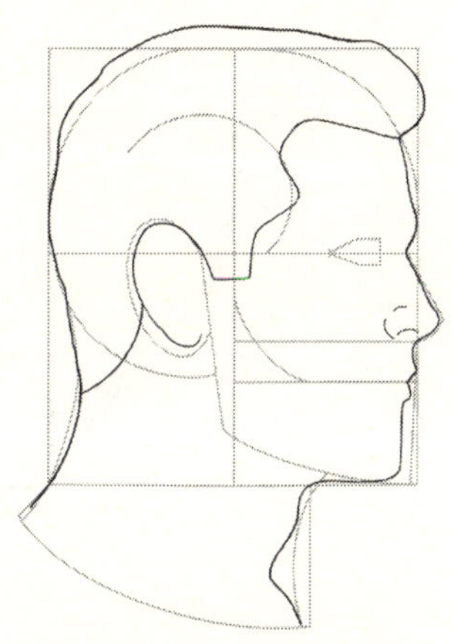

Using the grid, sketch the full profile outline — brow ridge, nose bridge, tip of the nose, upper lip, lower lip, and chin.

09

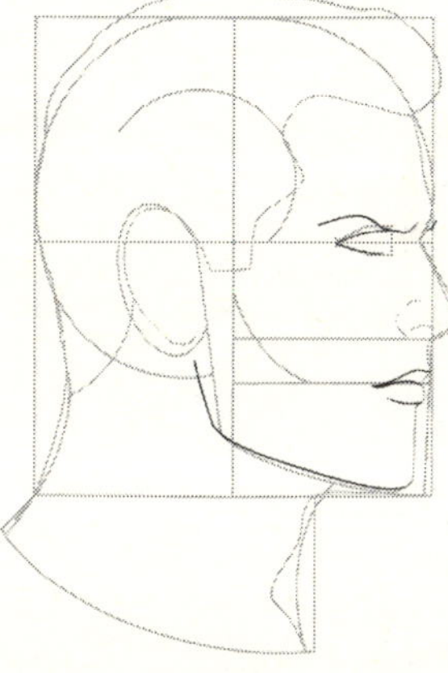

Tighten the eye shape, nose form, and mouth within the guide lines. The profile features should align to the horizontal measurements set in earlier steps.

10

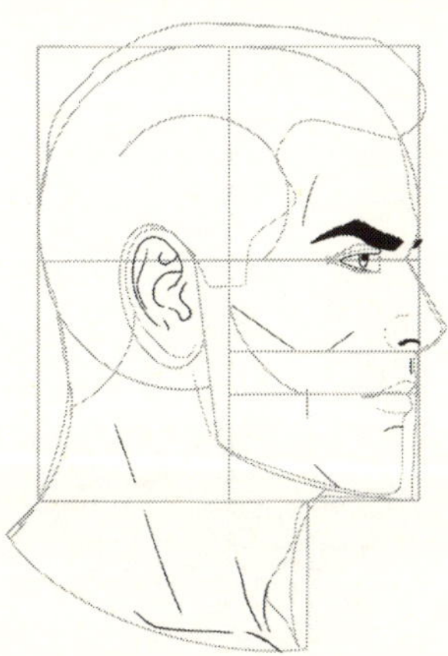

Draw the ear with internal cartilage detail — this is a key landmark. Carefully place the eye within its socket and define the brow ridge above it, as these give the face its character. Sketch in the neck shape below the jaw.

11

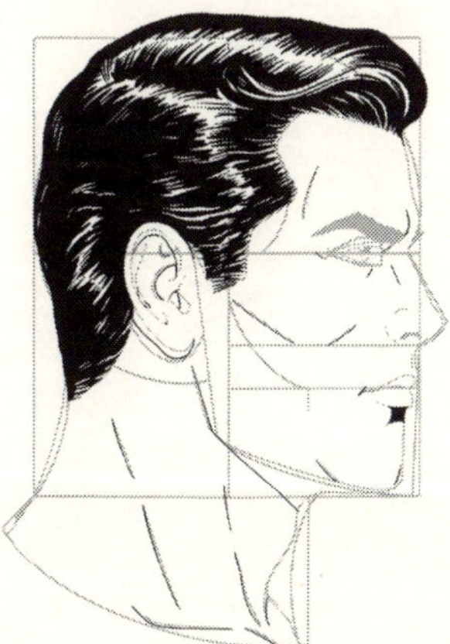

Block in the hair mass above and around the cranium. Begin adding shadow shapes beneath the brow, along the nose bridge, and under the chin using hatching or flat tones.

12

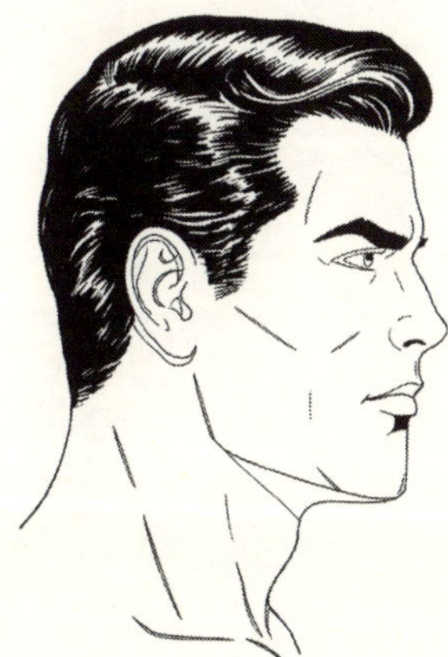

Remove construction lines. The finished face should show a clean profile silhouette with rendered hair, defined facial features, and tonal shading.

DRAWING THE MALE FACE IN 3/4 VIEW

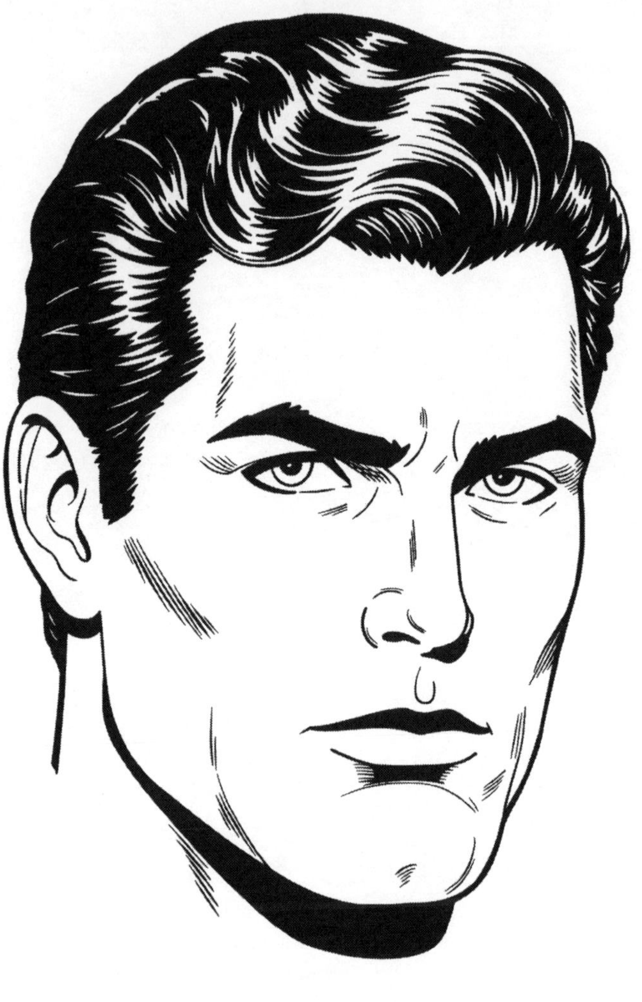

Pro Tip: In a 3/4 view the vertical centre line curves with the face, shifting toward the far side. Use it to anchor the nose and mouth to the turn of the head, keeping the face feeling truly three-dimensional.

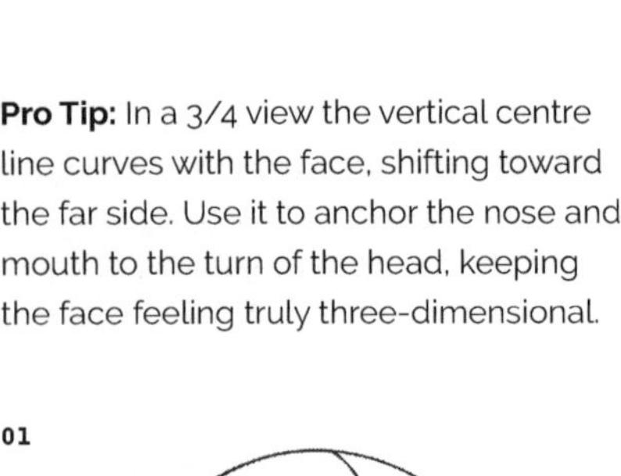

01

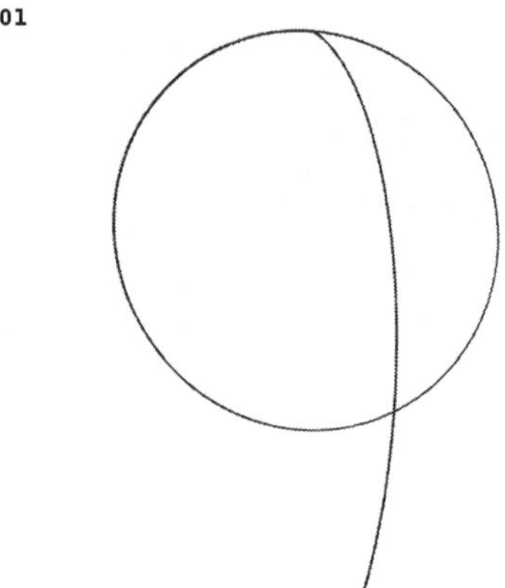

Draw an arced line downward from the top the circle. The line should extend past the base approximately 50% of the height of the circle.

02

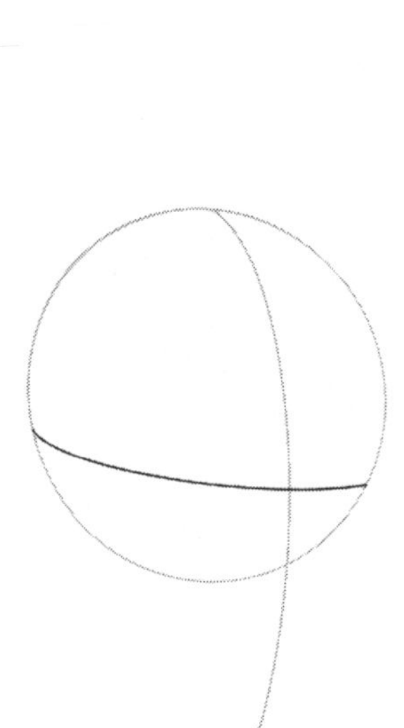

Draw a horizontal arced line on a slight leftward leaning slant approximately 1/3 of the height of the circle from the base. This will be the eyeline.

03

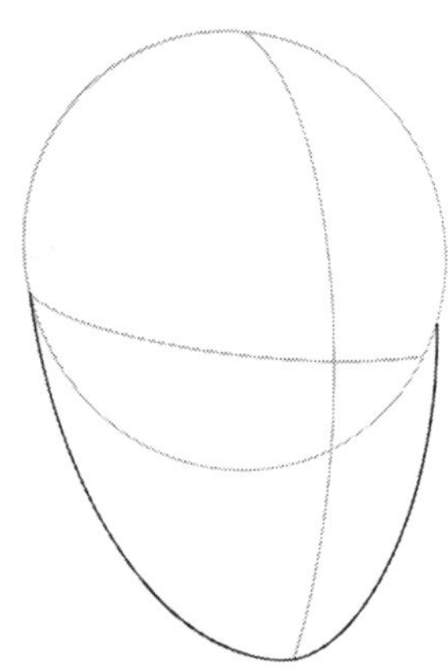

Sketch in the chin shape by connecting an arced line from each point of the eyeline. Note that on the left, it extends just above the eyeline. Be sure to include this detail.

04

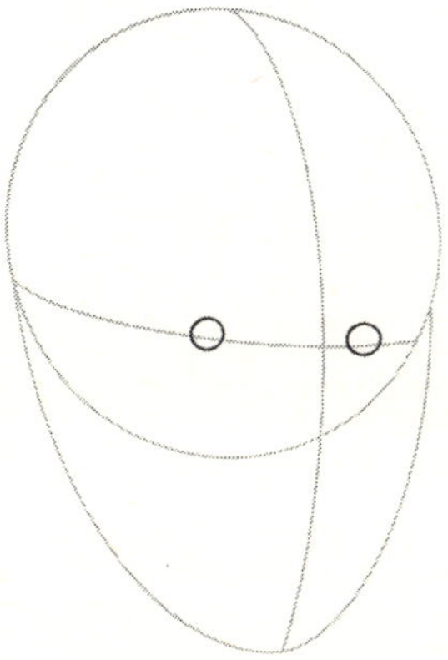

Place the eyes on the eyeline just like the reference above.

05

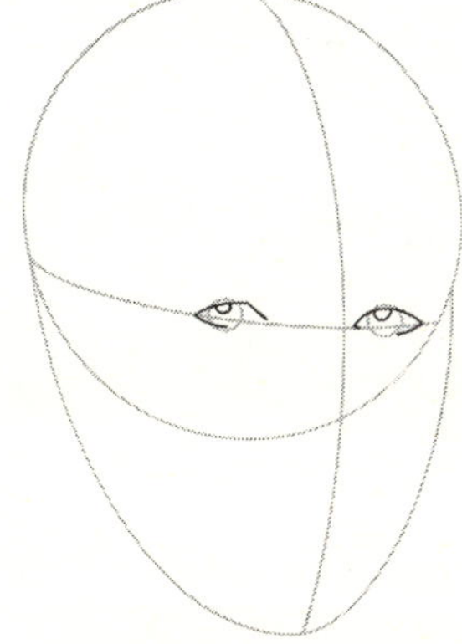

Sketch the in the eyelids to start giving the eyes some structure.

06

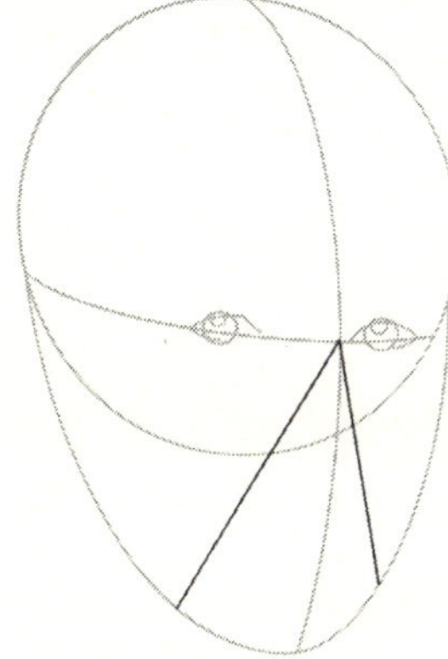

Draw a triangle shape from the centre point of the intersecting lines. This will help you determine the width and position of the nose and mouth.

07

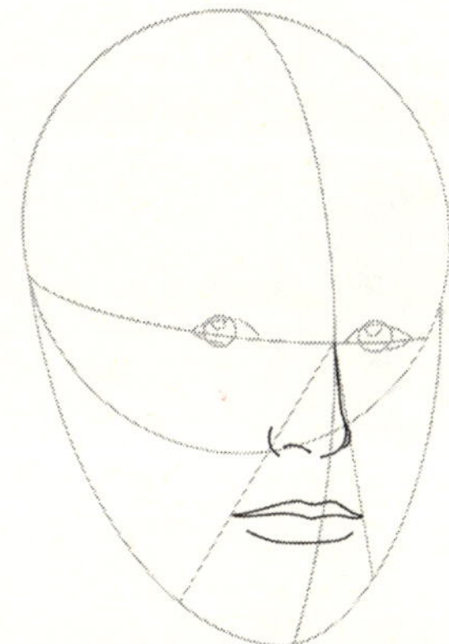

The mouth sits approximately halfway down the triangle.

08

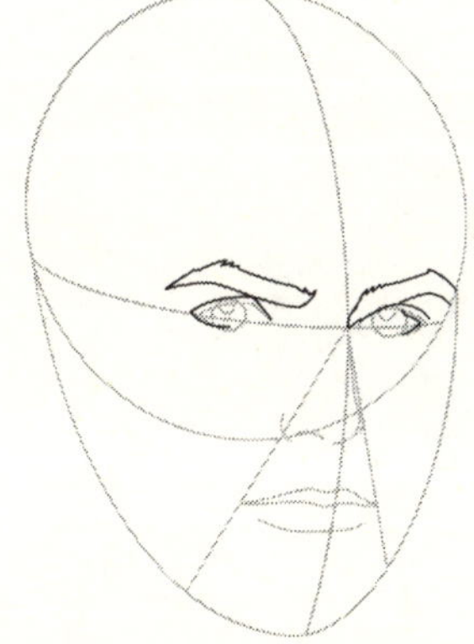

Sketch in the eyebrows. Add an additional fold line above the eyeline for a more natural look.

09

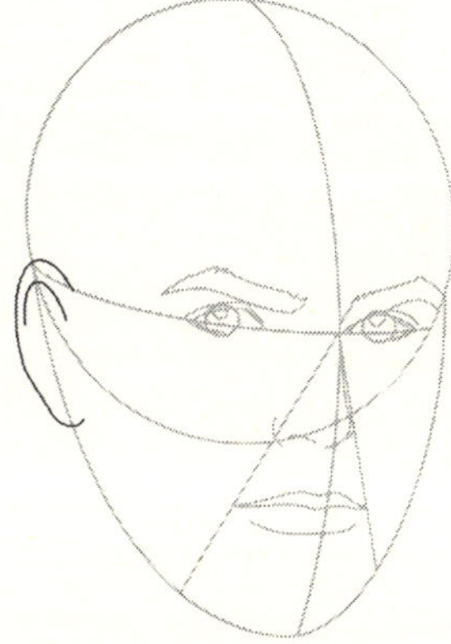

It's important that you draw the ears set in from the edge of the circle. If you do not, it will look as though the ear is placed behind the skull.

10

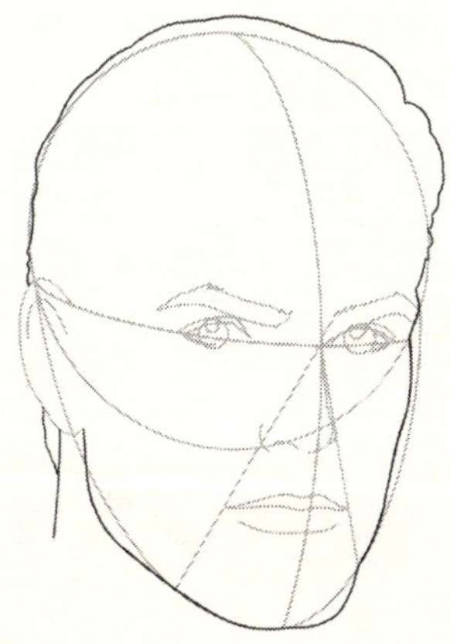

It's time to add a more natural-looking structure to the face. On the right, at the eyeline, notice that the contour of the line goes in and then back out again. This captures the definition of the cheekbones and brow.

11

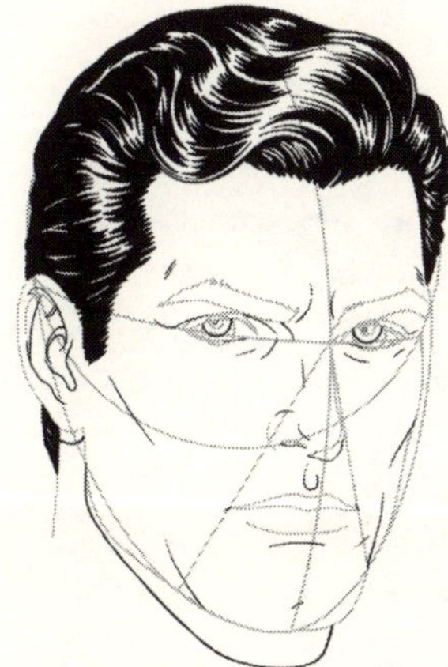

Using an inking brush, outline the hair and facial features.

12

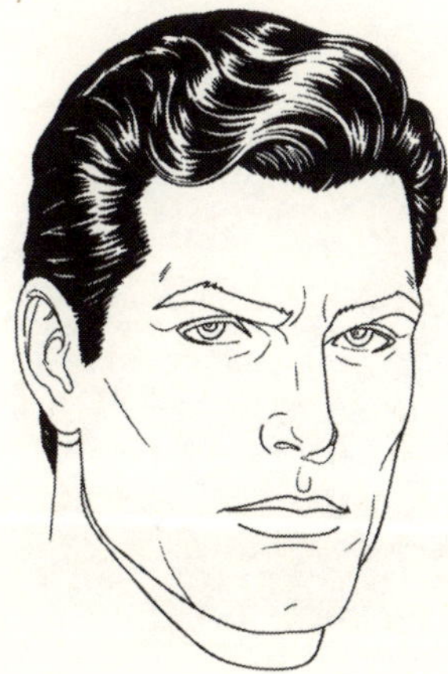

Erase your construction lines and prepare the illustration for rendering.

DRAWING THE MALE FACE FROM VARIOUS ANGLES

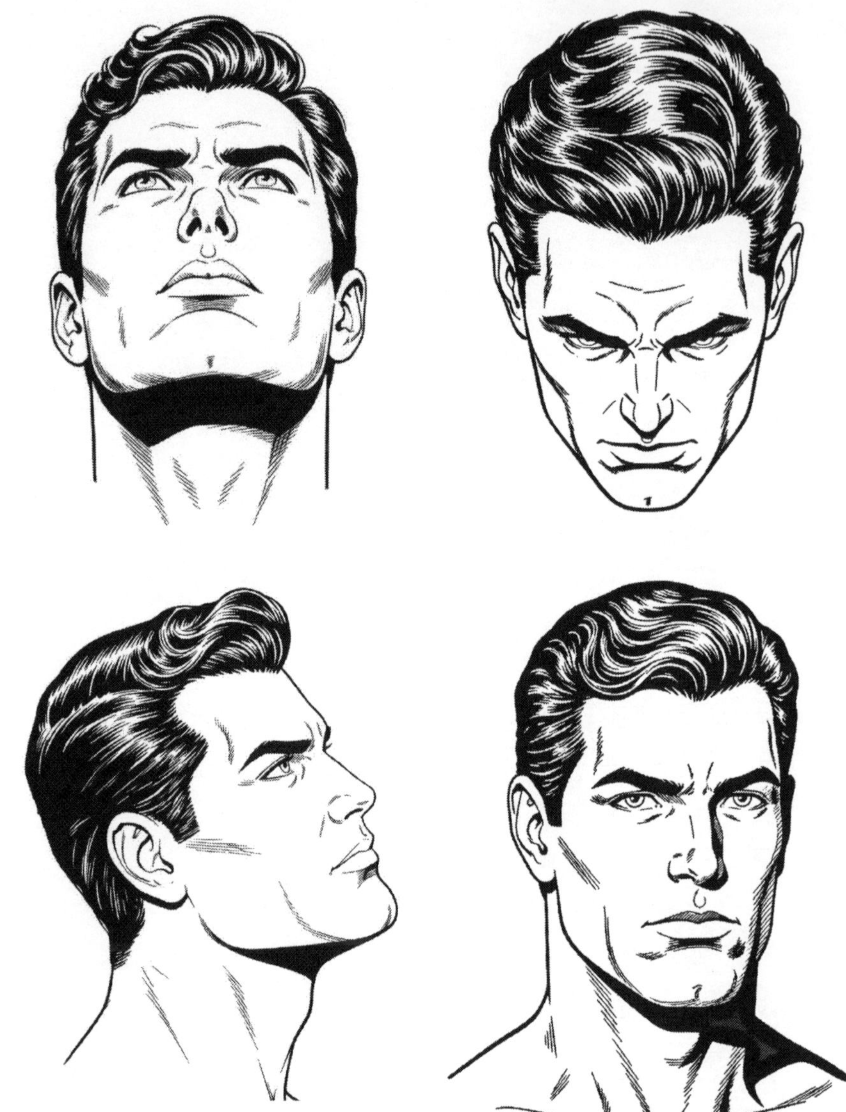

Pro Tip: When drawing the head from extreme angles, use perspective lines to guide proportion. Keep features aligned to maintain structure and avoid distortion.

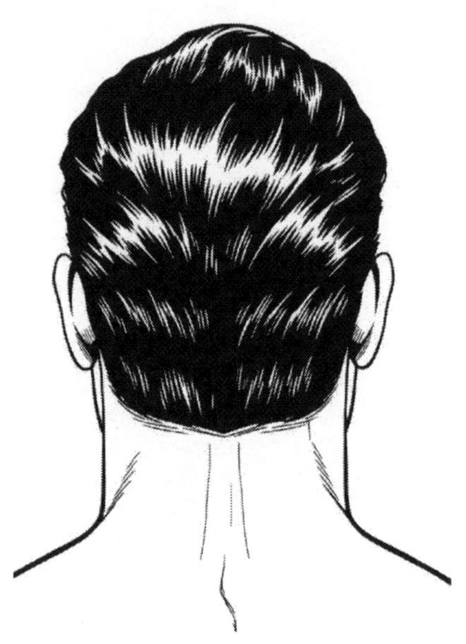

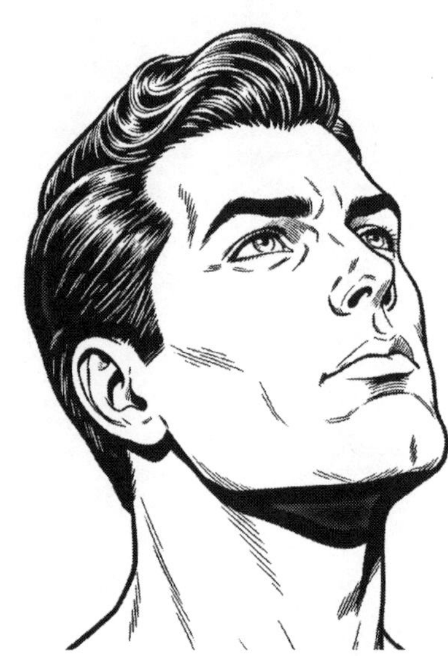

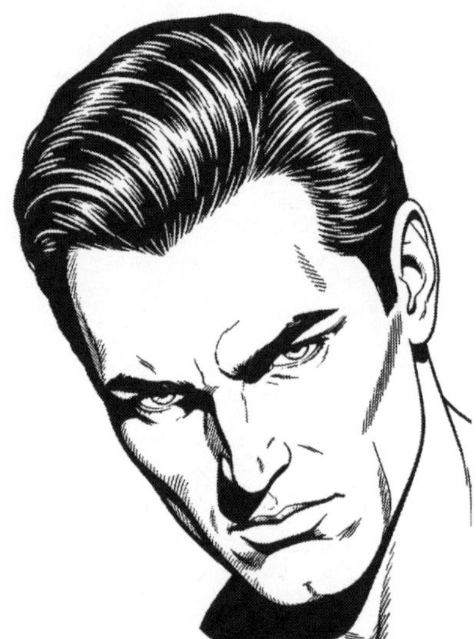

DRAWING MALE FACIAL EXPRESSIONS

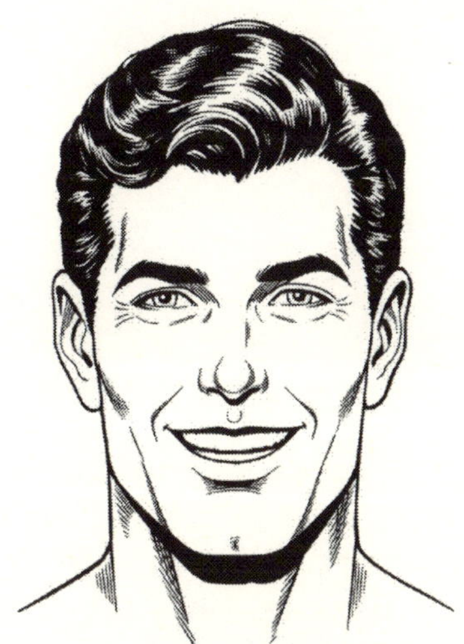

HAPPINESS

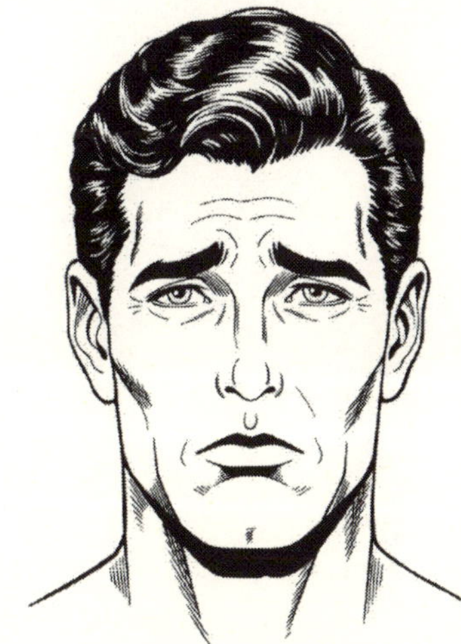

SADNESS

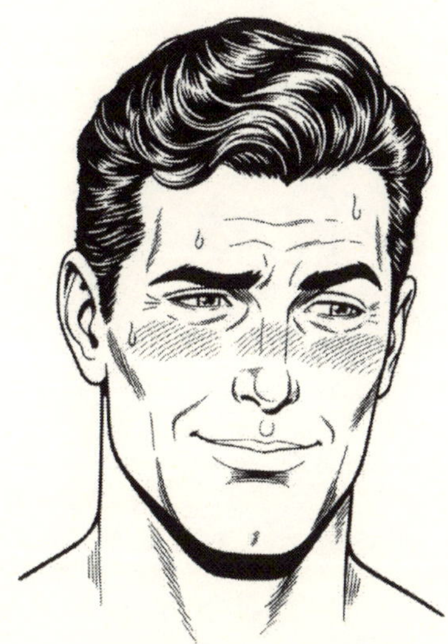

EMBARRASSED

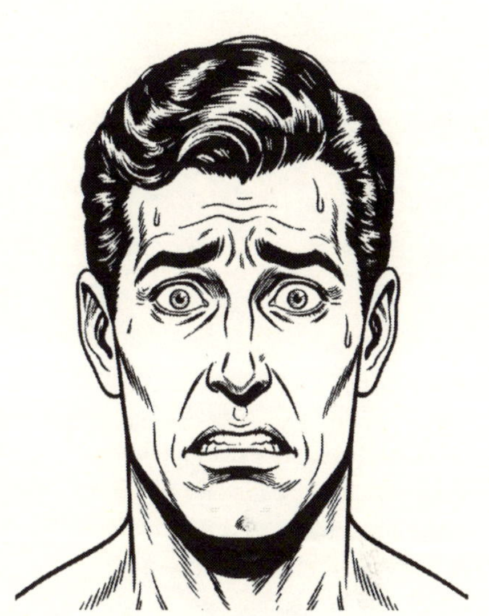

FEAR

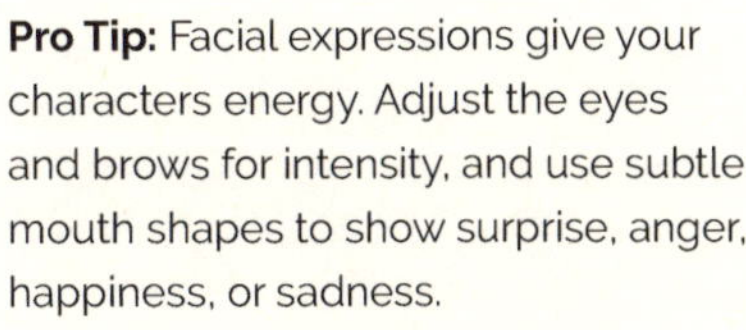

Pro Tip: Facial expressions give your characters energy. Adjust the eyes and brows for intensity, and use subtle mouth shapes to show surprise, anger, happiness, or sadness.

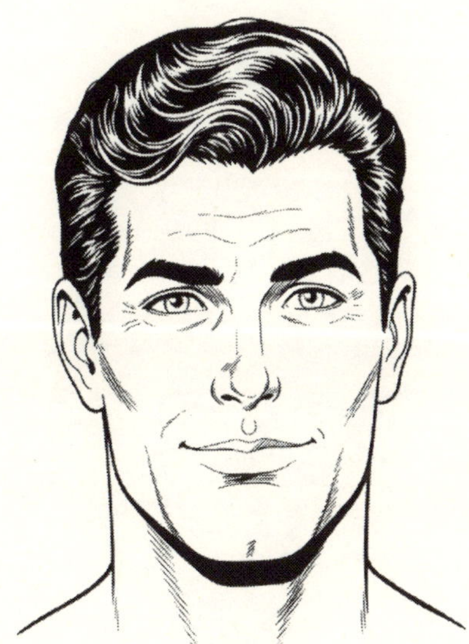

LOVE

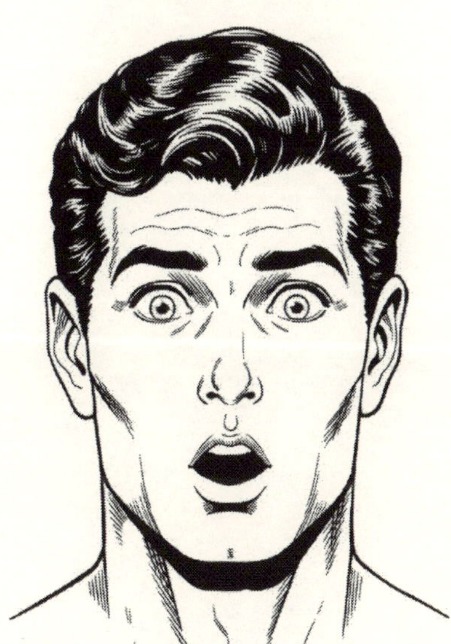

SURPRISED

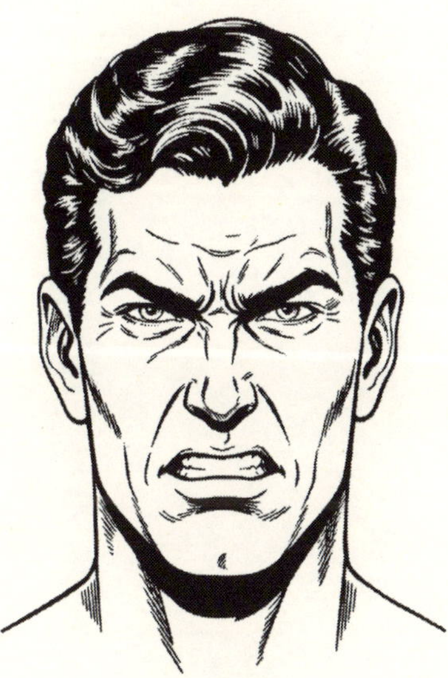

ANGER

A SIMPLIFIED APPROACH TO DRAWING THE HAND

01

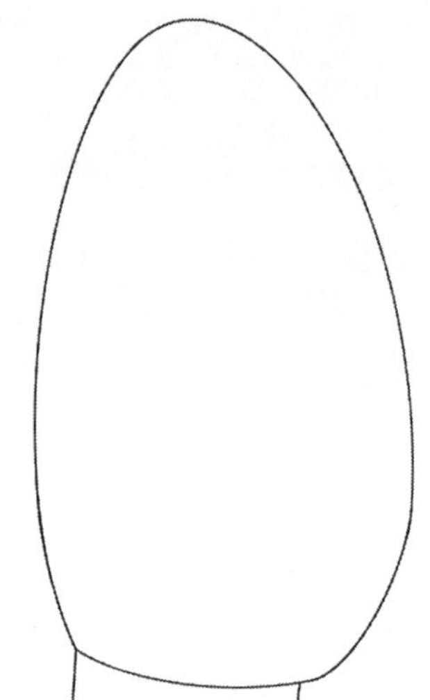

02

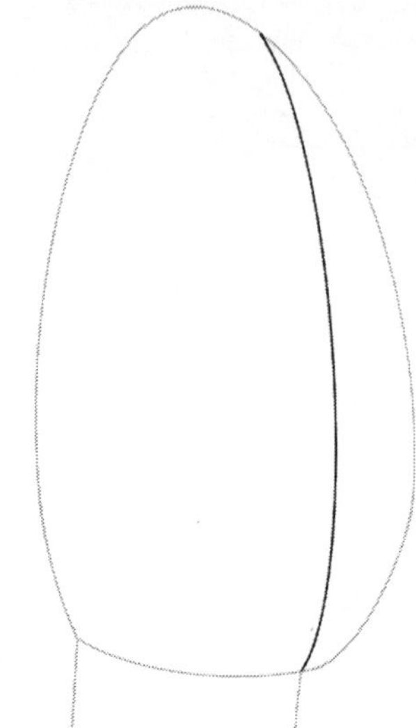

03

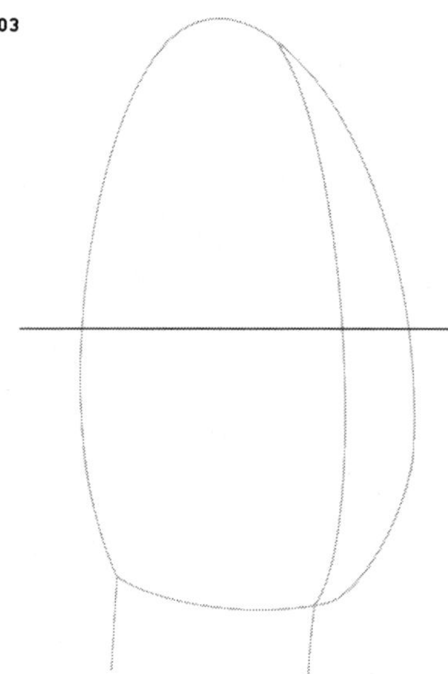

04

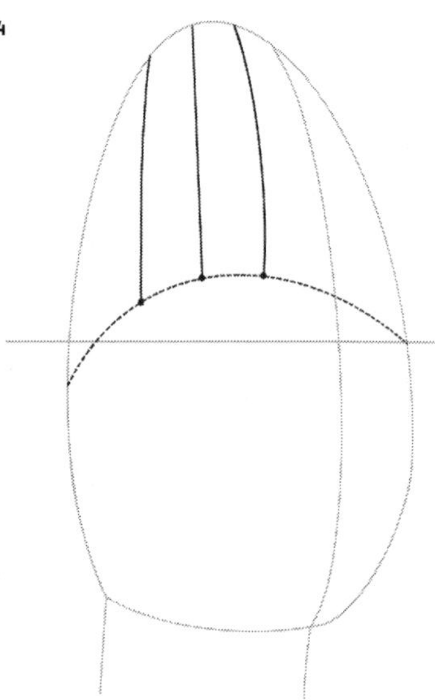

Drawing the hand is one of the most challenging yet rewarding studies for any artist. It combines structure, movement and expression. By breaking it into simple shapes and understanding its proportions, you can capture its form and expressive character.

05

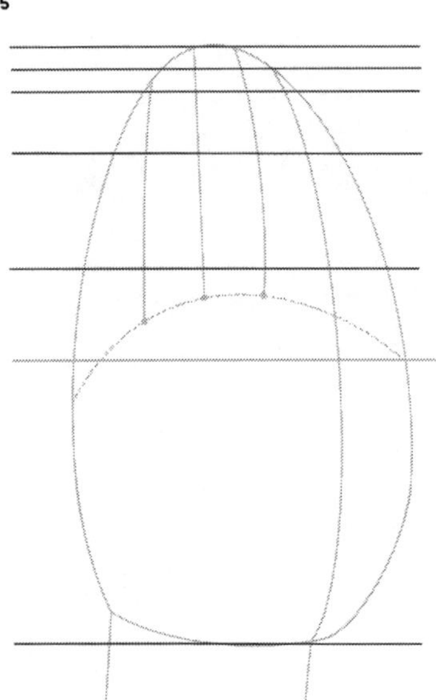

06

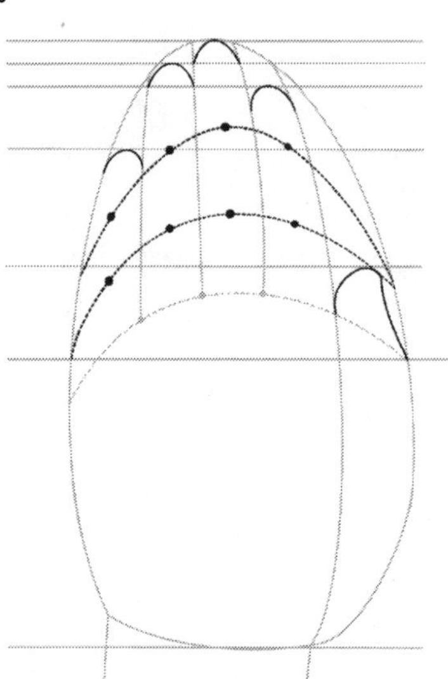

07

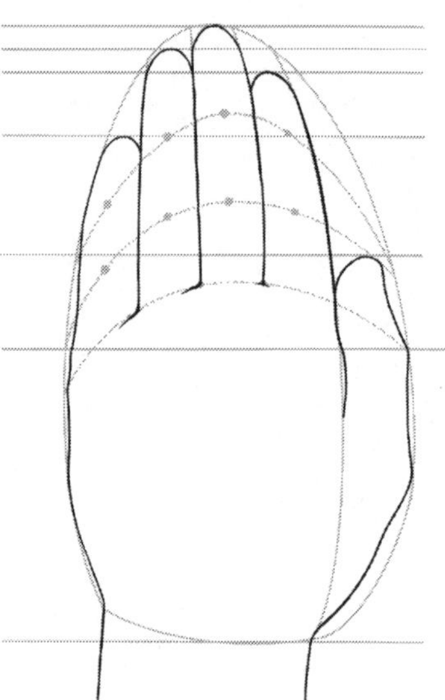

Step.1
Start by sketching an oval shape for the palm. Think of it as a smooth pebble—solid and slightly flattened. This shape represents the main mass of the hand and gives you a base to build on.

Step.2
Extend a short line from the bottom centre of the oval to suggest the wrist. The thumb attaches at an angle from the side, and curves naturally towards the character's fingers.

Step.3
Draw a horizontal line halfway between the top and bottom of the oval. This will help you place the base of the fingers in proportion to the rest of the hand.

Step.4
Above this halfway line, draw a curved guide to mark where the fingers begin. The curve should dip slightly below the line at the little finger's base and rise at the index finger's base.

Step.5
Use this curve to measure the finger lengths. The middle finger is usually the longest, the index and ring fingers are roughly equal, and the little finger is shorter. The thumb starts slightly higher than the base curve of the fingers.

Step.6
Round off the fingertips, keeping each finger slightly tapered. Imagine three arcs running across the hand: one arc for the knuckles, one arc for the middle joints, and one arc for the fingertips. The thumb connects along these same curves, completing the natural rhythm of the character's hand.

Step.7
At the base of the fingers, notice a short, curved fold of skin that runs across the palm. This crease follows the natural arc where the fingers bend and helps define the base of the palm.

Step.8
When the hand is flat and the thumb is curved inward, you'll see a deep crease running from the thumb's base toward its top joint. This forms an inverted "T" shape with the main fold of the palm and defines the thumb's movement.

Step.9
Add the two main crease lines across the palm as indicated. The small pits between the finger bases can be slightly darkened, and you might include a subtle fold line running across the wrist for added realism.

Step.10
Some hands show double lines at the finger joints, depending on size and flexibility. A single line will usually do, but adding a faint secondary crease can suggest more realism.

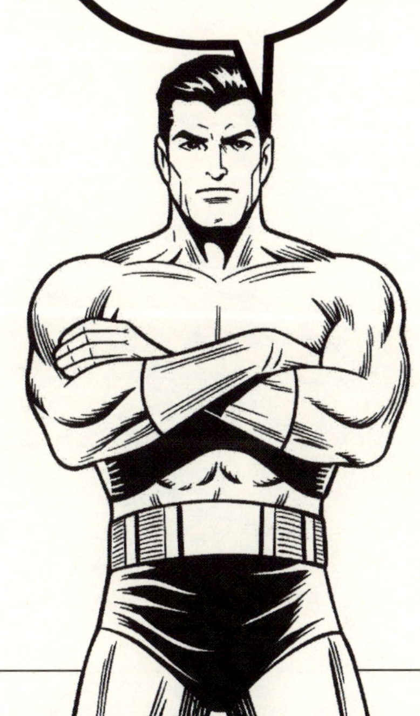

08

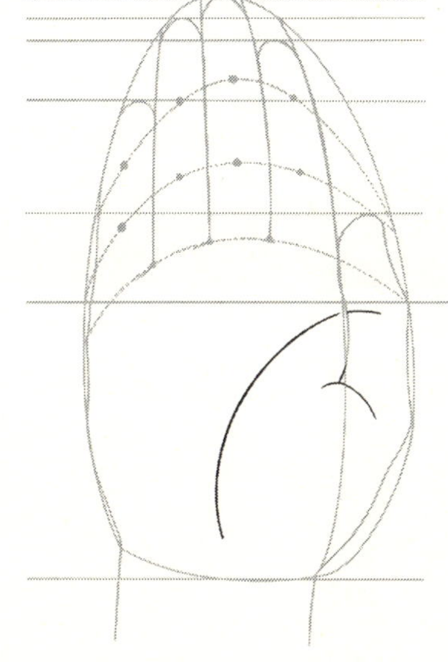

09

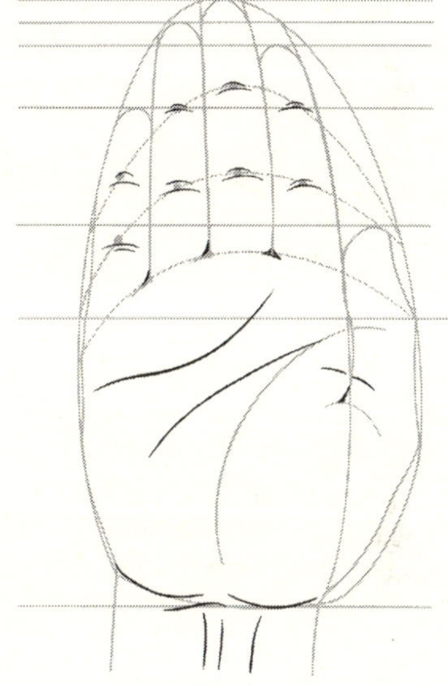

10

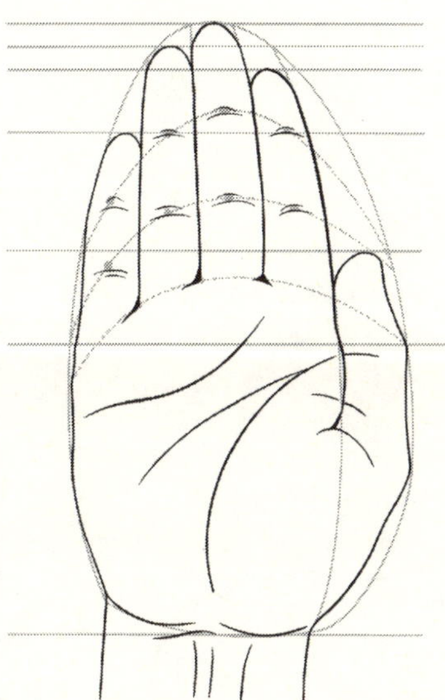

A SIMPLIFIED APPROACH TO DRAWING THE HAND

01

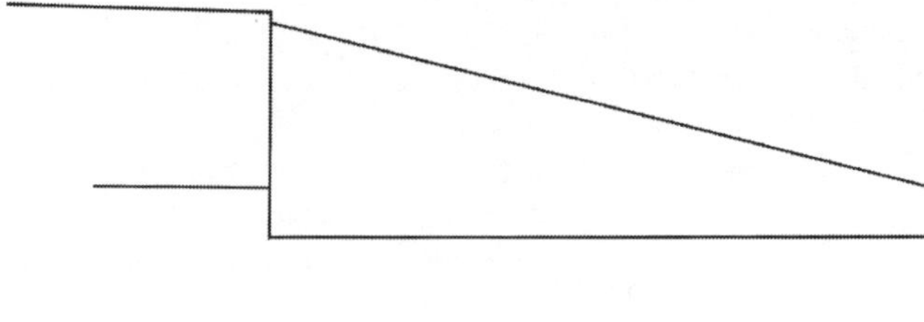

02

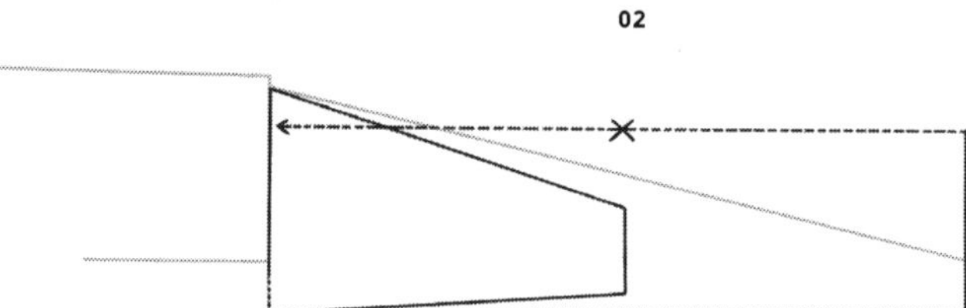

Understanding the hand from the side view is essential for capturing its structure and movement. From this angle, the hand reveals its subtle planes, step-downs, and the powerful form of the thumb base. By simplifying it into basic geometric shapes, you can grasp its proportions more easily while building a solid foundation for drawing hands in any position.

03

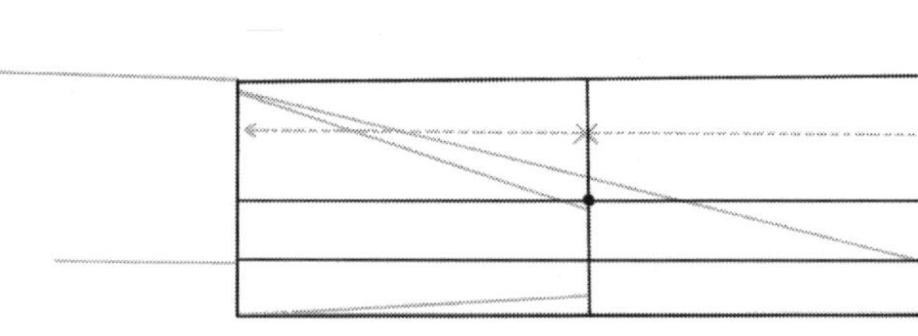

04

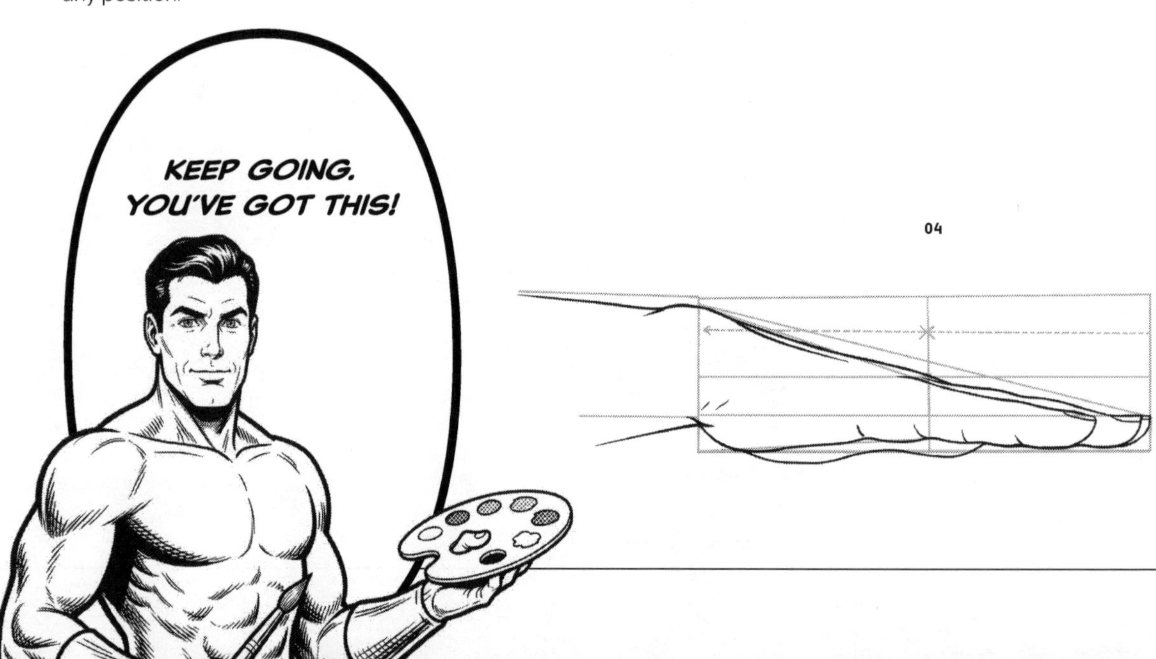

Step.1
From the side, the hand can be simplified into a tapered trapezoid. The base on the little finger side is thicker than on the thumb side. Notice the clear step down where the wrist meets the hand—there's always a change in direction at this point.

Step.2
A smaller trapezoid runs from the wrist to the base of the little finger, about half the overall length of the hand.

Step.3
You can establish proportions by drawing a rectangle around the hand. The midpoint marks the hand's thickness, while the lower quarter indicates where the wrist connects. This also helps define the width of the fingers.

Step.4
The completed side view should look sleek and dynamic, with a smooth, aerodynamic contour.

Step.5
On the thumb side, the wrist and palm meet with a more pronounced drop, forming a subtle curve on the underside of the hand.

Step.6
The thumb's knuckles align with the nail joint, showing a strong step down between the wrist and thumb. Remember, the ball of the thumb is a prominent feature and gives the hand much of its power and shape.

Step.7
Because the thumb base drops lower, the hand appears slightly wider when viewed from this angle. The halfway point across the thumb aligns roughly with its top knuckle.

Step.8
When the thumb rests against the hand, its base contracts slightly, creating an elliptical shape that makes the muscle fold inward.

05

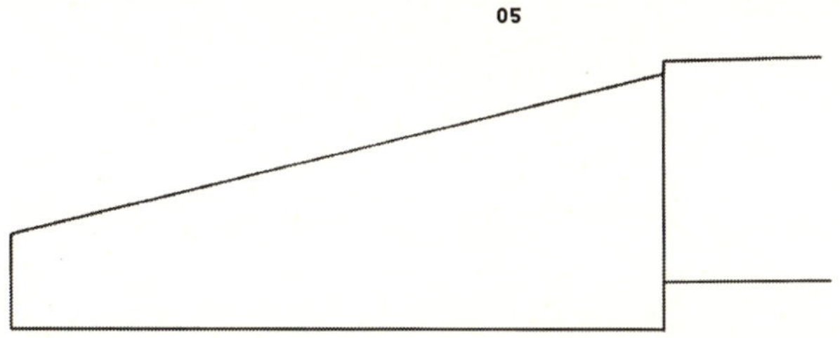

06

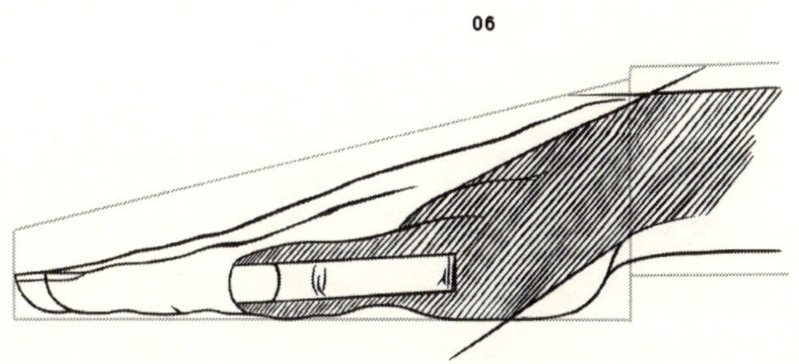

07

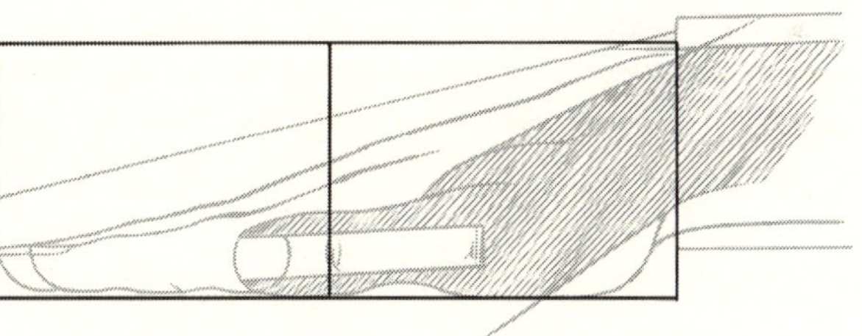

08

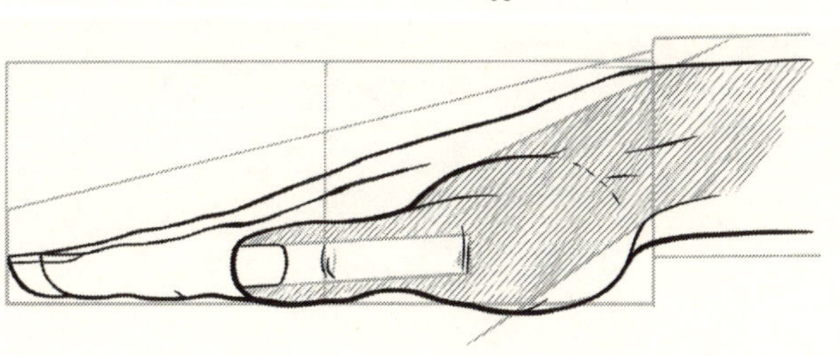

OPEN HAND

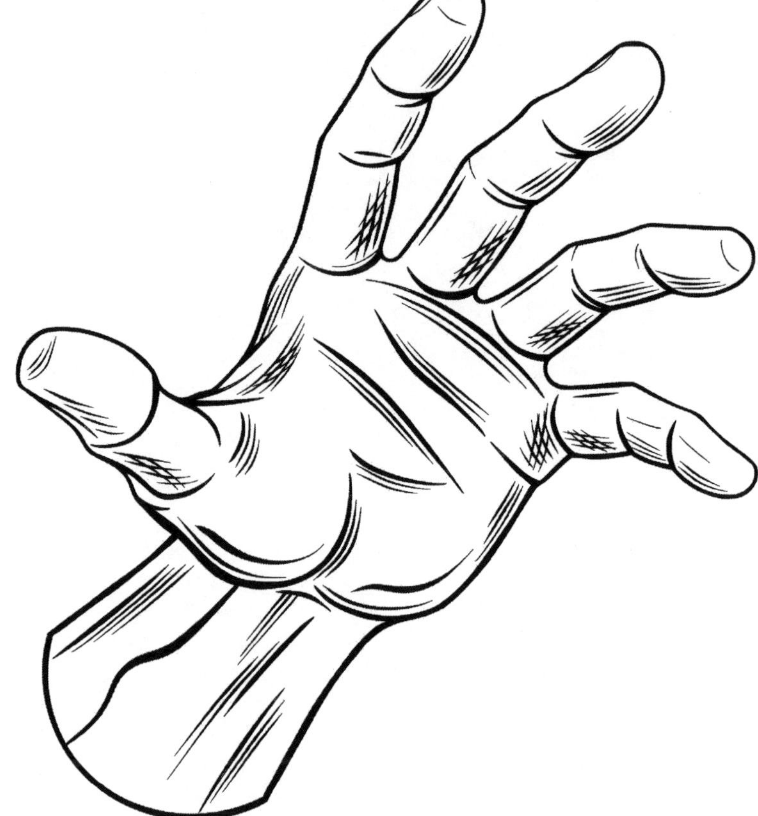

Pro Tip: The four fingers follow a gentle arc across the knuckles, with the middle finger roughly half the length of the palm. The thumb sits lower and at a wider angle, about one thumb-width away from the index finger.

01

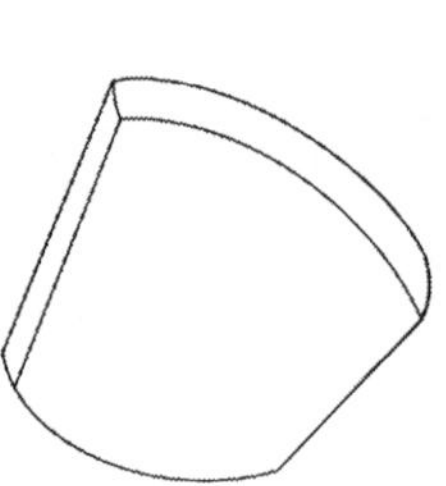

02

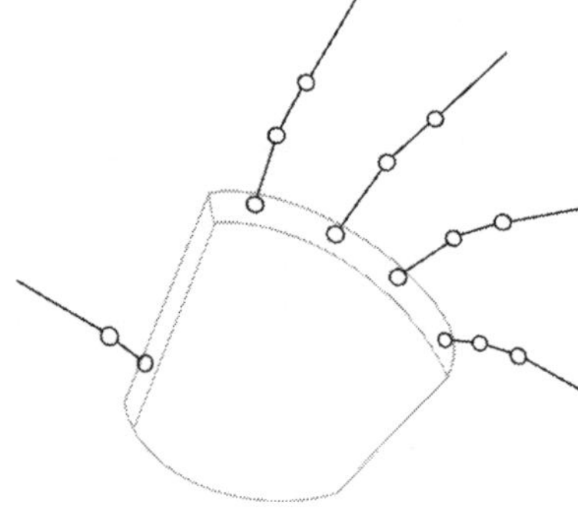

03

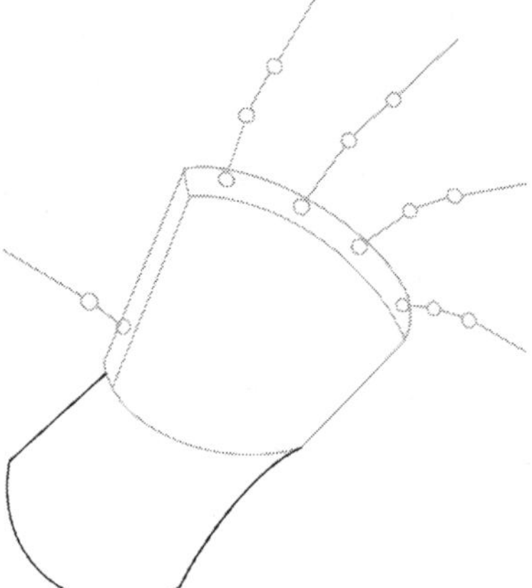

04

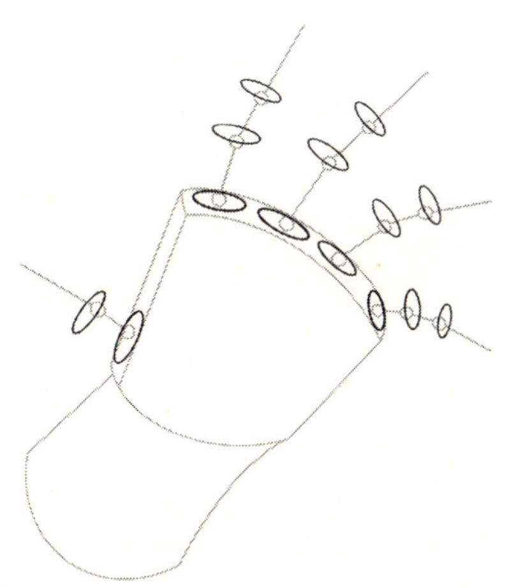

05

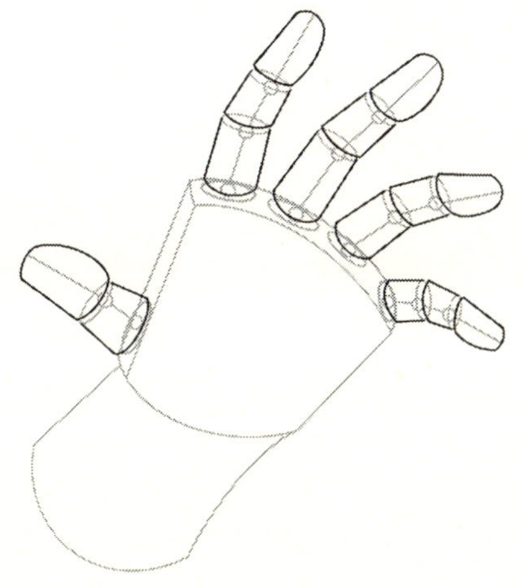

06

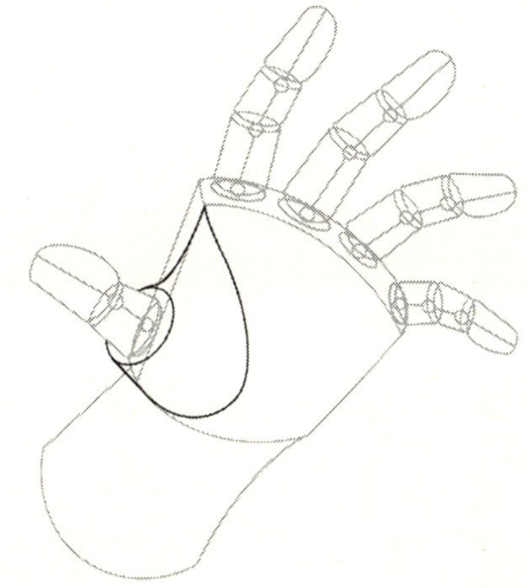

07

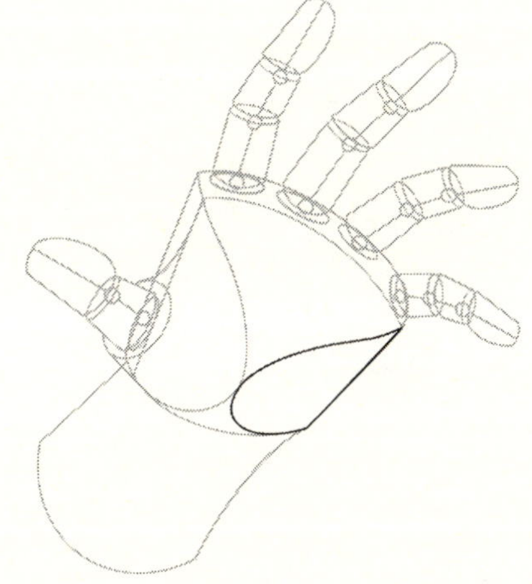

08

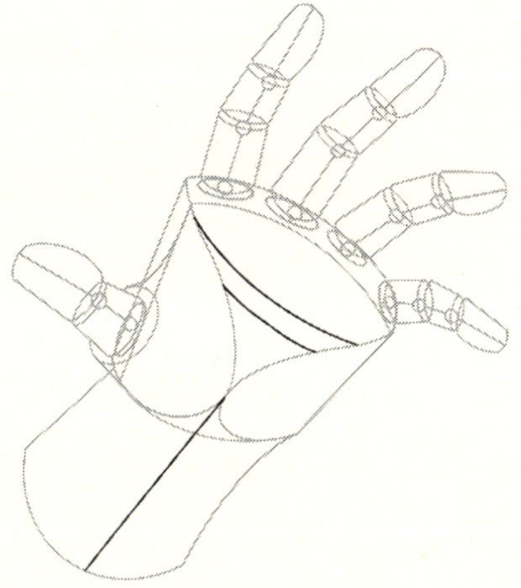

09

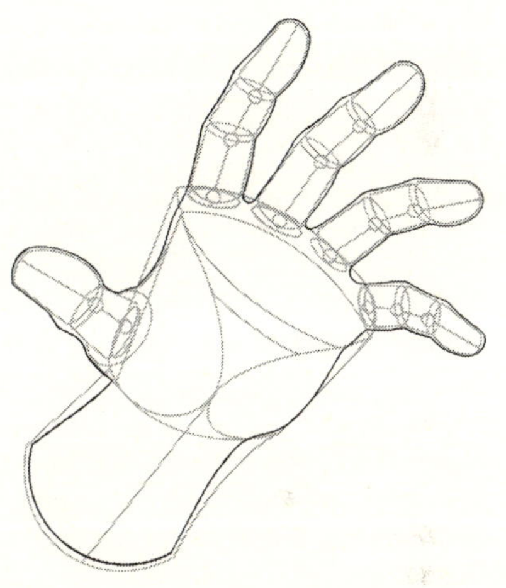

10

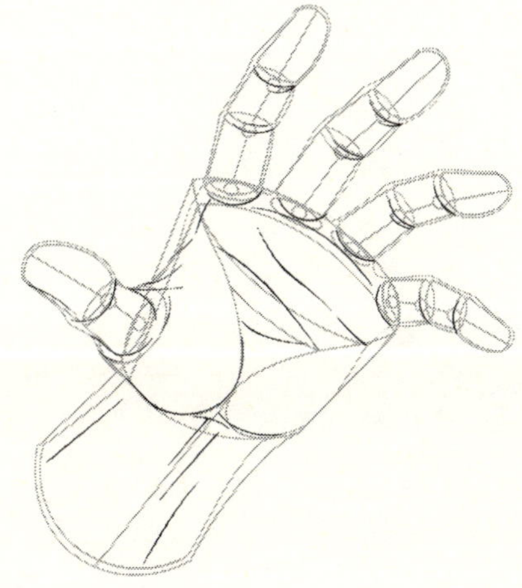

11

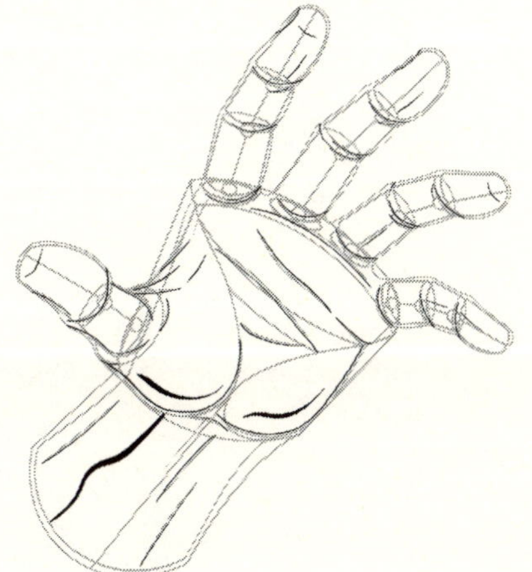

12

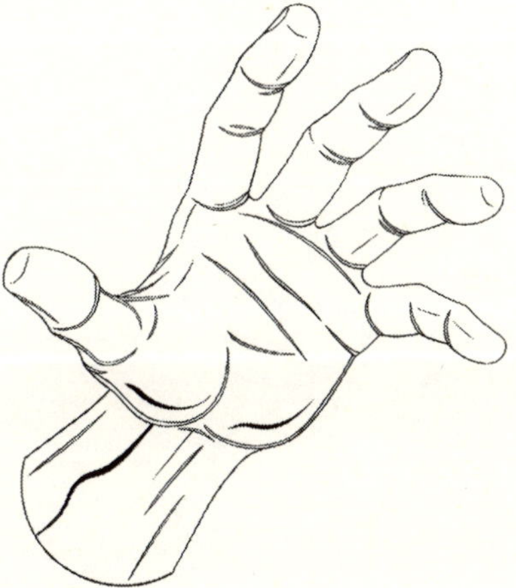

A SIMPLIFIED APPROACH TO DRAWING THE FOOT

Pro Tip: The ankle isn't level—its inner side sits higher than the outer. This happens because the tibia (inner ankle bone) extends lower than the fibula (outer ankle bone). When drawing the foot, use an angled line across the ankle to show this tilt. It instantly makes your figure feel more grounded and anatomically correct.

01

02

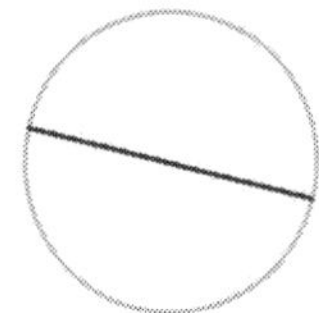

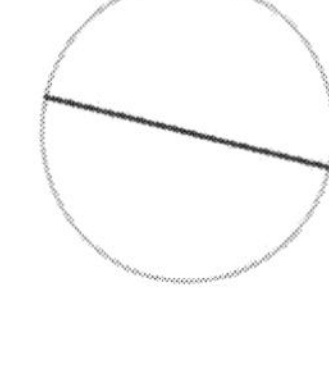

03

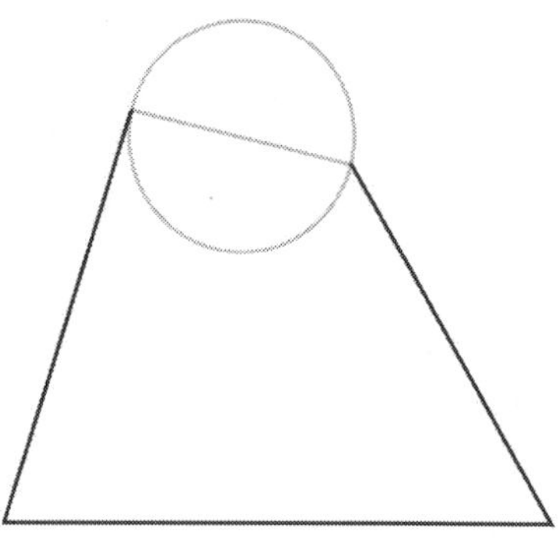

04

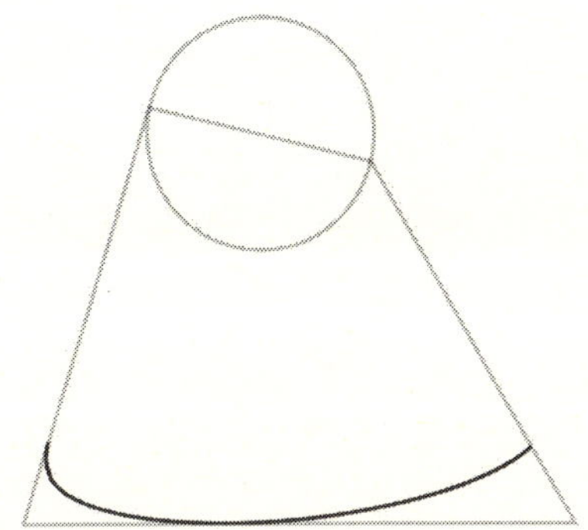

05

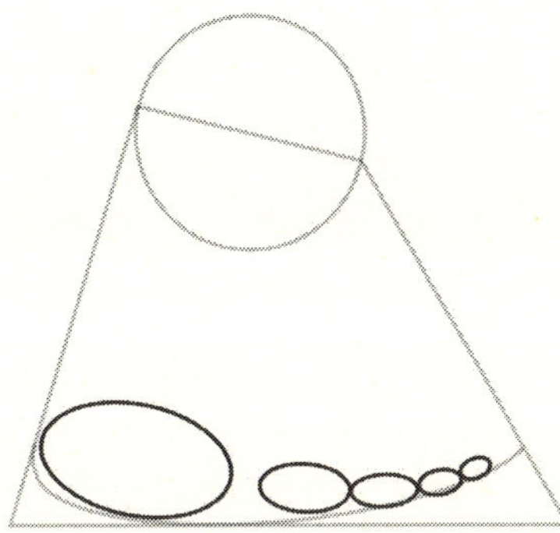

06

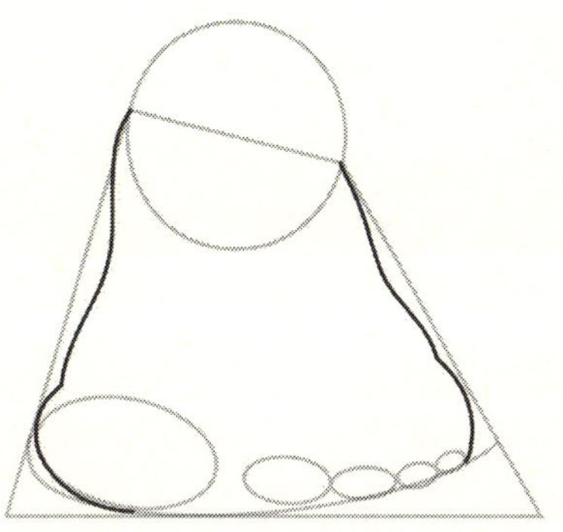

07

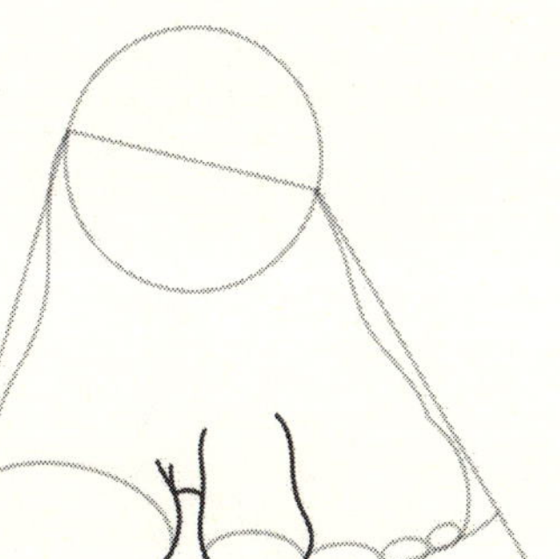

08

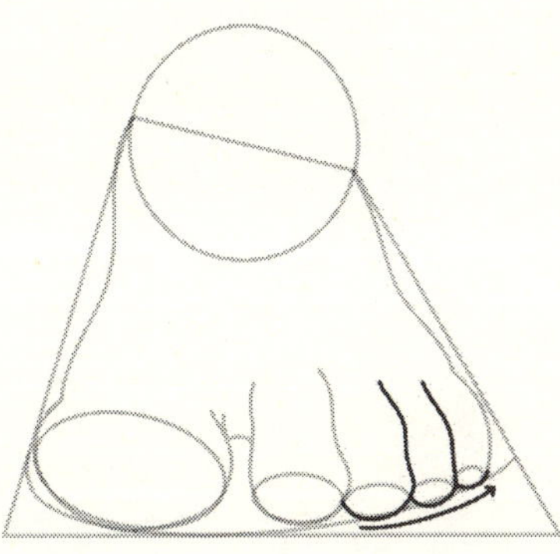

09

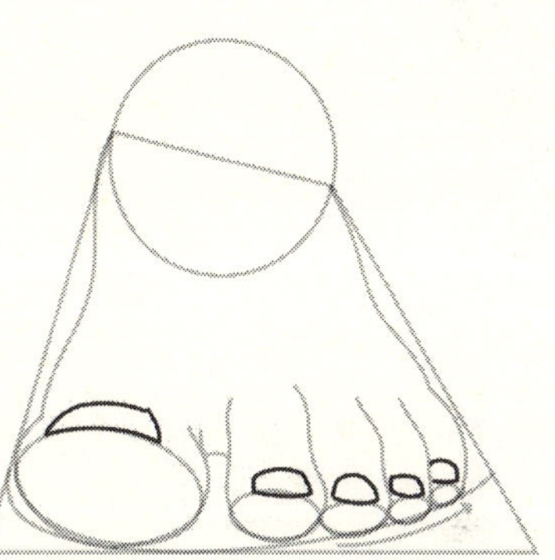

10

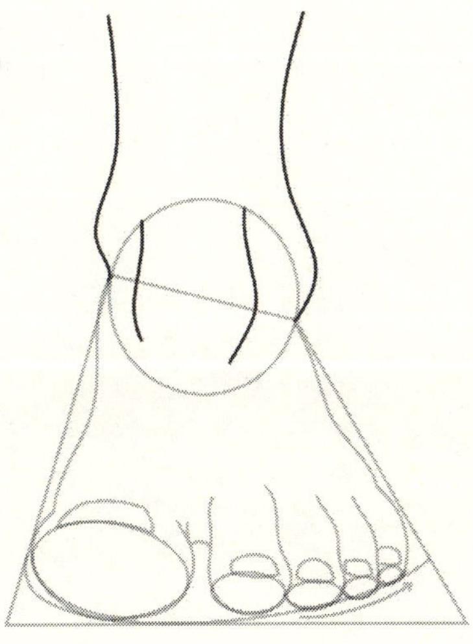

11

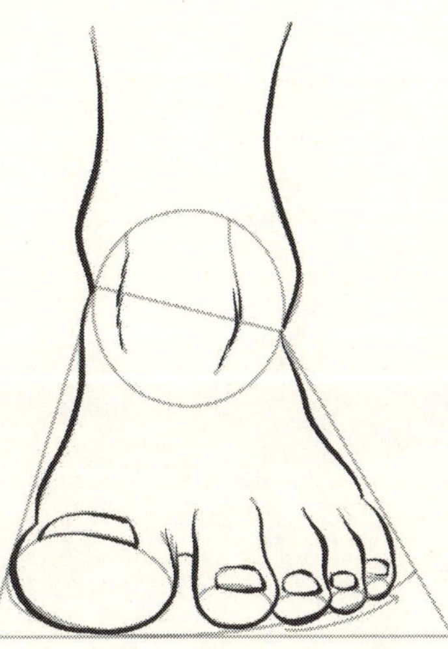

12

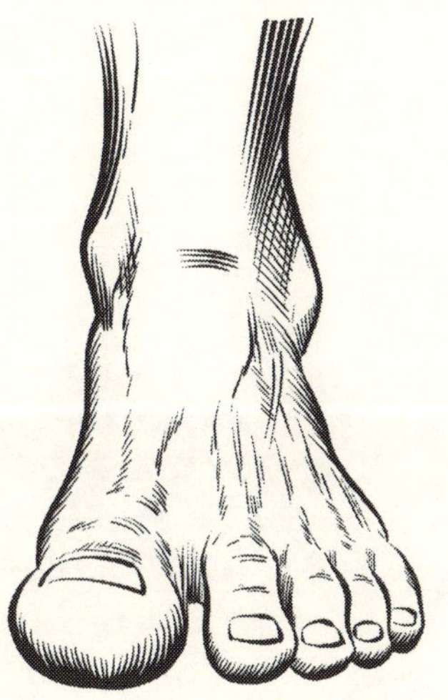

A SIMPLIFIED APPROACH TO DRAWING THE FOOT

Pro Tip: The foot supports the entire body, yet its form is often misunderstood. By reducing it to simple geometric shapes, you can grasp its structure and proportions before adding detail. This exercise will help you build the foot from the ground up, focusing on balance, rhythm and the relationship between the heel, arch and toes.

01

02

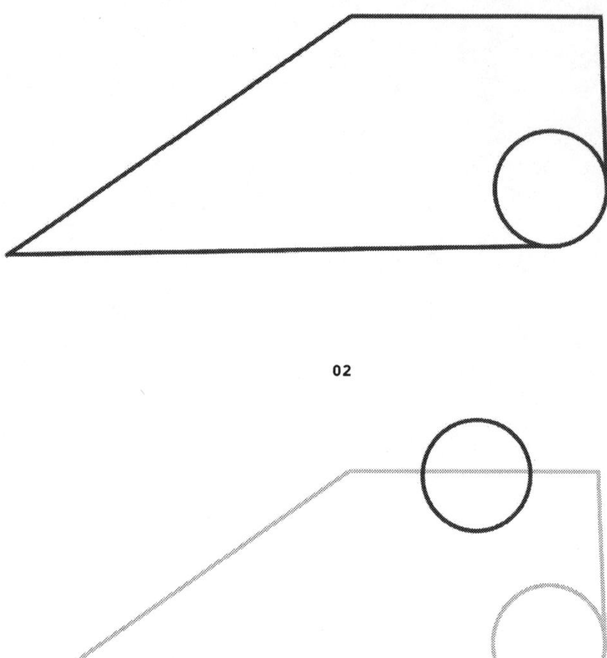

03

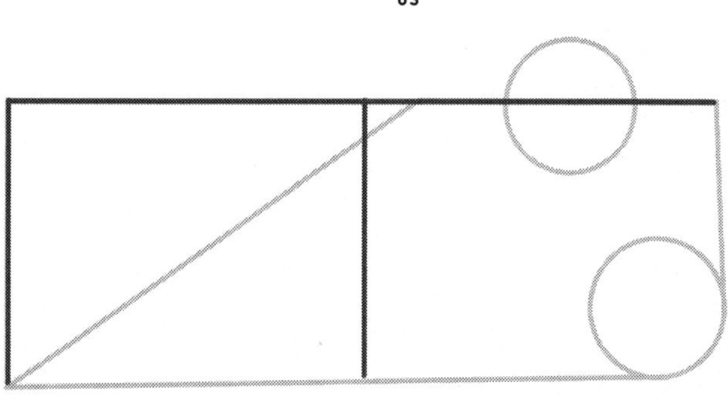

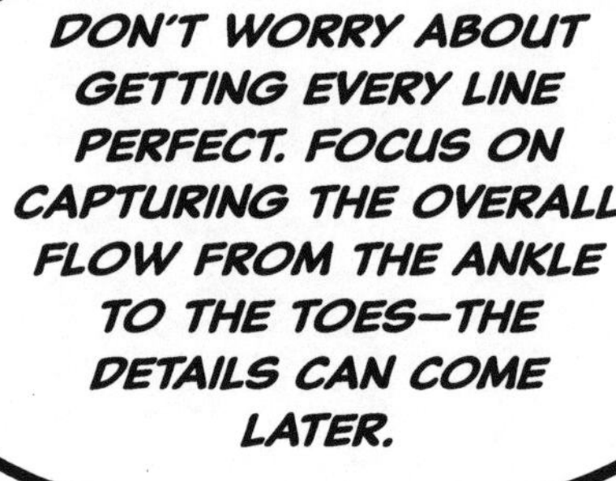

04

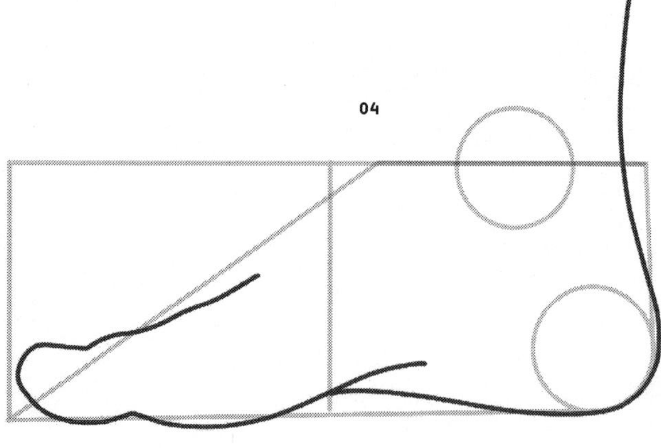

Step.1
Begin with a simple wedge shape to represent the foot's overall form. The top edge tilts slightly downward, showing the slope from the ankle to the toes. Add a circle at the back to mark the heel.

Step.2
Add another smaller circle slightly higher and forward from the heel to indicate the ankle joint. This second circle helps you understand how the ankle connects to the foot and sets the angle for the leg.

Step.3
Enclose the shape in a rectangle to define the proportions. The front half represents the forefoot (toes and ball), and the back half represents the arch and heel. The diagonal line across the box helps visualise the downward slope from the ankle to the toes.

Step.4
Begin sketching the foot's contour over the guide shapes. Use the lower line for the sole and the upper slope for the top plane of the foot. Keep the arch slightly raised and the toes angled downward.

Step.5
Add the front plane of the leg and refine the joint connection. The top circle marks where the ankle meets the leg, while the lower circle still defines the heel mass. Keep the lines light and structural.

Step.6
Outline the ankle bones and refine the curves around the top of the foot. Remember, the inner ankle sits higher and more forward than the outer one—this subtle tilt gives the foot its natural, grounded appearance.

Step.7
Refine the drawing with more confident contour lines. Emphasise the weight-bearing structure of the foot: the heel, arch, and ball. Notice how the line from the ankle to the toes flows in one continuous rhythm.

Step.8
Finish with surface details such as tendons with subtle shading.

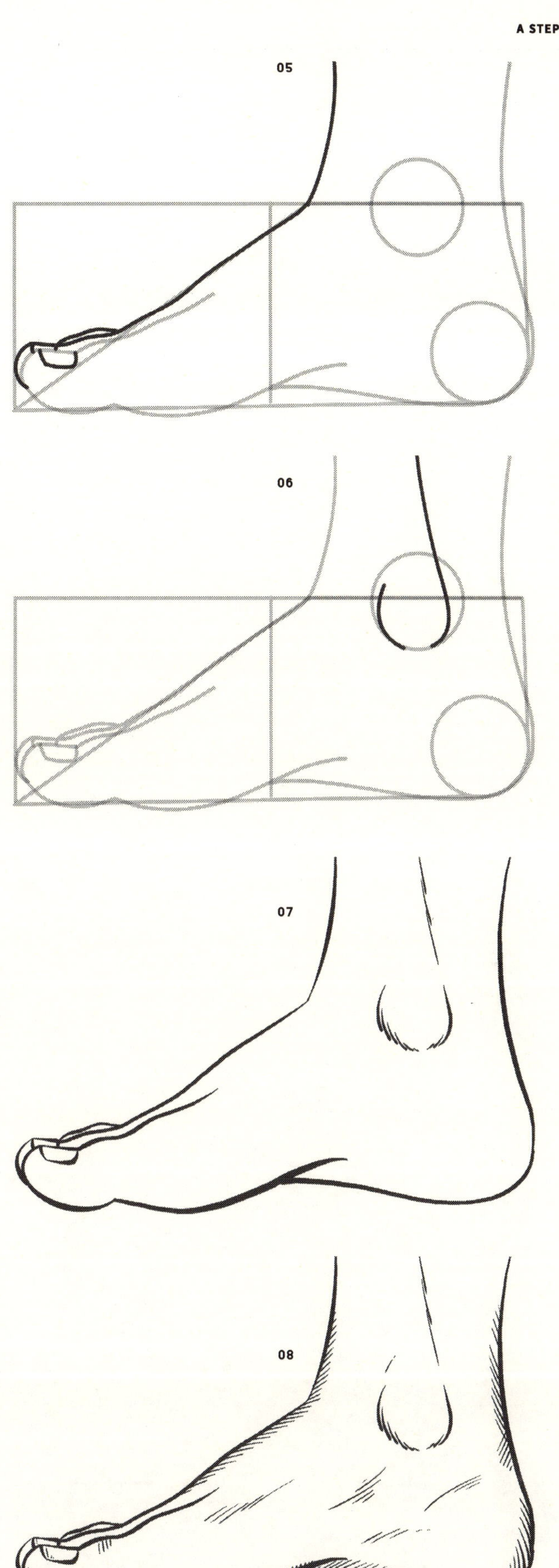

DRAWING FEET AND HANDS FROM VARIOUS ANGLES

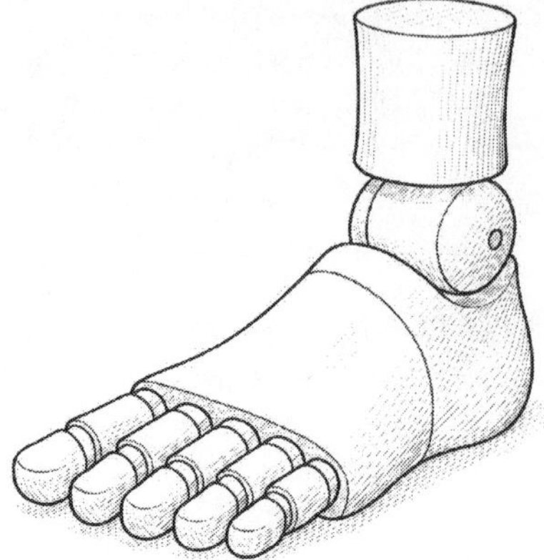

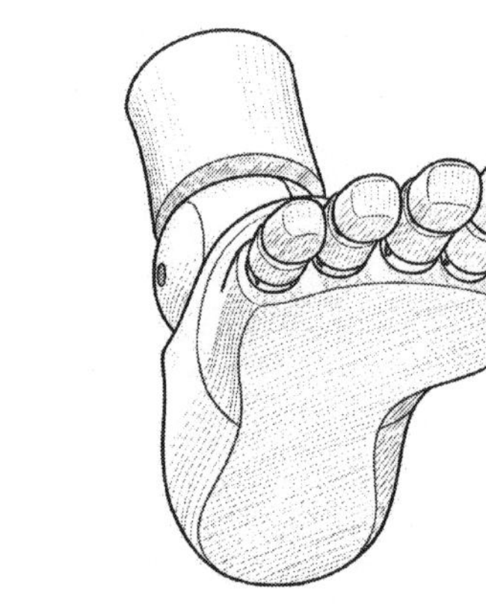

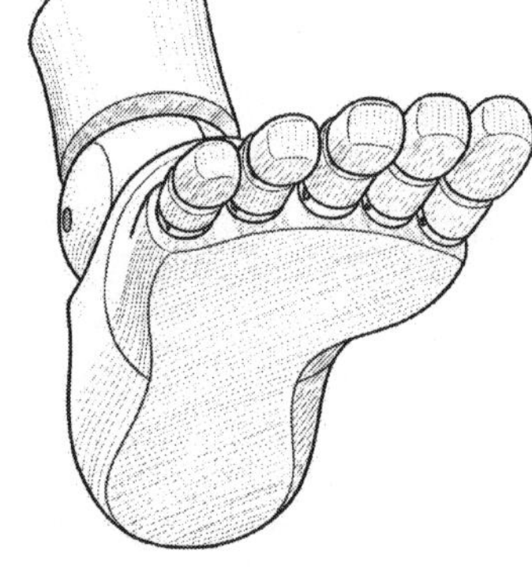

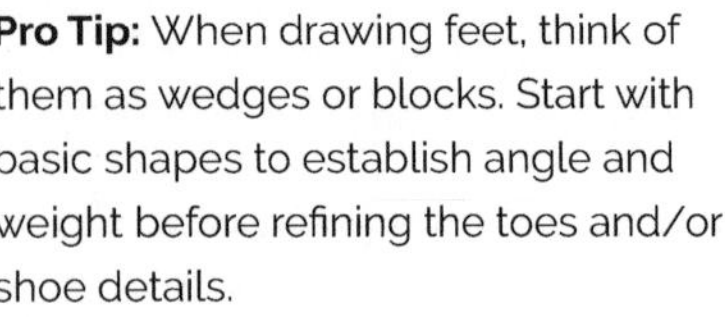

Pro Tip: When drawing feet, think of them as wedges or blocks. Start with basic shapes to establish angle and weight before refining the toes and/or shoe details.

01

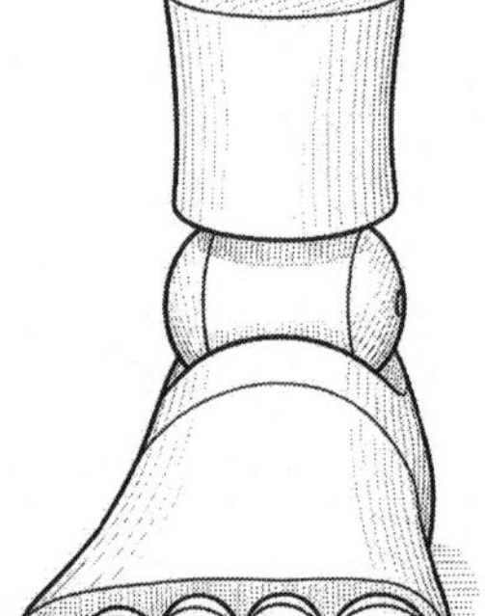

02

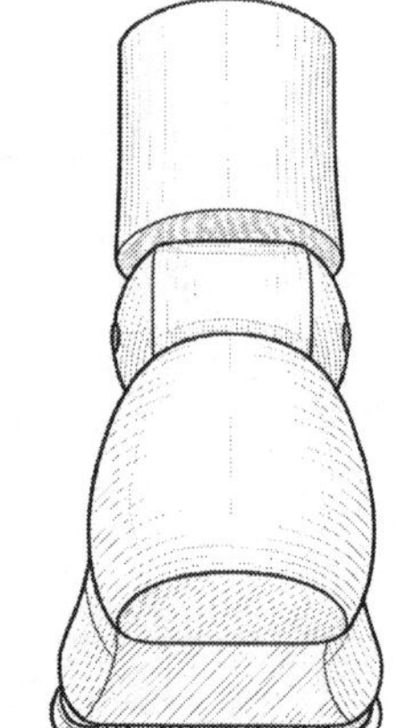

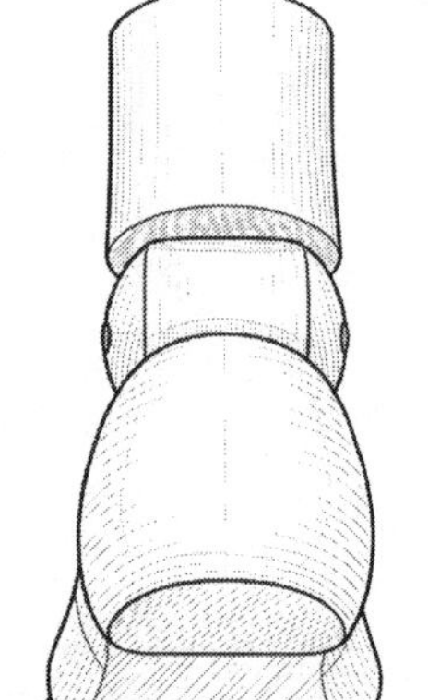

03

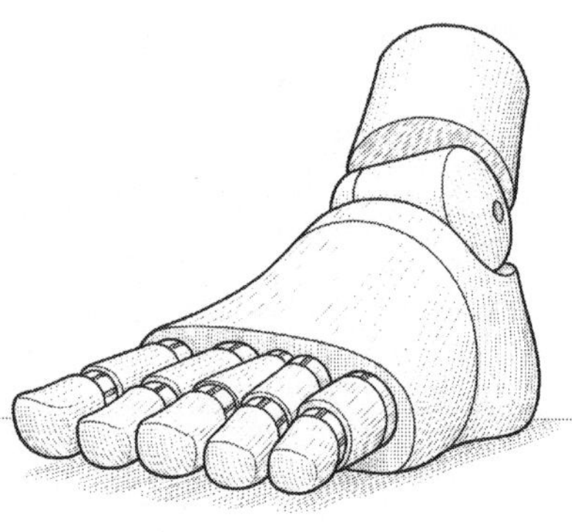

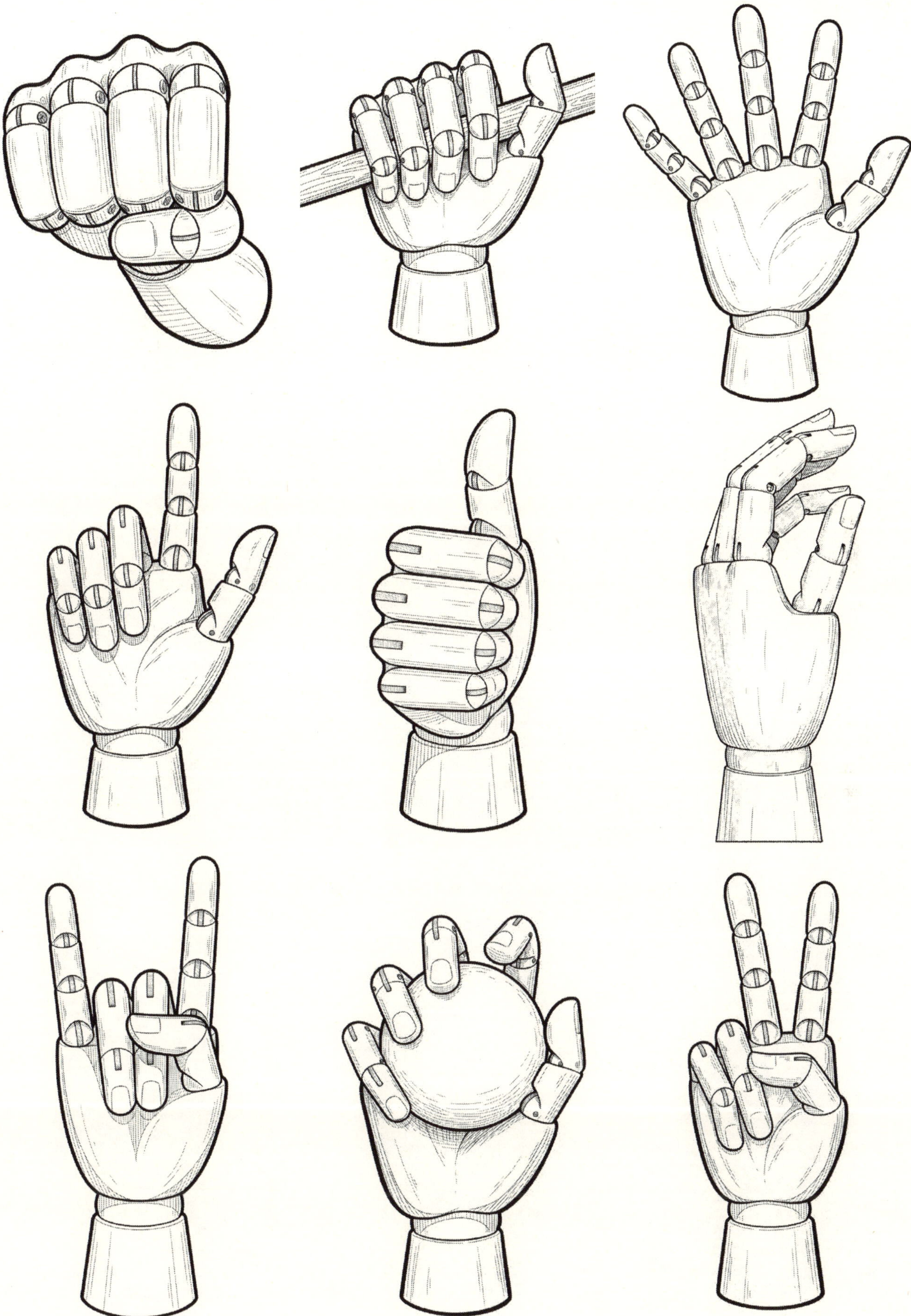

UNDERSTANDING PROPORTIONS OF THE MALE ANATOMY

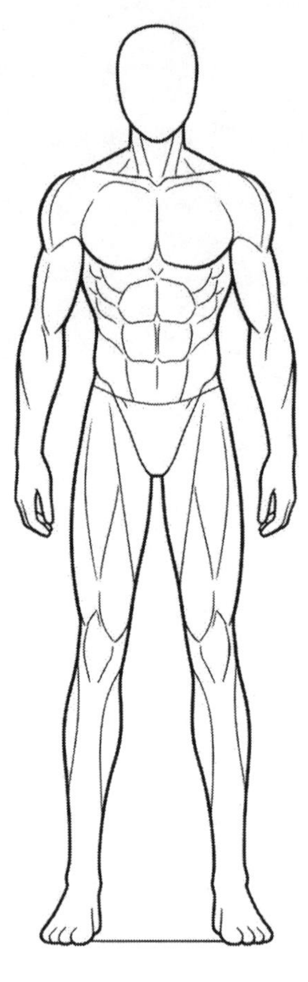

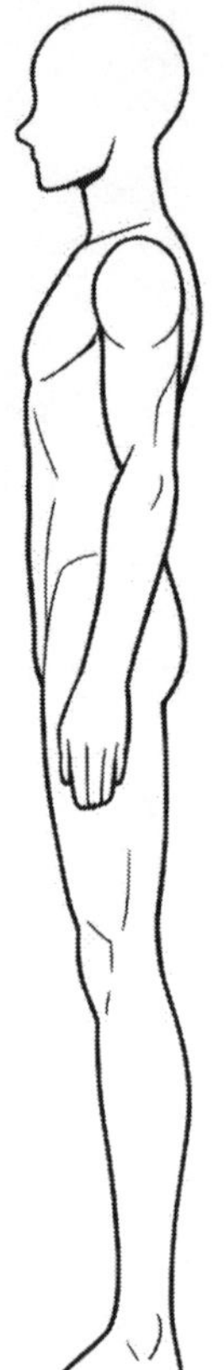

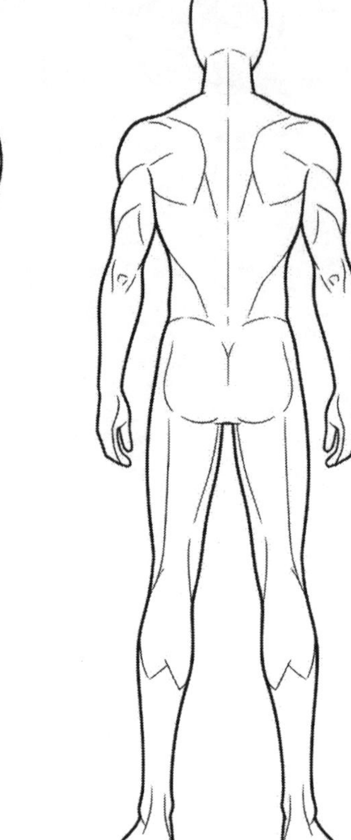

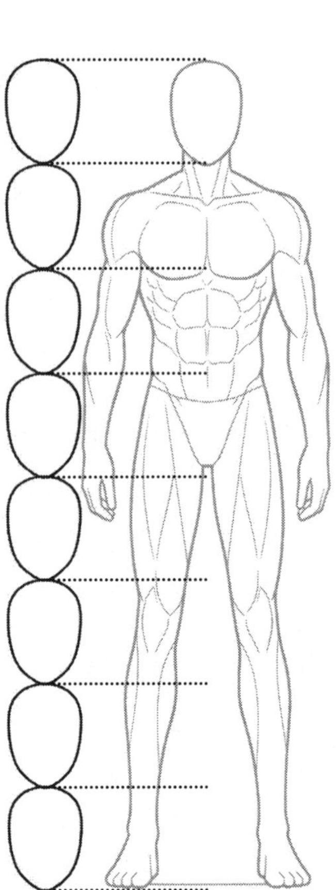

The average male superhero measures approximately 8 heads tall. Use the head as a unit to keep proportions consistent.

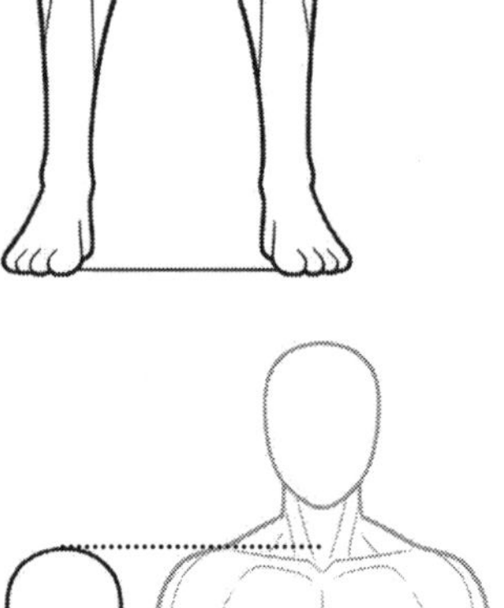

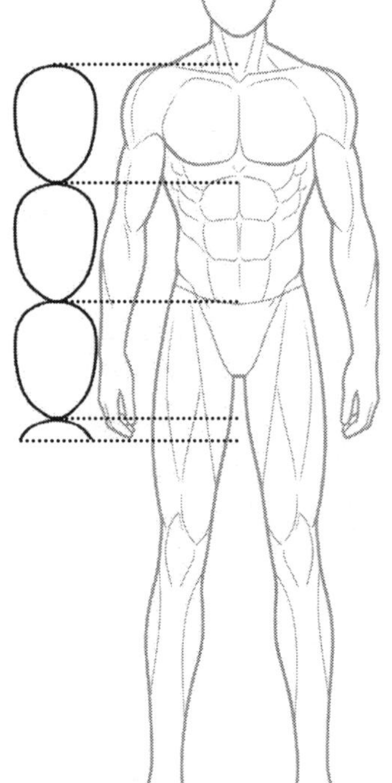

The arm should be approximately $3\frac{1}{3}$ heads in length.

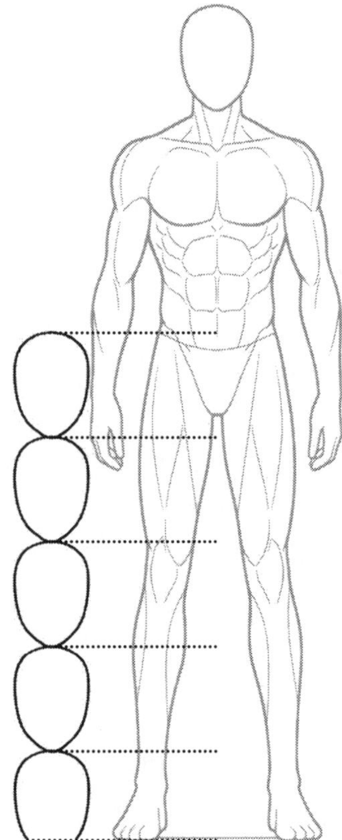

From the hips to the feet, the lower body measures approximately 5 heads.

Pro Tip: When drawing the human figure, start by establishing the head first. Once you've drawn it, you've created a unit of measurement that can be used to map out the rest of the body with accuracy and consistency.

Using head lengths as your universal measuring tool keeps the proportions of the figure balanced. For example, an average adult figure is roughly seven and to eight heads tall. This method helps you locate key landmarks, such as the position of the shoulders, chest, waist, hips, knees, and feet—relative to the size of the head. By stacking and comparing these head lengths as you work, you can build the entire figure confidently, maintaining harmony and realism throughout your drawing.

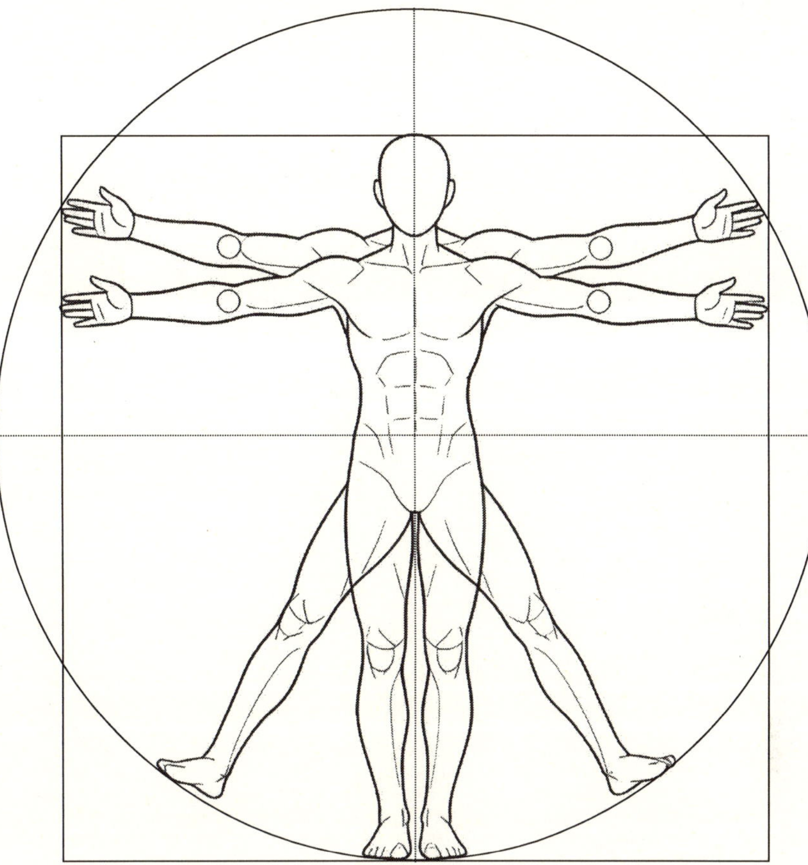

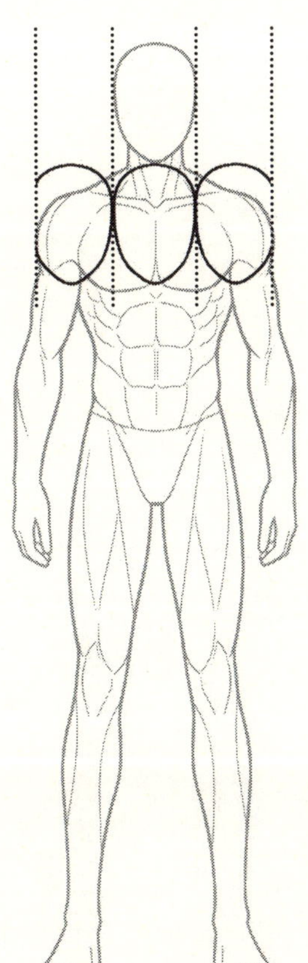

The shoulders sit approximately 3 head widths apart.

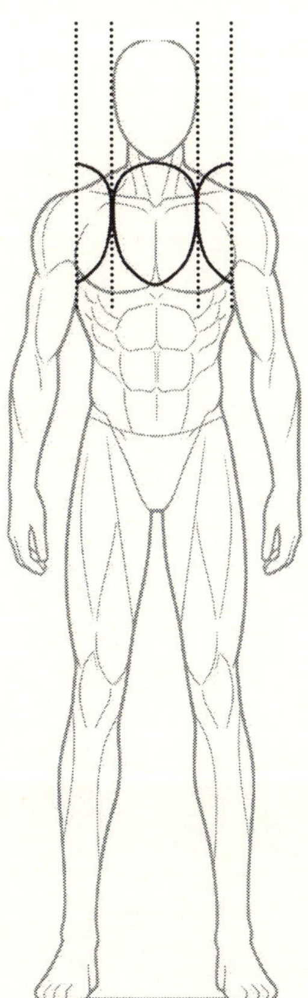

The chest spans approximately 2 head widths.

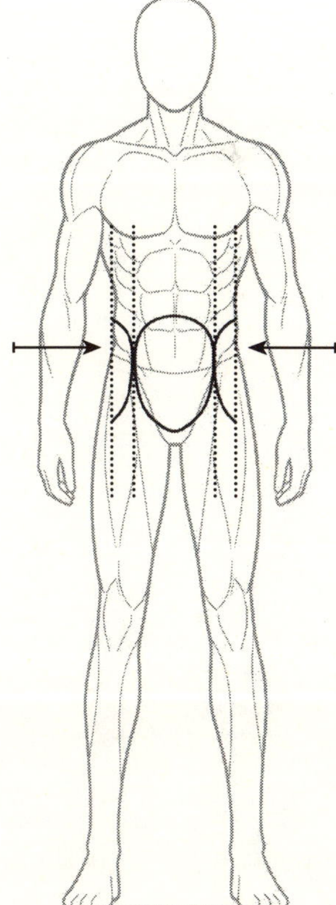

The waist measures approximately 1⅔ head widths at the top of the pelvis.

DRAWING THE MALE FIGURE IN DYNAMIC POSES

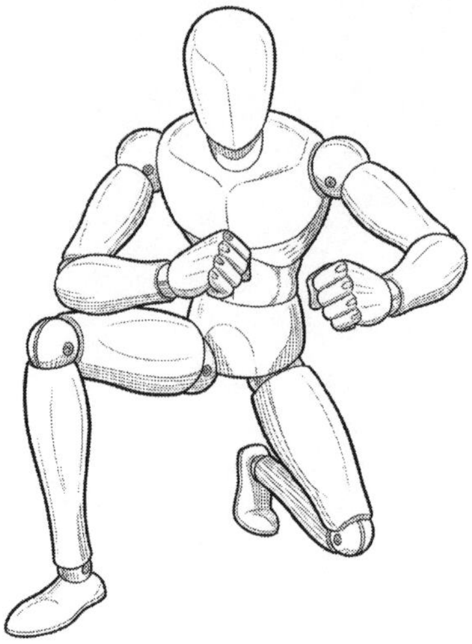

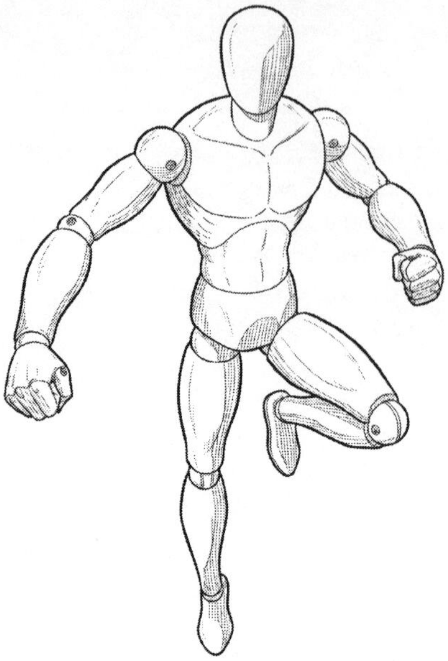

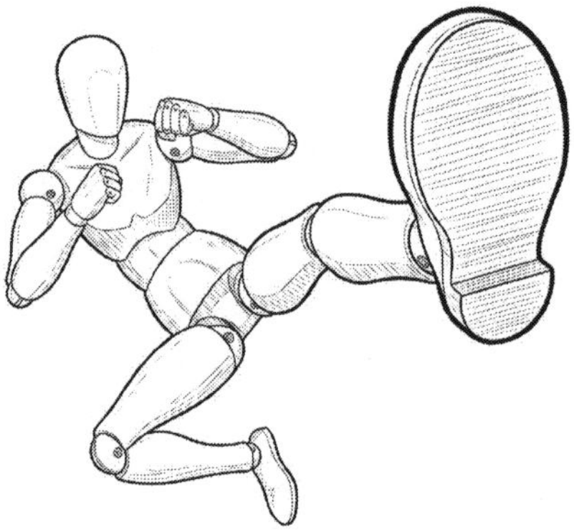

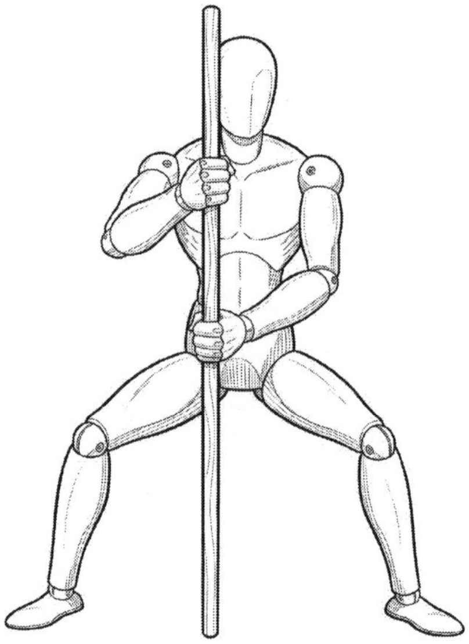

Pro Tip: Start with loose, sweeping lines to capture the movement before tightening the form. Keep the centre of gravity in mind to anchor your figure.

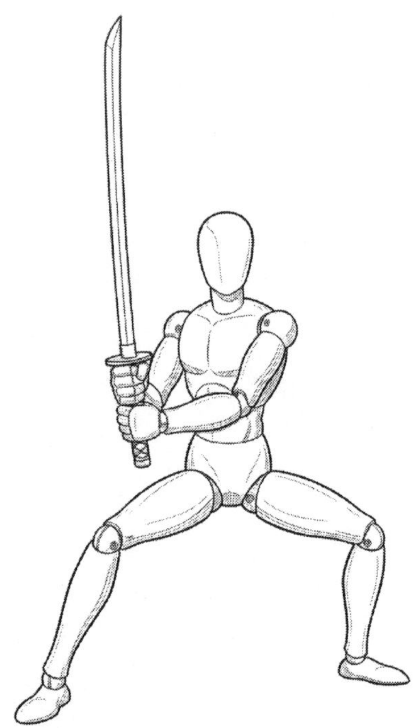

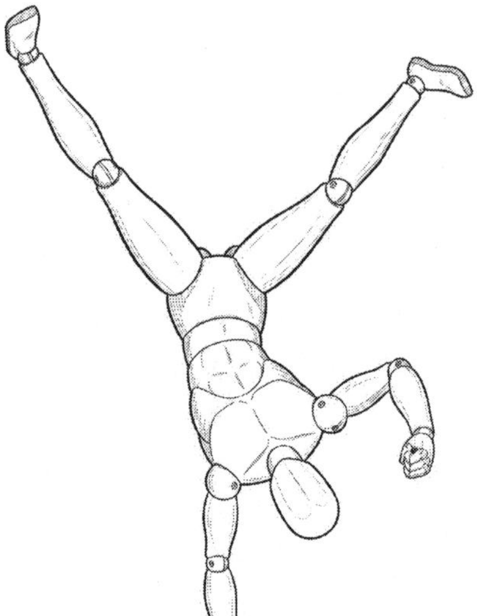

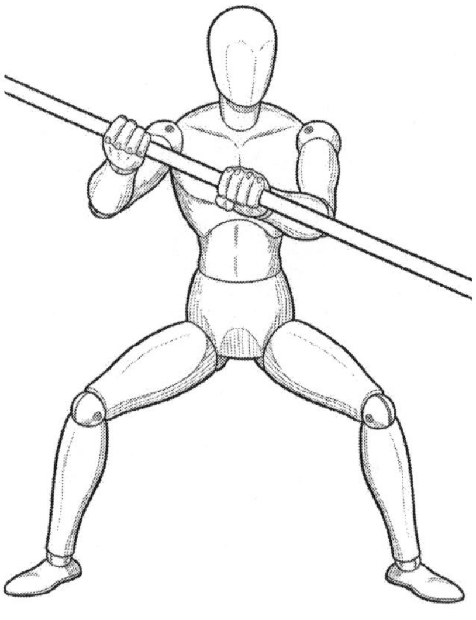

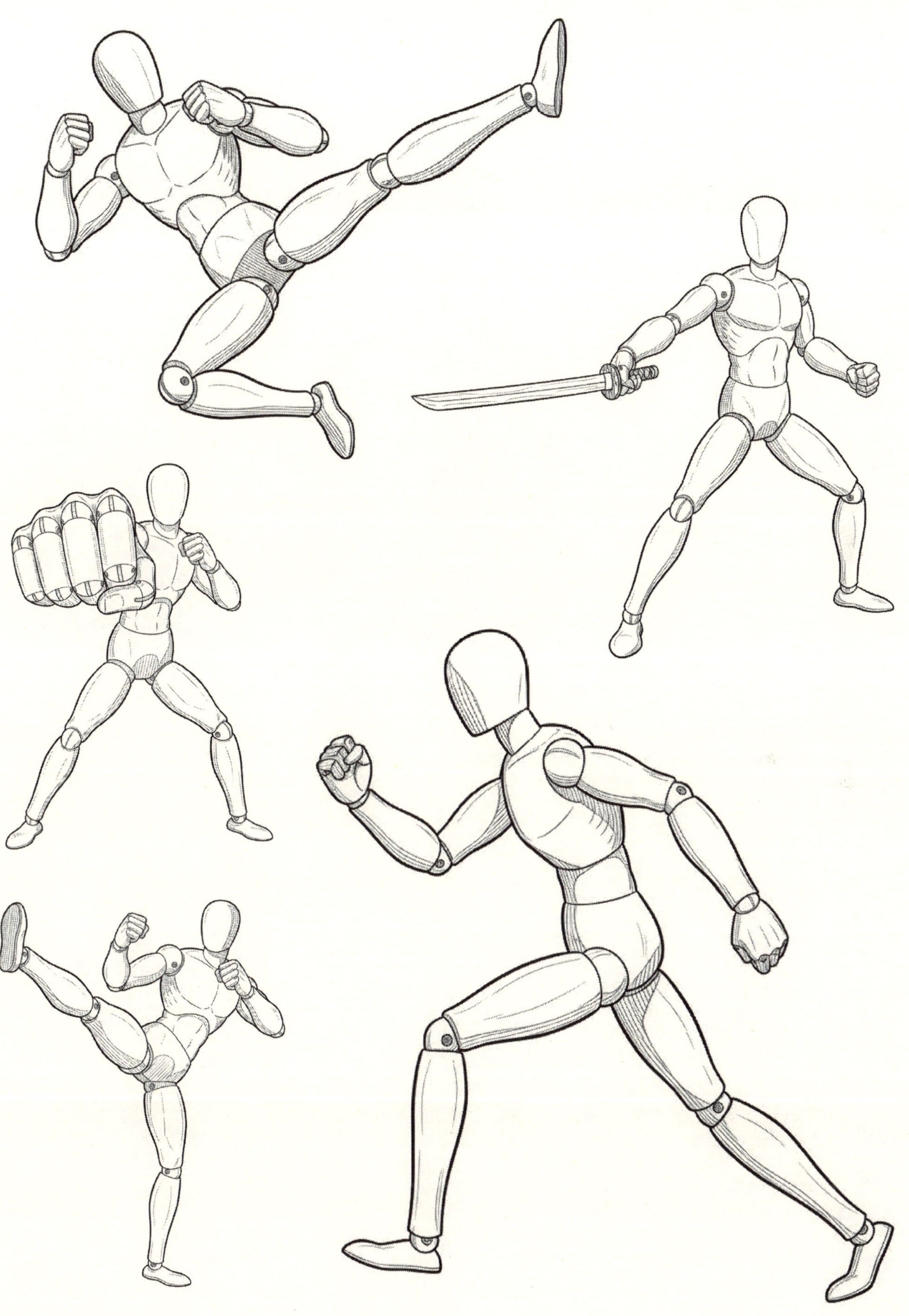

DRAWING THE FEMALE FACE

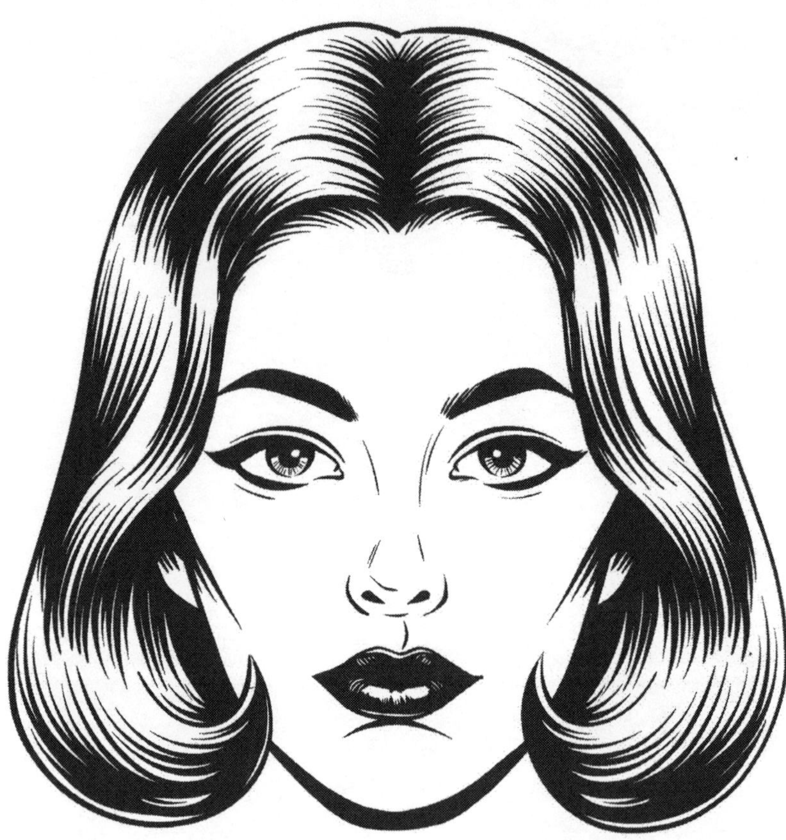

Pro Tip: Keep your construction lines light and consistent—these guides are the backbone of your drawing. Use them to check symmetry, balance, and alignment as you refine the features.

01

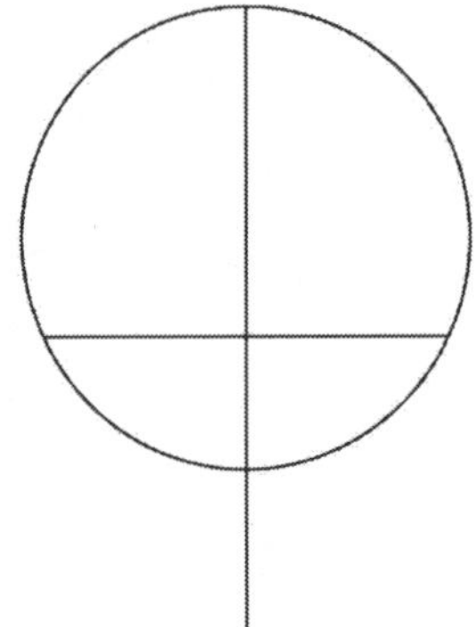

Start by drawing a circle that's evenly divided into quarters. Draw a line that extends from the bottom of the circle that measures 1/3 of the circle's height.

02

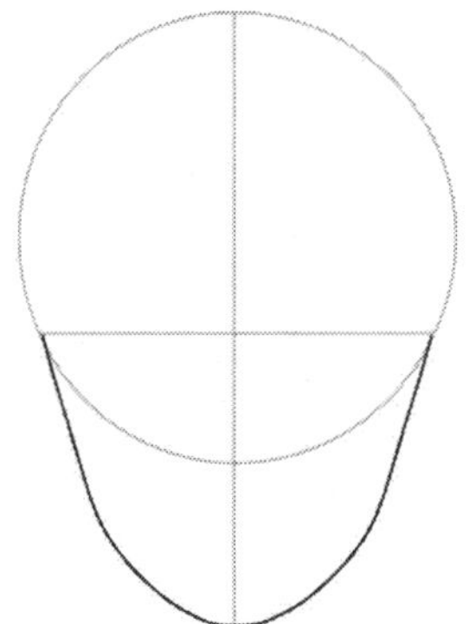

Now, draw in a chin shape that connects the left and right points of the circle with the line that extends from the bottom of the circle.

03

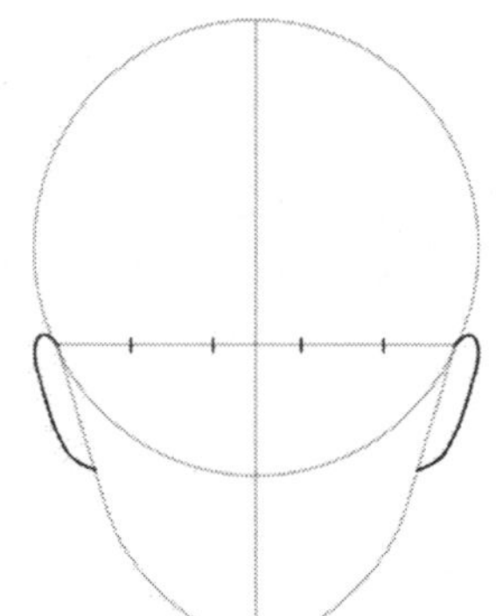

To determine the placement of the eye, know that the head will be 5 eyes wide. Divide the horiznotal line into 5 equal spaces.

04

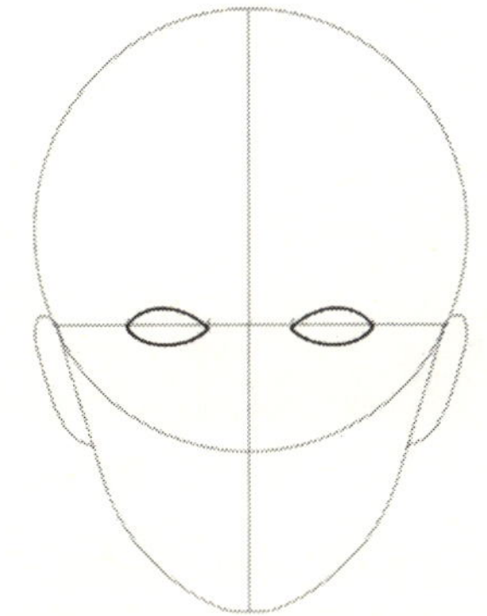

Place the eyes in the second and fourth spaces. The space between the eyes is always one eye width.

05

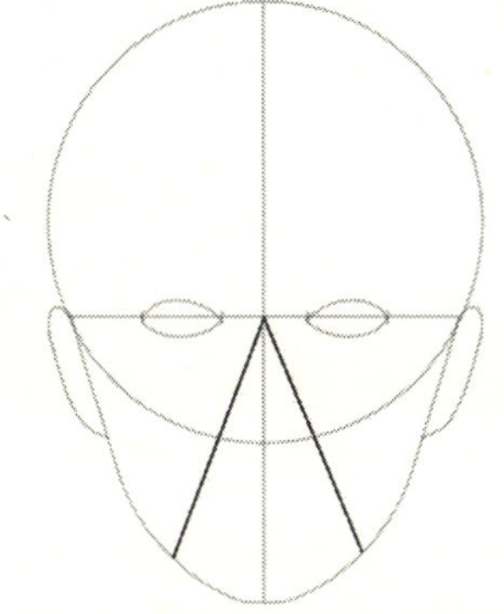

Draw a triangle extending downward from the bridge of the nose, just like the example above. This will define the width of the nose and mouth.

06

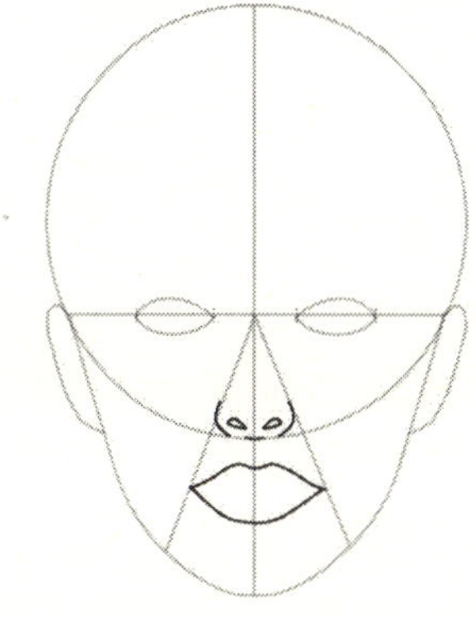

The mouth sits approximately halfway down the triangle. Note that the base of the nose is at the bottom of the circle.

07

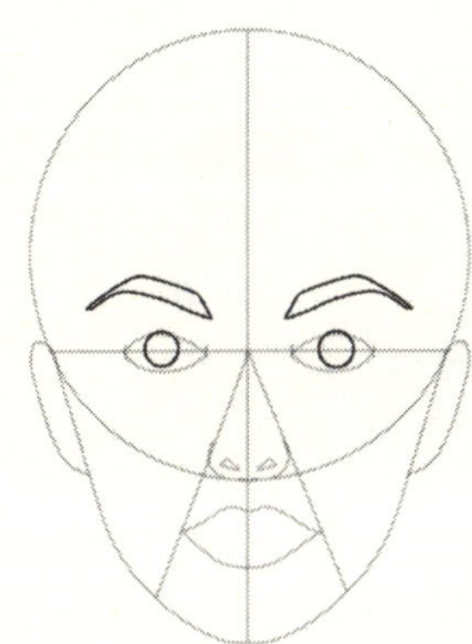

Sketch in the iris of the eyes, as well as the eyebrows.

08

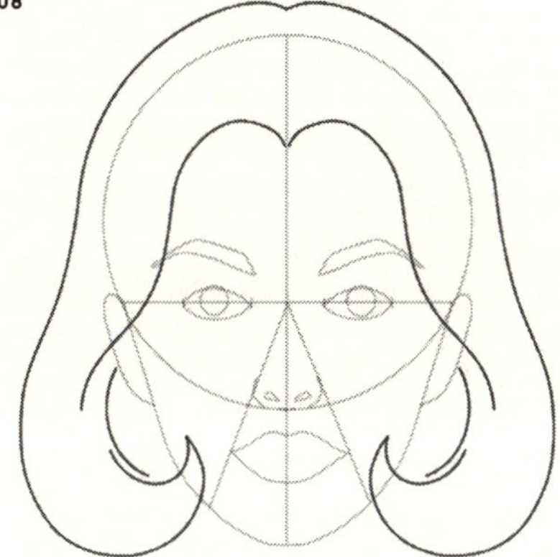

Add the guidelines for the hair. Let some flow over the ear for natural effect.

09

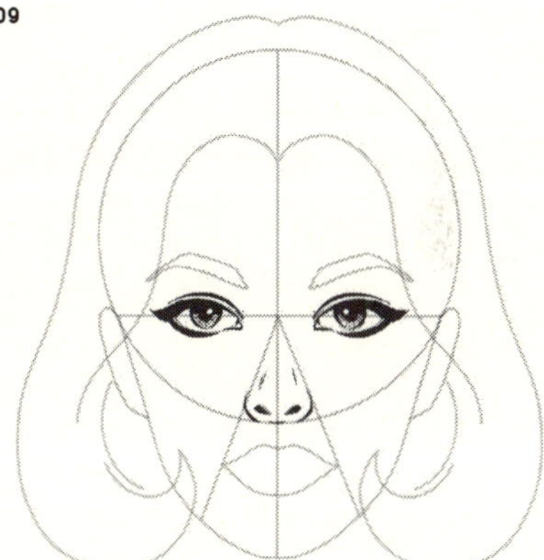

With an inking brush, start detailing the eyes. Don't draw lots of individual eyelashes, instead draw them as one volume.

10

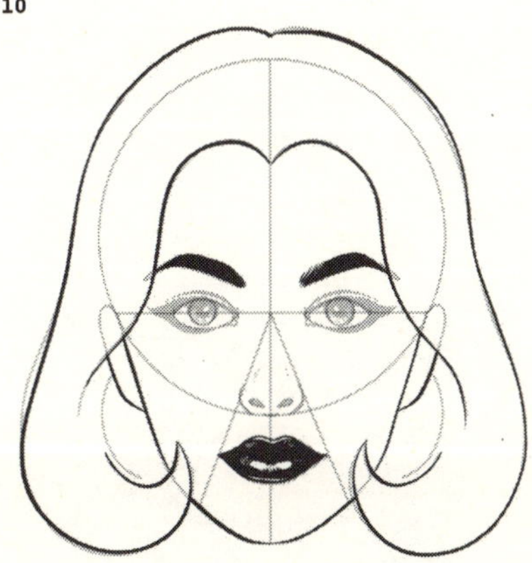

Ink the eyebrows, hair outline and mouth. Add reflections to the lips to avoid them from looking too heavy.

11

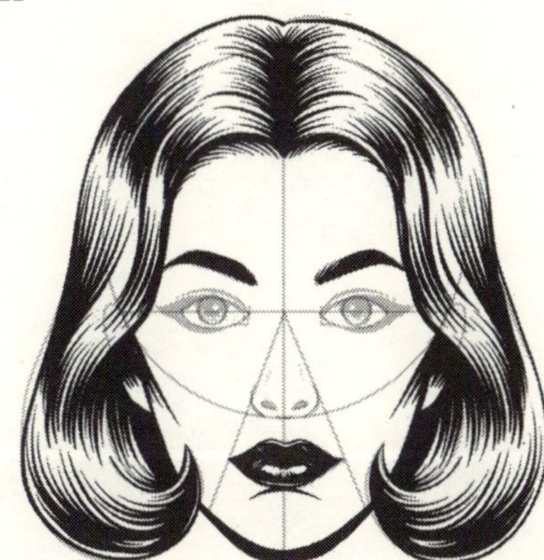

Complete the inking of the hair, adding highlights and shading. Note that it is darkest next to the ear where the hair flows over and blocks the light from entering. Also, add a gentle arced line beneath the lips to define the chin.

12

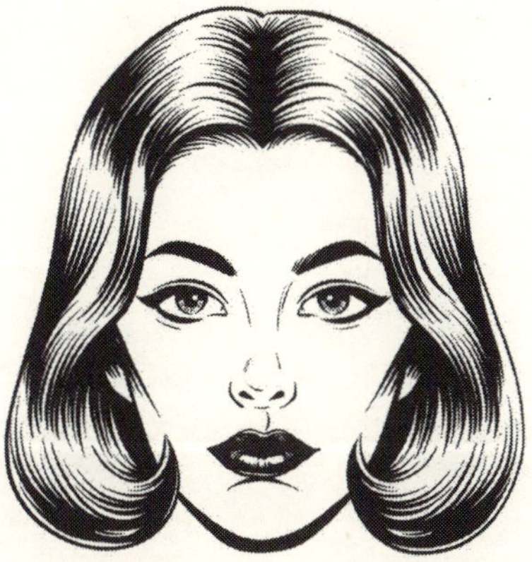

Remove all construction lines. The final drawing should have confident linework, full hair rendering, and strong tonal contrast.

DRAWING THE FEMALE FACE IN PROFILE VIEW

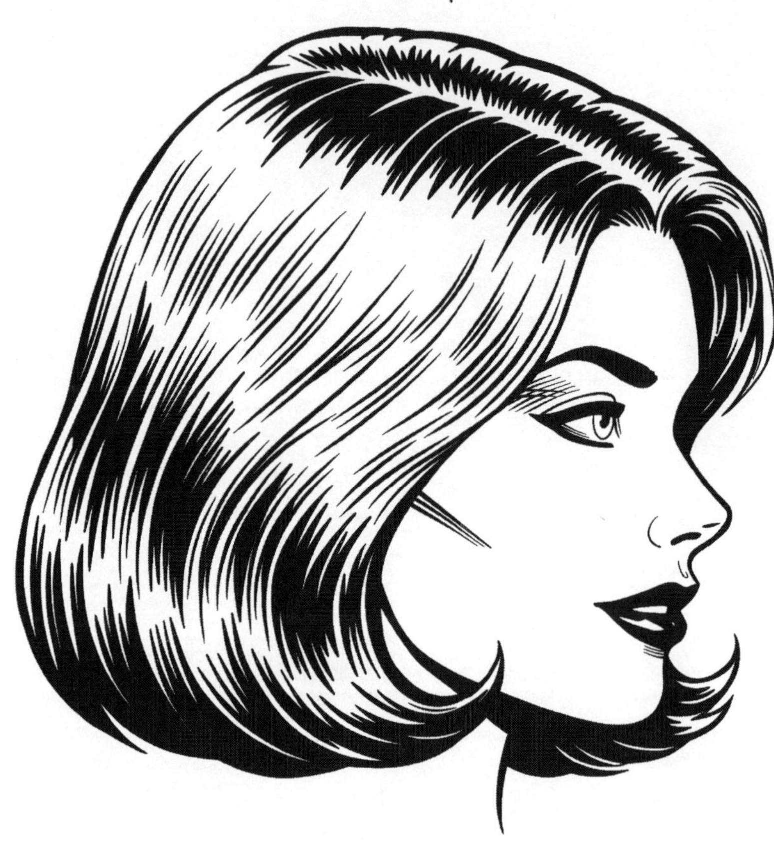

Pro Tip: When sketching in profile, focus on how each feature aligns along the vertical centre and horizontal lines. Visualising these relationships early helps maintain correct proportions.

01

Draw a square divided into four equal quadrants with a vertical and horizontal centre line. This is your proportional guide for the whole head.

02

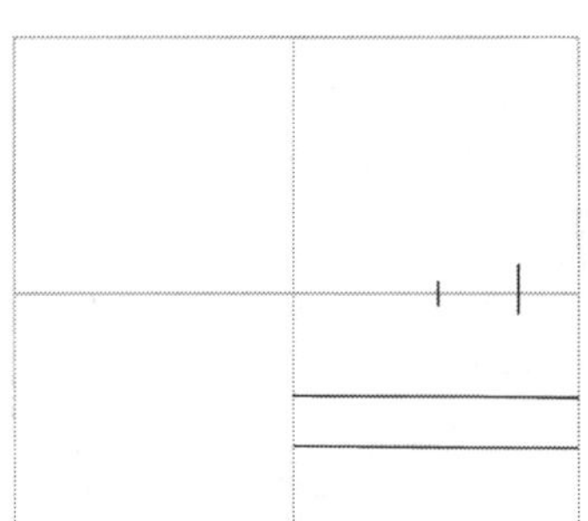

Place horizontal tick marks across the centre line to establish the brow, eye, nose, and mouth levels.

03

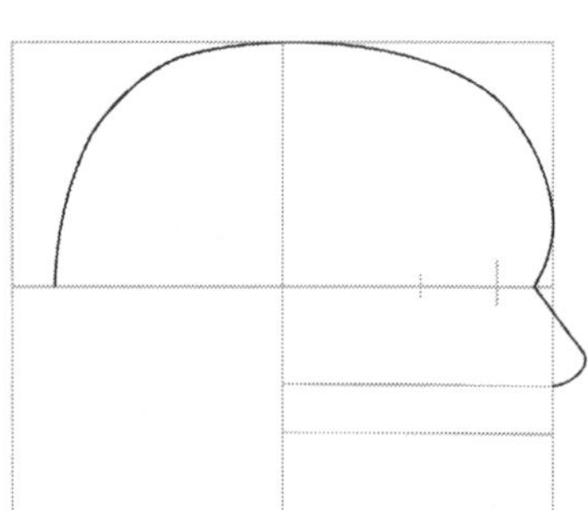

Draw a large D-shaped cranium filling the upper portion of the grid. Add a simplified nose shape extending below.

04

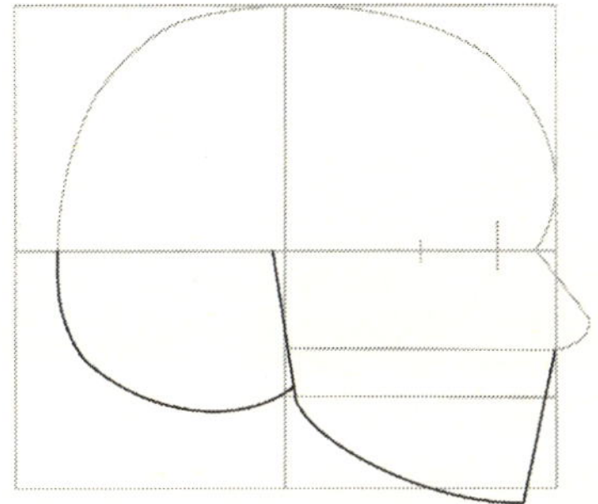

Round out the back of the cranium into a smooth curve. Add the chin shape below the jaw.

05

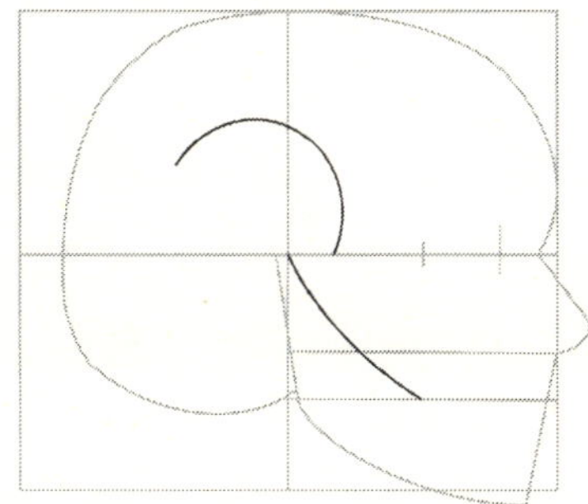

Sketch in the cheekbones and the side plane of the head.

06

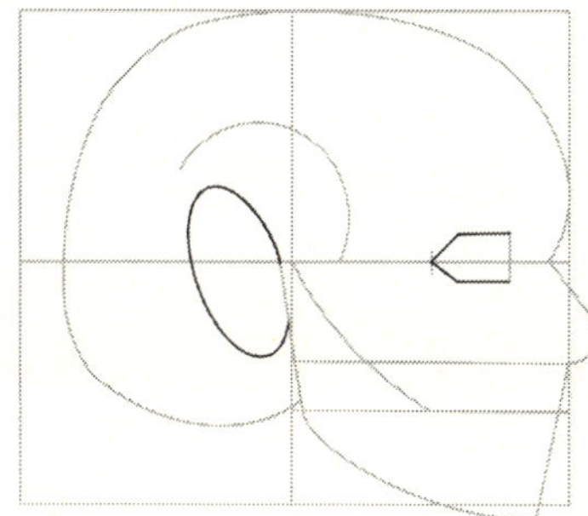

Add the ear at the horizontal centre line where the cranium meets the face. Draw in a socket for the eye to sit within.

07

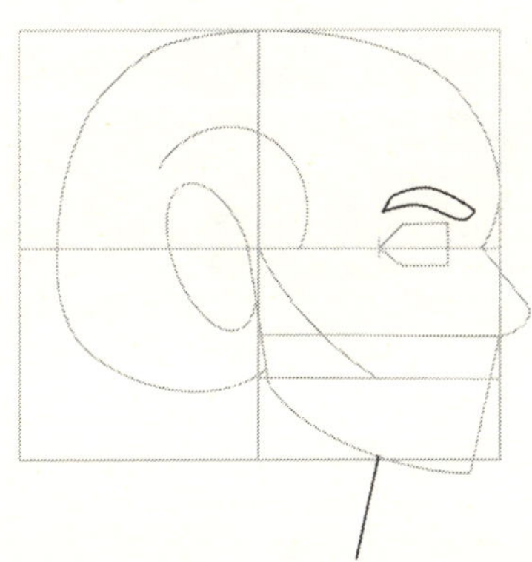

Sketch in the brow and draw a neck line extending down from the chin.

08

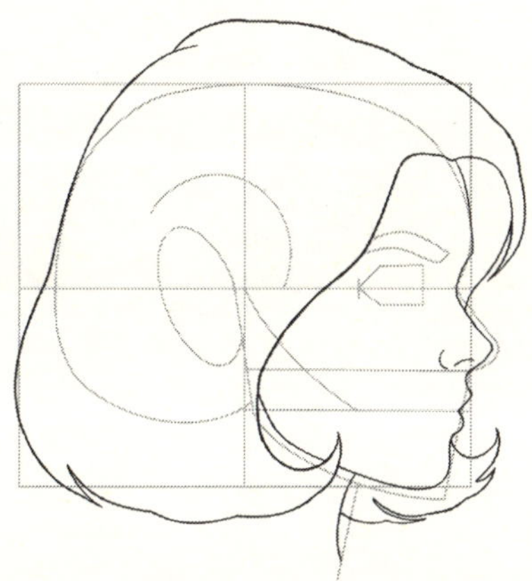

The full hair mass and profile silhouette (nose, lips, chin, neck) are drawn in with confident lines over the construction.

09

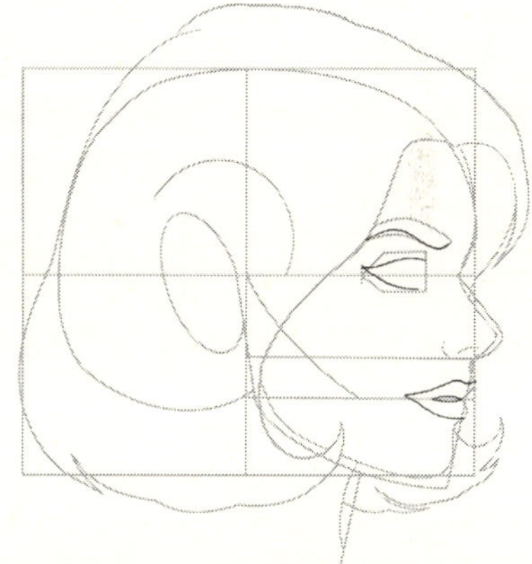

Now tighten the profile by drawing the shape of the eye and lips.

10

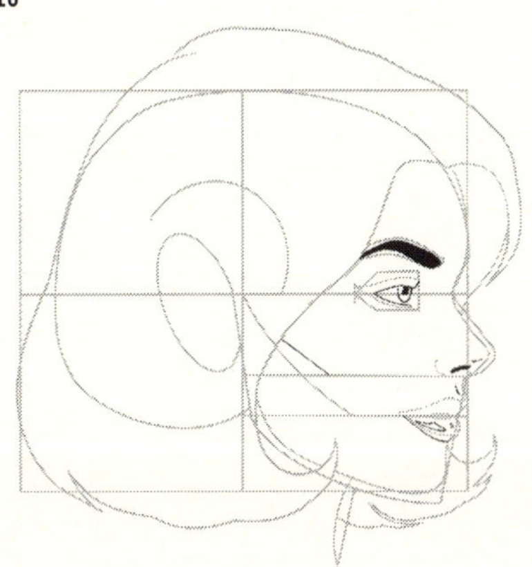

Draw the details brow, eye and nose.

11

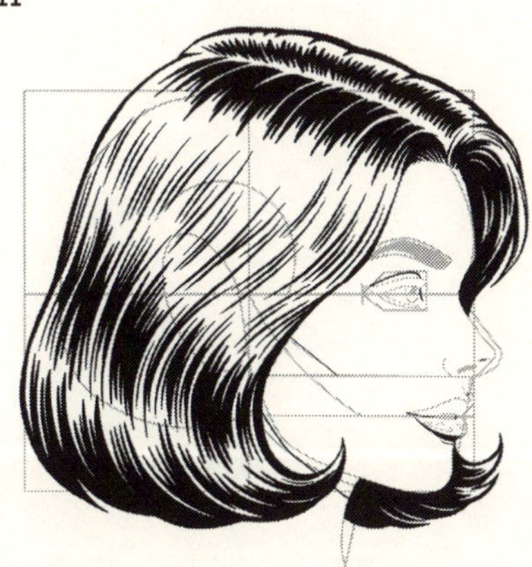

Render the hair with bold strand lines and heavy shadow.

12

Remove all construction lines. The image is now ready for final rendering.

DRAWING THE FEMALE FACE IN PROFILE VIEW

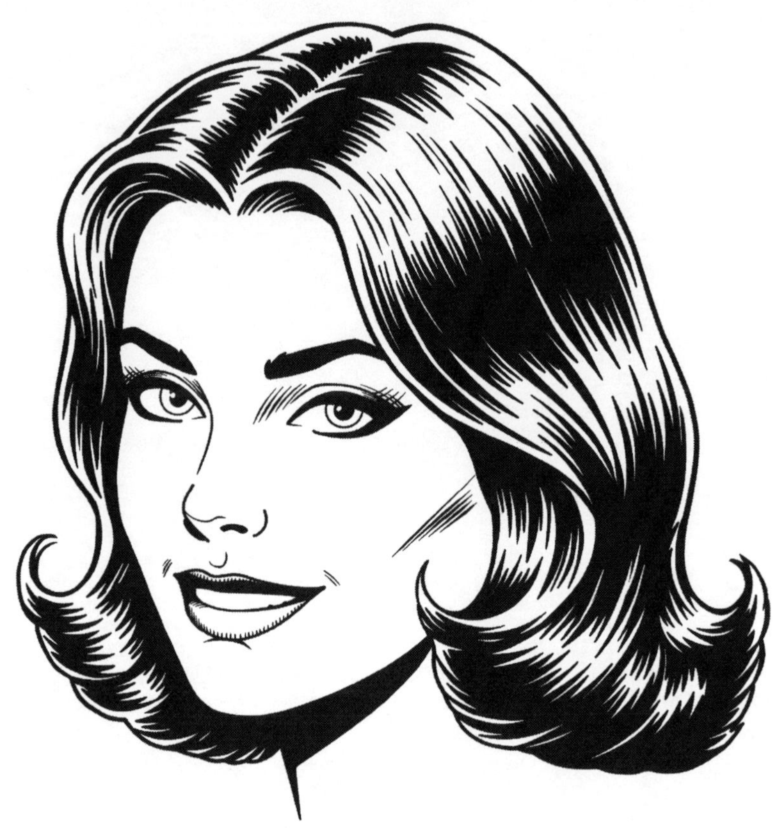

Pro Tip: In step 10, on the left at the eyeline, notice that the contour of the line goes in and then back out again. This captures the definition of the cheekbones and brow. Be sure to include this detail.

01

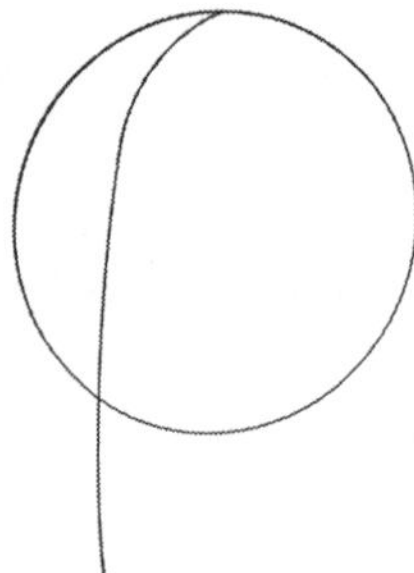

Draw an arced line downward from the top the circle. The line should extend past the base approximately 50% of the height of the circle.

02

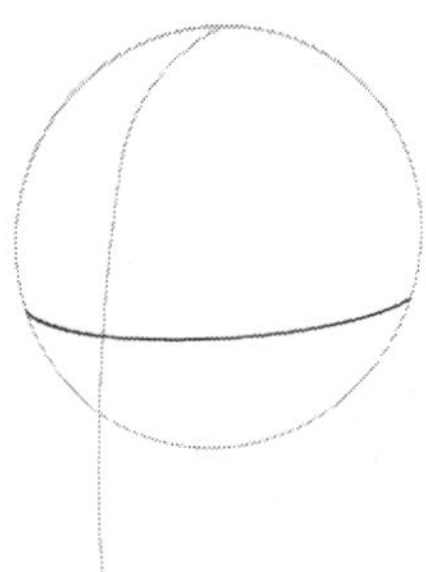

Draw a horizontal arced line on a slight leftward leaning slant approximately 1/3 of the height of the circle from the base. This will be the eyeline.

03

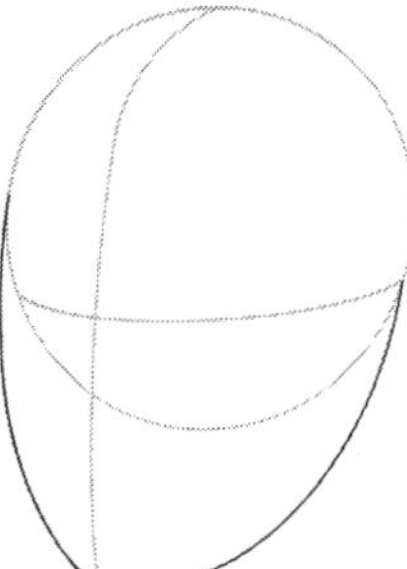

Sketch in the chin shape by connecting an arced line from each point of the eyeline. Note that on the left, it extends just above the eyeline. Be sure to include this detail.

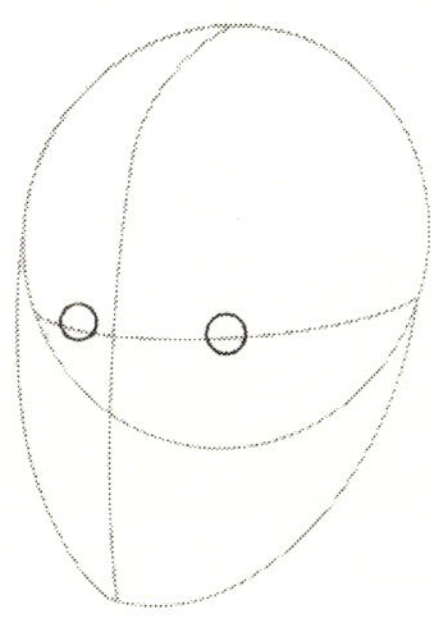

Place the eyes on the eyeline just like the reference above.

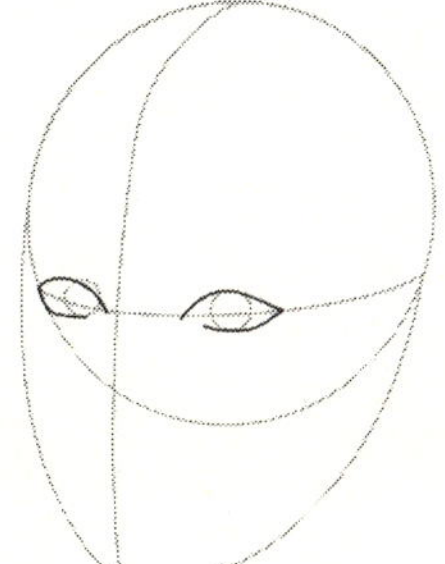

Sketch the in the eyelids to start giving the eyes some structure.

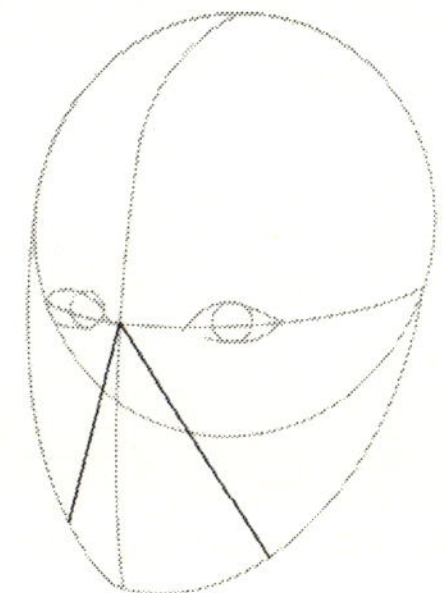

Draw a triangle shape from the centre point of the intersecting lines. This will help you determine the width and position of the nose and mouth.

07

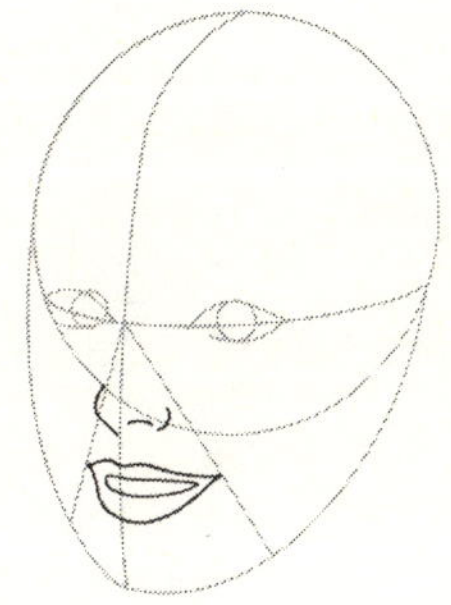

The mouth sits approximately halfway down the triangle.

08

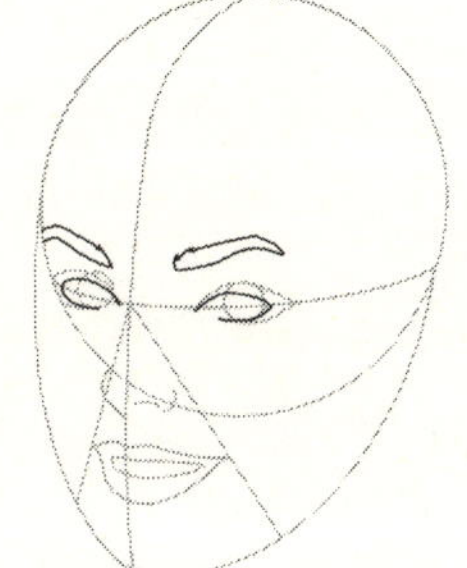

Sketch in the eyebrows. Add additional fold lines above the eyeline for a more natural look.

09

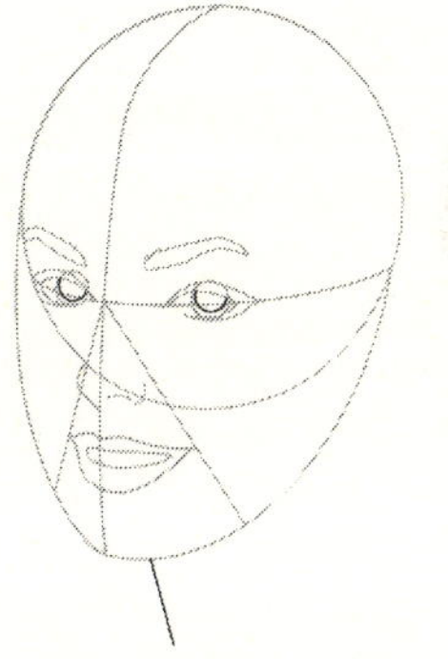

Sketch in the eyeballs and draw a neck line extending down from the chin.

10

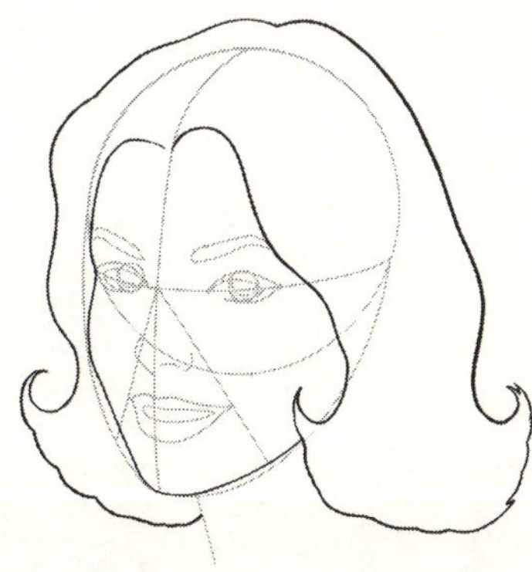

The full hair mass and profile silhouette are drawn in with confident lines over the construction.

11

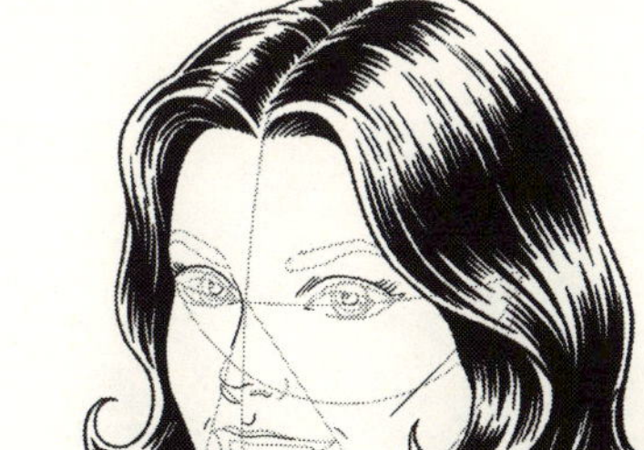

Using an inking brush, outline the hair and facial features.

12

Remove all construction lines. The image is now ready for final rendering.

DRAWING THE FEMALE FACE FROM VARIOUS ANGLES

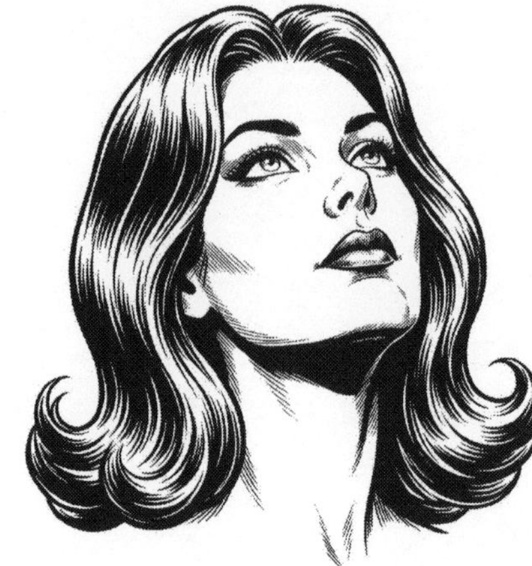

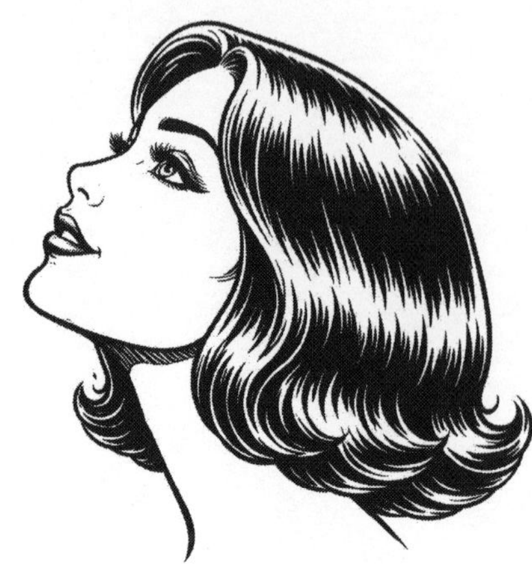

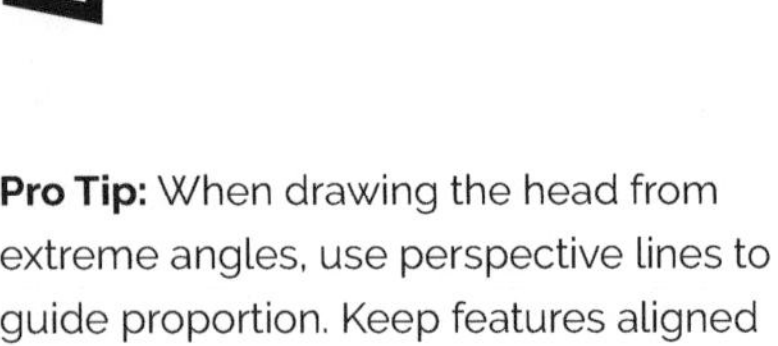

Pro Tip: When drawing the head from extreme angles, use perspective lines to guide proportion. Keep features aligned to maintain structure and avoid distortion.

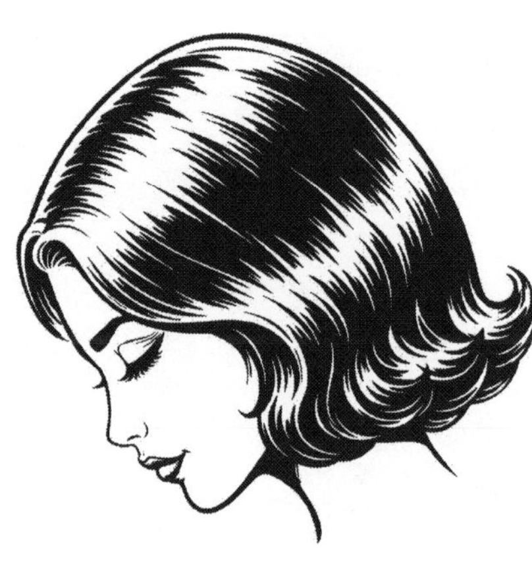

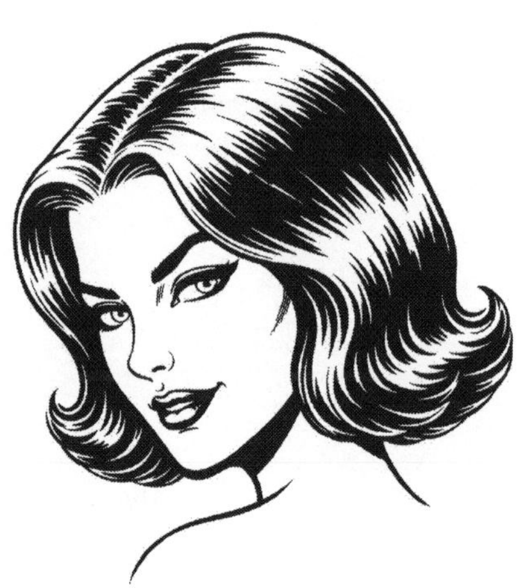

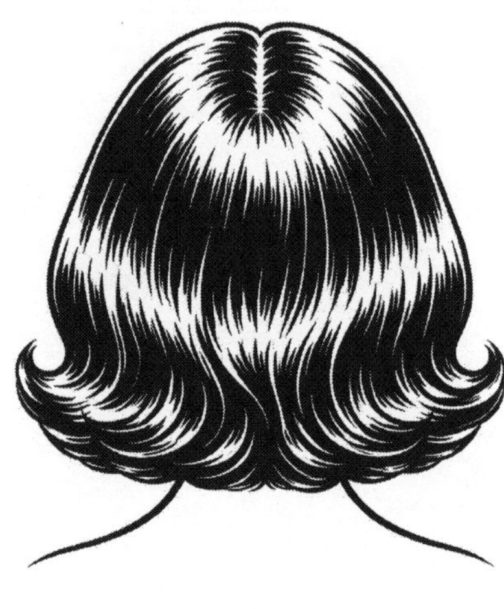

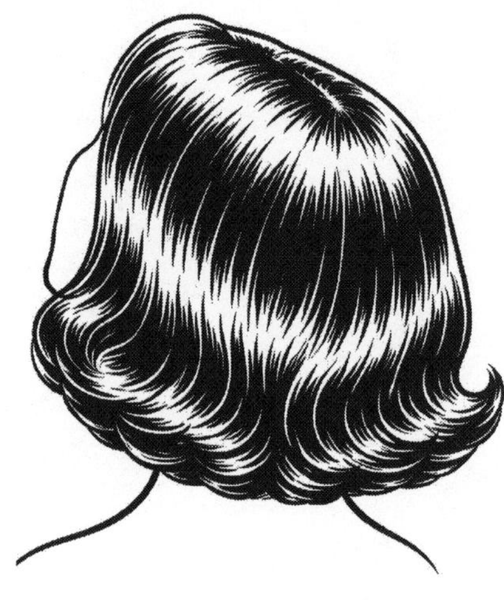

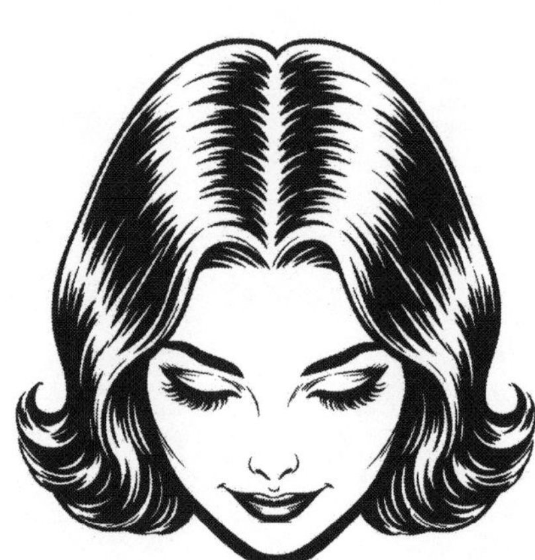

DRAWING FEMALE FACIAL EXPRESSIONS

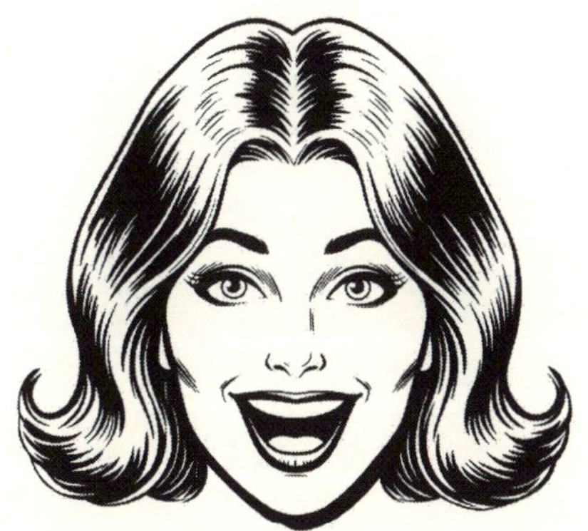

HAPPINESS

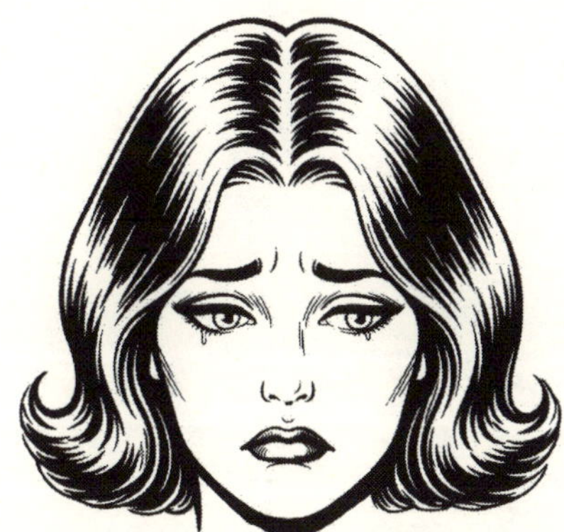

SADNESS

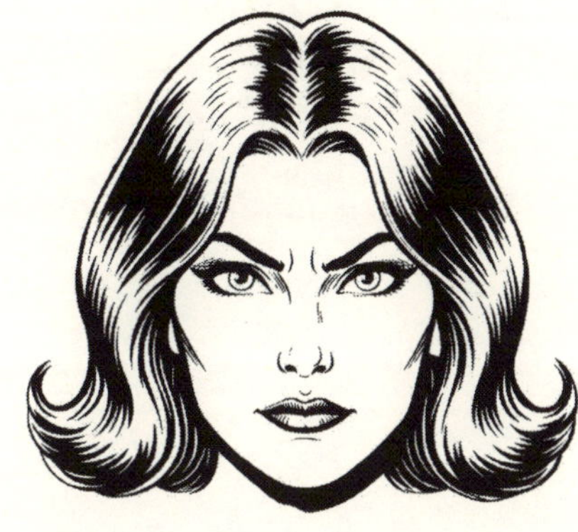

DETERMINED

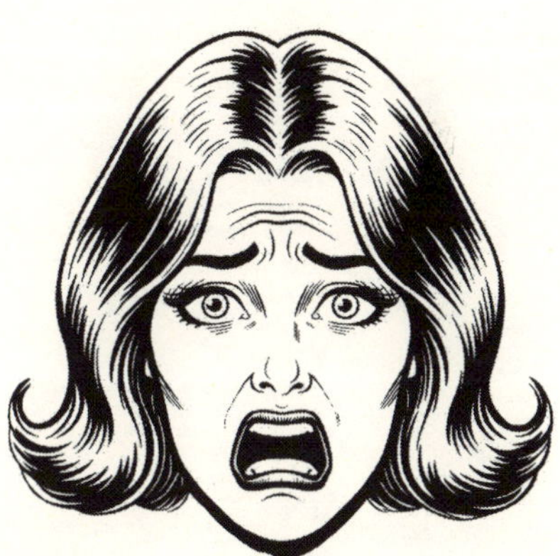

FEAR

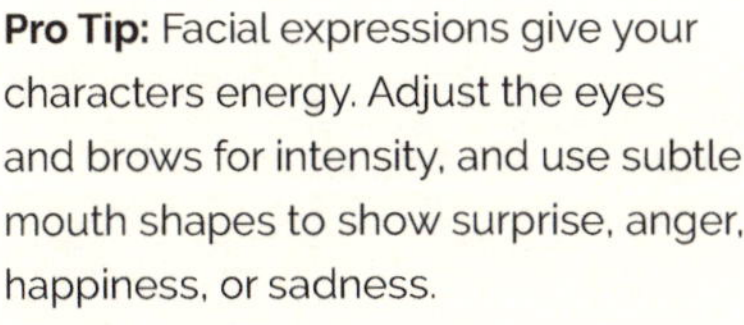

Pro Tip: Facial expressions give your characters energy. Adjust the eyes and brows for intensity, and use subtle mouth shapes to show surprise, anger, happiness, or sadness.

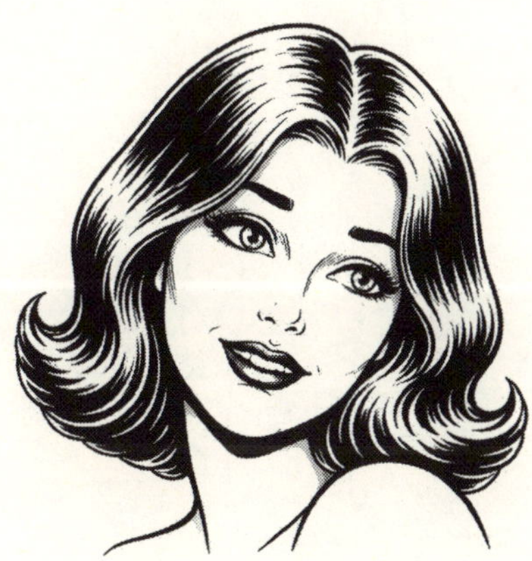

LOVE

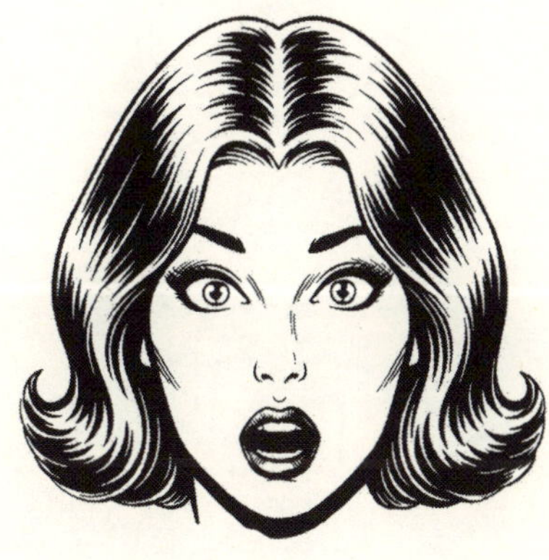

SURPRISED

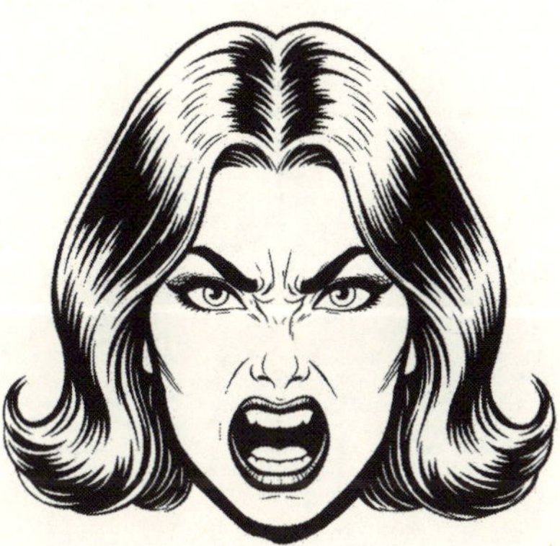

ANGER

UNDERSTANDING PROPORTIONS OF THE FEMALE ANATOMY

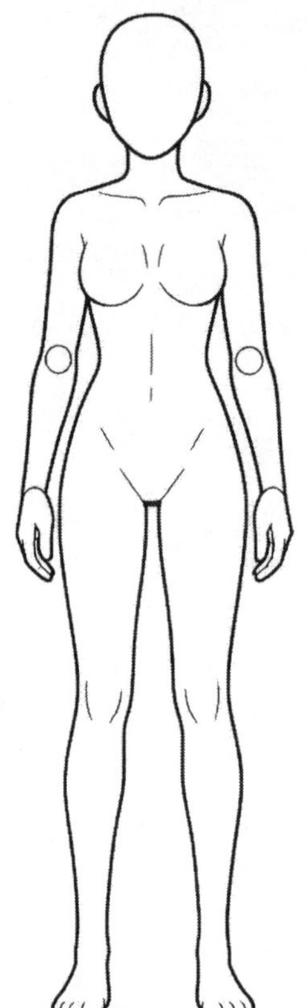

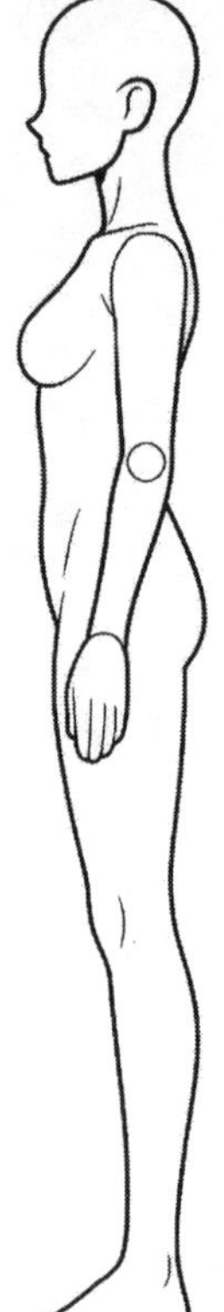

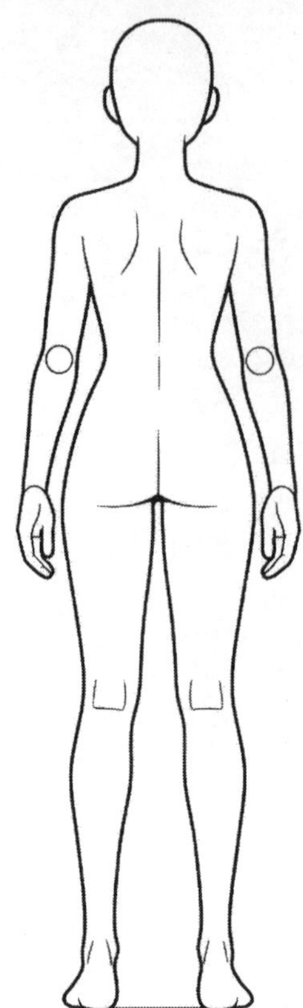

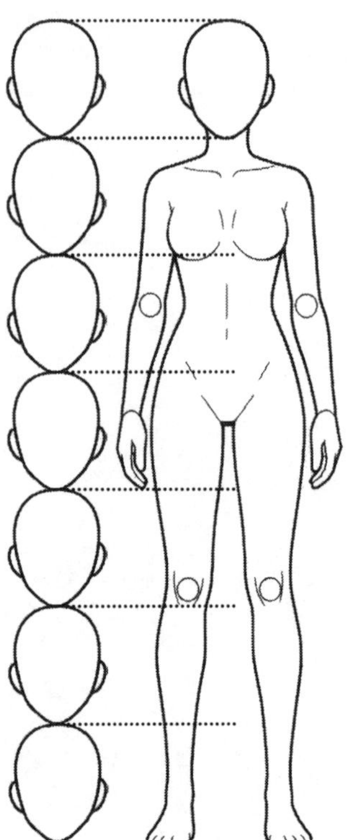

The average female superhero stands 7 heads tall.

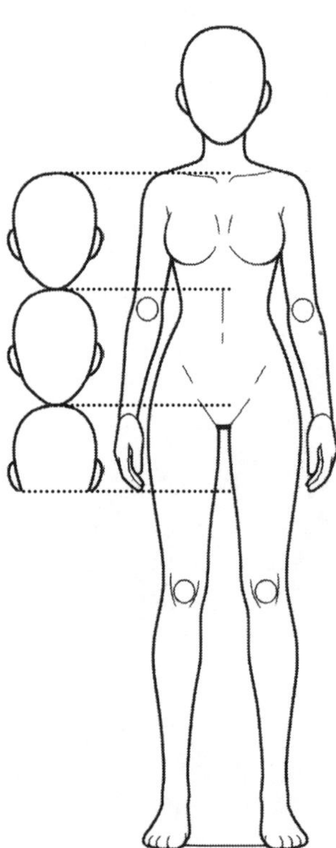

The arm, from the shoulder to the top of the fingers, measures roughly 2½ heads.

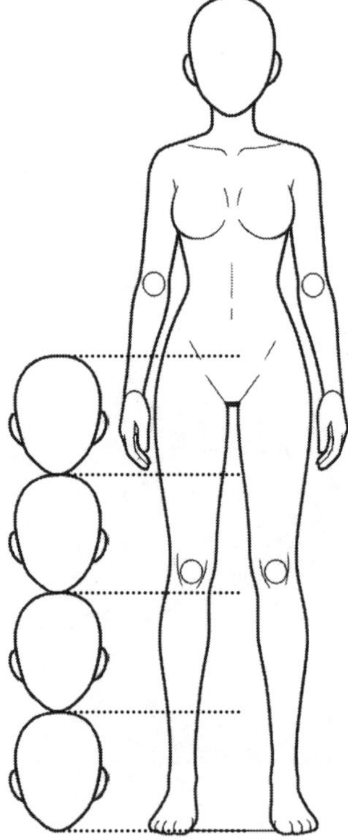

From the hips to the feet, the lower body measures approximately 4 heads.

Pro Tip: When drawing the female figure, begin by sketching the head first. This gives you a reliable unit of measurement for building the rest of the body in proportion.

Using head lengths as your guide ensures the figure remains balanced and graceful. The average female figure is about seven heads tall. This approach helps you place key features—like the shoulders, bust, waist, hips, knees, and feet—in the correct relationship to one another. By stacking these head lengths as you draw, you can construct a well-proportioned figure with natural rhythm and flow.

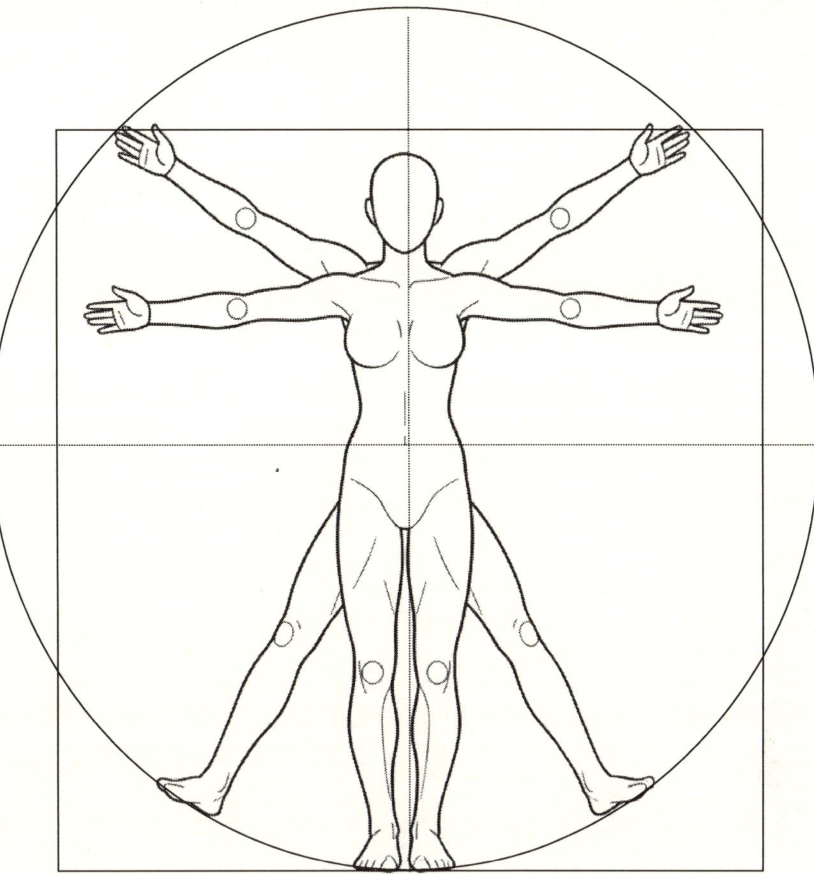

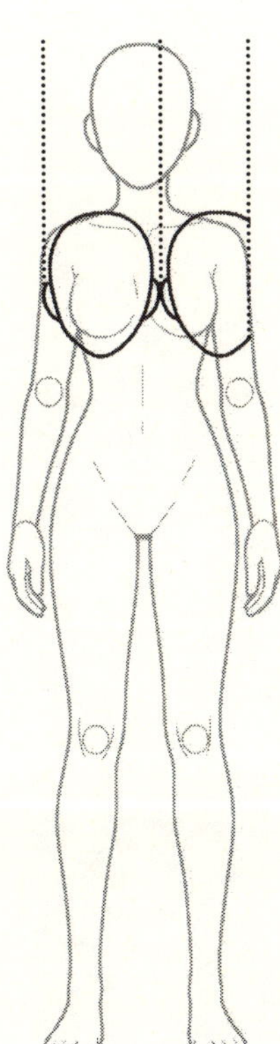

The shoulders sit approximately 1¾ head widths apart.

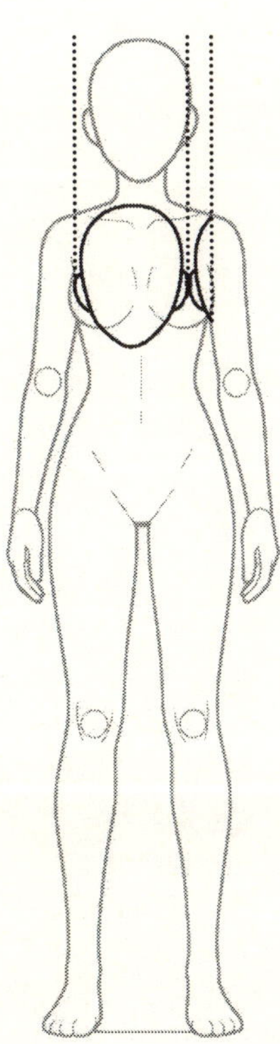

The chest measures the width of approximately 1¼ heads.

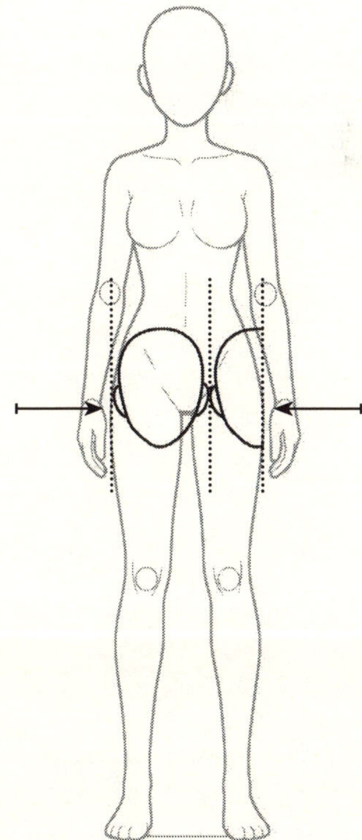

The waist measures approximately 1½ head widths at the top of the pelvis.

DRAWING THE FEMALE FIGURE IN DYNAMIC POSES

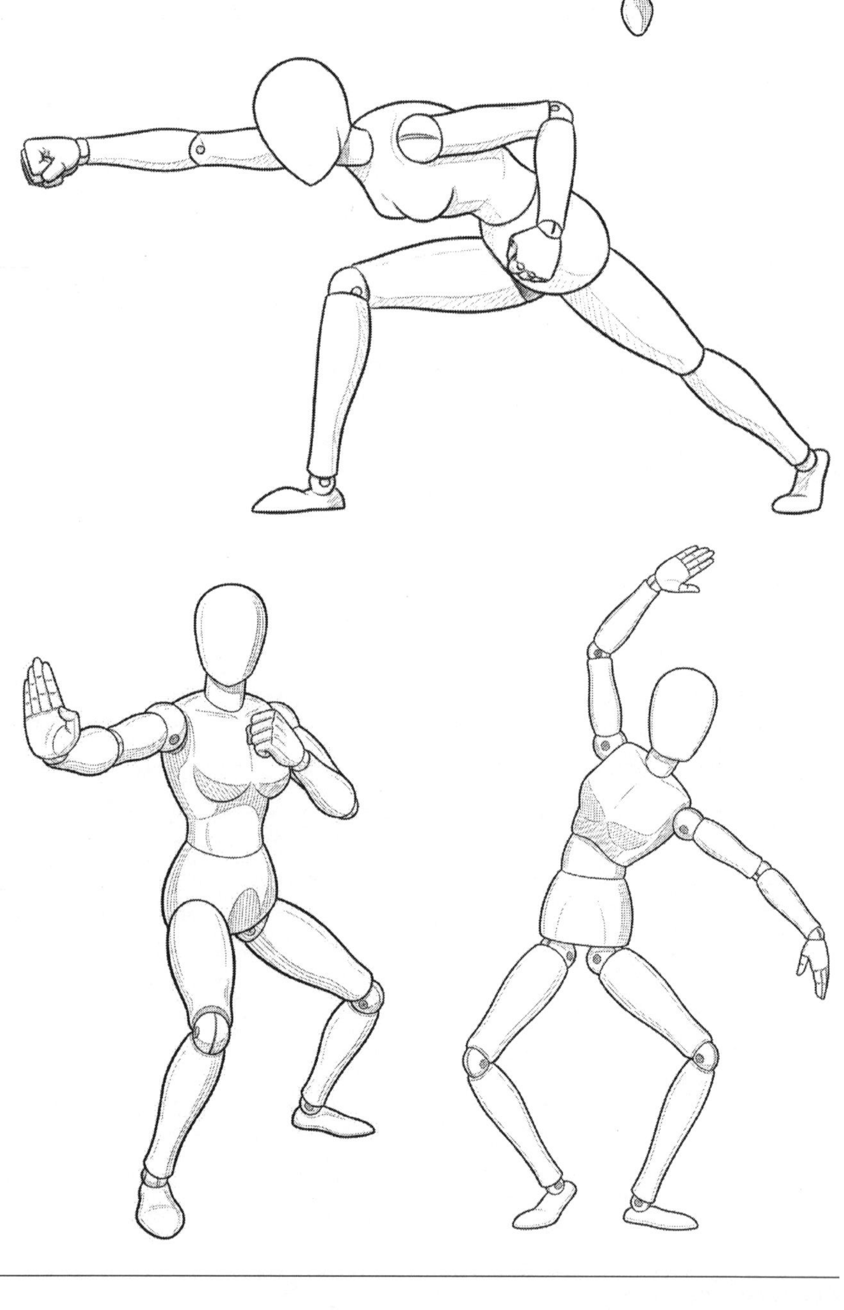

Pro Tip: Begin with loose, flowing lines to capture the gesture and rhythm of the pose before refining the form. Focus on balance and flow—keeping the centre of gravity in mind.

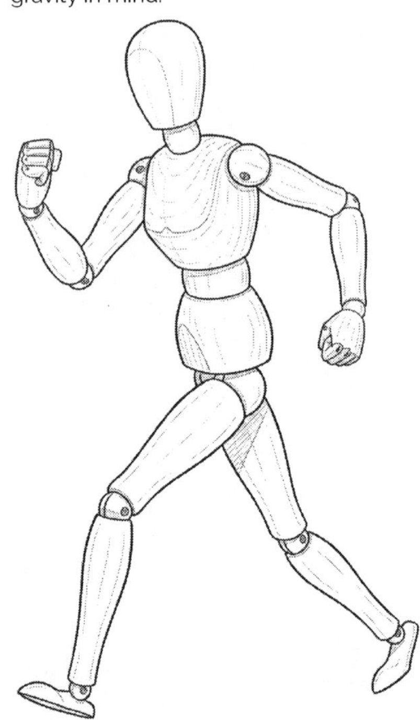

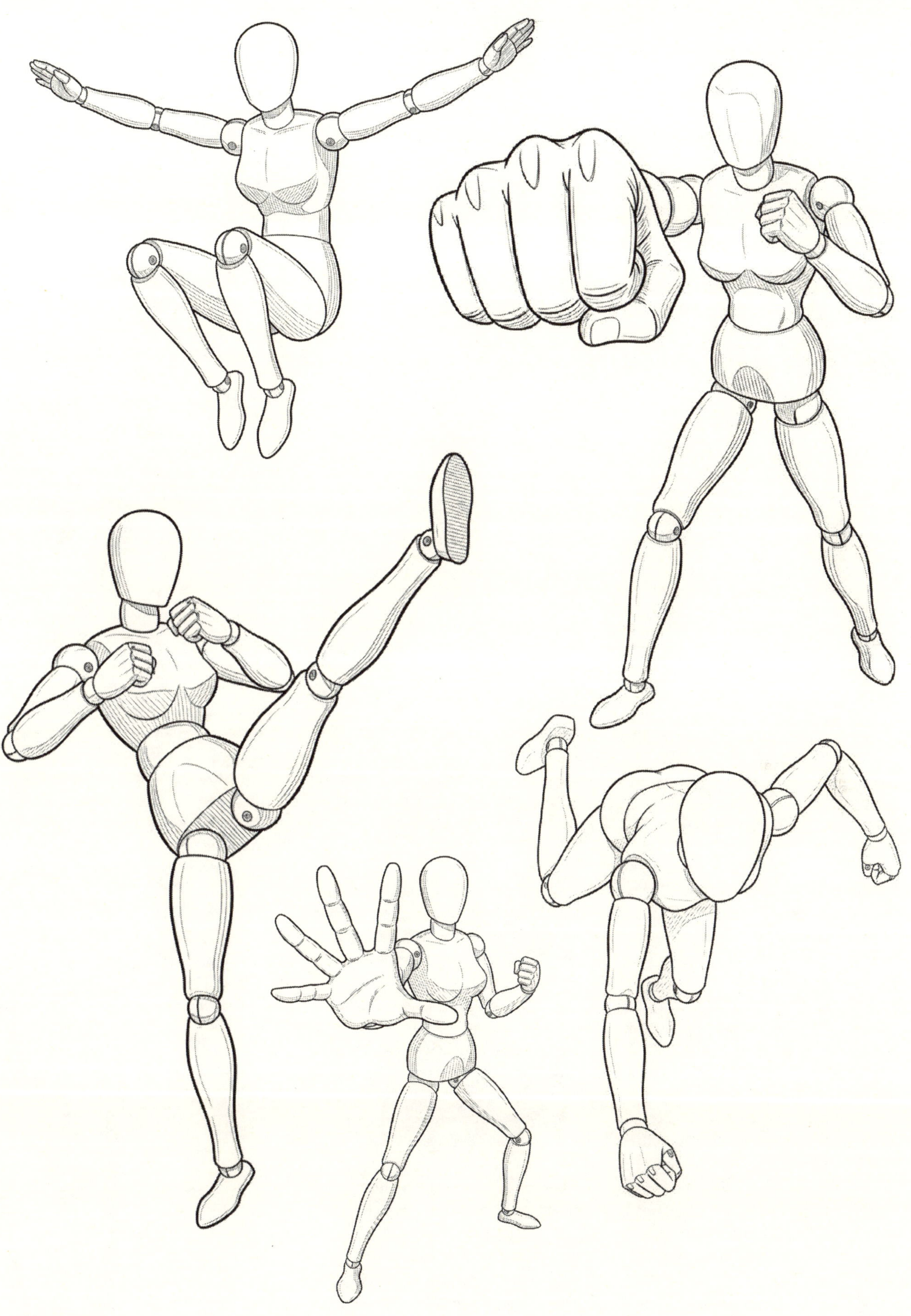

02| DRAWING SUPERHEROES

ACTION AND HEROIC POSES

You've got the fundamentals down. You understand the figure, you can map out proportions, and your faces and hands are taking shape. Now it's time to put that knowledge in motion, literally. This is where your characters stop standing still and start leaping off the page.

Action and heroic poses are the heartbeat of comics. They're the frozen moments that tell the whole story in a single panel, the hero launching a punch before it lands, the villain caught mid-kick, the caped figure silhouetted against the sky. Getting these poses right is what separates a flat drawing from one that crackles with energy and drama.

Think about the comics images that have stayed with you. The ones that lodged themselves in your memory long after you put the book down. Chances are they weren't quiet moments. They were figures in motion, bodies twisted with effort, caught at the exact peak of an action. That is the power of a great pose. It doesn't just show what a character is doing, it tells you who they are. The way a hero plants their feet before a fight, the angle of their shoulders as they take to the sky, the defensive stance of someone who has been hit before and knows how to take another, all of it communicates character without a word of dialogue.

It's worth understanding what makes an action pose work before we start drawing them. The key is what artists call line of action, an invisible line that runs through the entire figure and gives a pose its sense of direction and energy. A straight line of action produces a stiff, static figure. A curved or diagonal line of action produces movement, tension and life. Every great action pose is built around a strong line of action and we'll show you how to find it and build your entire figure around it so that energy and momentum feel baked into your character from the very first mark you make.

In this chapter, we'll walk you through the poses that define the superhero genre, breaking each one down into clear, achievable steps. Whether your character is on the offensive, holding the line, or soaring above the city, you'll have the tools to draw it with confidence. More than that, you'll understand the principles behind each pose well enough to adapt them, push them further, and eventually develop the instinct to create dynamic, convincing action from your imagination.

The fundamentals got you here. Now let's see what you can do with them.

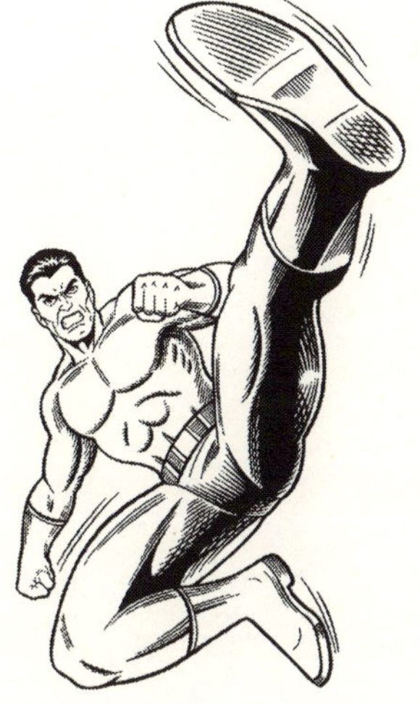

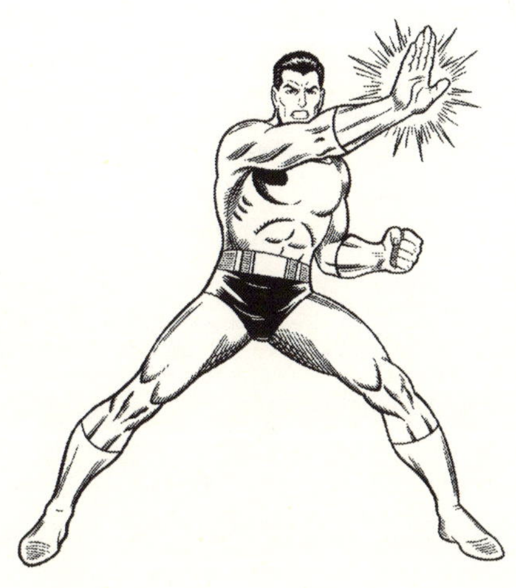

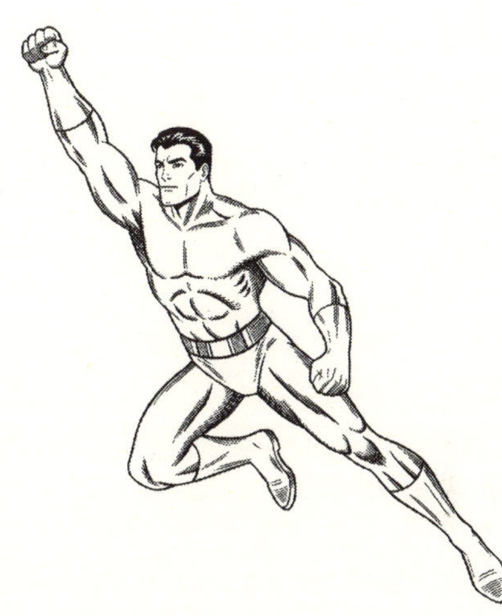

Heroic and Combat Poses: From the classic stances that communicate power and authority before a single punch is thrown, to the raw explosive energy of striking and kicking, we'll walk you through the poses that define a fighter. A heroic stance needs to tell the reader instantly that this person is powerful, capable and not to be taken lightly, all before the action has even begun. We'll show you how to use the position of the feet, the set of the shoulders and the angle of the body to project exactly the kind of presence your character demands. From there we move into combat, covering the mechanics of punching, striking and kicking in a way that translates genuine physical force onto the page. You'll learn how to use the whole body rather than just the limbs to sell the weight and momentum behind every move, keeping your figures balanced and believable even at the peak of the action.

Blocking and Defence: Heroes take hits as well as they give them, and a well drawn defensive pose can be every bit as powerful and compelling as any offensive one. Defence tells its own story. It speaks of experience, resilience and the kind of hard won toughness that makes a hero worth rooting for. We'll walk you through the body mechanics of a convincing block, how weight shifts, how the arms and hands position themselves, and how the whole figure responds to the anticipation of impact. Because in any great action sequence the push and pull between attack and defence is what creates the rhythm and tension that keeps a reader gripped from one panel to the next.

Flying and Aerial Poses: Nothing says superhero like defying gravity. The image of a figure soaring through the sky is one of the most iconic in all of comics, and also one of the most technically challenging to pull off convincingly. Without a ground plane to anchor them, figures can easily look like they are floating rather than moving through space at speed. We'll show you how to use the angle of the body, the position of the limbs to communicate velocity and direction. Whether your character is hovering, diving or launching upward, by the end of this section the sky will feel like exactly where they belong.

BLOCKING THE STRIKE 'THE DEFLECTOR'

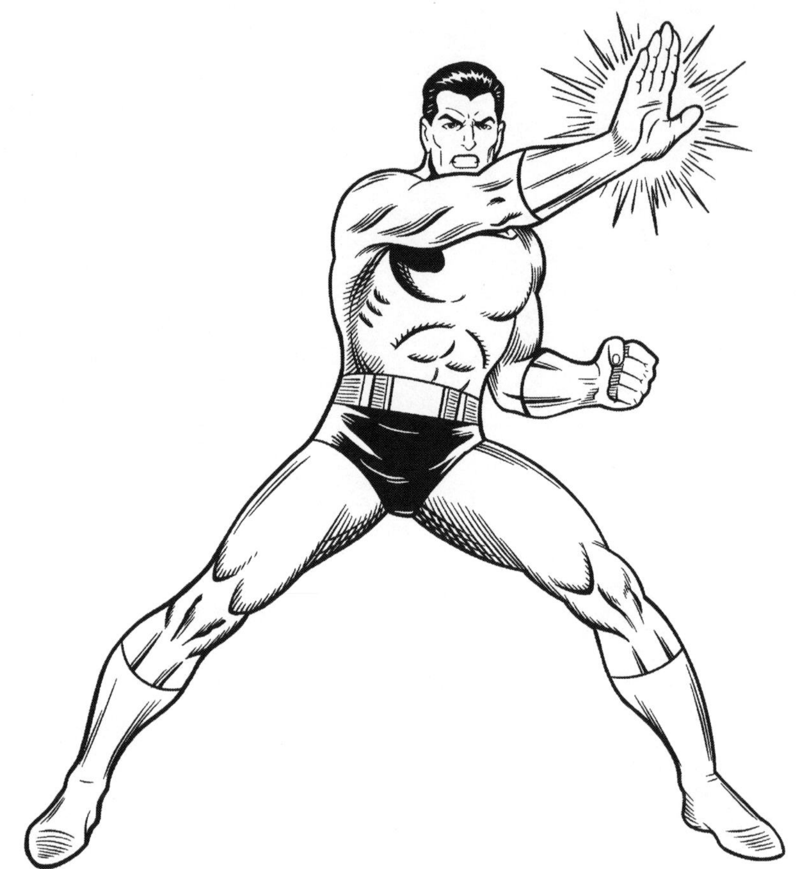

Pro Tip: Check that your figure's weight feels grounded. The wide leg stance should create a strong triangular base. If the pose looks unstable, widen the feet slightly and ensure the torso leans slightly into the blocking arm.

01

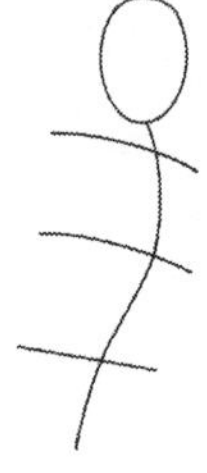

02

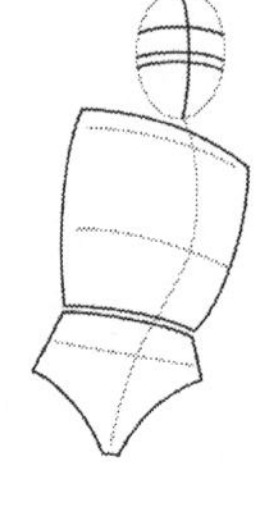

03

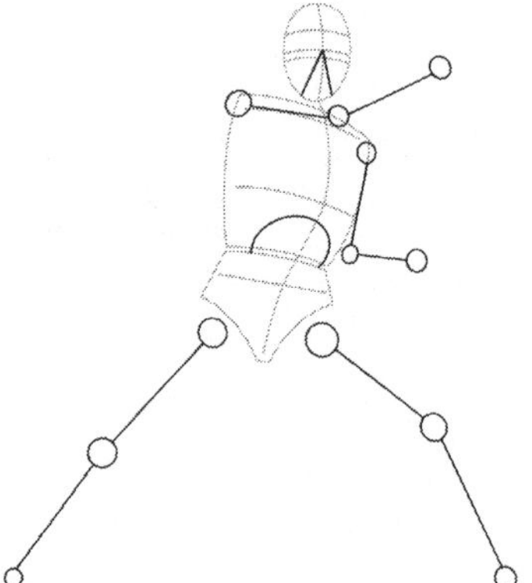

04

05

06

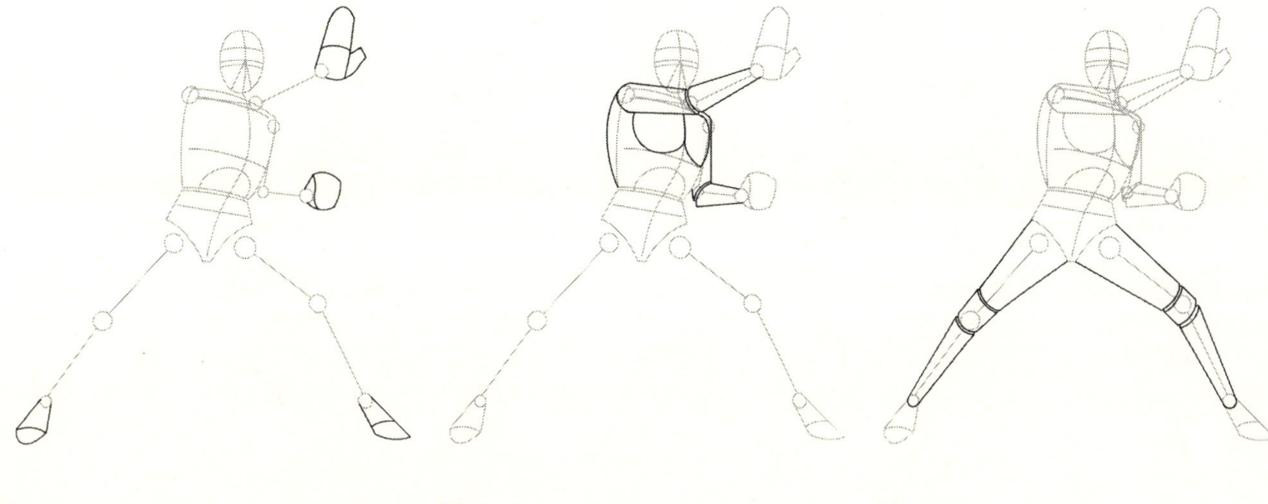

07

08

09

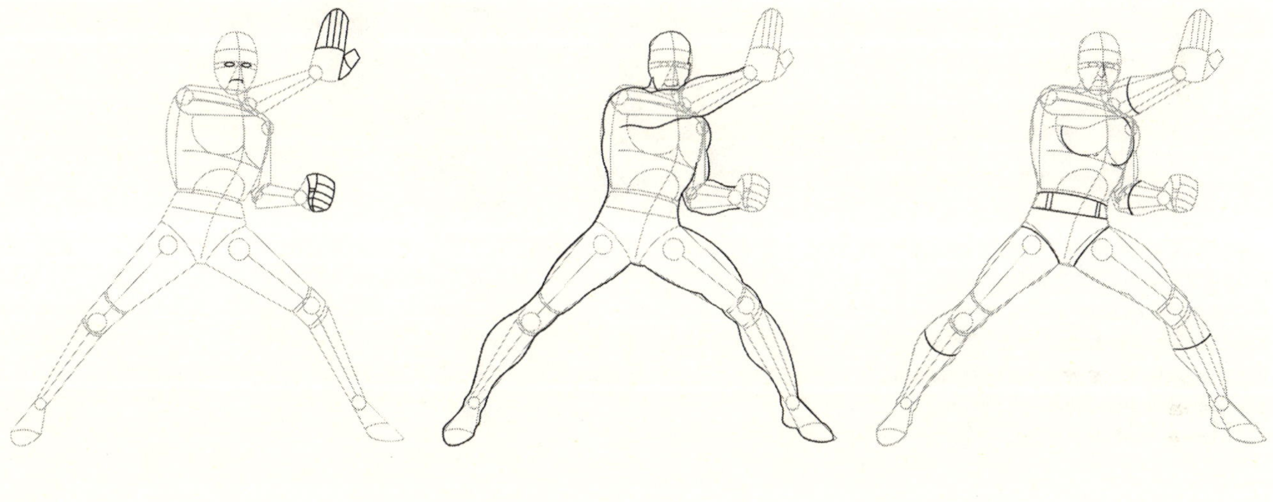

10

11

12

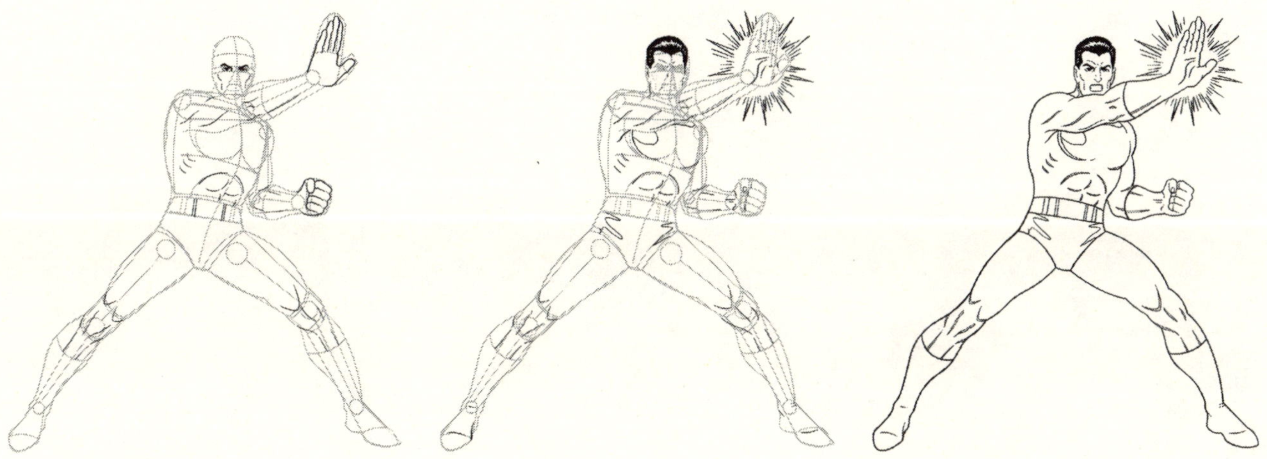

FLYING KICK 'THE OBLITERATOR'

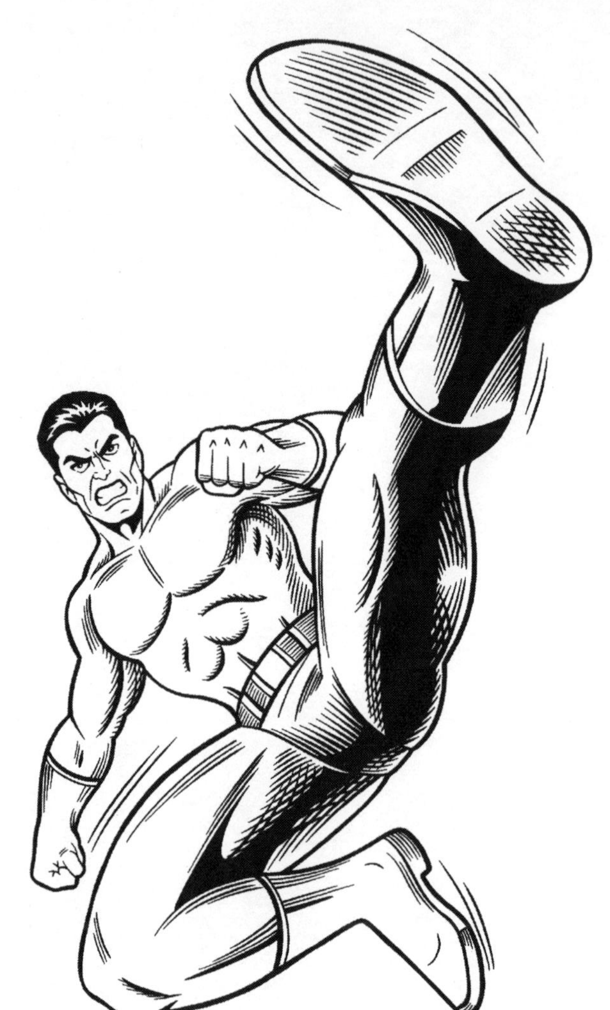

Pro Tip: Use foreshortening on the extended kicking leg to drive it toward the viewer and sell the impact. Tilt the torso slightly to suggest momentum and forward propulsion through the air.

01

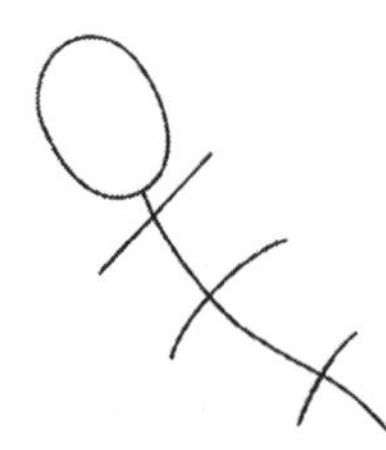

02

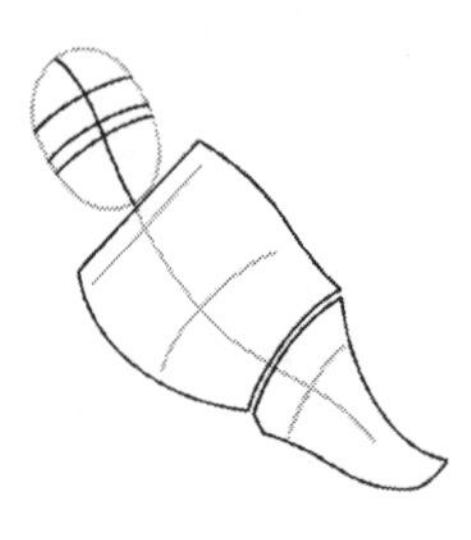

03

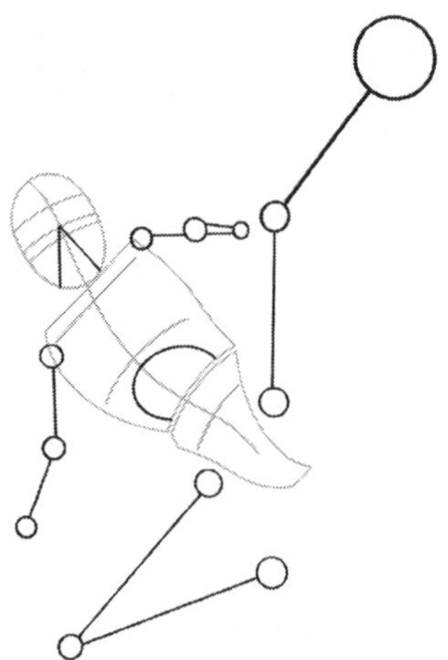

04

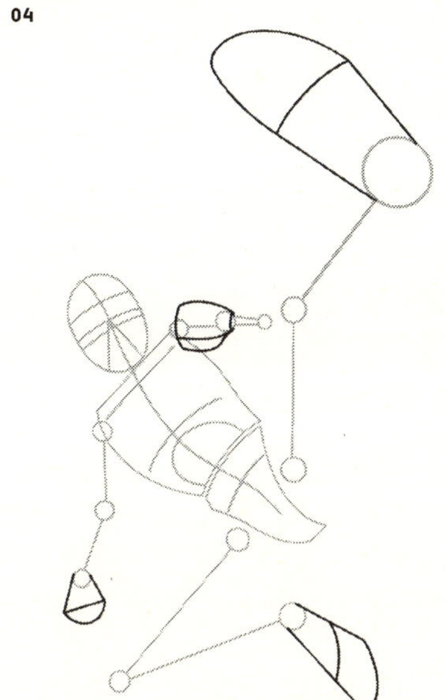

05

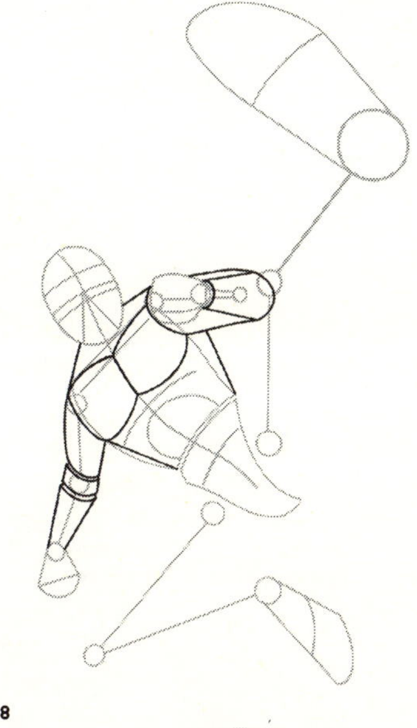

06

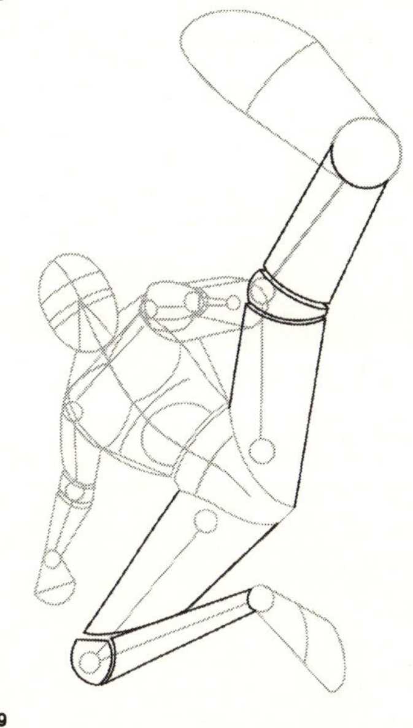

07

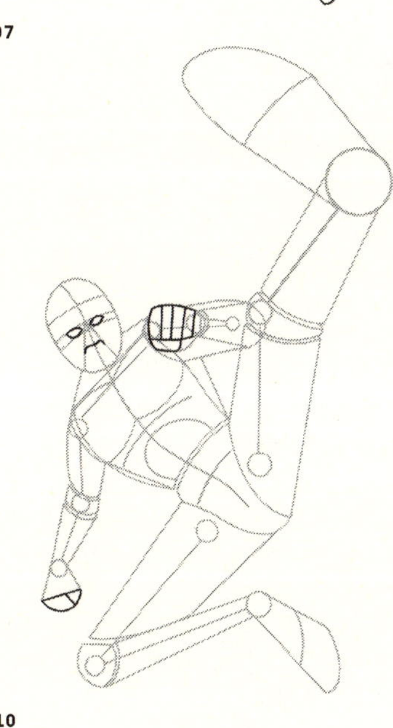

08

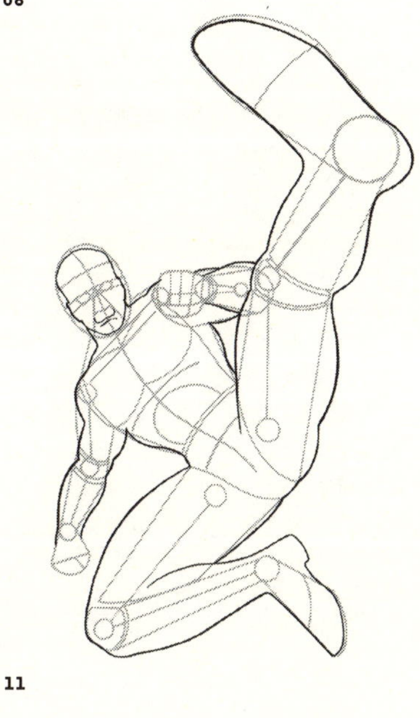

09

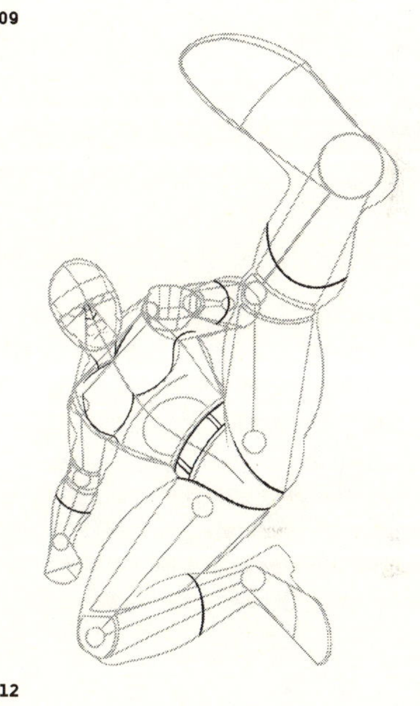

10

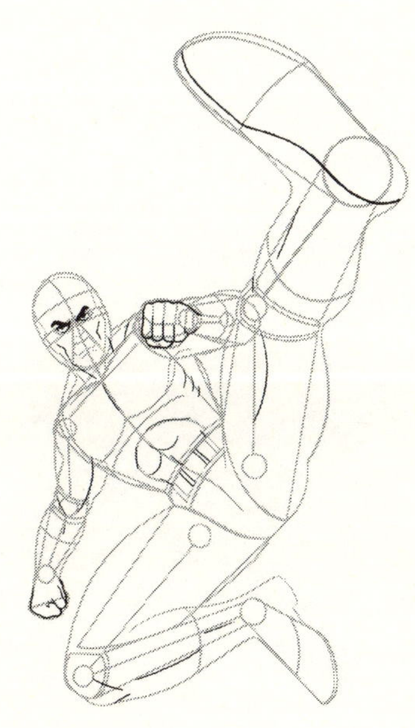

11

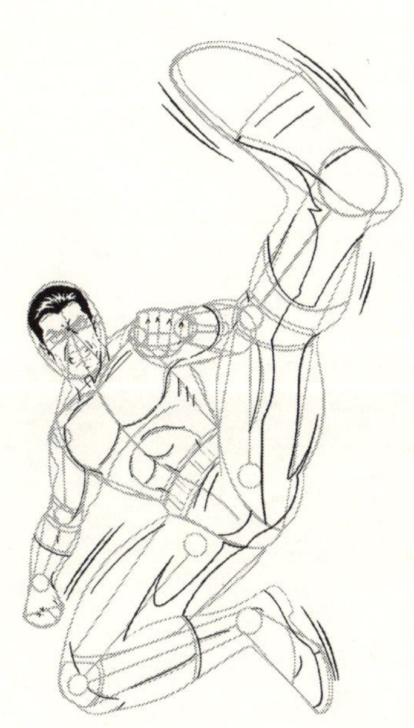

12

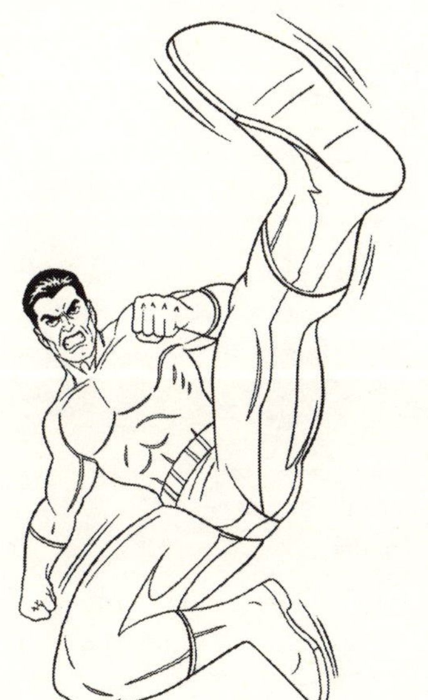

GRABBING THE ENEMY 'THE CLUTCH'

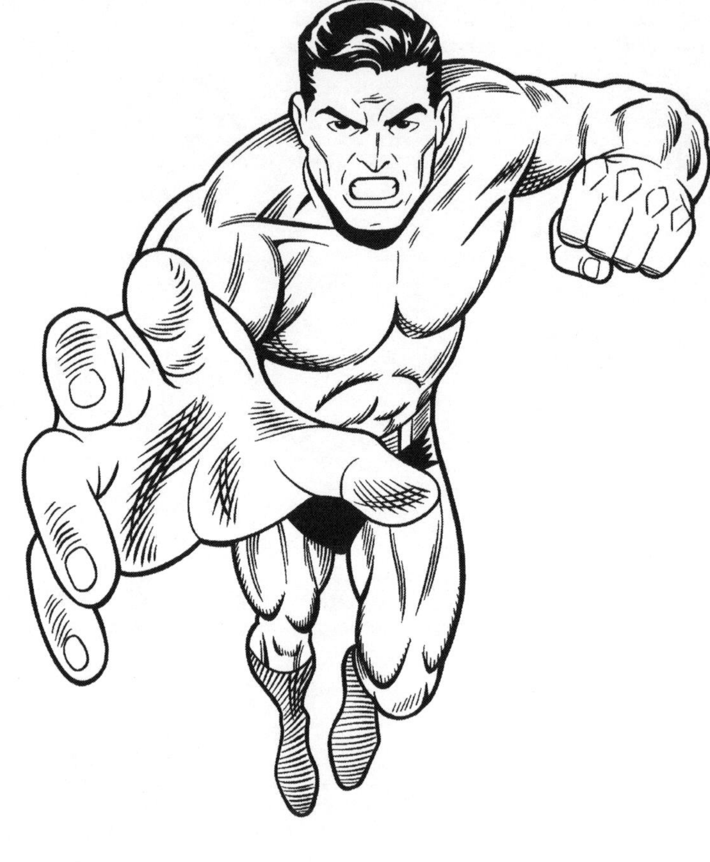

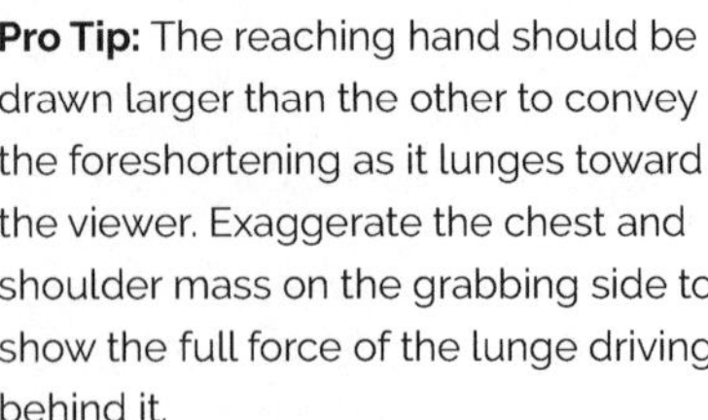

Pro Tip: The reaching hand should be drawn larger than the other to convey the foreshortening as it lunges toward the viewer. Exaggerate the chest and shoulder mass on the grabbing side to show the full force of the lunge driving behind it.

01

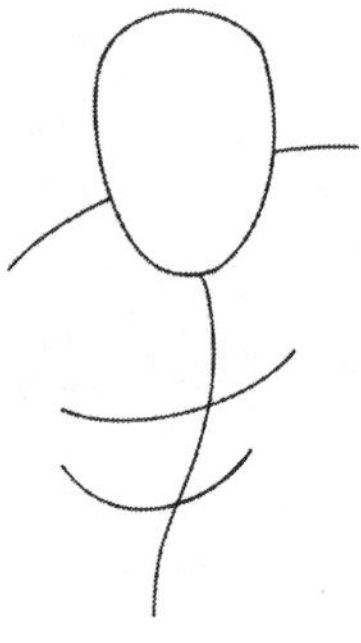

02

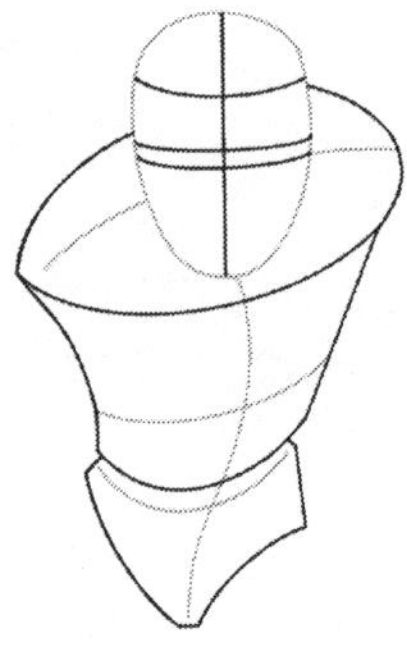

03

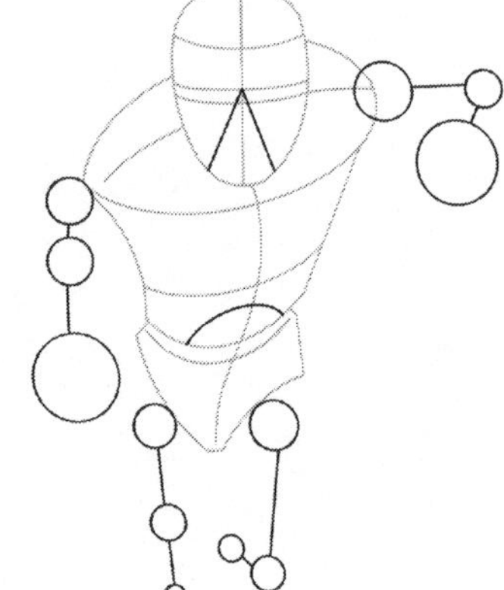

04

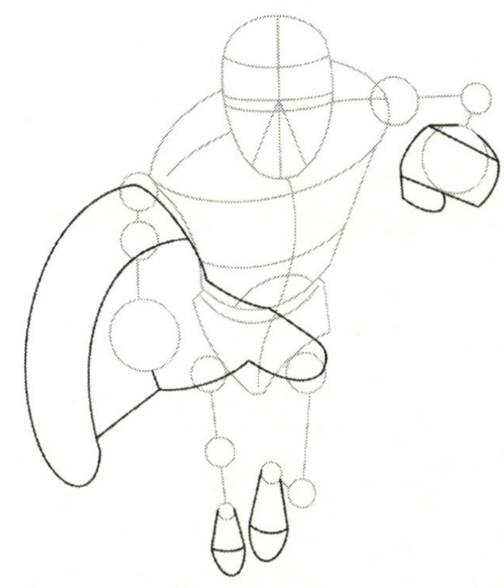

05

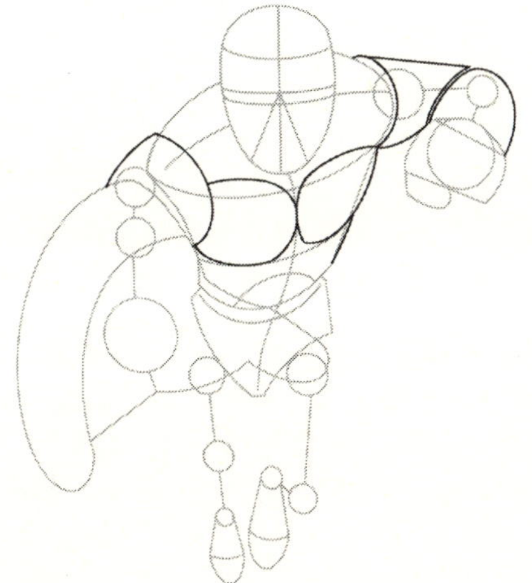

06

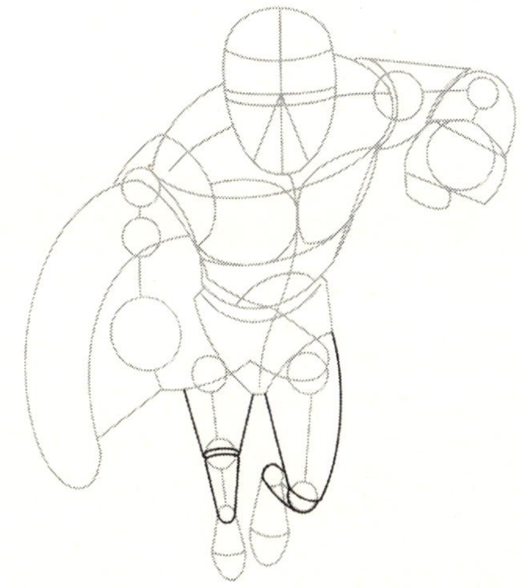

07

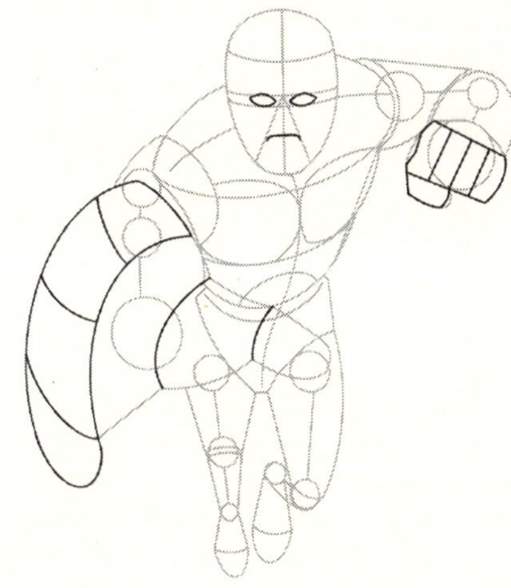

08

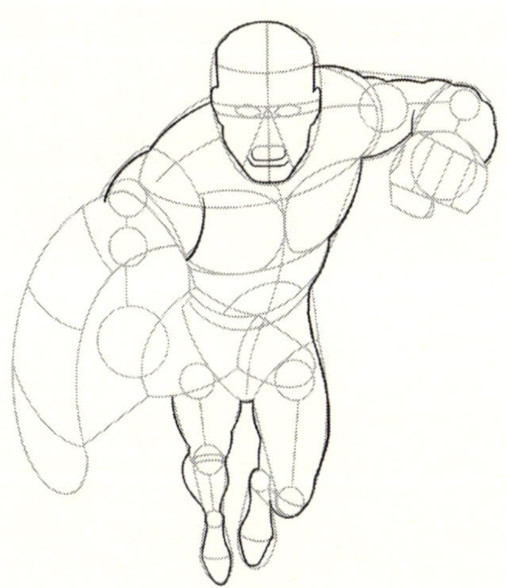

09

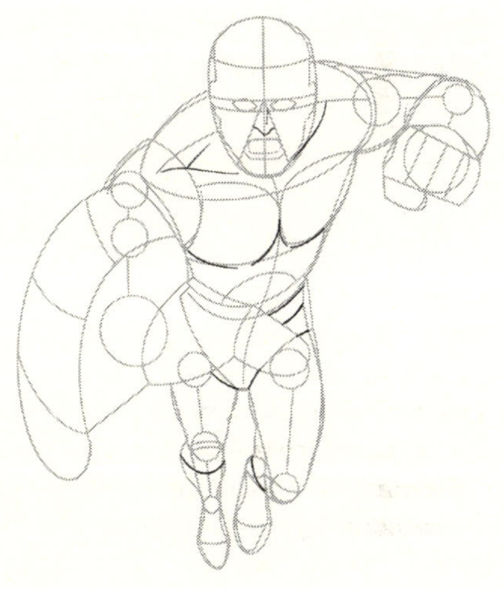

HOW TO DRAW SUPERHEROES

10

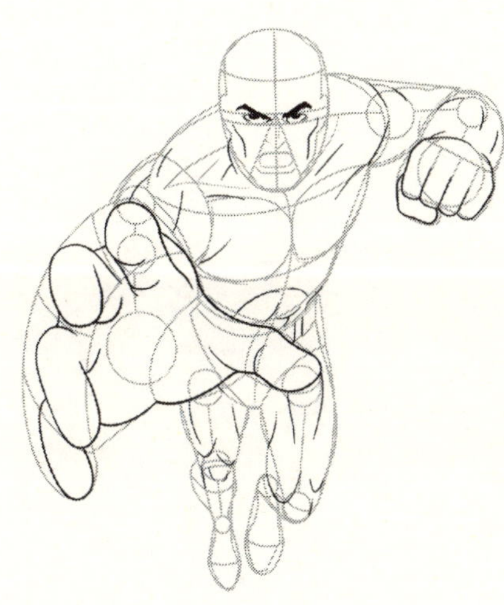

11

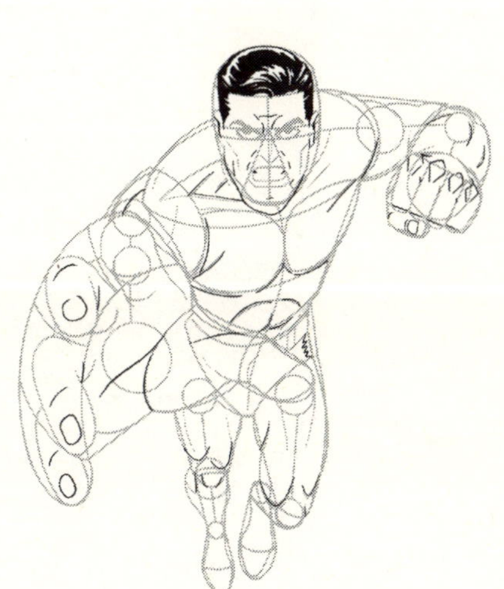

12

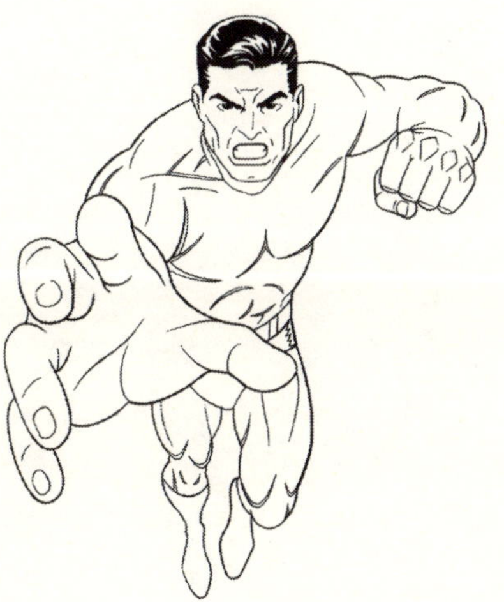

PUNCHING OVERHEAD 'THE FINISHER'

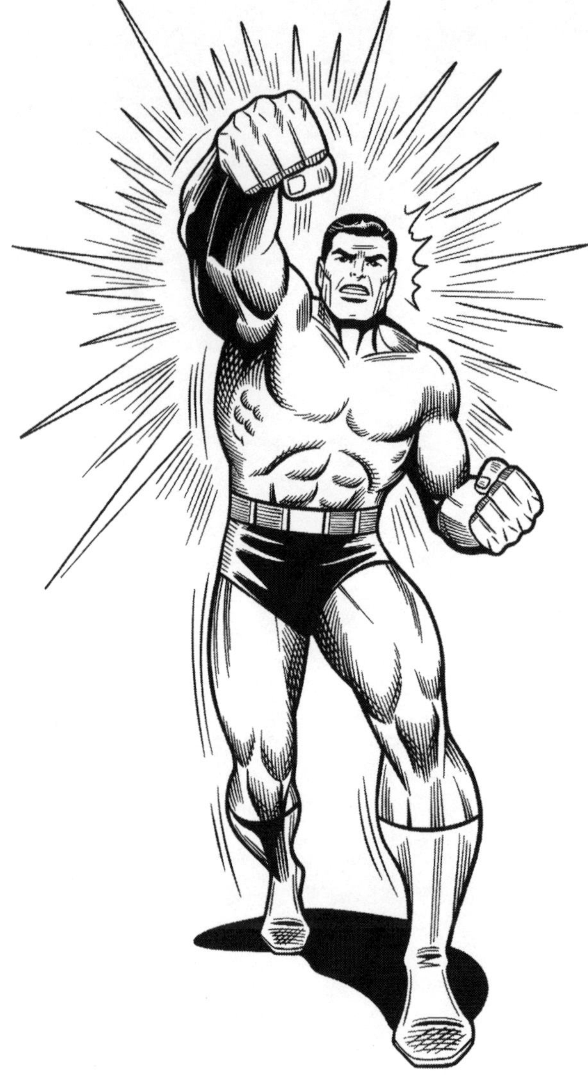

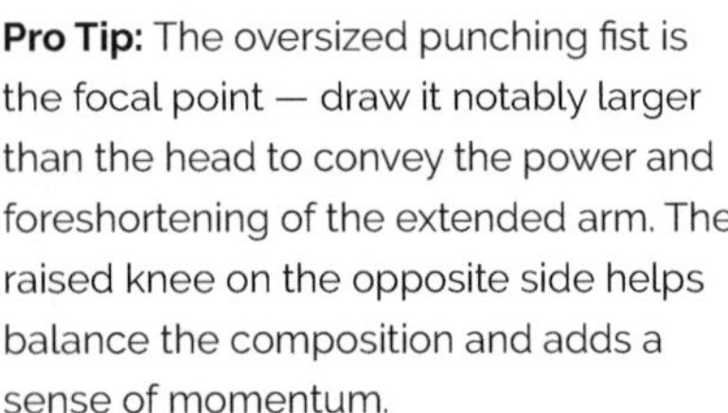

Pro Tip: The oversized punching fist is the focal point — draw it notably larger than the head to convey the power and foreshortening of the extended arm. The raised knee on the opposite side helps balance the composition and adds a sense of momentum.

01

02

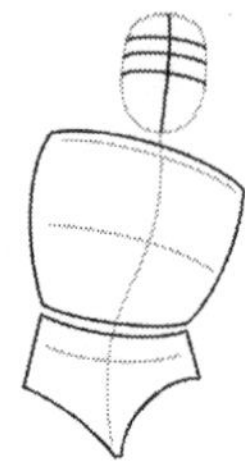

03

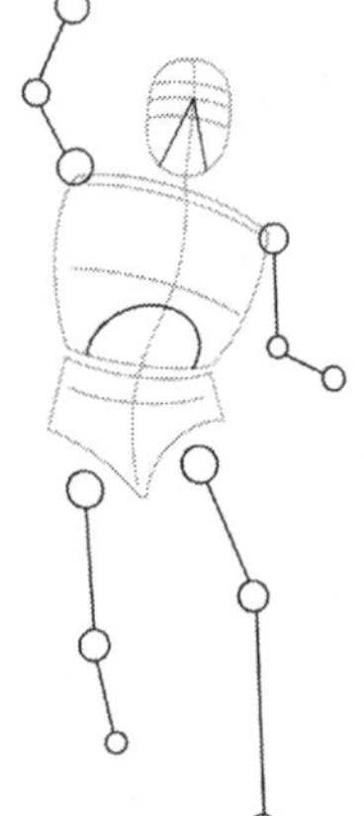

04

05

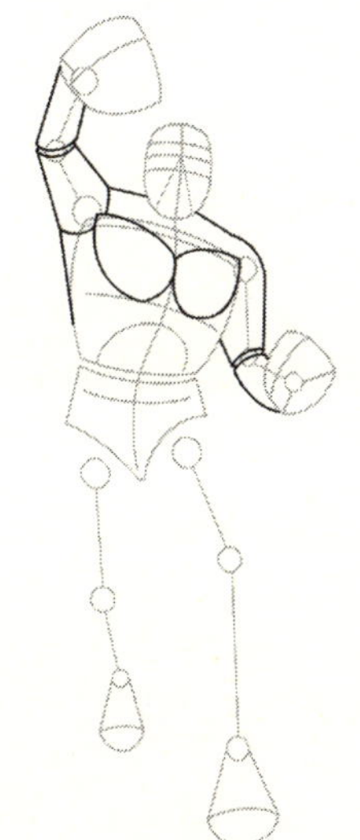

06

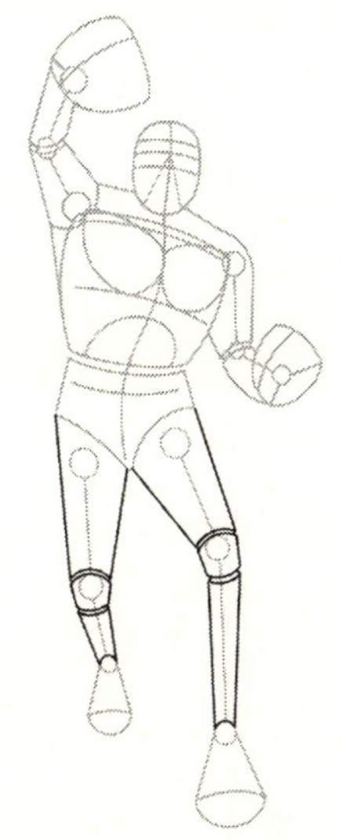

07

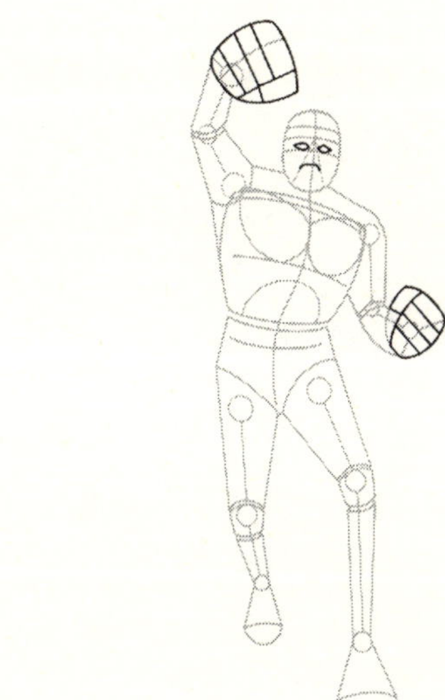

08

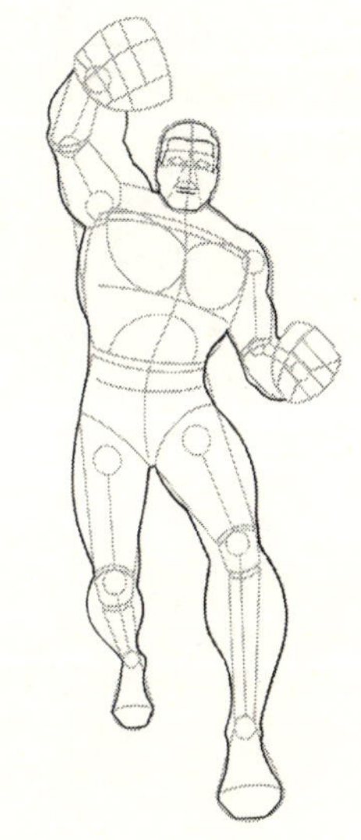

09

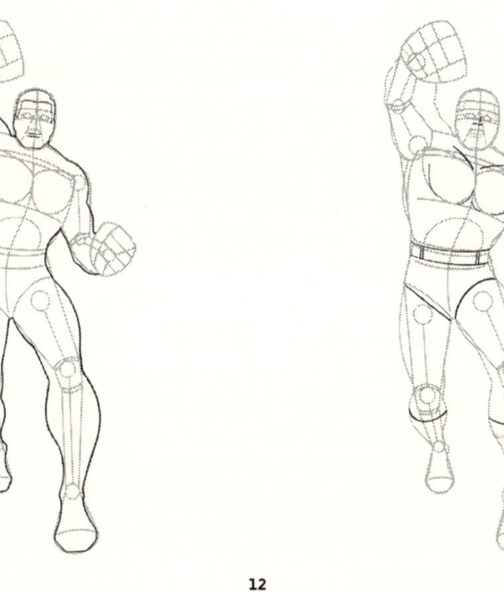

10

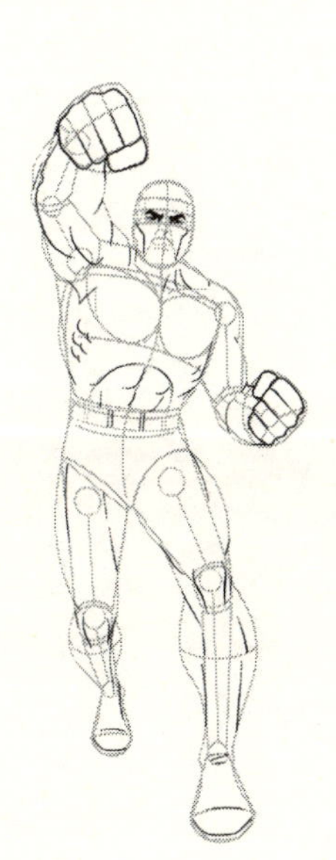

11

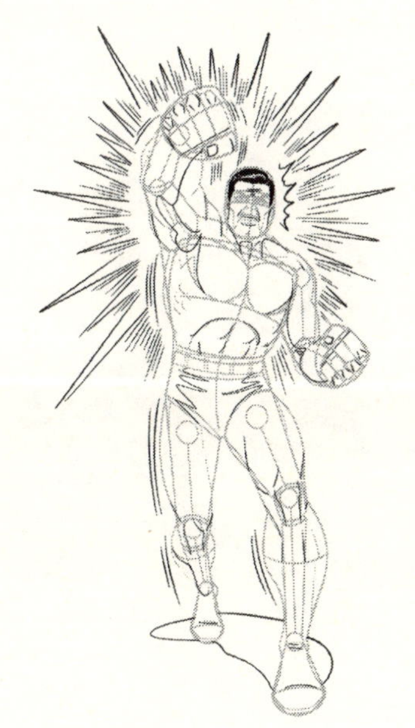

12

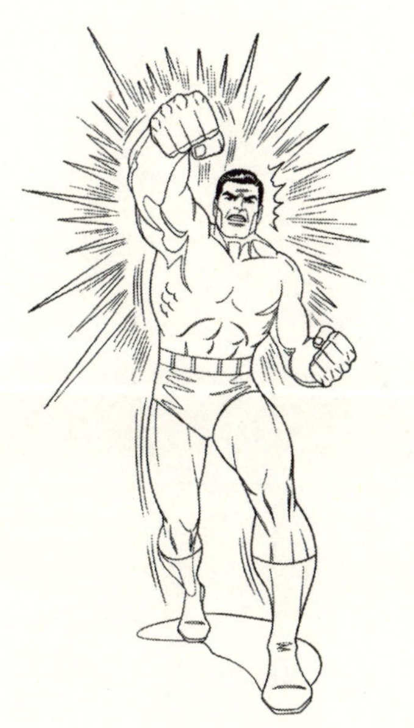

PUNCHING DOWNWARD 'THE GROUNDBREAKER'

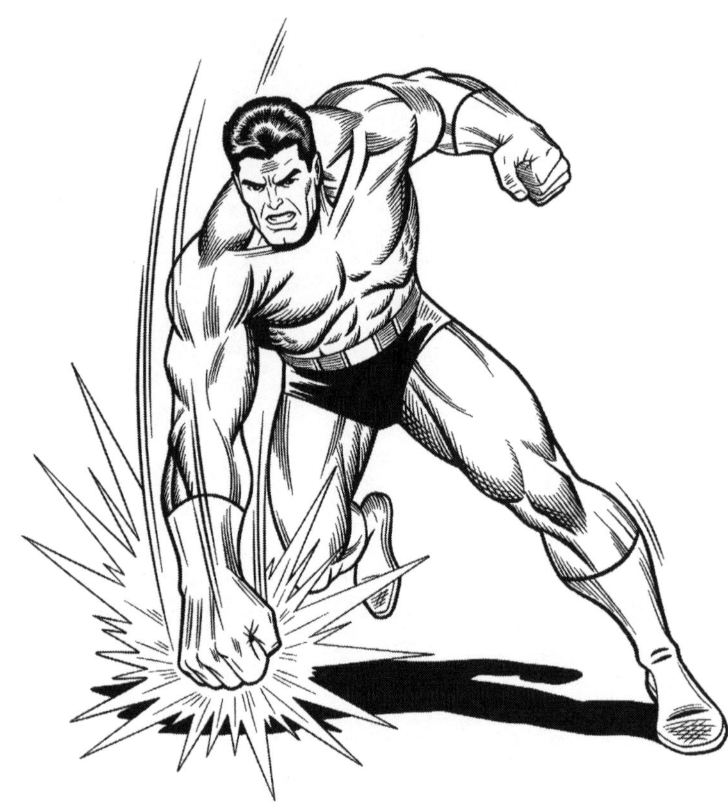

Pro Tip: The power of this pose comes from the steep forward lean — the spine should angle at roughly 45 degrees, with the punching fist reaching all the way down to ground level.

01

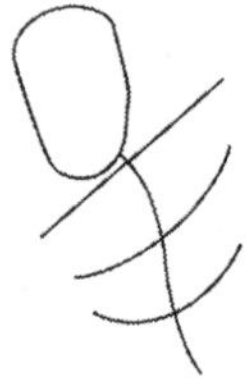

02

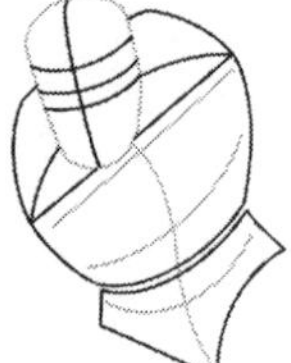

03

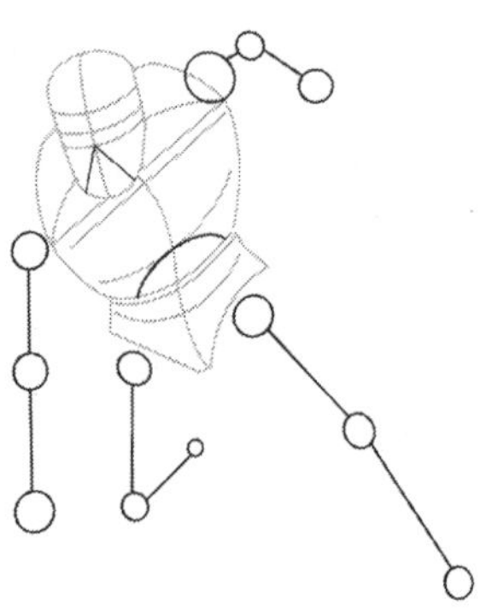

04

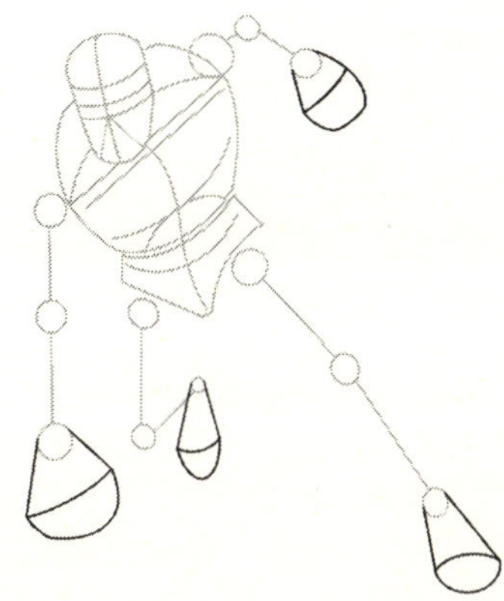

05

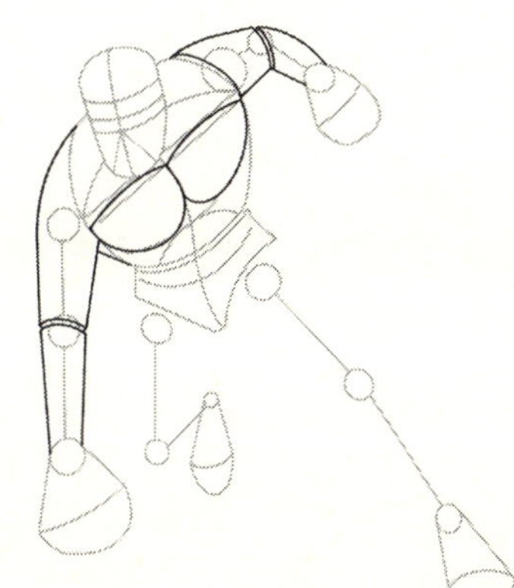

06

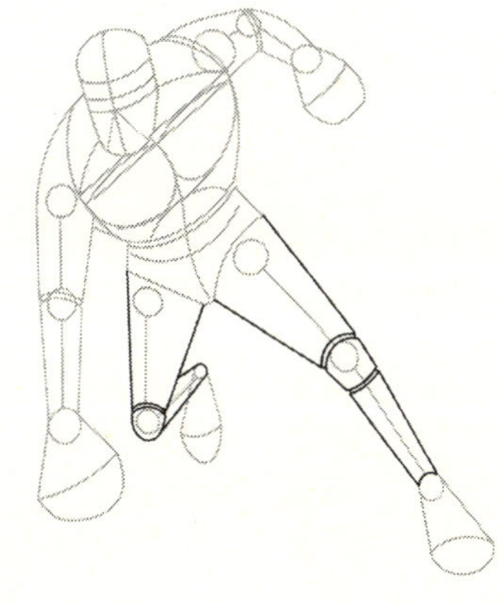

07

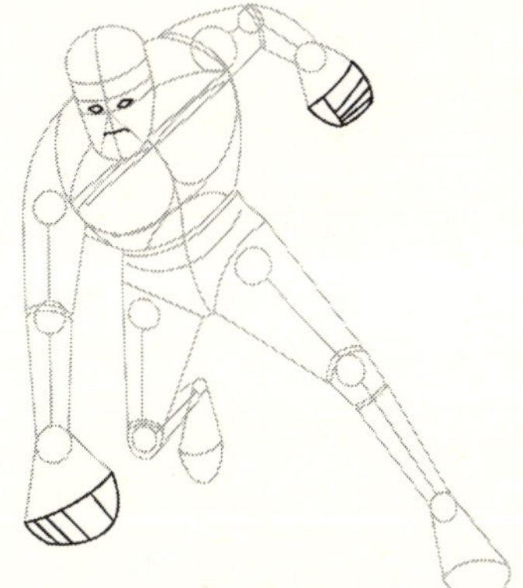

08

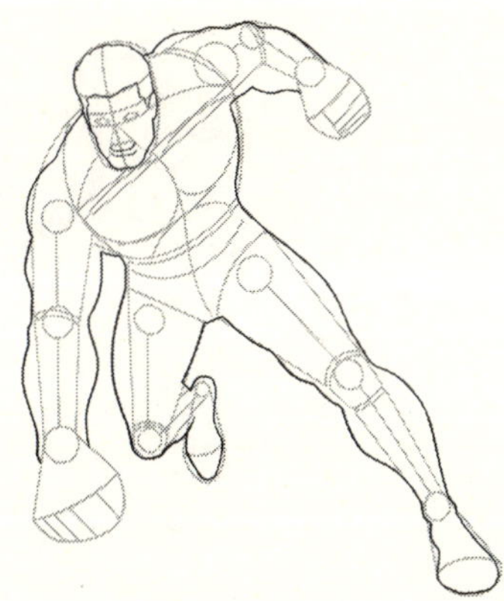

09

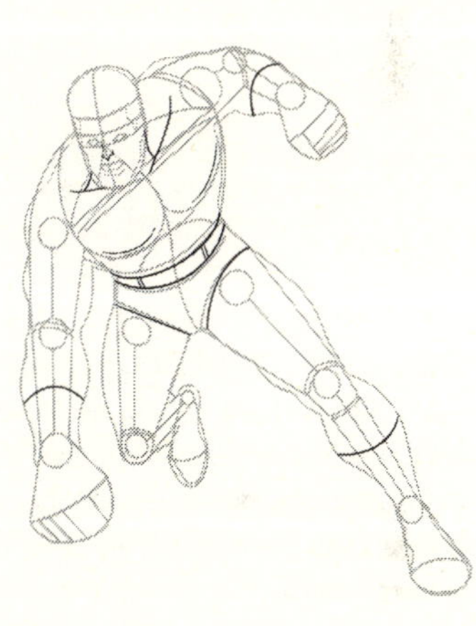

10

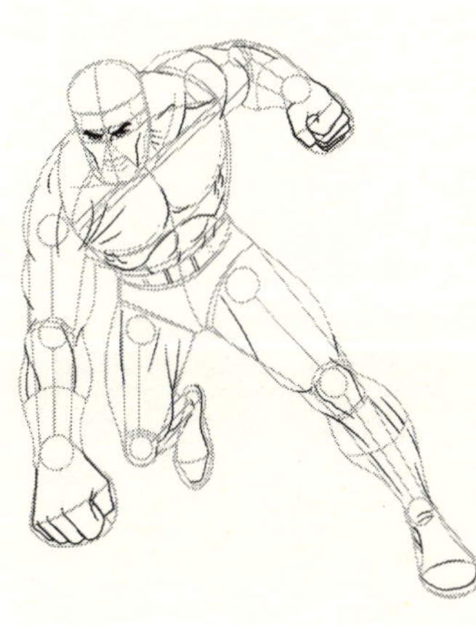

11

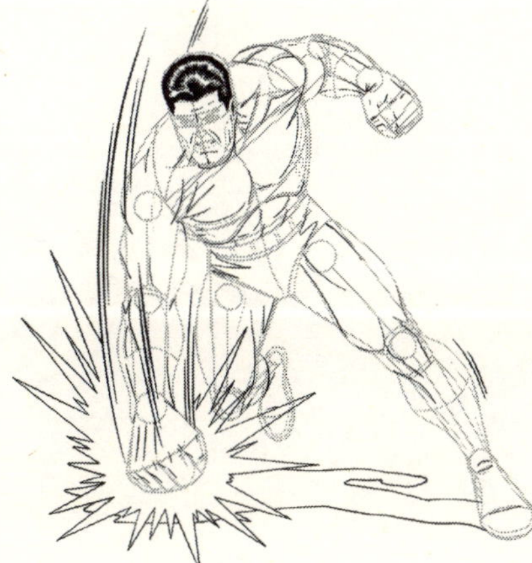

12

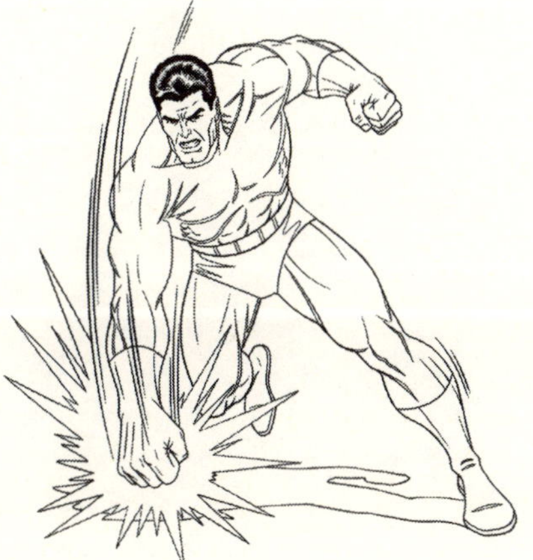

FLYING PUNCH 'THE CLOSER'

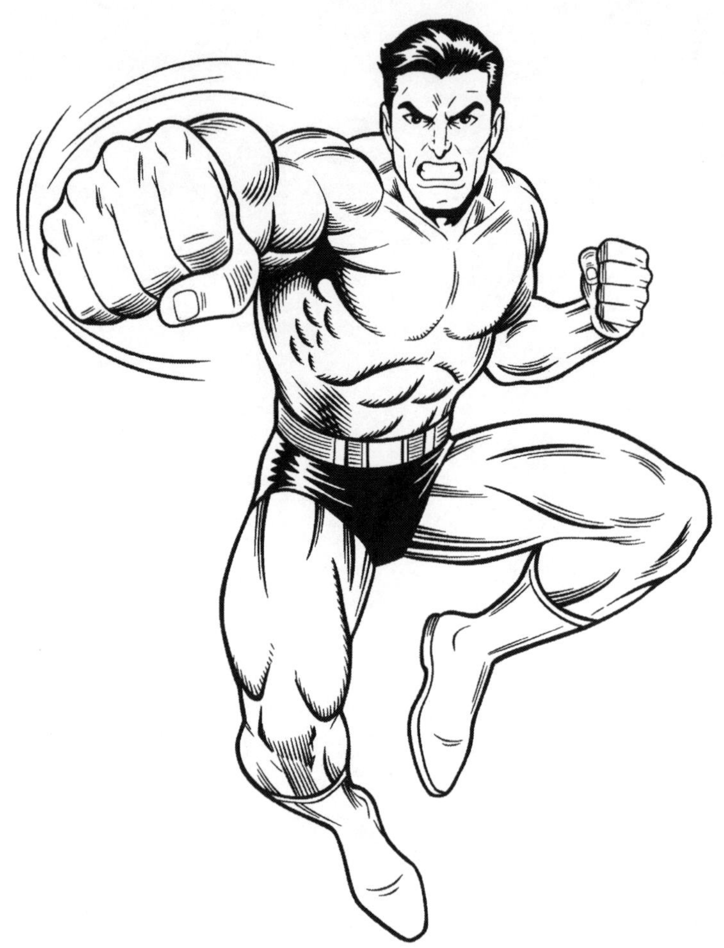

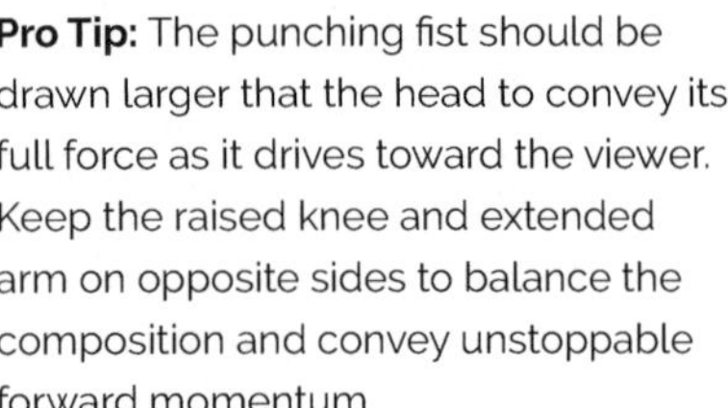

Pro Tip: The punching fist should be drawn larger that the head to convey its full force as it drives toward the viewer. Keep the raised knee and extended arm on opposite sides to balance the composition and convey unstoppable forward momentum.

01

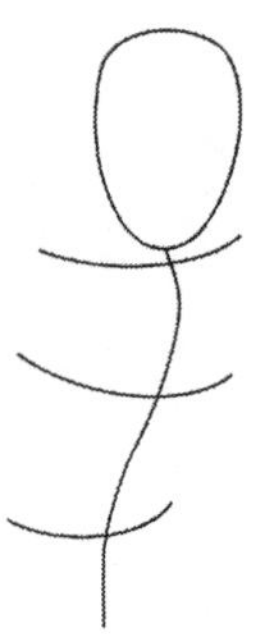

02

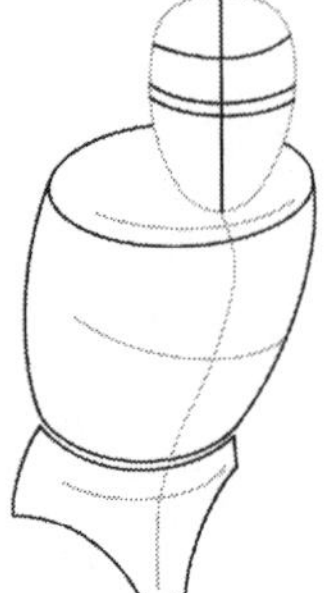

03

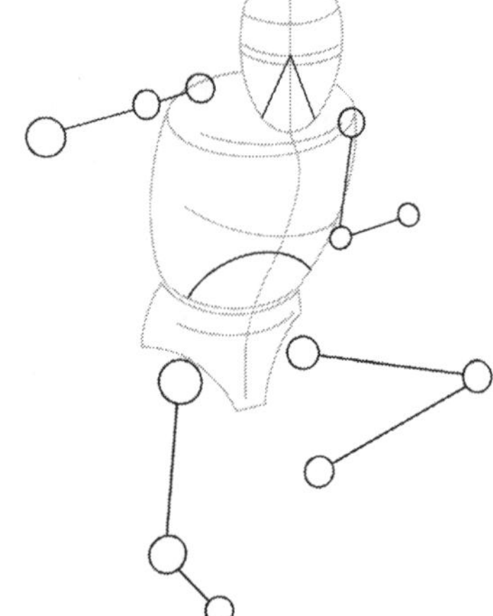

04

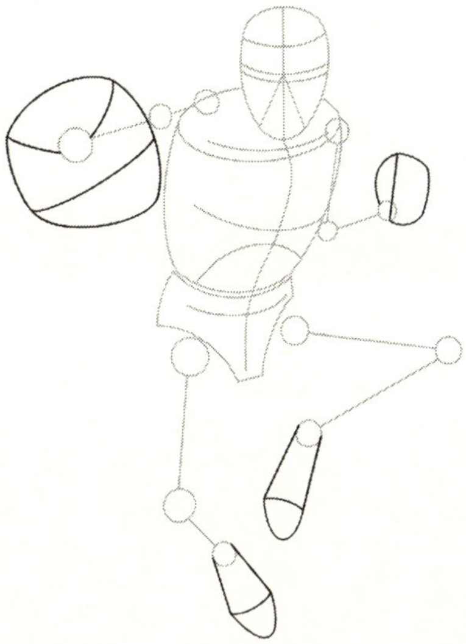

05

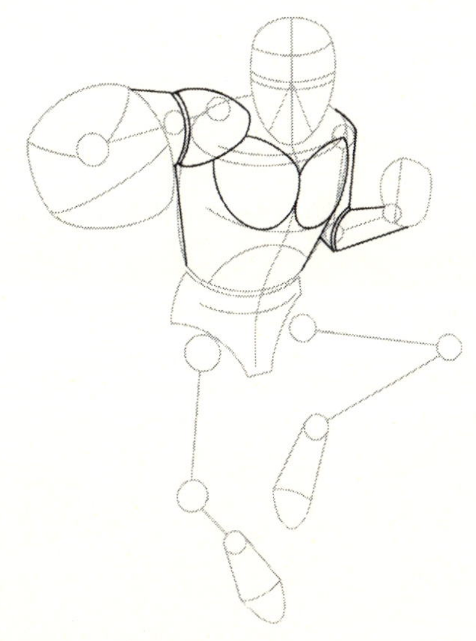

06

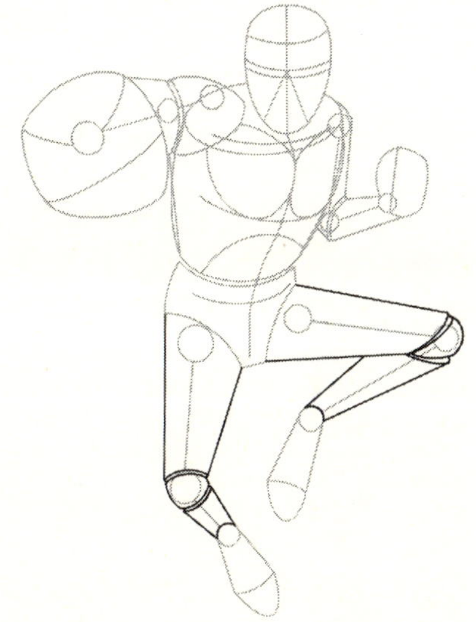

07

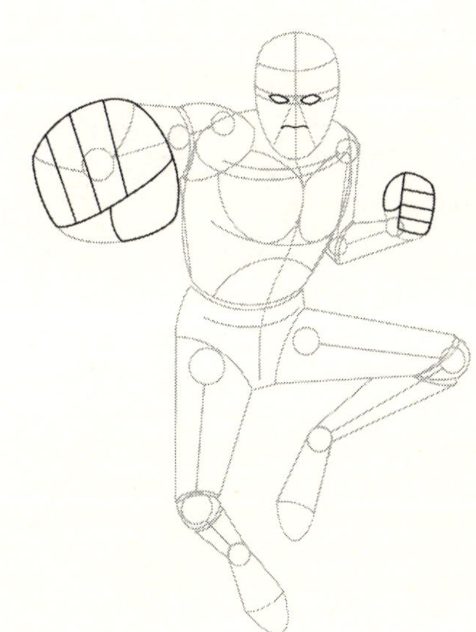

08

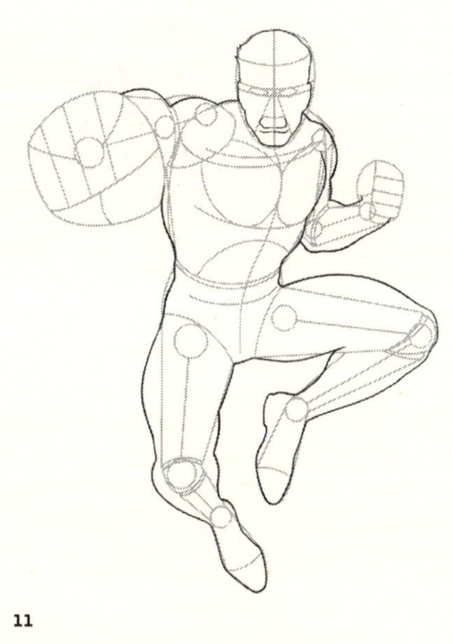

09

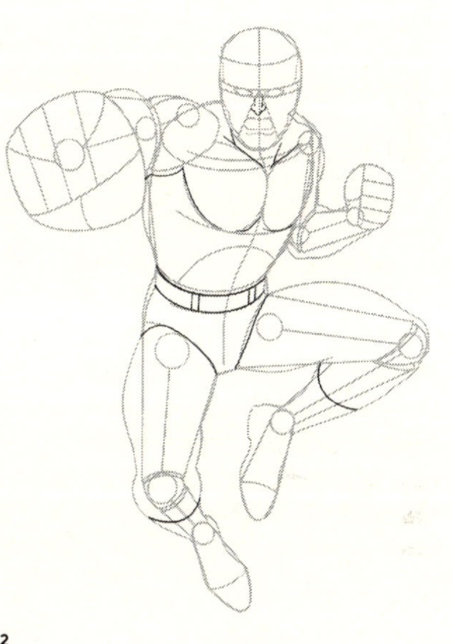

10

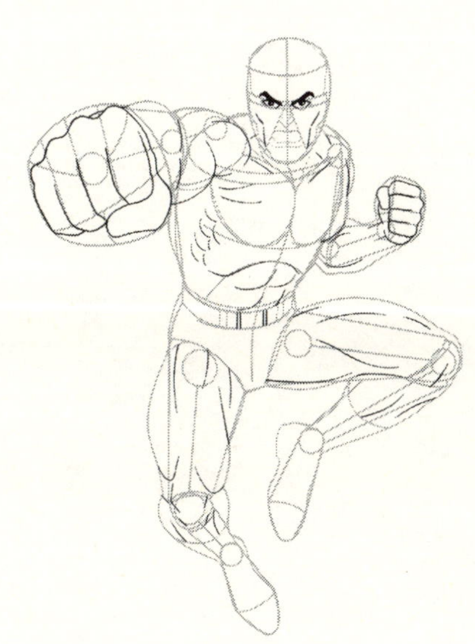

11

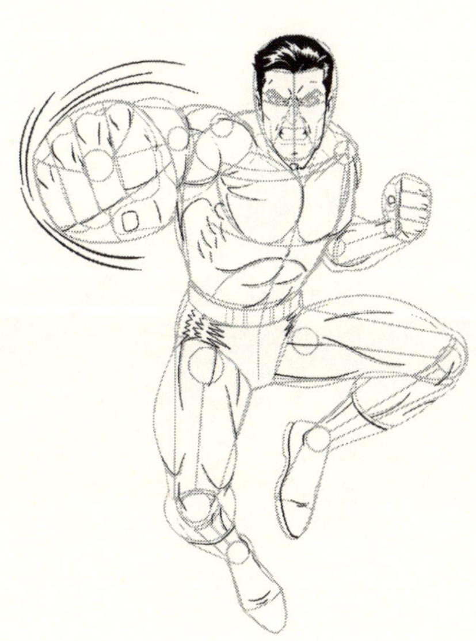

12

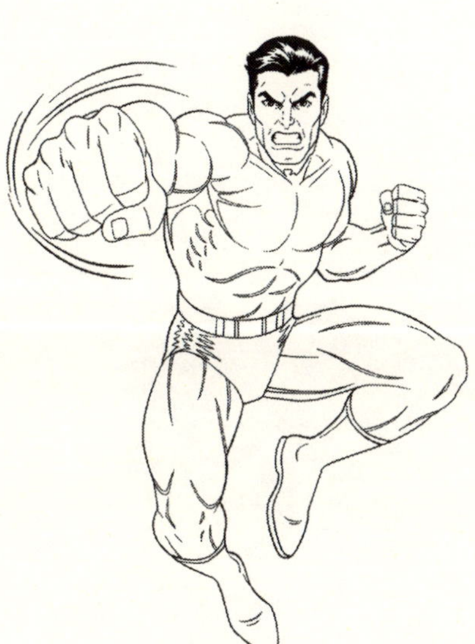

FLYING FIST-FIRST 'THE SOARER'

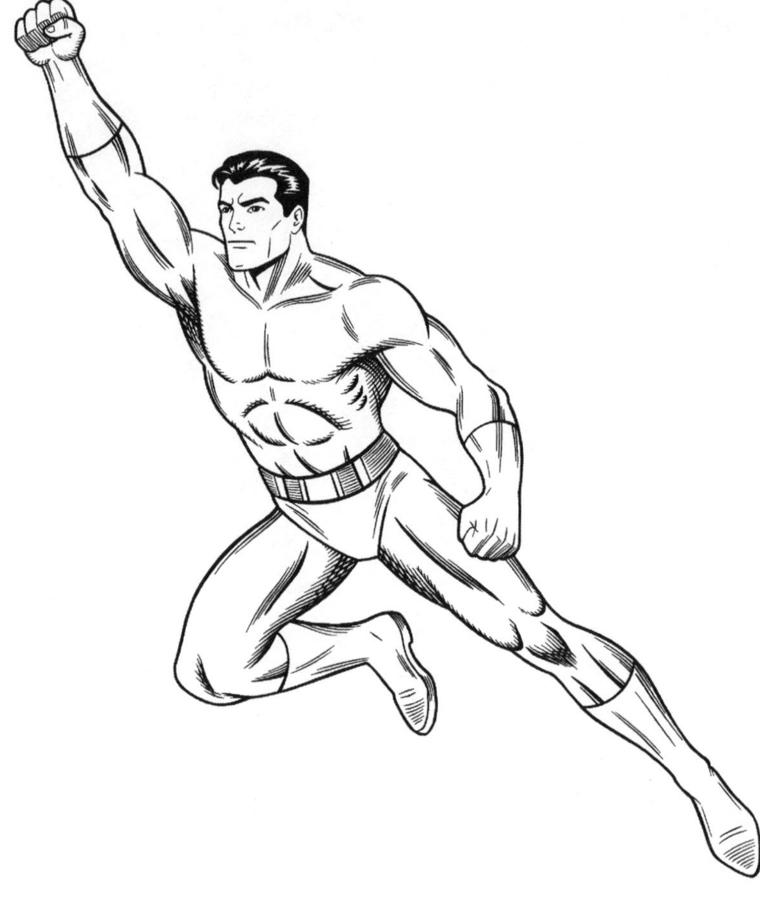

Pro Tip: The raised fist leads the composition, telling the viewer the figure is soaring. Keep the body on a strong diagonal line from fingertip to trailing leg to convey speed and momentum.

01

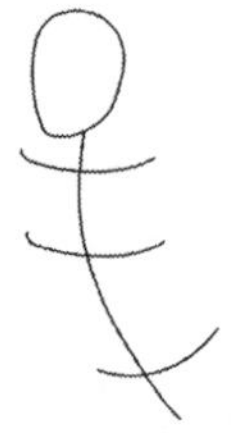

02

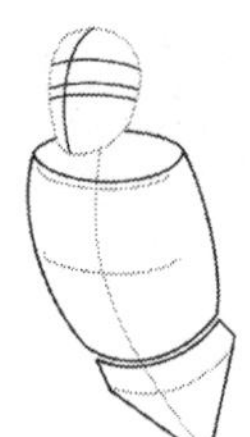

03

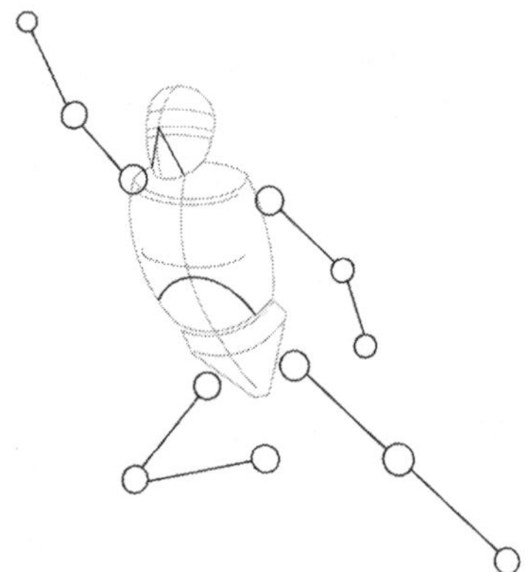

04

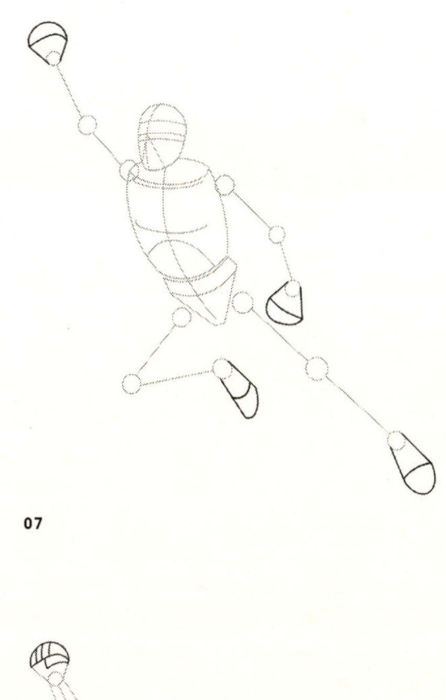

05

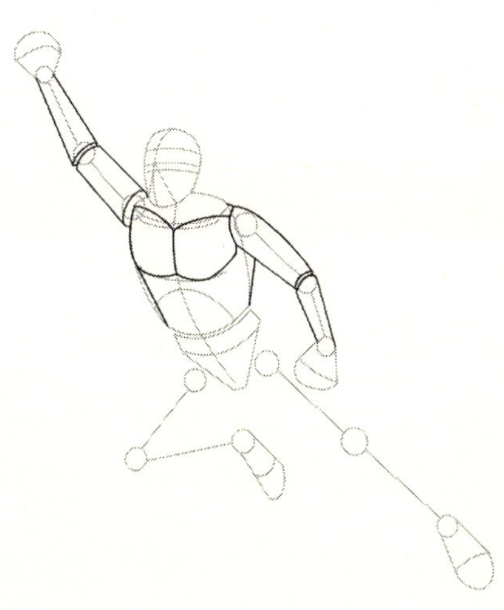

06

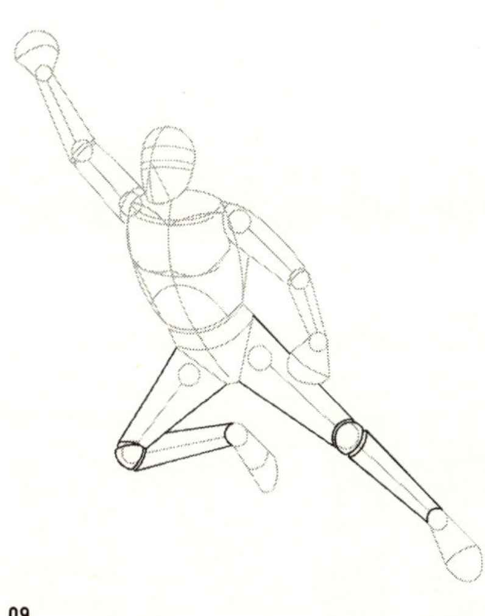

07

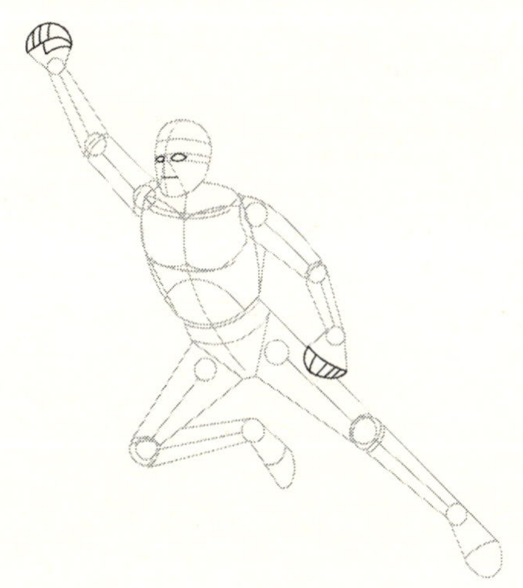

08

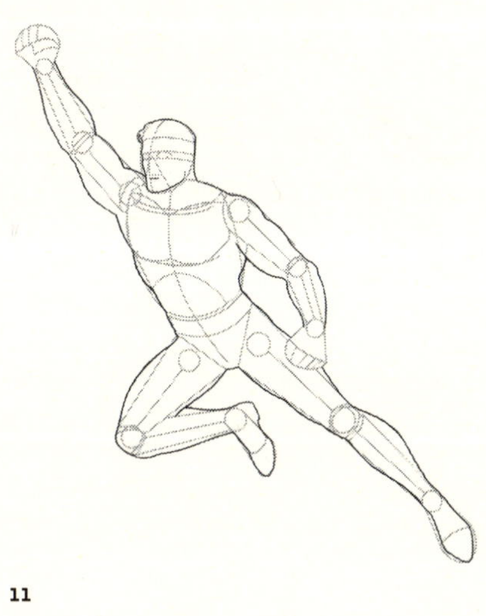

09

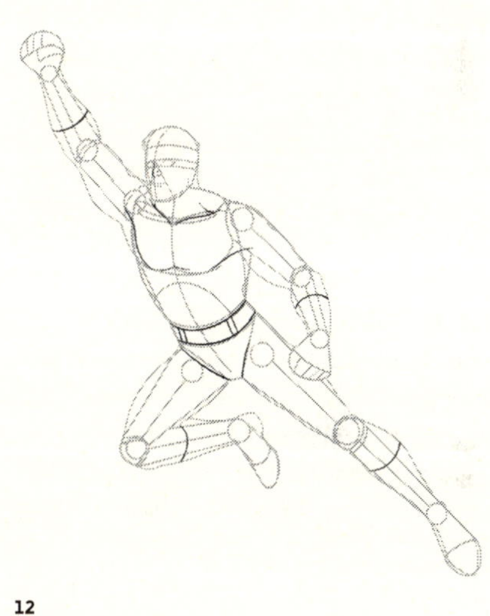

10

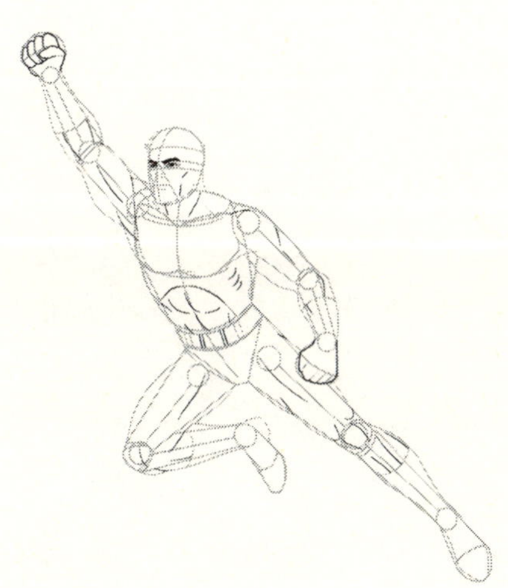

11

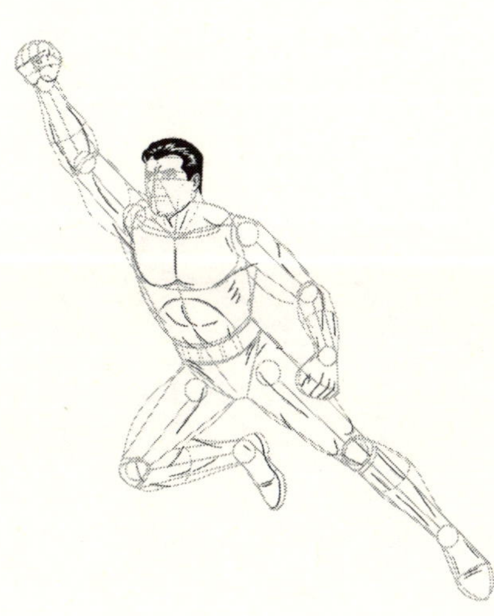

12

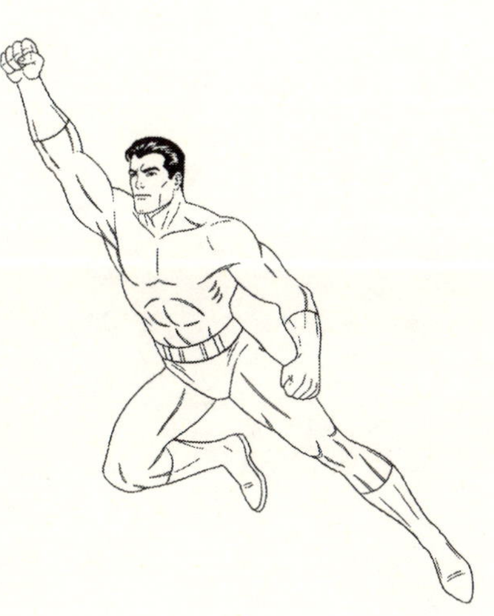

HIGH-SPEED RUNNING 'THE REDLINE'

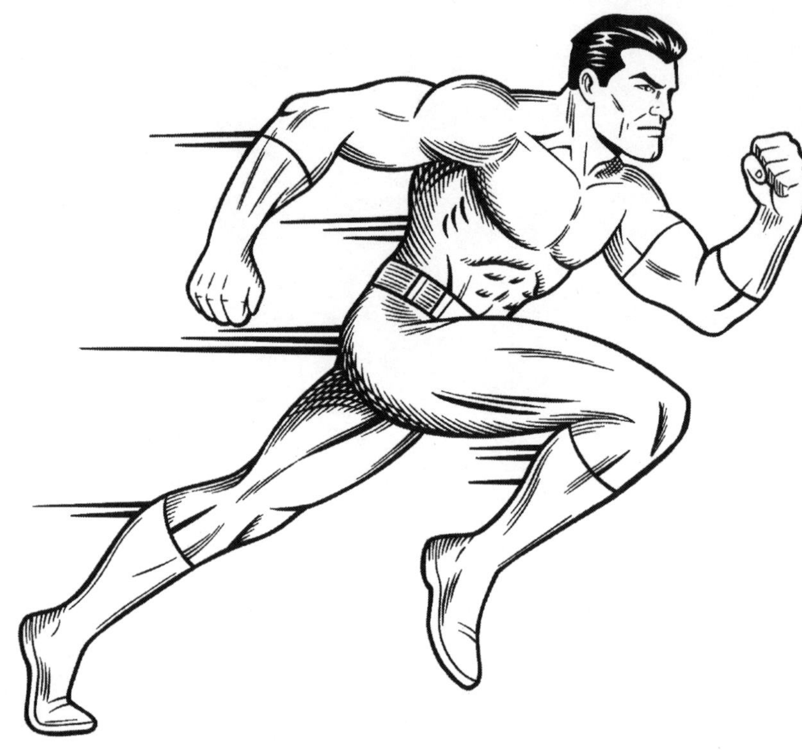

Pro Tip: A convincing run is all about opposing diagonals — the arms and legs should swing in opposite directions to convey natural motion. Keep the torso leaning forward and the stride long and low to suggest speed and urgency.

01

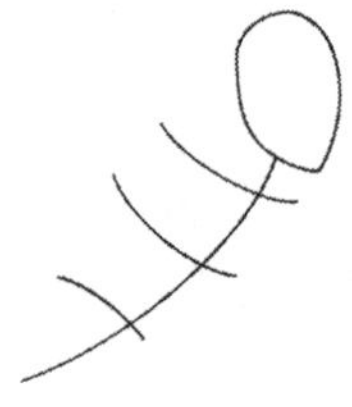

02

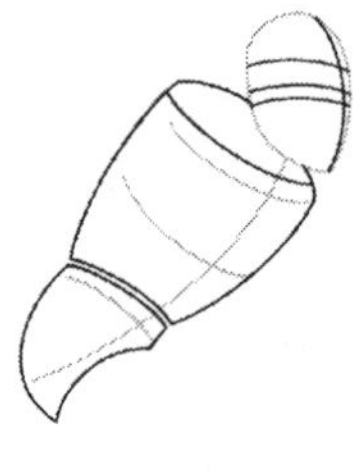

03

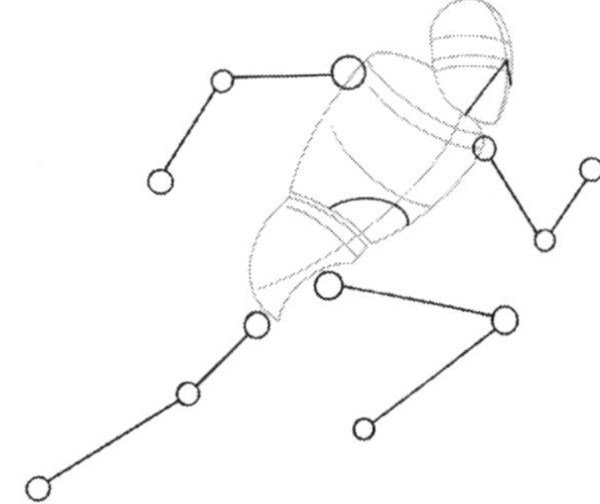

04

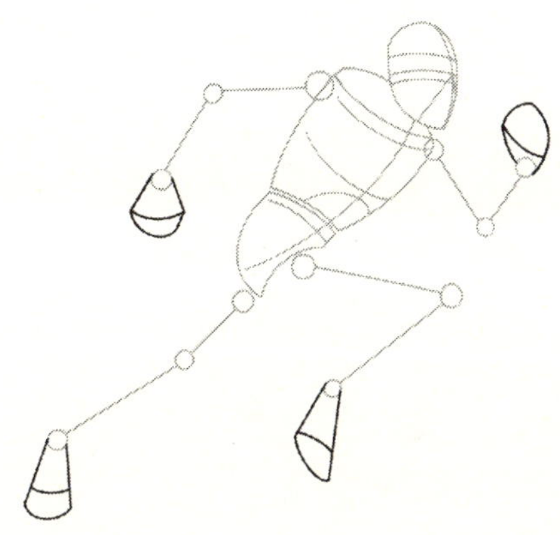

05

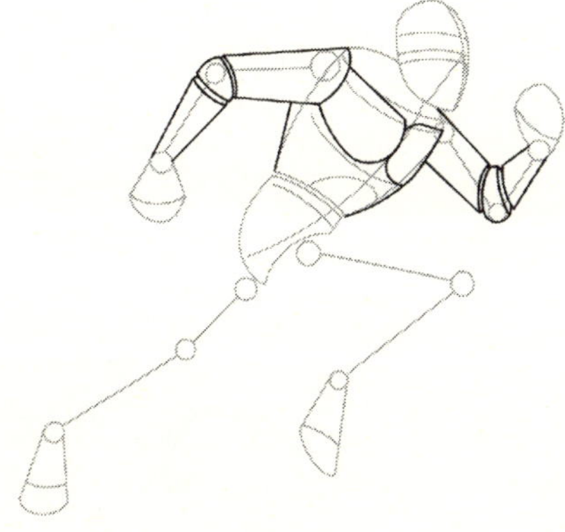

06

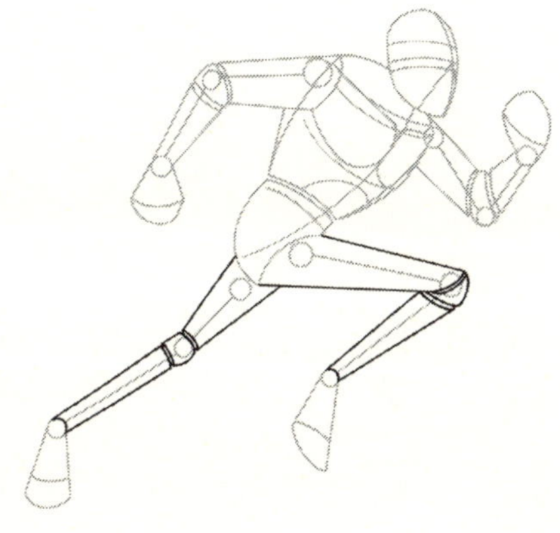

07

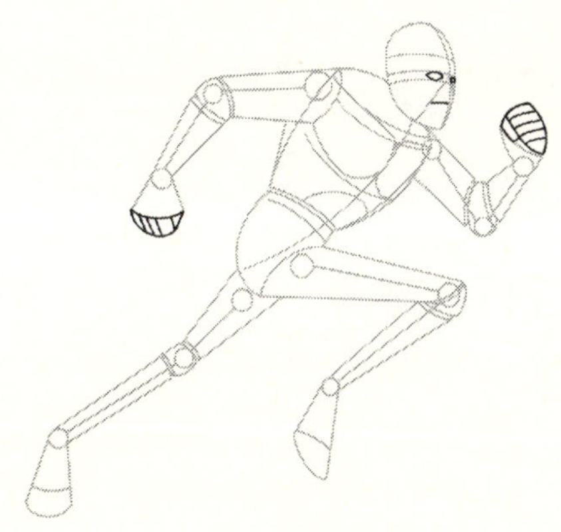

08

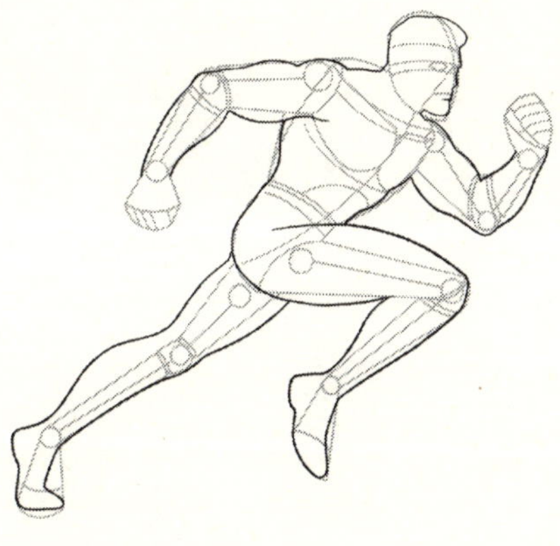

09

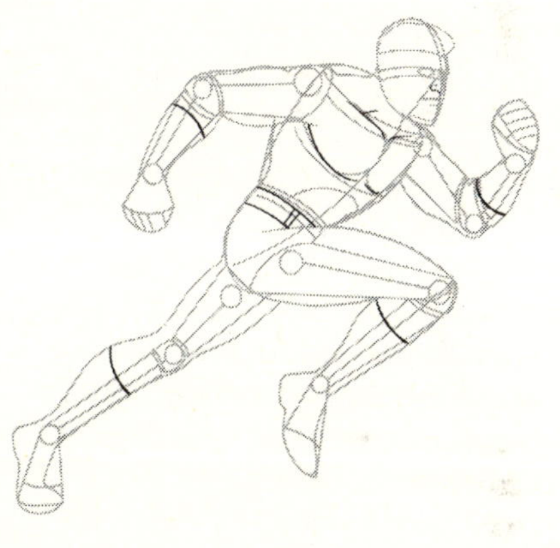

10

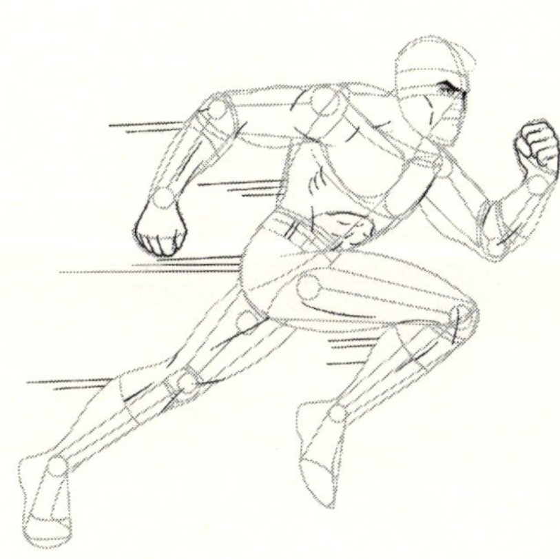

11

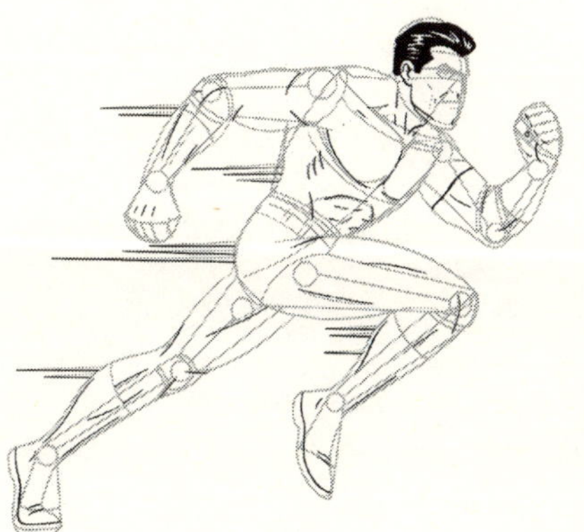

12

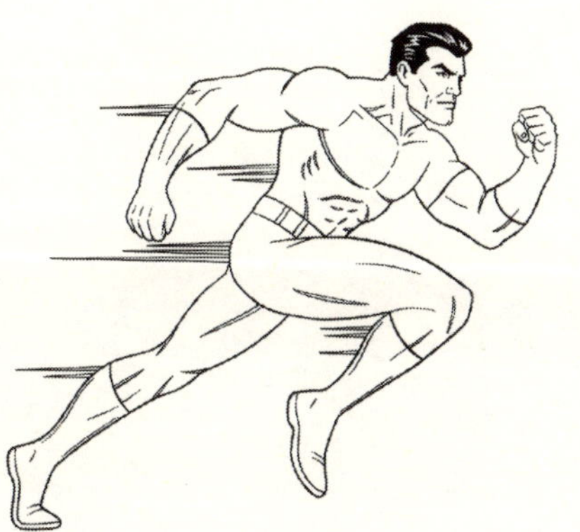

POWERLIFTING 'THE TITAN'

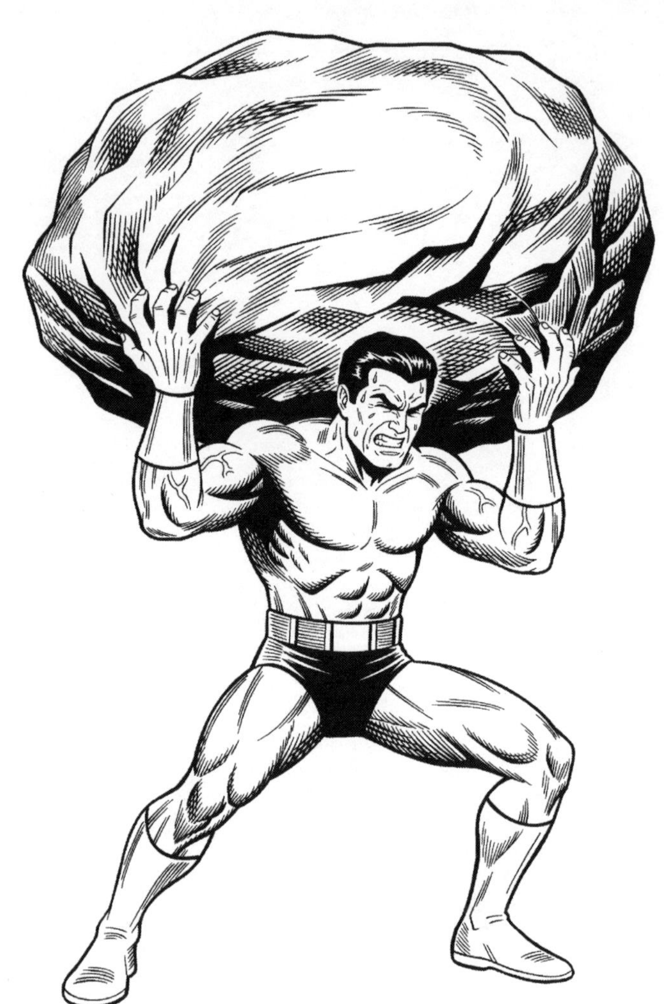

Pro Tip: Keep the legs wide and deeply bent, with the knees tracking over the feet, to give the stance a stable, straining base that sells the superhuman effort.

01

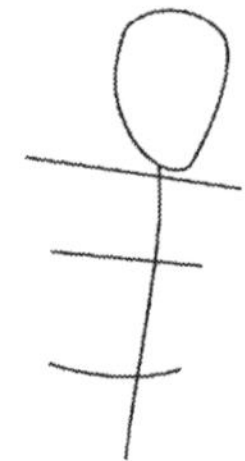

02

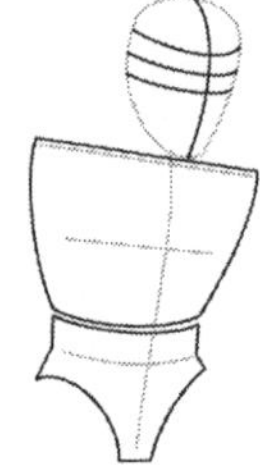

03

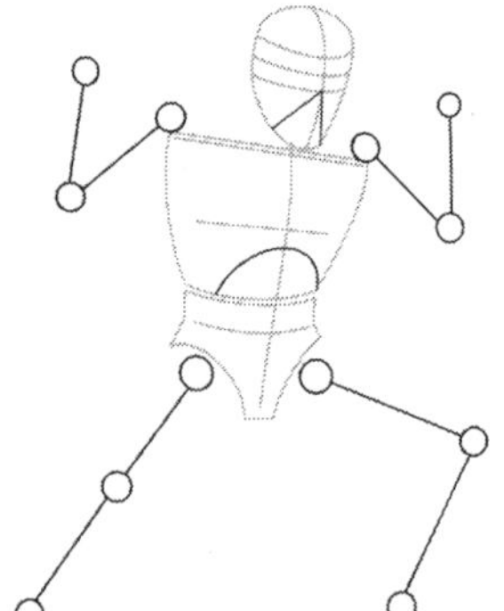

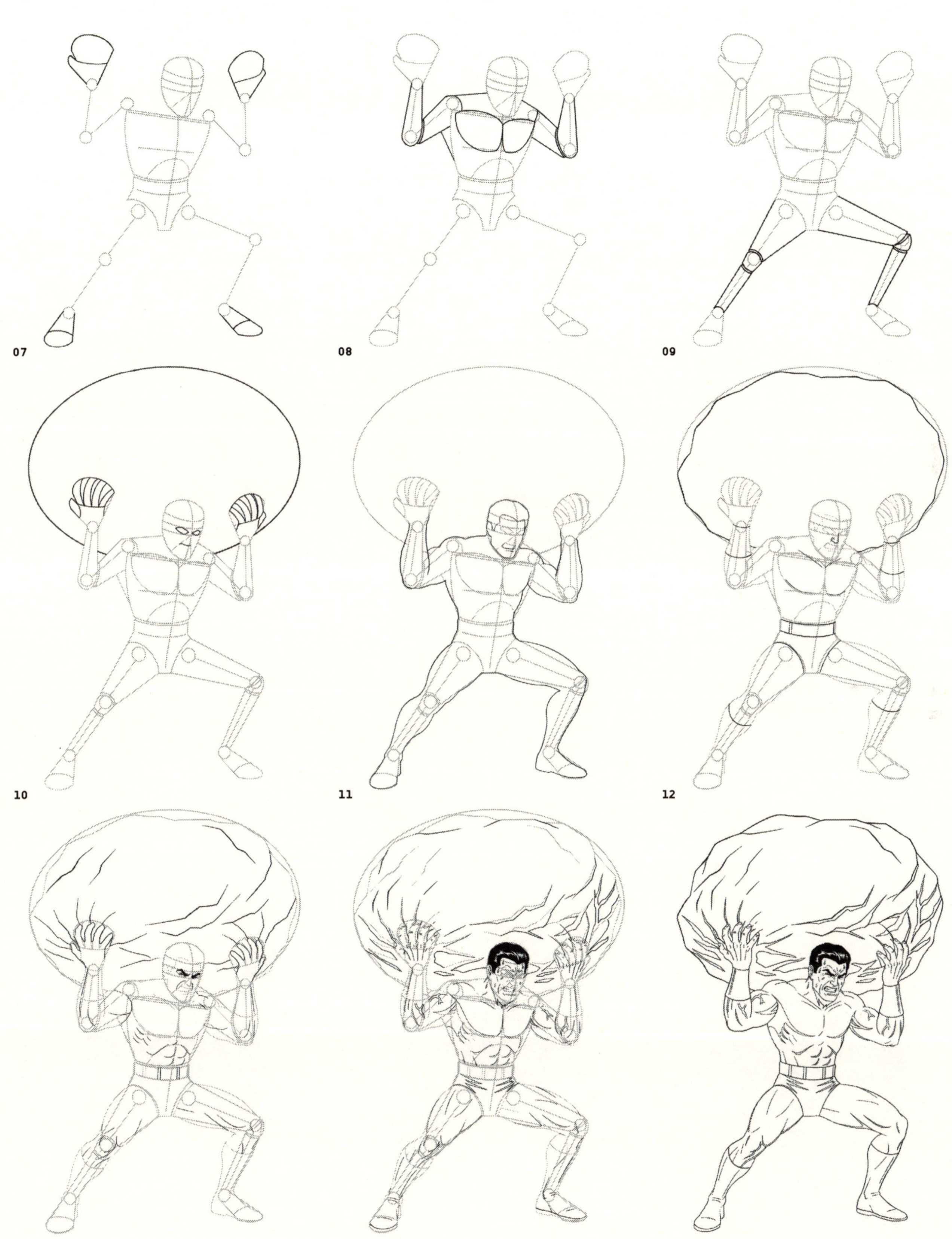
04
05
06
07
08
09
10
11
12

THREE-POINT LANDING 'THE TOUCHDOWN'

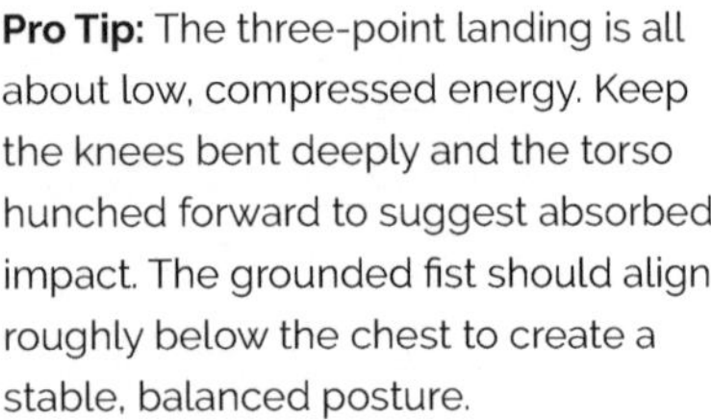

Pro Tip: The three-point landing is all about low, compressed energy. Keep the knees bent deeply and the torso hunched forward to suggest absorbed impact. The grounded fist should align roughly below the chest to create a stable, balanced posture.

01

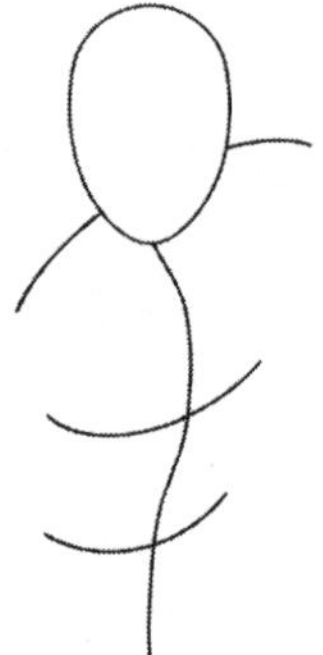

02

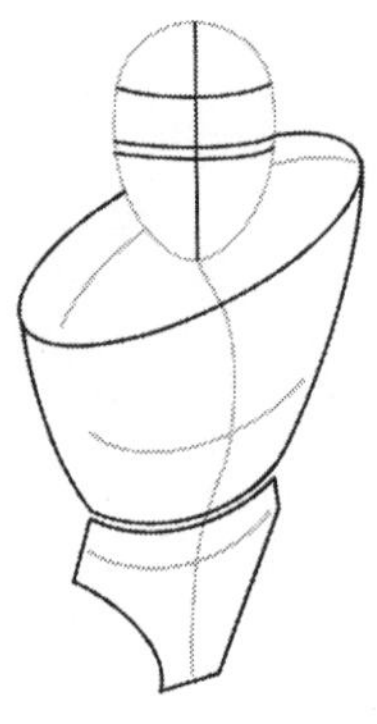

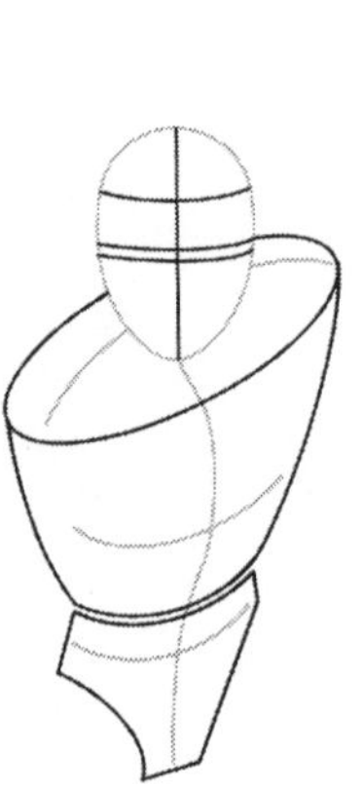

03

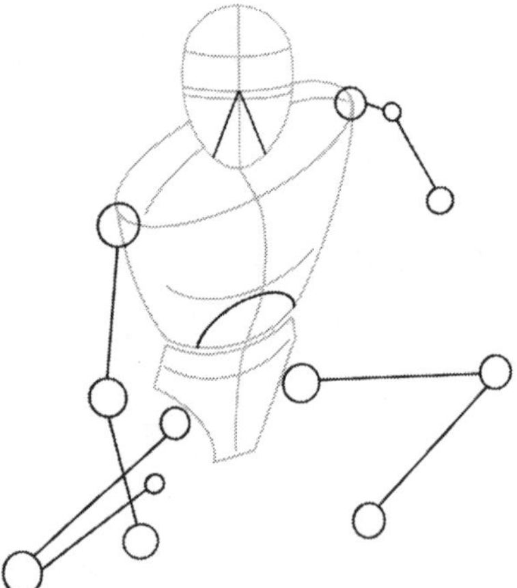

04

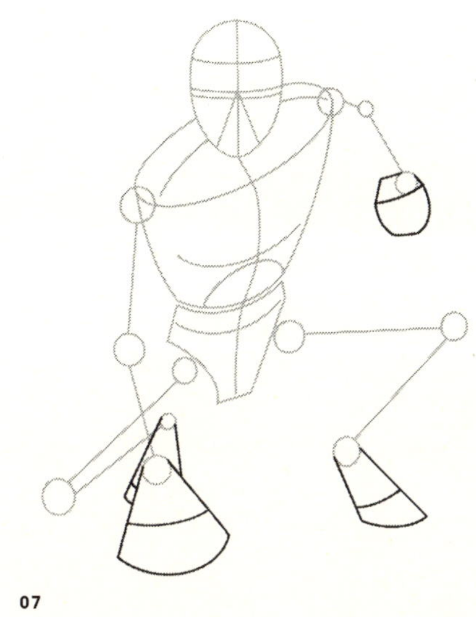

05

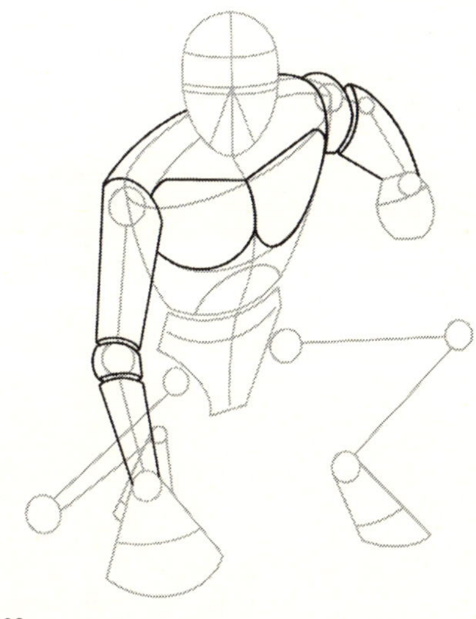

06

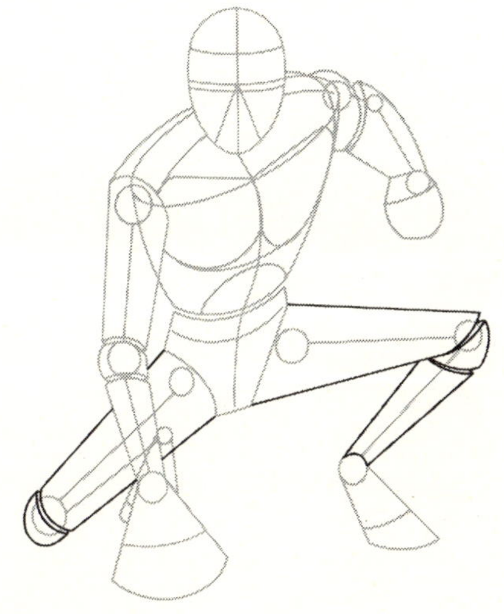

07

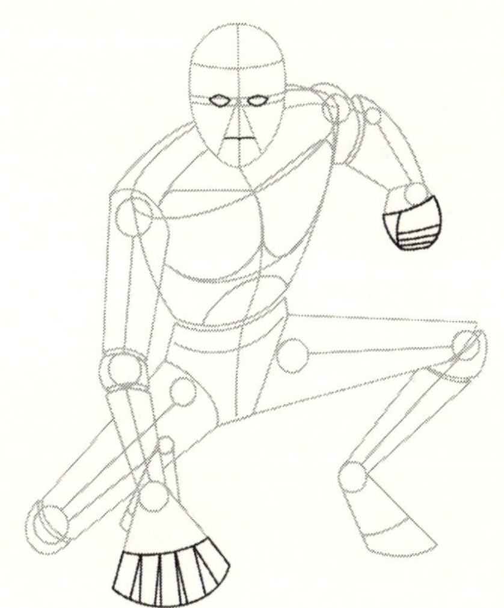

08

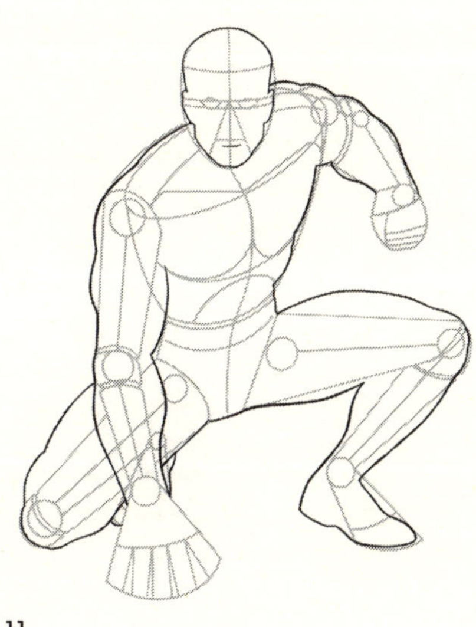

09

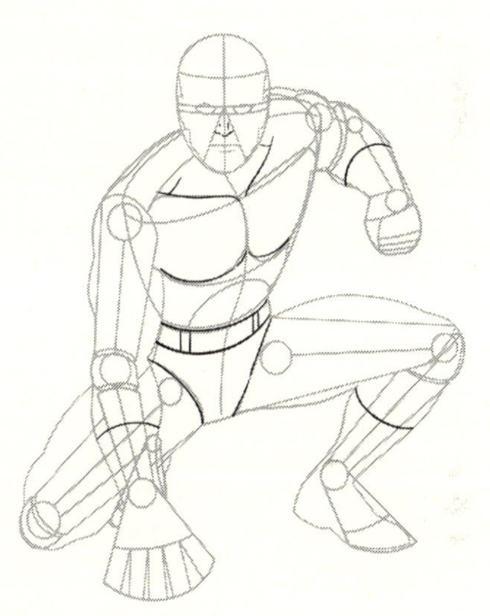

10

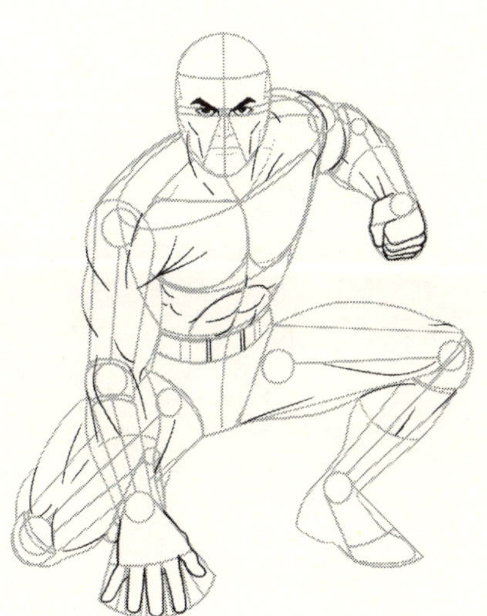

11

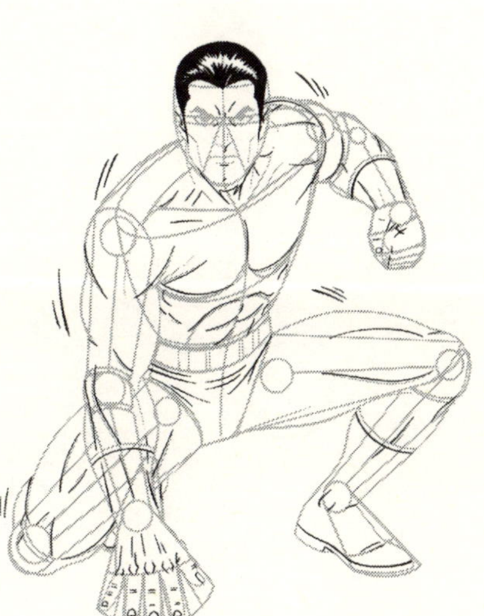

12

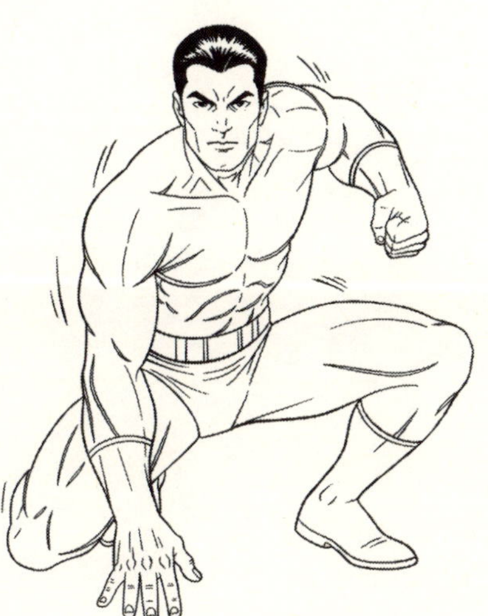

STANDING ARMS CROSSED 'THE COMMANDER'

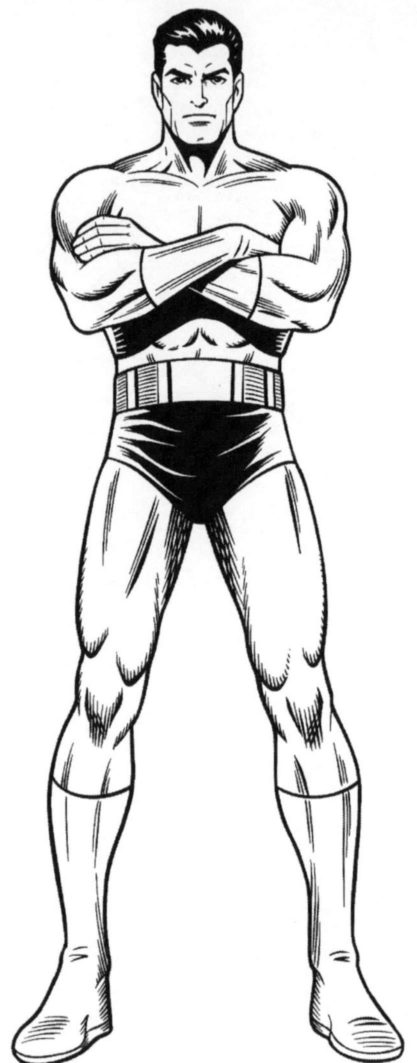

Pro Tip: Drawing from just below eye level instantly adds dominance and stature. Keep the shoulders wide and arms crossed high on the chest. The legs should taper subtly downward to enhance the towering effect.

01

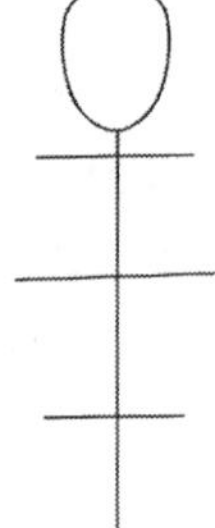

02

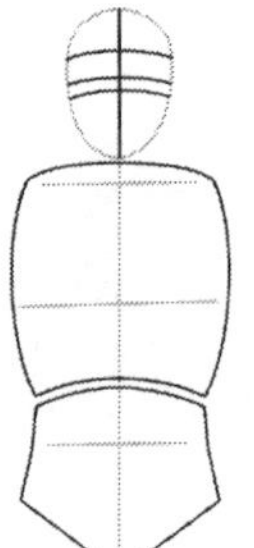

03

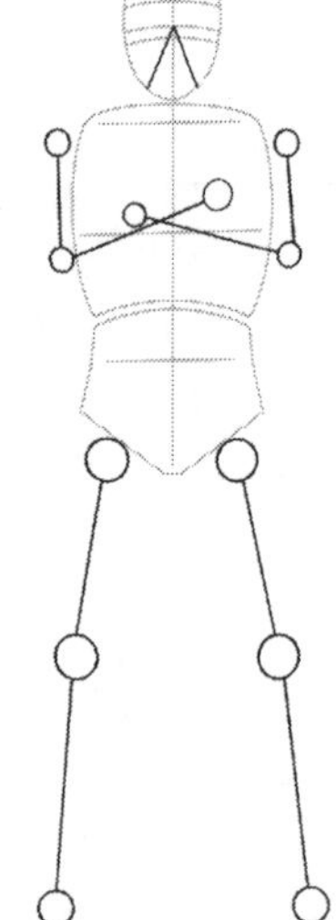

04

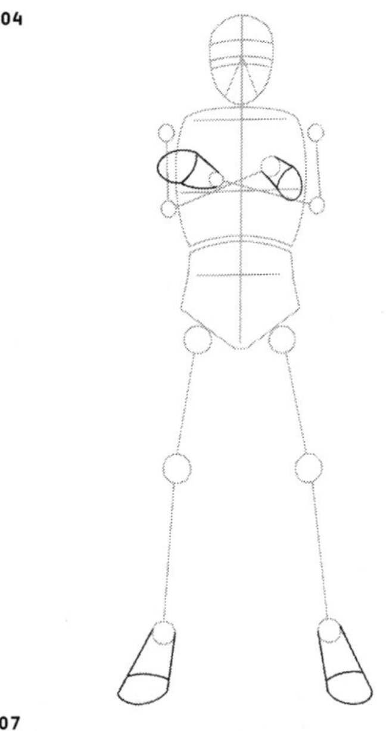

05

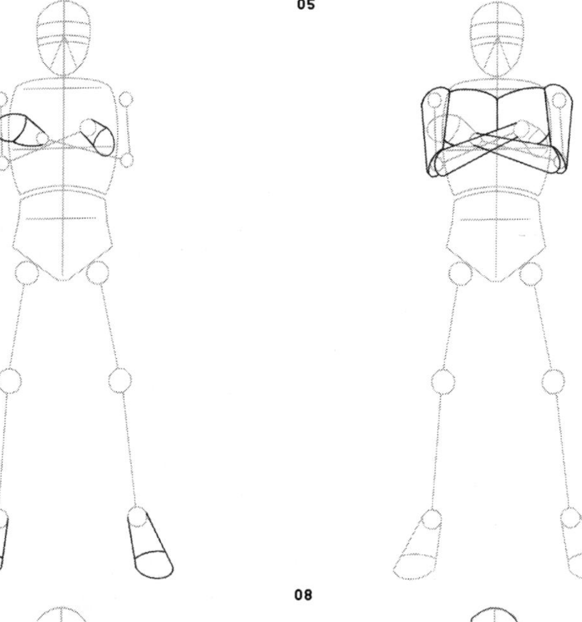

06

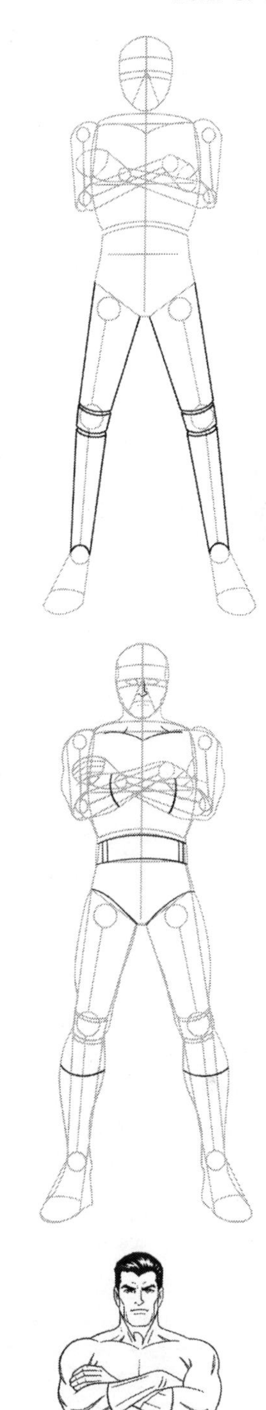

07

08

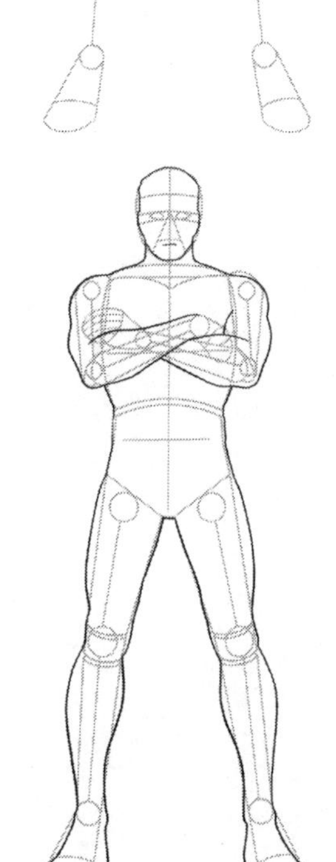

09

10

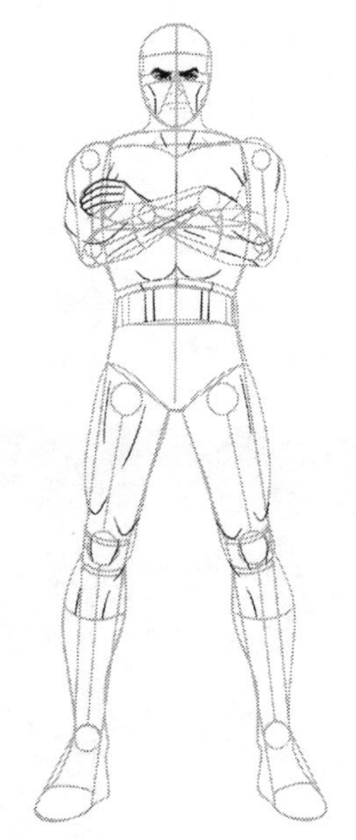

11

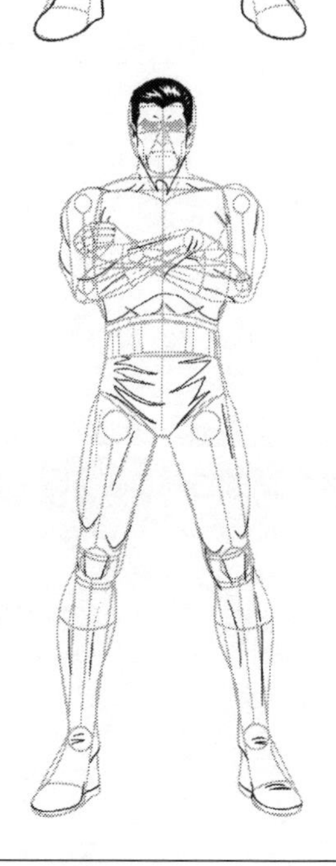

12

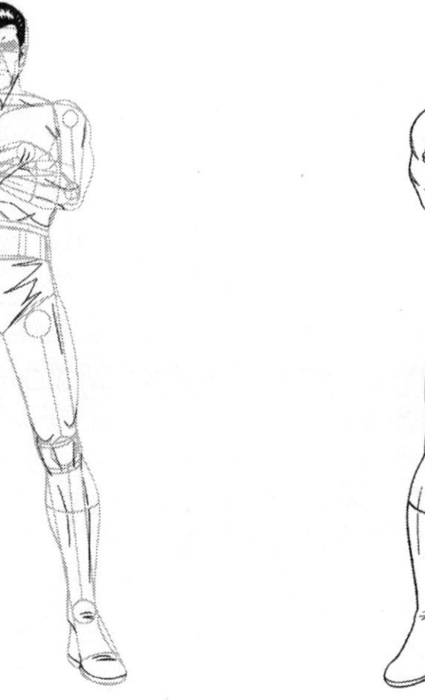

03| DESIGNING YOUR OWN SUPERHERO

GOING BEYOND HUMAN

You can draw the figure. You can capture power and movement in a single pose. Now comes the most exciting part of the entire journey: creating a character that is entirely, uniquely yours. This is where the artist in you gets to run wild.

Designing a superhero from scratch can feel overwhelming at first. Where do you even begin? The answer, as it turns out, is all around you. The natural world is bursting with colour, texture, form, and ferocity, and for centuries, artists and storytellers have looked to it for inspiration. In this chapter, we're going to do exactly that, and show you how to transform what you find into compelling, original superhero designs.

The truth is that no great character design exists in a vacuum. Every memorable hero or villain you've ever seen was born from a spark of inspiration that the artist found somewhere in the world around them, a silhouette, a texture, a behaviour, a colour, something that caught their eye and refused to let go. Learning to look at the world as a source of raw creative material is one of the most valuable skills you can develop as a comics artist, and it is a skill that never stops giving. Once you start seeing the design potential in a beetle's armour, the fluid grace of a deep sea creature, or the jagged geometry of a crystal formation, you will never be short of ideas.

The secret is in the blend. A character inspired by a single idea can be interesting, but a character that fuses a concept with the human form in a thoughtful, creative way becomes something truly memorable. This is where design thinking comes in. It's not enough to simply place animal features onto a human body and call it done. The best hybrid designs feel inevitable, as though the character could not possibly look any other way. Achieving that takes a understanding of how shapes, silhouettes and textures interact, how to take the essence of your inspiration and weave it into the figure in a way that feels cohesive, purposeful and alive. That is exactly what this chapter will teach you.

By the time you've worked through these pages you'll have a design process you can apply to absolutely anything. A storm, a predator, a mineral pulled from the earth: all of it becomes potential. All of it becomes material. And the most exciting realisation of all is that you are only ever limited by how widely you're willing to look.

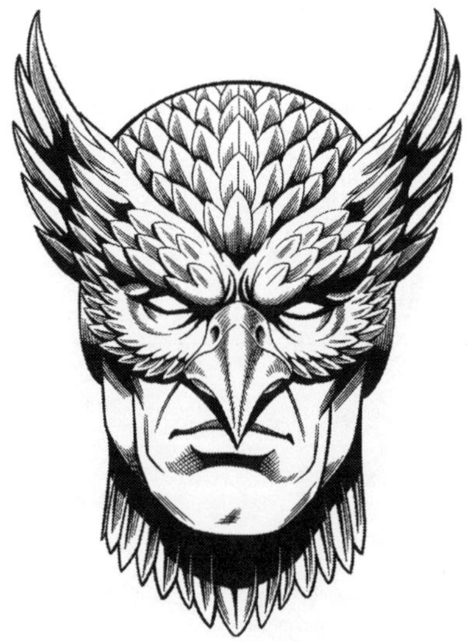

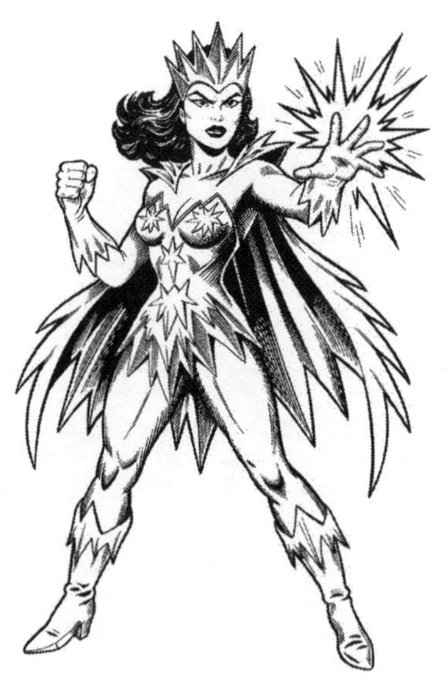

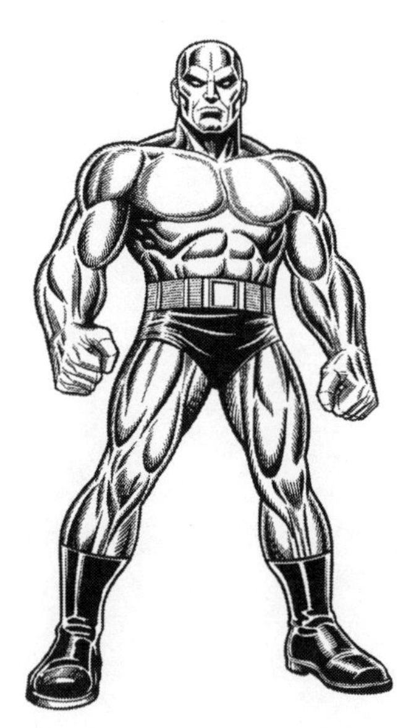

The Natural World: From the raw power of a predator to the alien geometry of an insect, the fluid grace of an aquatic creature, to the vivid colours of a tropical bird, the natural world is one of the richest design libraries on the planet. Every creature that has ever evolved has done so with a purpose, and that purpose is written into every scale, feather, fang and fin. Millions of years of adaptation have produced forms of breathtaking variety, and as a character designer your job is simply to look, to really look, and ask yourself what each creature is communicating through its appearance. Danger. Speed. Camouflage. Dominance. These are the same qualities you want your characters to project, and nature has already done the hard work of figuring out how to express them visually. We'll show you how to look beyond the surface and identify the shapes, textures, silhouettes and behaviours that can be borrowed, adapted and woven into your character designs.

Elements: What does a character who commands fire actually look like? How do you make ice feel cold on the page, or lightning feel genuinely dangerous? The elemental forces of the natural world offer some of the most dramatic and visually striking inspiration available to a character designer, and they come with something that organic inspiration sometimes lacks: instant readability. A character built around fire reads as fire. A character built around ice reads as ice. That clarity of concept is enormously powerful in a visual medium where a reader has only a fraction of a second to absorb a new character and understand what they're about. We'll explore how to translate fire and ice into costume design, body structure and visual effects, showing you how to capture the essence of each element in a way that feels dynamic and convincing. A character built around an elemental concept should feel inseparable from it, as though the power doesn't just belong to them but runs through every line of their design.

Metals and Minerals: The jagged edges of a crystal, the reflective sheen of gold, the raw imposing weight of stone. The mineral world offers a treasure trove of texture, colour and form that can give a character an instantly distinctive visual identity. Minerals bring a geometric quality to character design, hard edges, repeating patterns and crystalline structures that can make a figure look genuinely unlike anything else on the page. There is also a psychological dimension to mineral inspired design that is worth considering. Gold reads as wealth and power. Obsidian reads as darkness and threat. Diamond reads as invulnerability. And then there are the metals that speak purely of strength, dense, unyielding, industrial materials like tungsten, titanium and steel that communicate raw physical power before a character has thrown a single punch. These associations are deeply embedded in the way we respond to materials, and a designer who understands them can use them to enormous effect.

BIRD OF PREY 'SKY HUNTER'

Pro Tip: A predatory bird's key design elements — hooked beak, layered feathers and fierce brow ridge. These can be woven into a costume as a sharp helmet, overlapping chest plating and a heavy visor to communicate speed and aerial dominance.

01

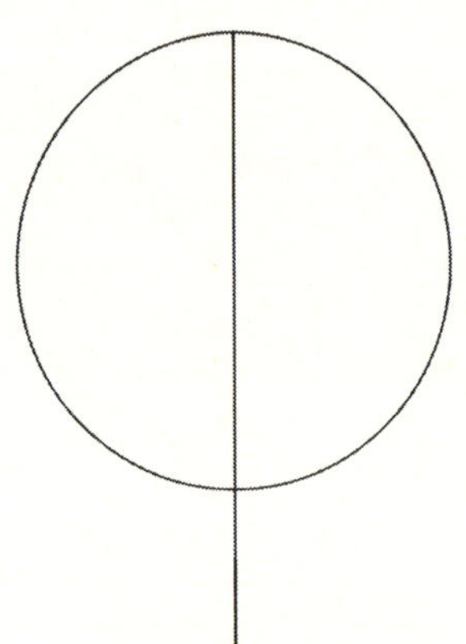

02

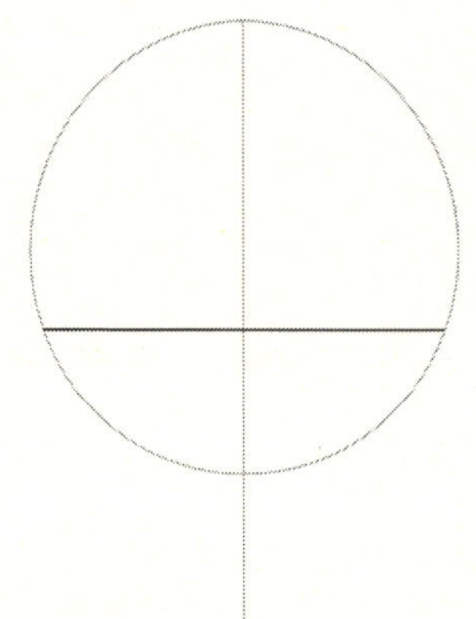

03

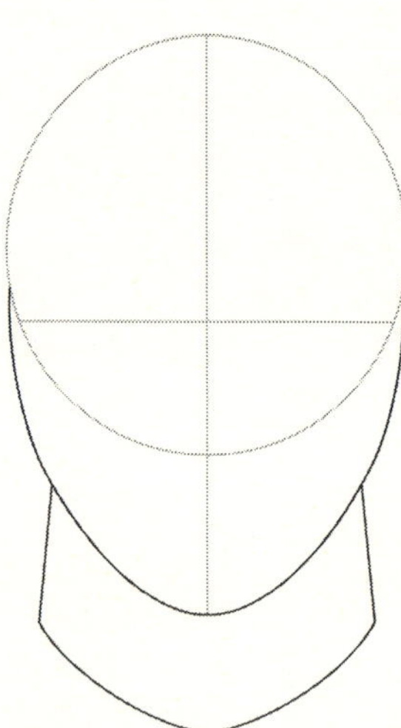

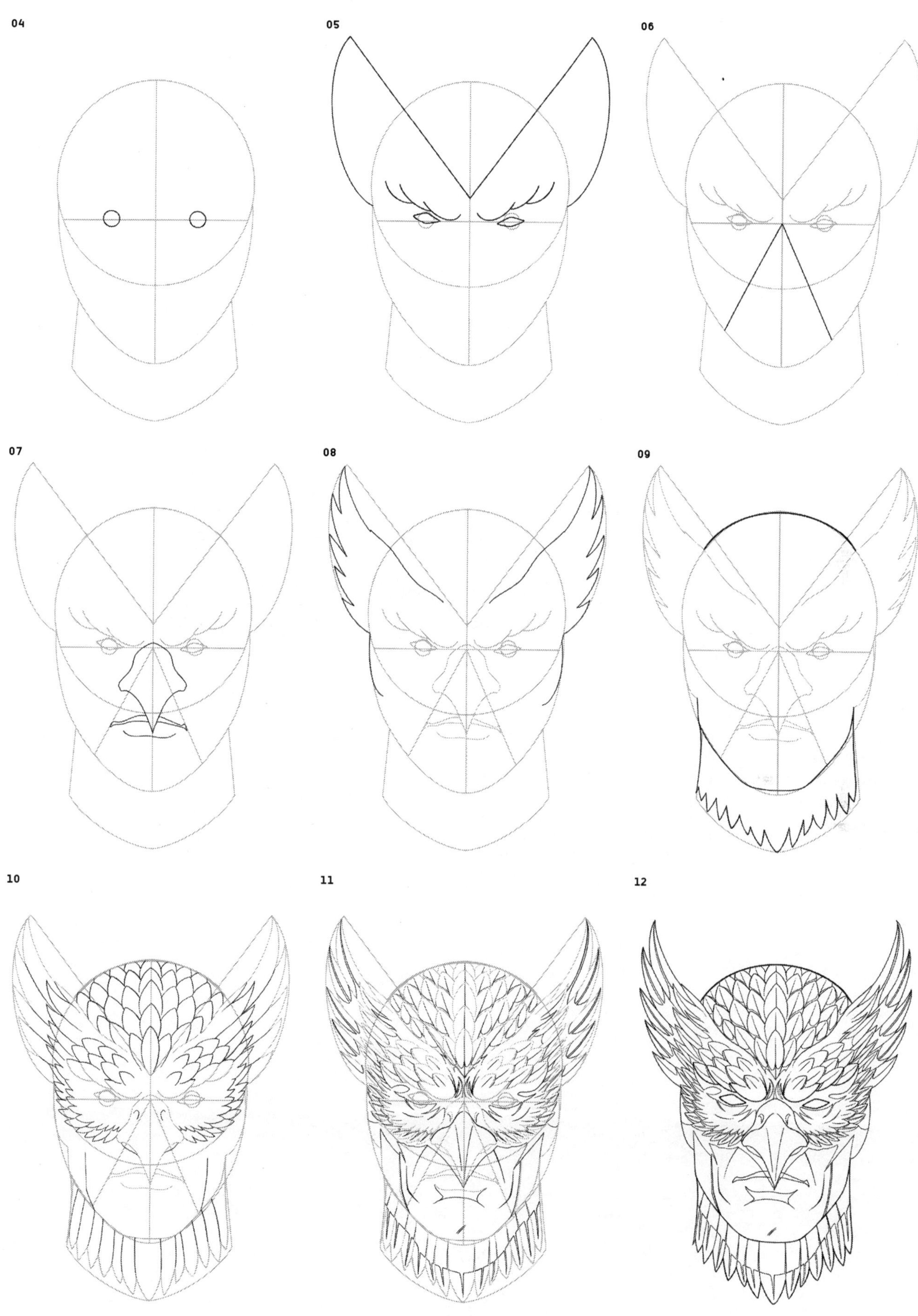
04
05
06
07
08
09
10
11
12

INSECT 'STRIKEWING'

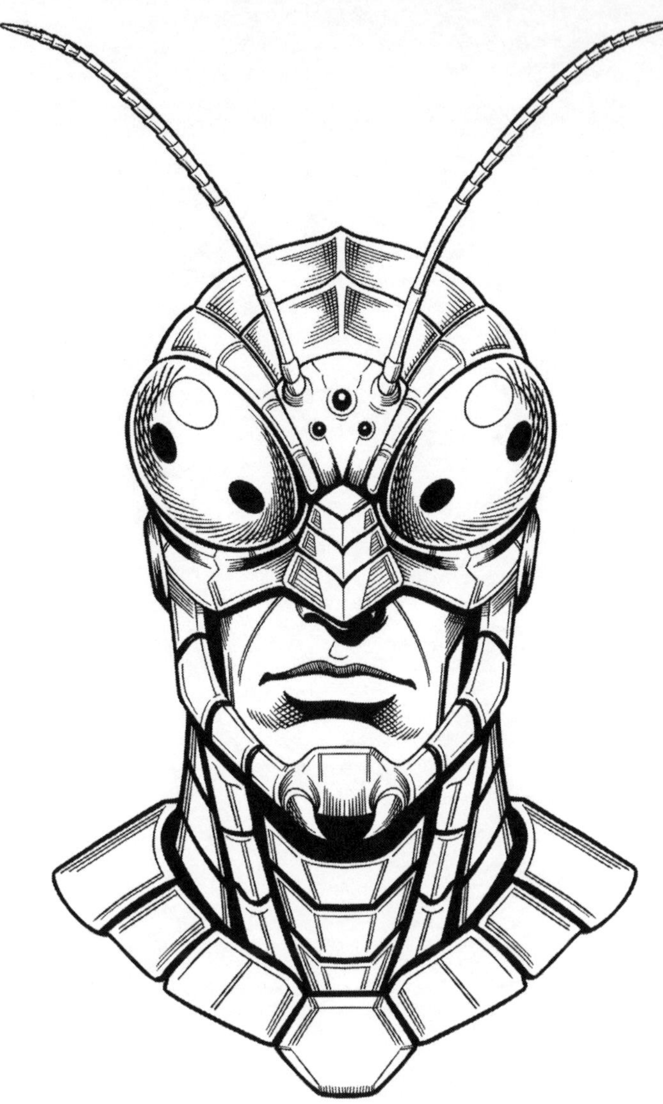

Pro Tip: The insect world offers a uniquely unsettling design language — compound eyes become a multi-lensed visor, a segmented exoskeleton becomes body armour, and antennae become sensor arrays, communicating precision, stealth and lightning reflexes.

01

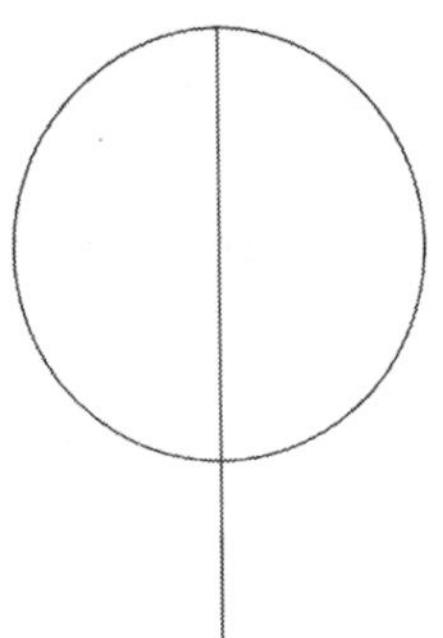

02

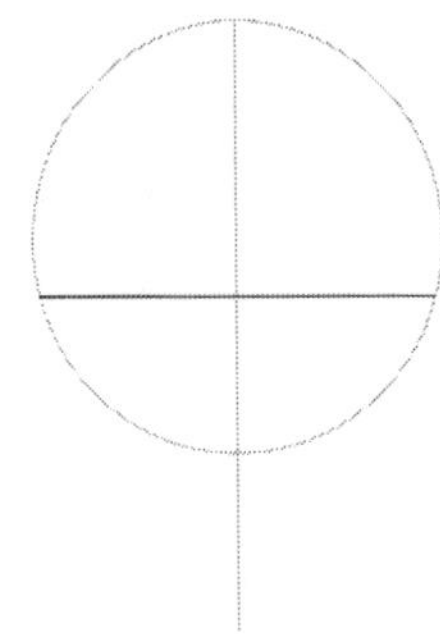

03

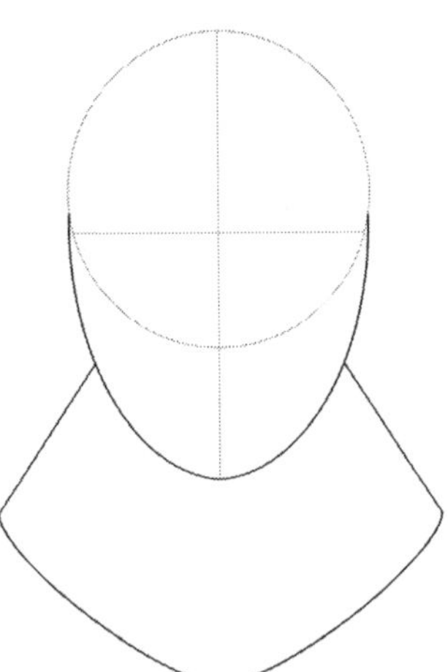

04

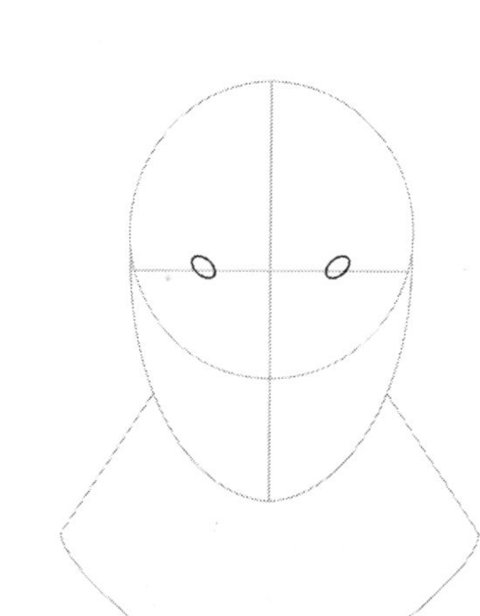

05

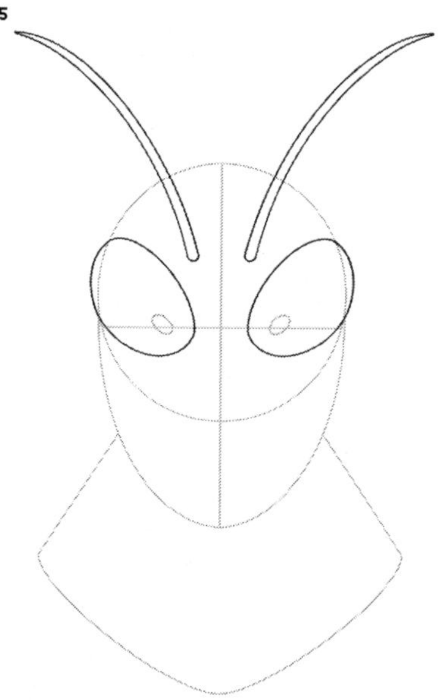

06

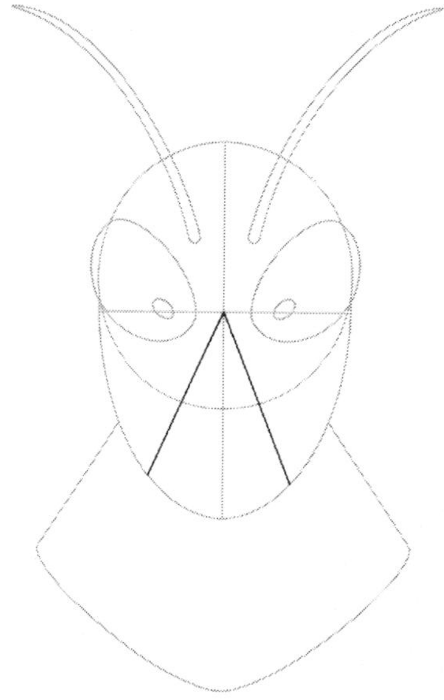

07

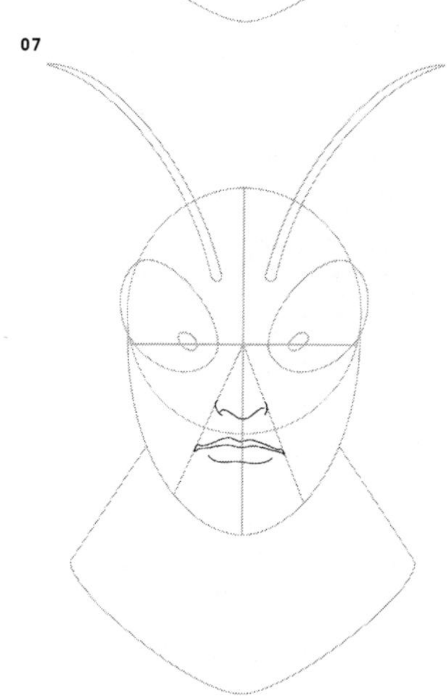

08

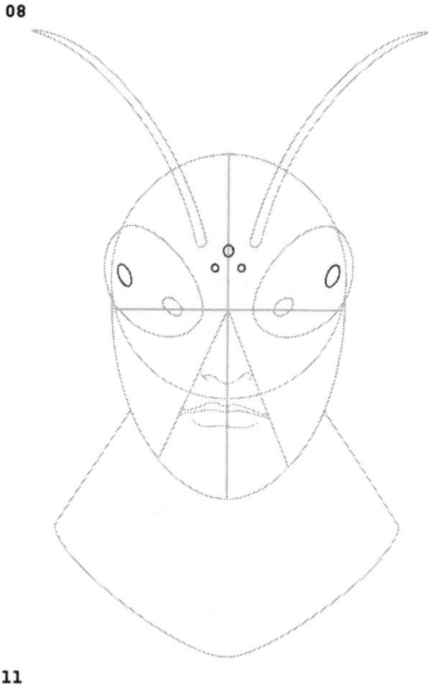

09

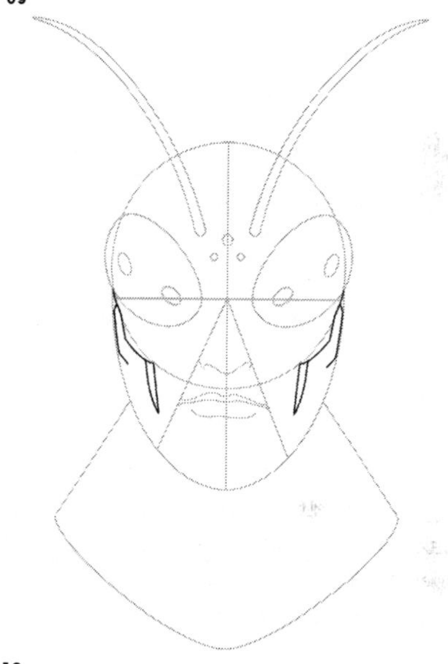

10

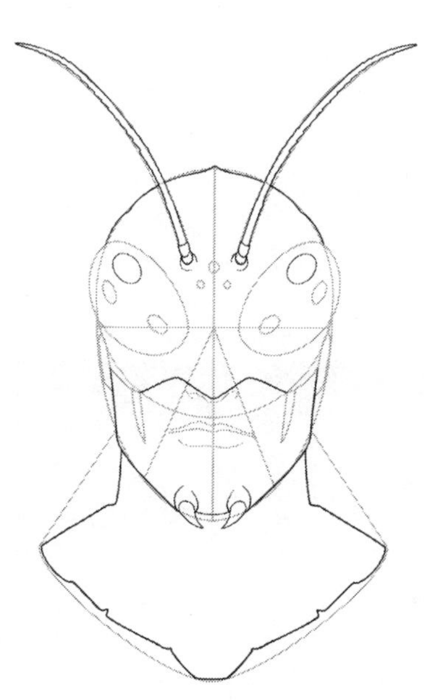

11

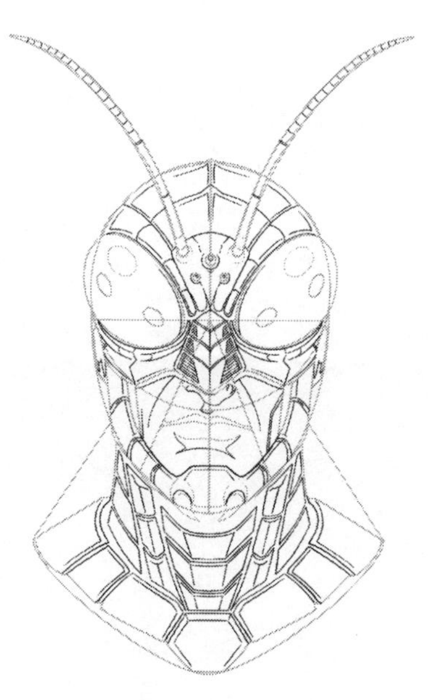

12

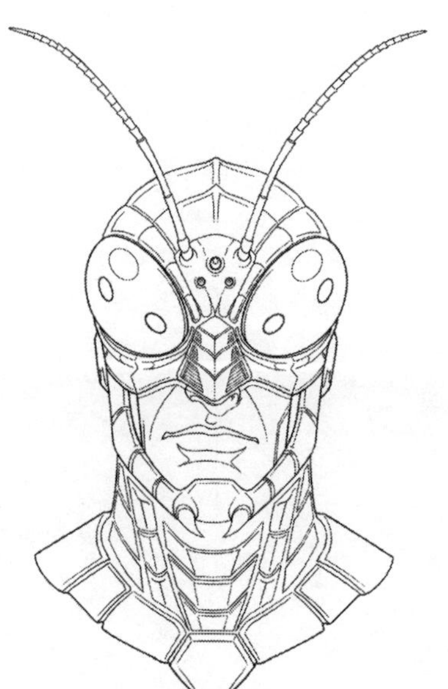

SHARK 'THE APEX'

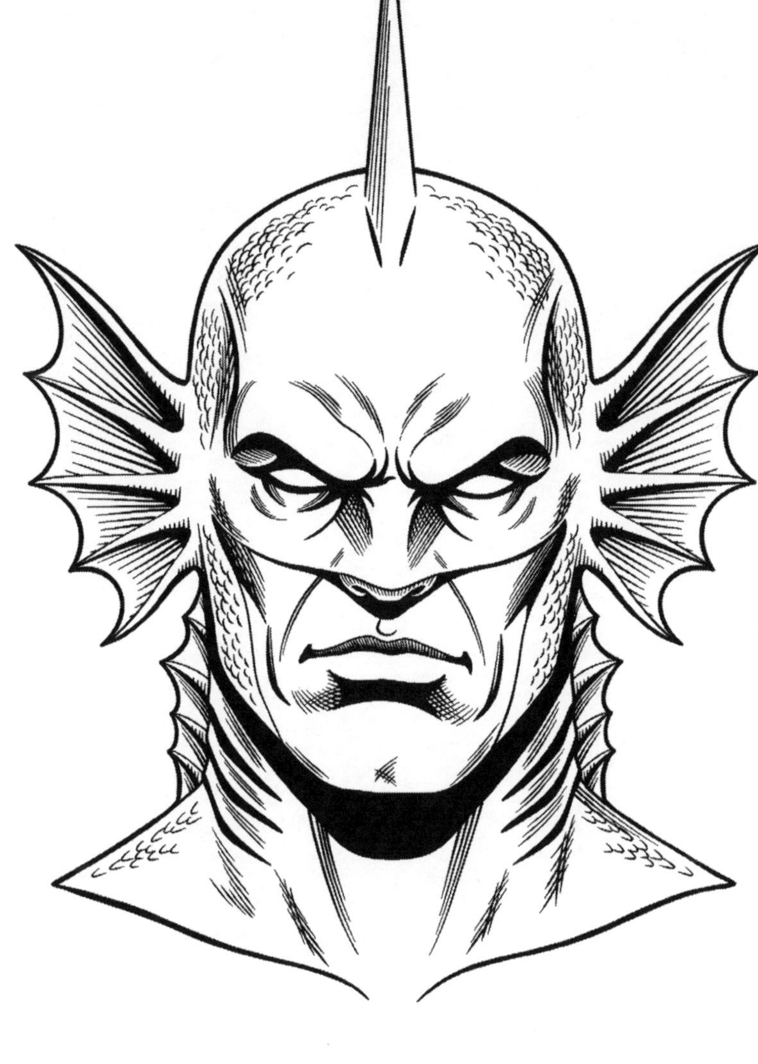

Pro Tip: The shark offers a primal design language — scaled skin becomes textured armour plating, the dorsal fin a crown-like spike, and webbed gill fins become sweeping side guards, communicating raw power, cold aggression and dominance.

01

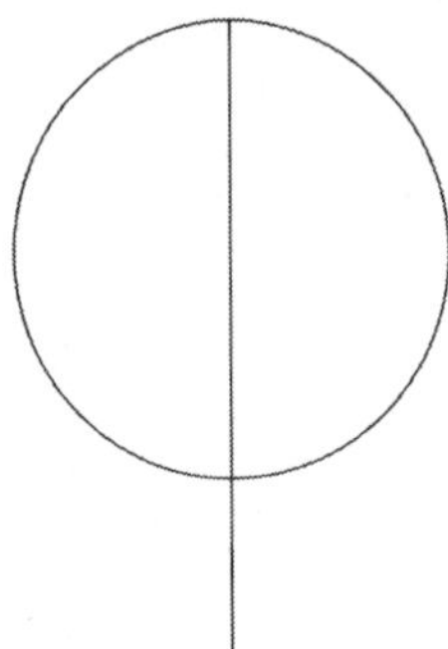

02

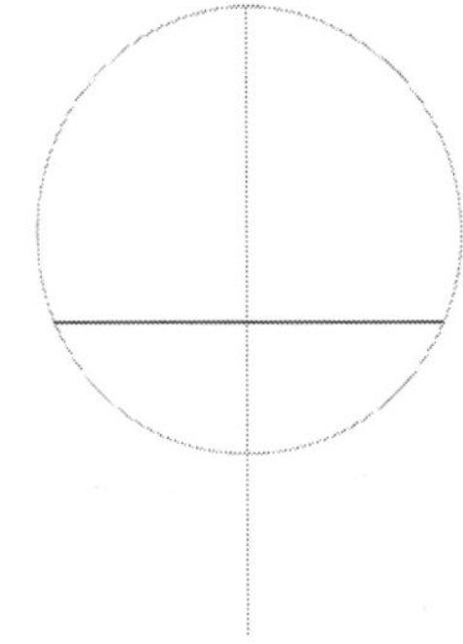

03

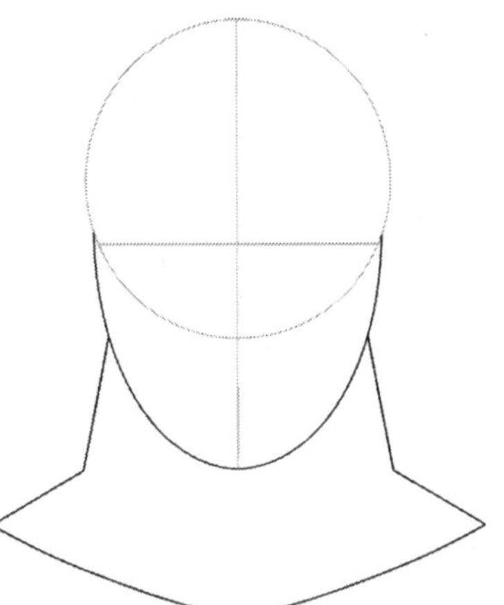

04

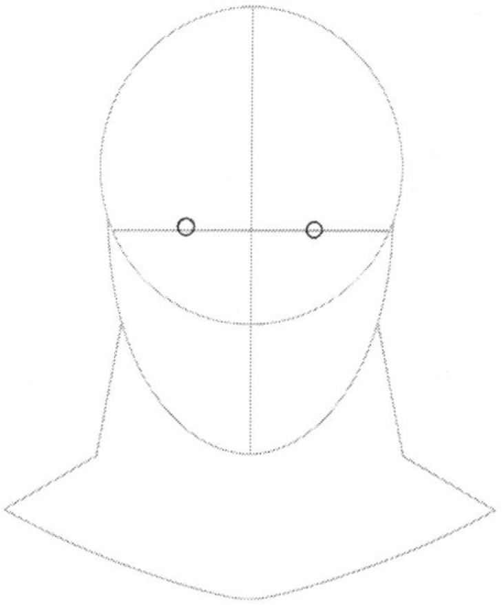

05

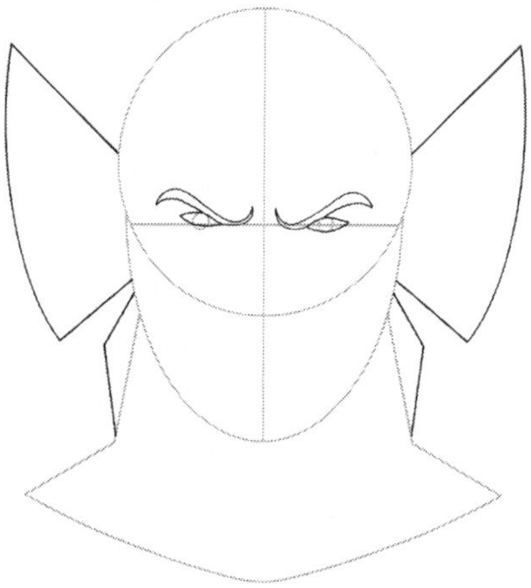

06

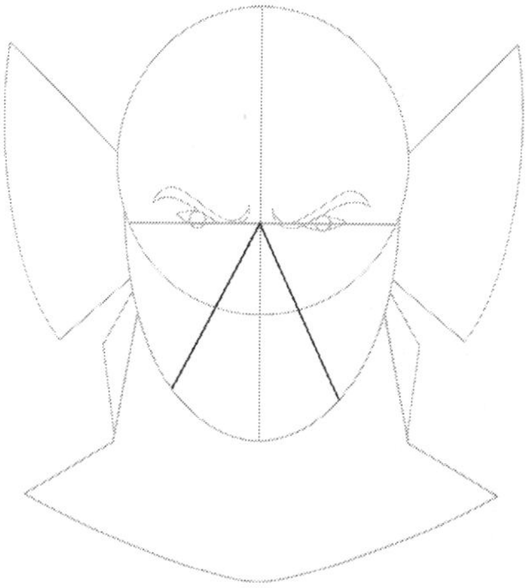

07

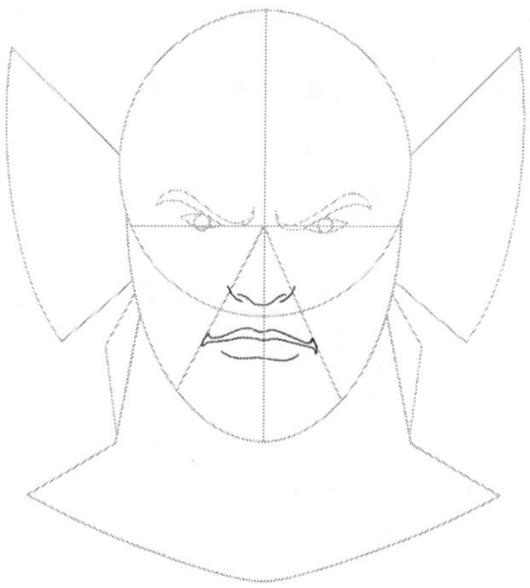

08

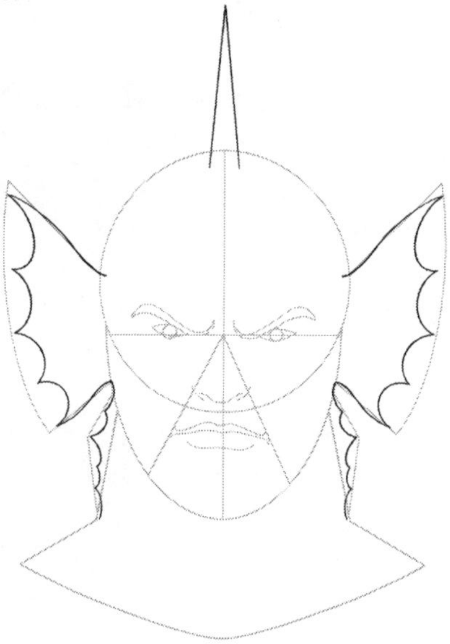

09

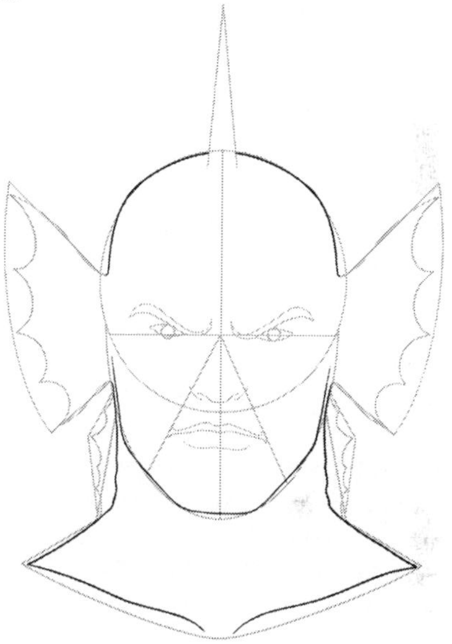

10

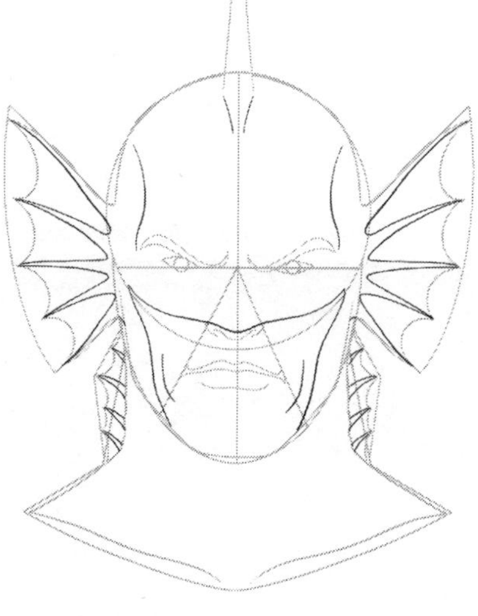

11

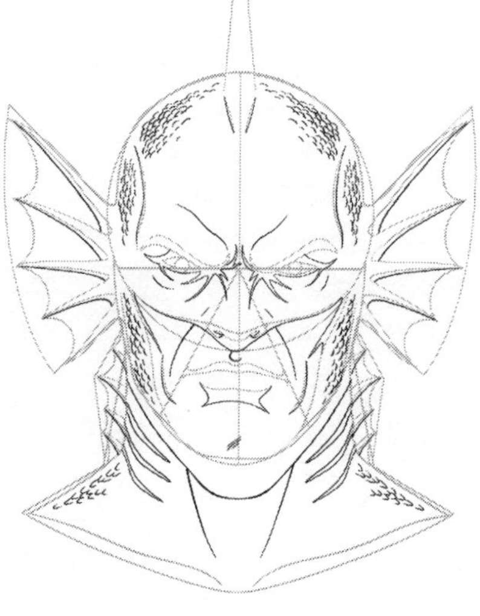

12

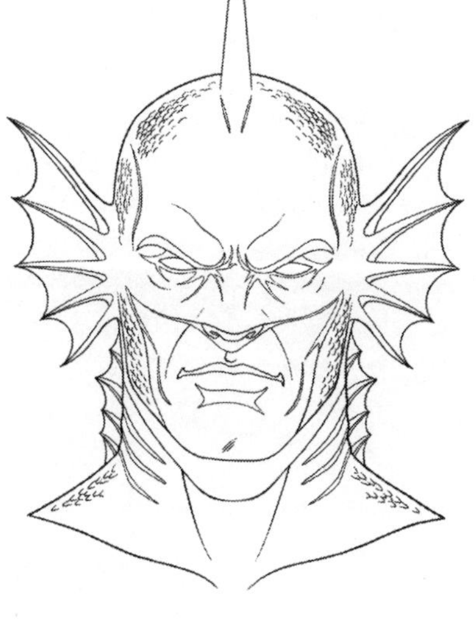

SNAKE 'THE KING COBRA'

Pro Tip: The cobra's design language is built on threat and deception — the flared hood becomes a dramatic raised collar, scaled skin becomes ribbed body armour, and the sleek tapered form communicates coiled power, patience and lethal precision.

01

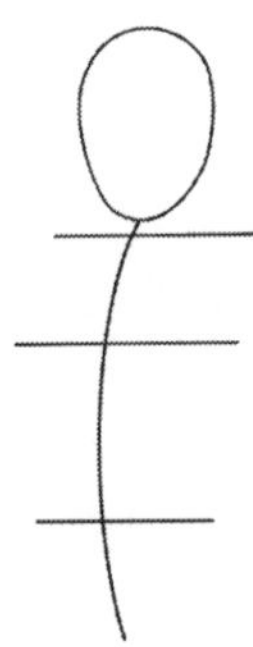

02

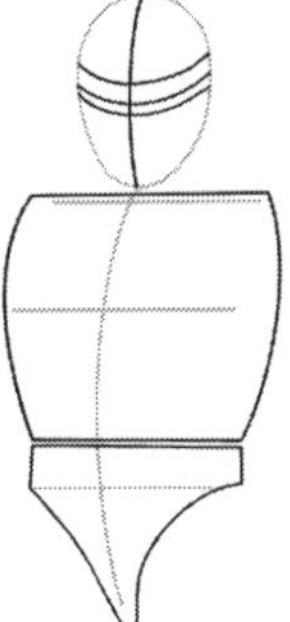

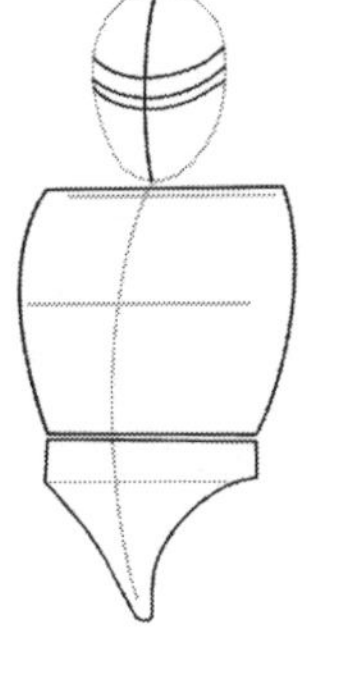

03

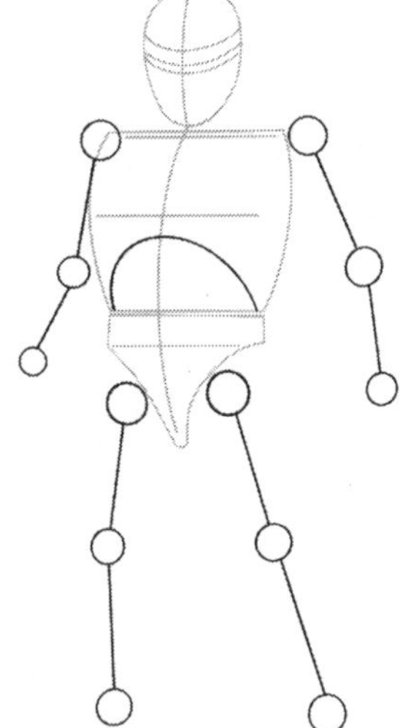

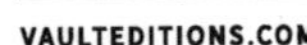

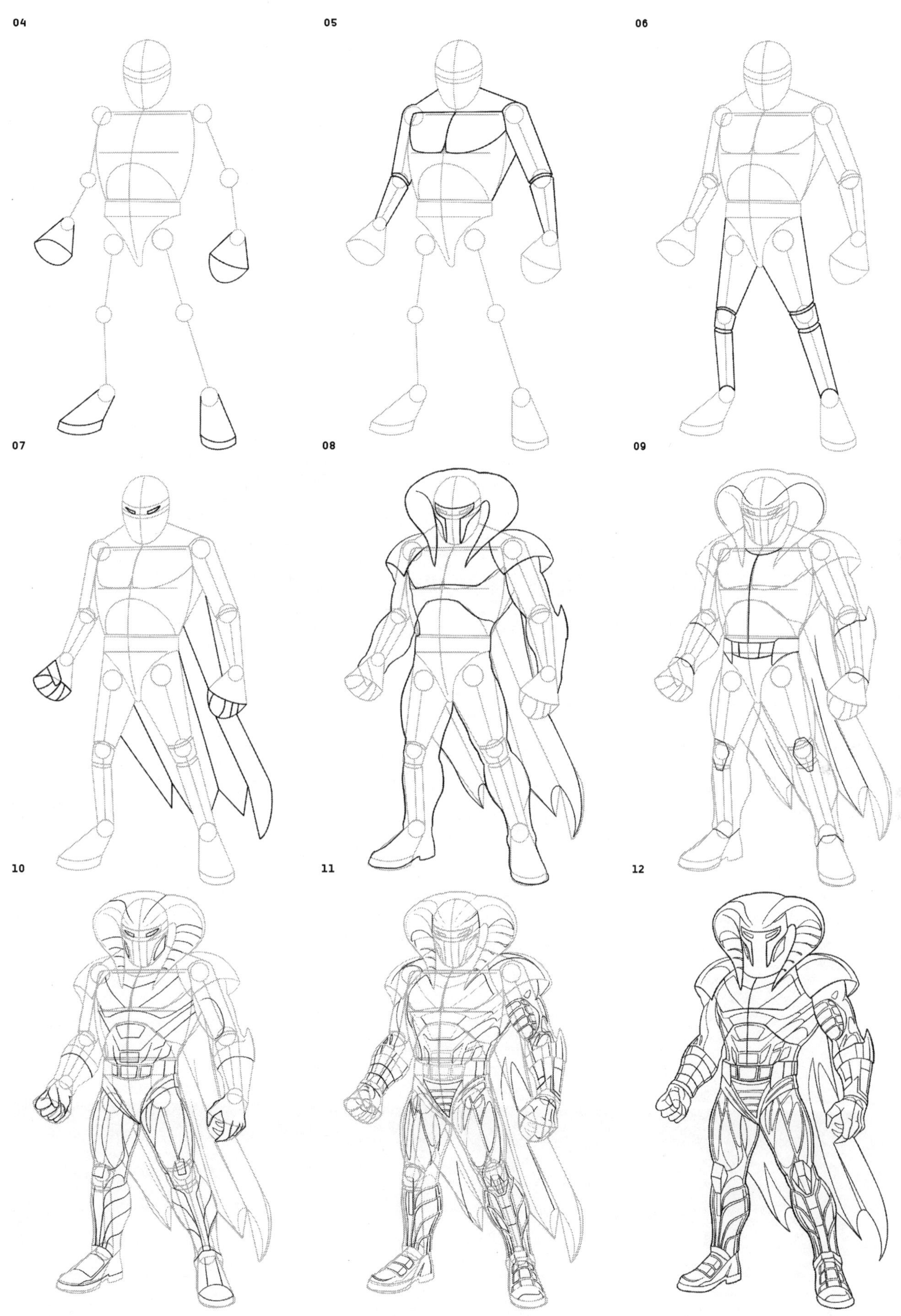

04
05
06
07
08
09
10
11
12

BIRDS 'THE SWIFT'

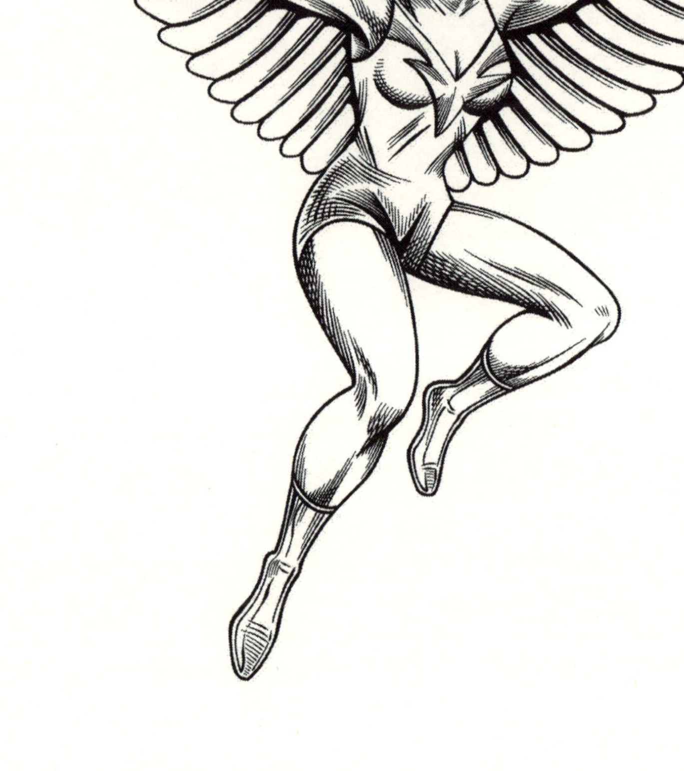

Pro Tip: The swift's design language blends grace with speed — sleek streamlined feathers become a form-fitting costume, swept-back wings become a dramatic cape, and effortless aerial agility communicates pure, unstoppable velocity.

01

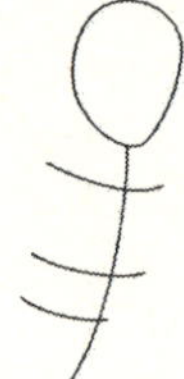

02

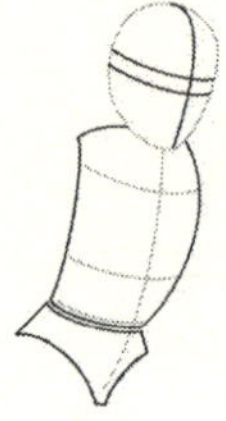

03

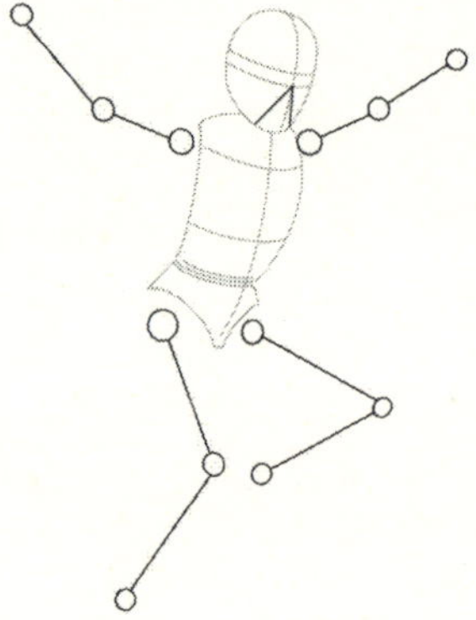

04

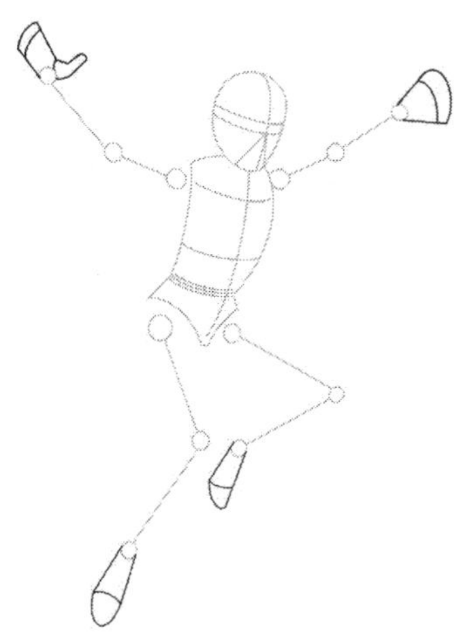

05

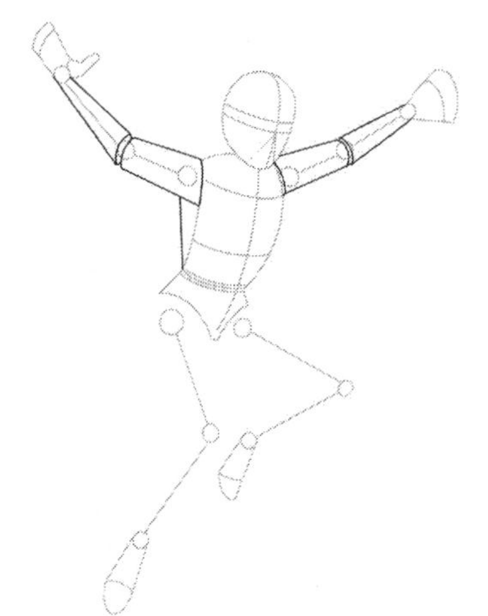

06

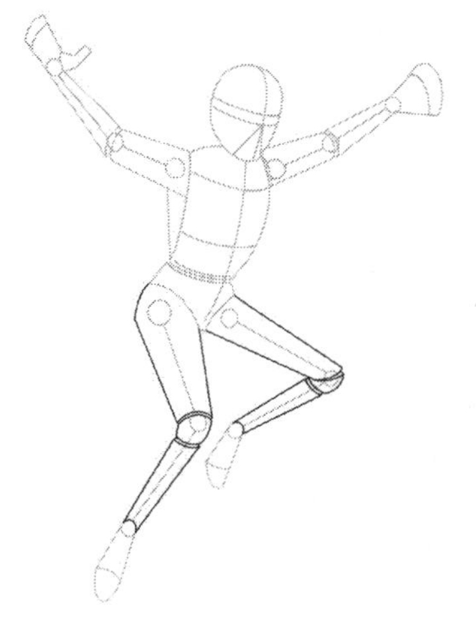

07

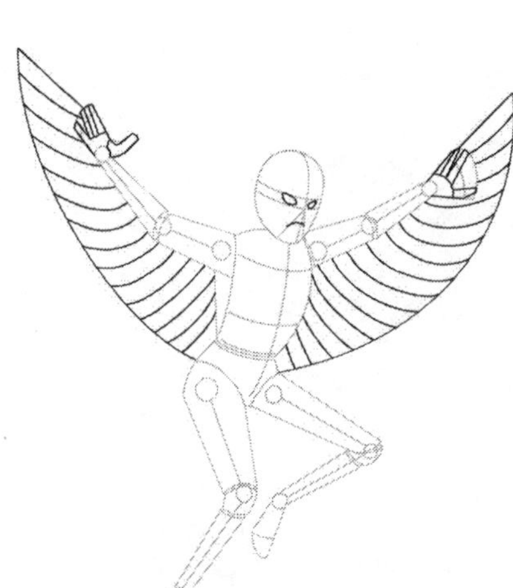

08

09

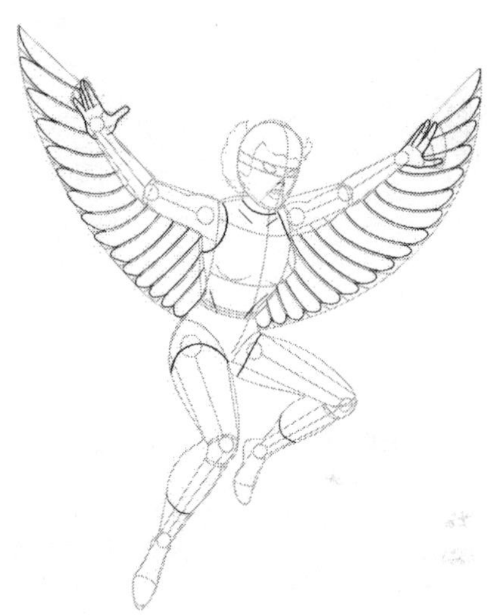

10

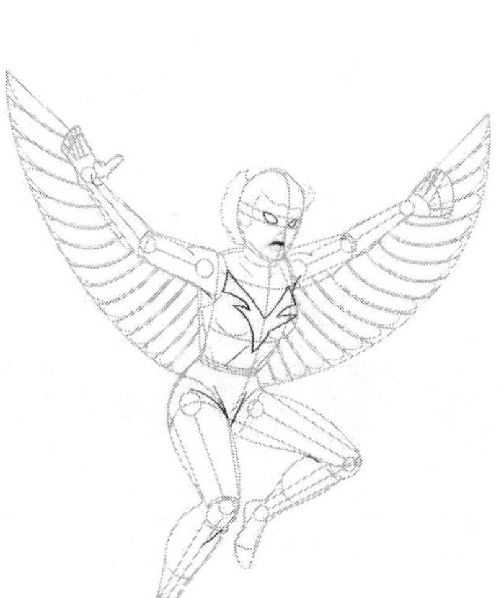

11

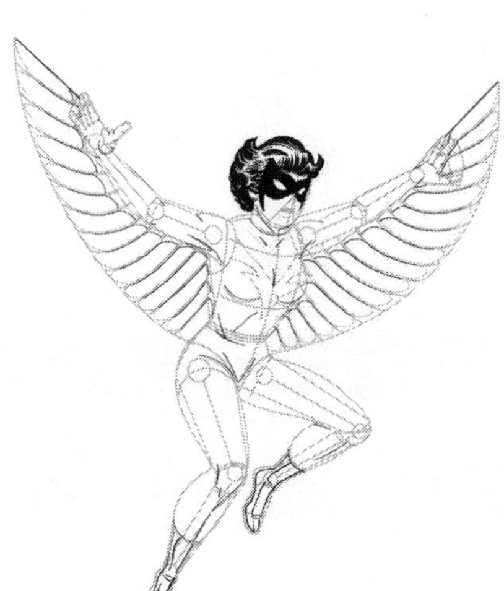

12

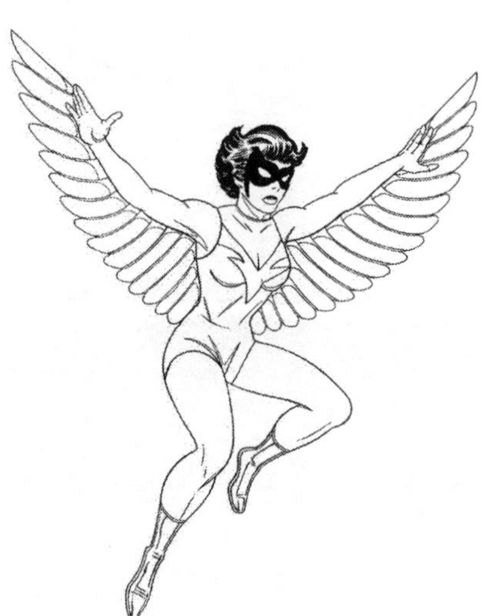

ICE 'THE FROST QUEEN'

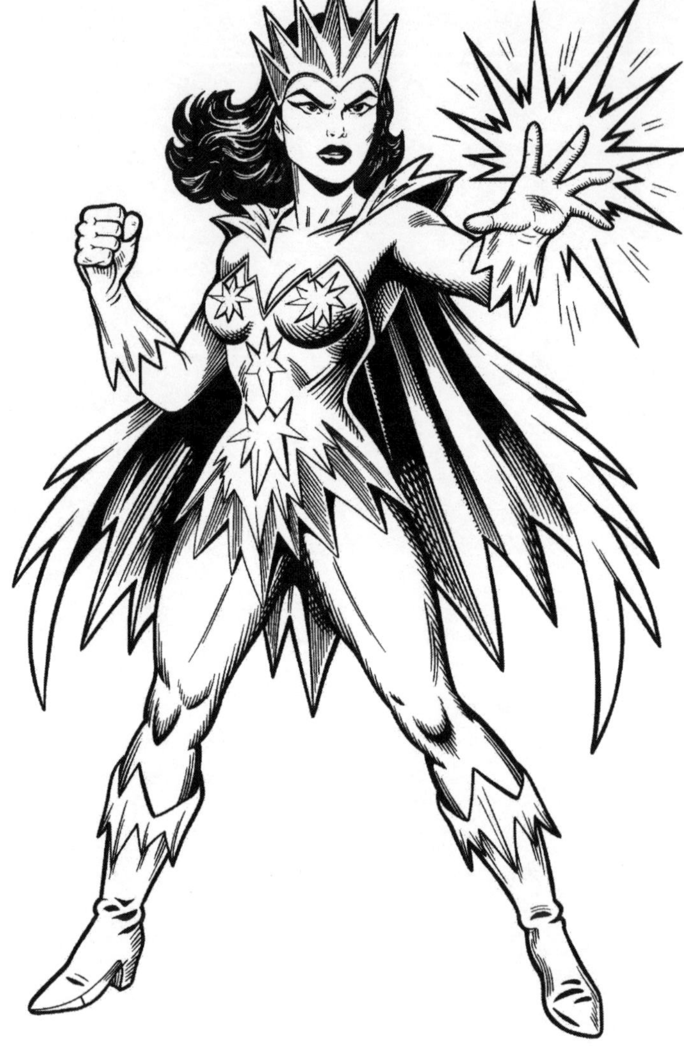

Pro Tip: Ice as a design element is all about sharp, fractured geometry — crystalline spikes become a jagged crown and costume edges, the shattering quality of frozen water becomes starburst chest details.

01

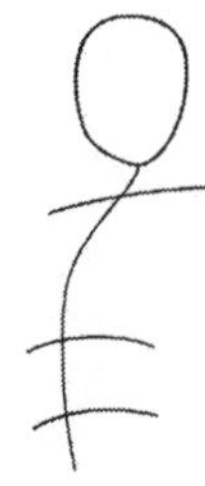

02

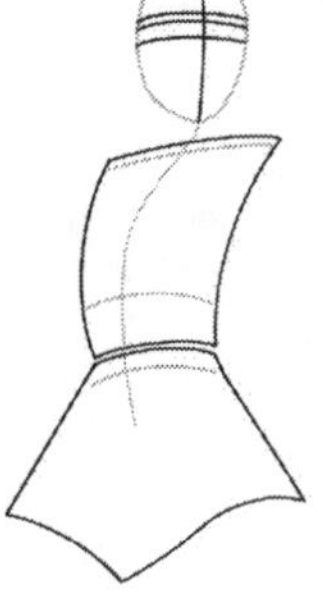

03

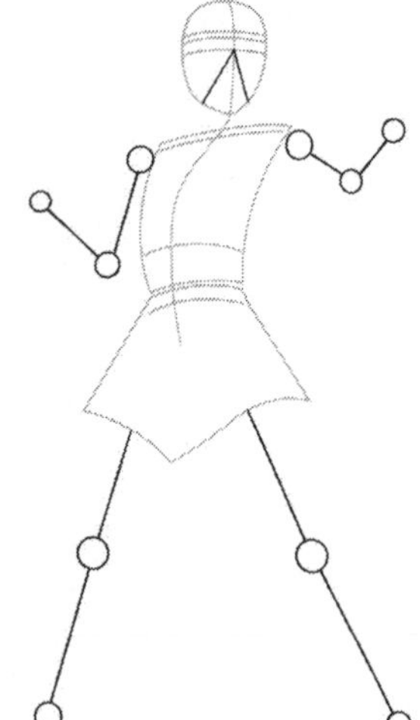

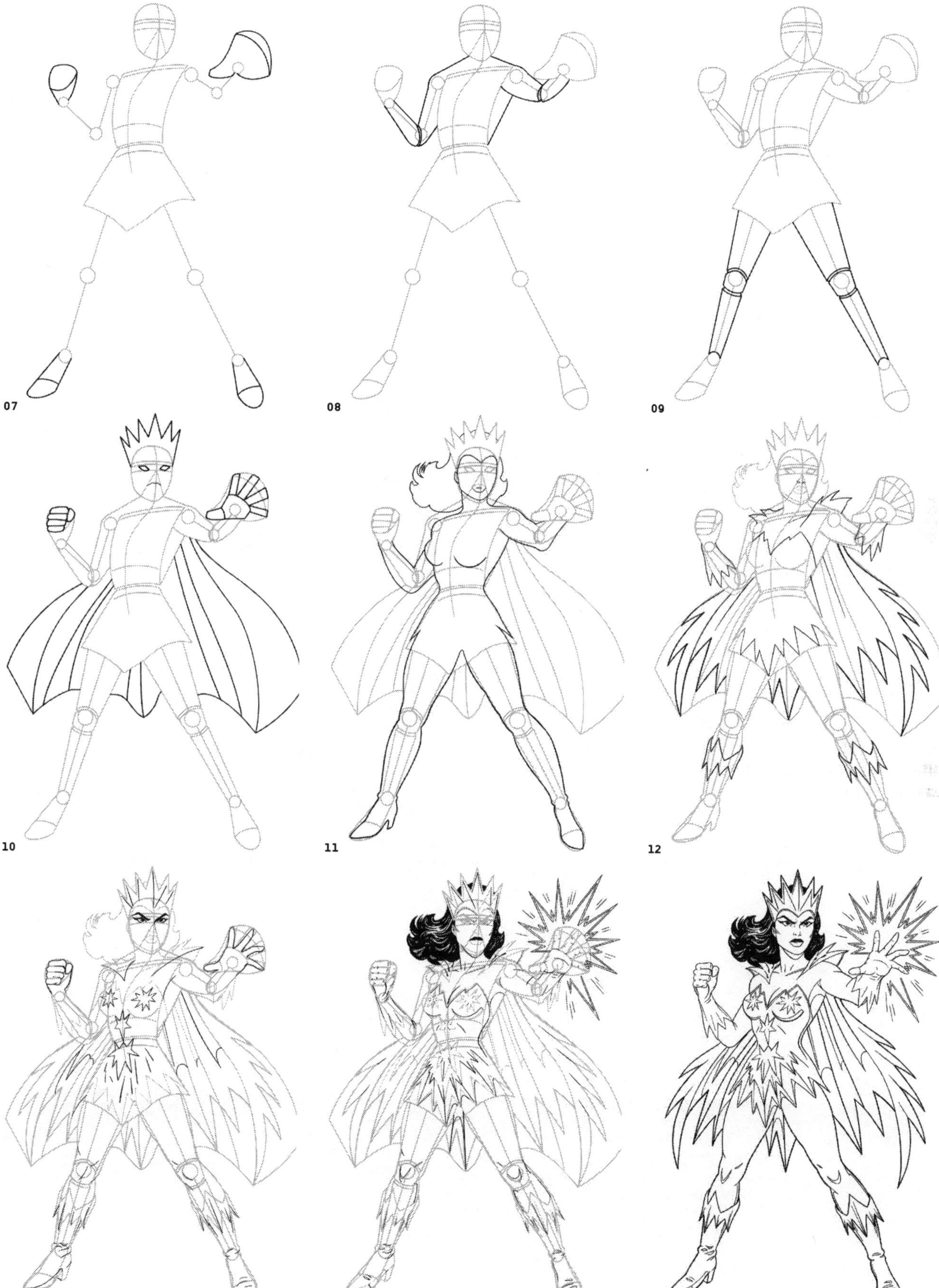
04
05
06
07
08
09
10
11
12

FIRE 'THE INFERNO'

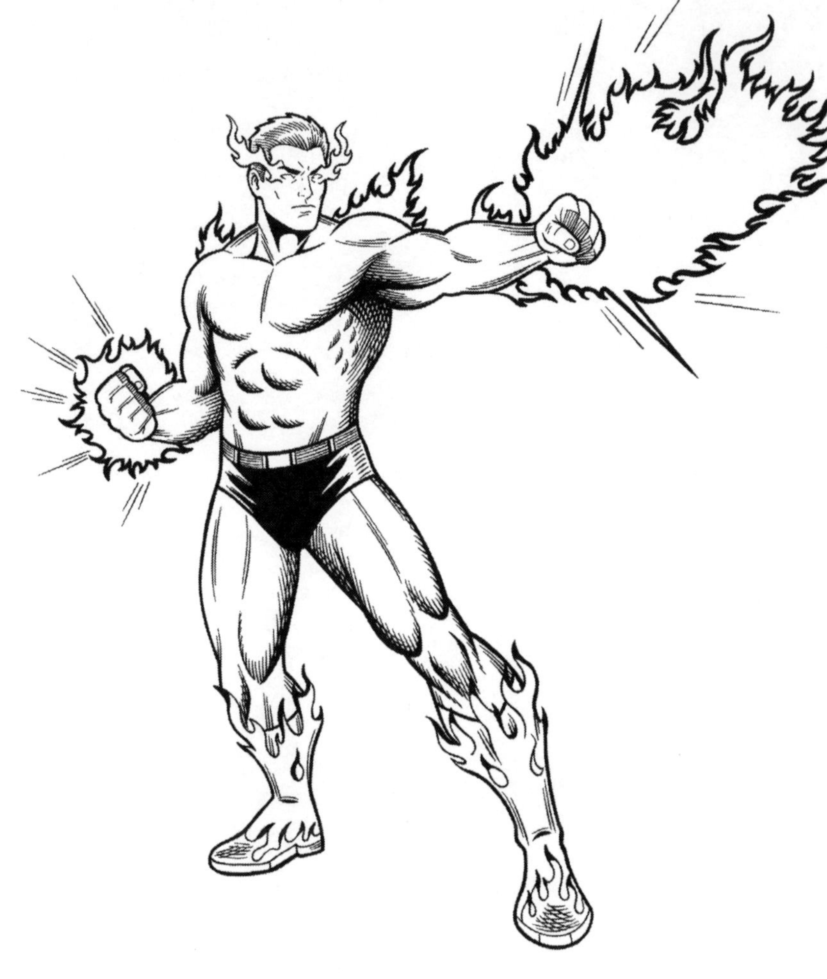

Pro Tip: Fire as a design element is fluid and untameable — dancing flame shapes become costume edges and hair, the explosive outward energy of combustion becomes trailing arcs of fire, and the intense heat at the core communicates raw, barely contained destructive power.

01

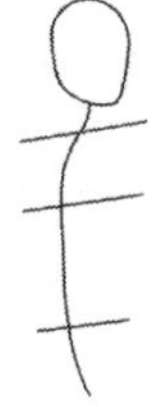

02

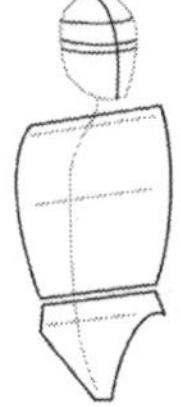

03

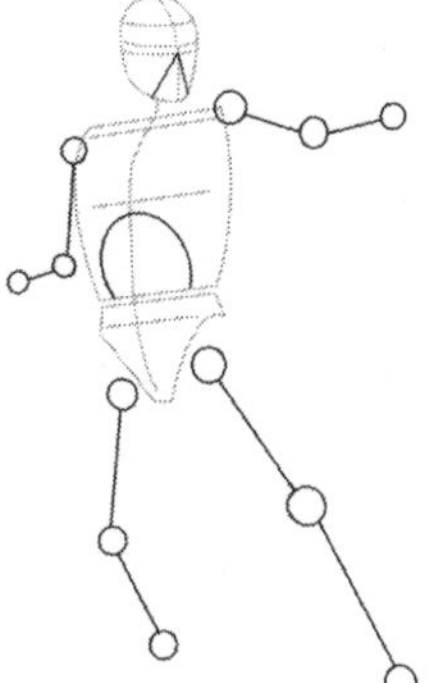

04

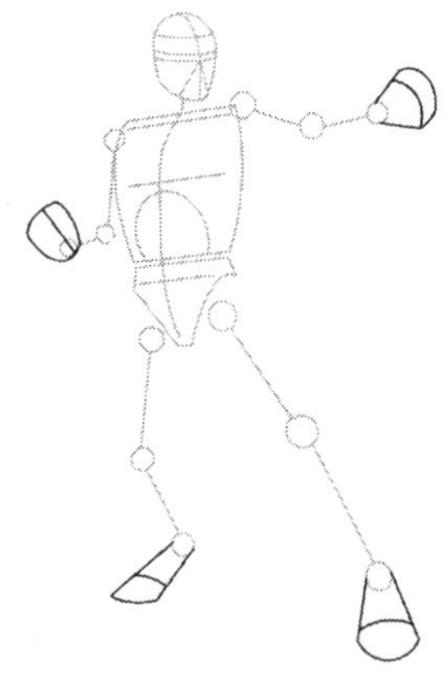

05

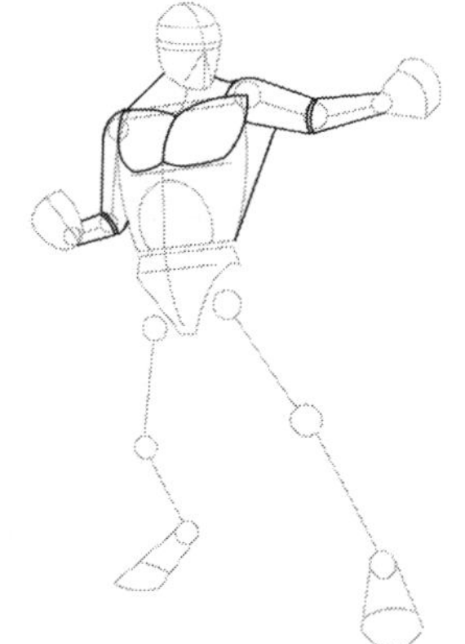

06

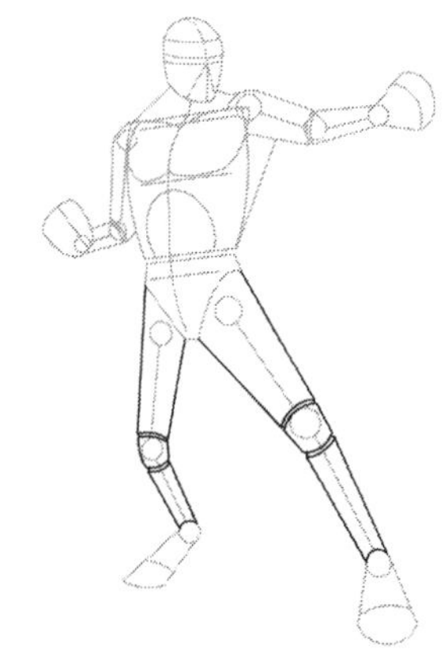

07

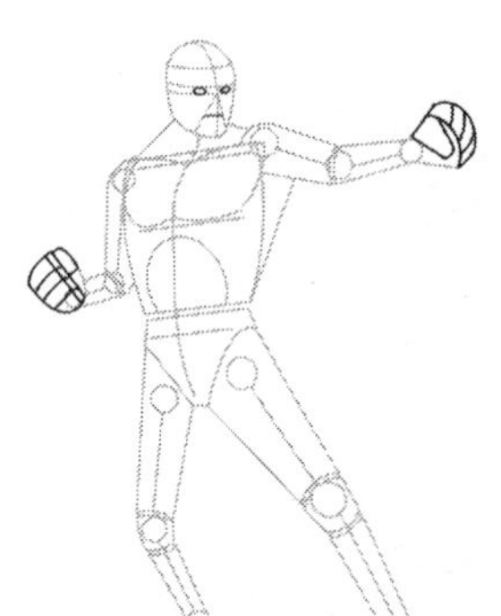

08

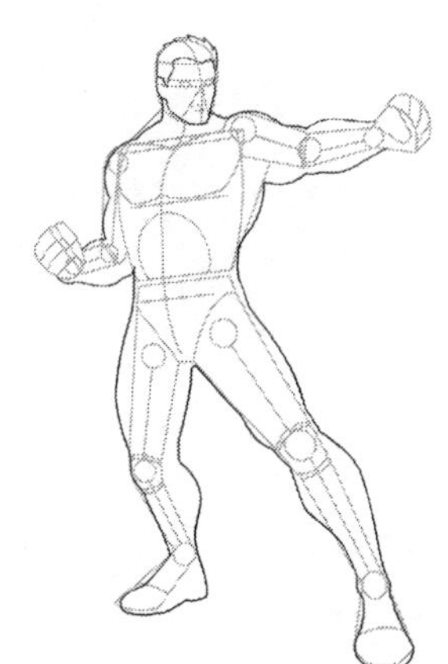

09

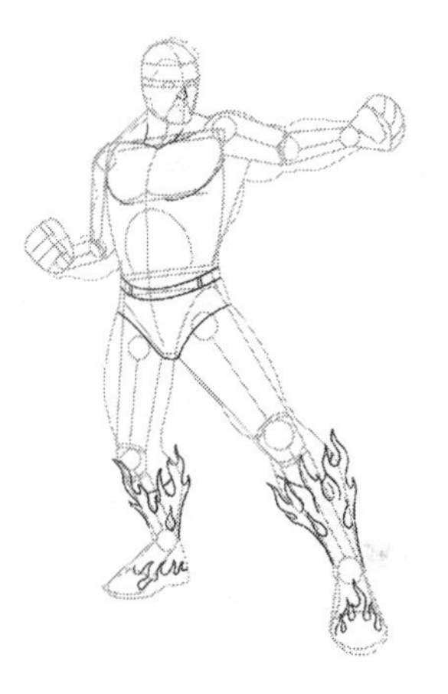

10

11

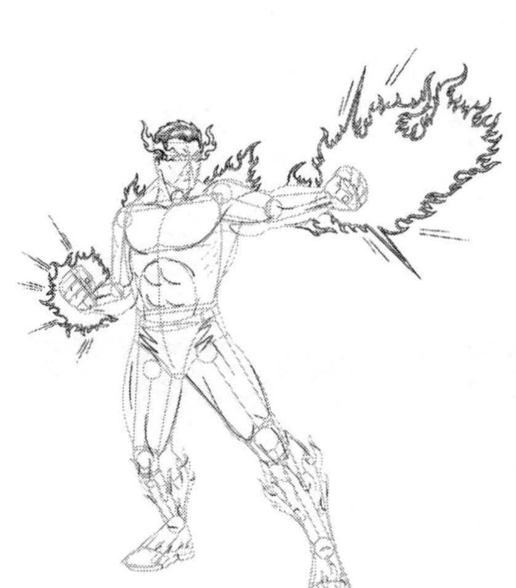

12

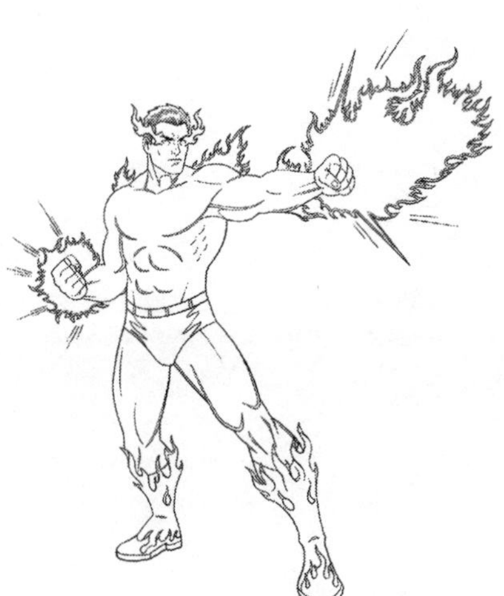

METAL 'THE FORGER'

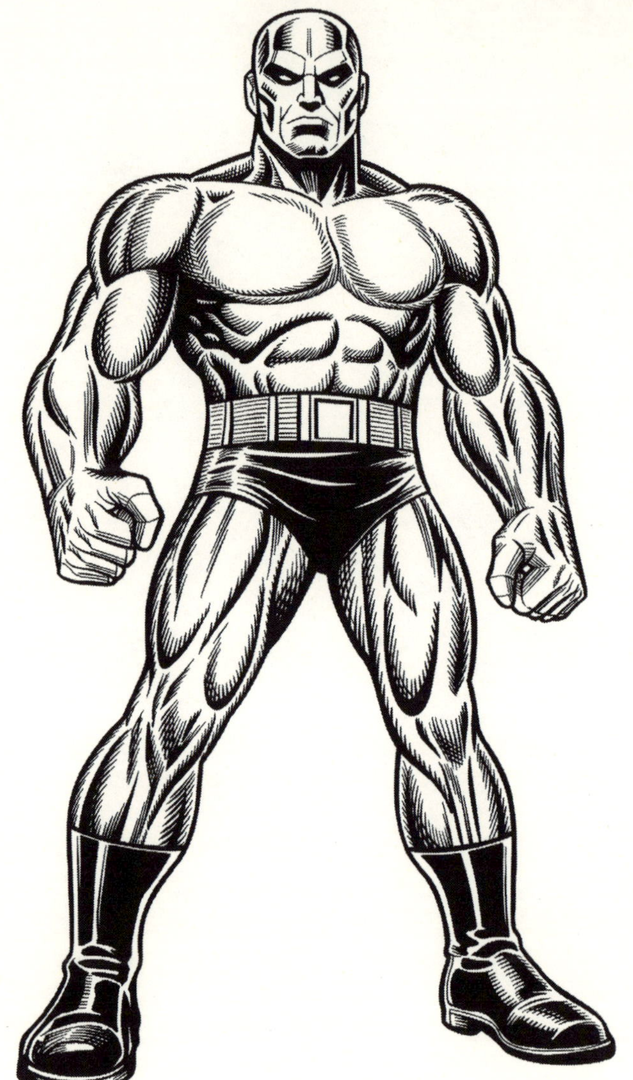

Pro Tip: Metal as a design element speaks of strength and permanence — forged steel inspires hard, rigid edges across the whole body, while the density of raw iron is reflected in thick, immovable limbs that communicate unstoppable, indestructible force.

01

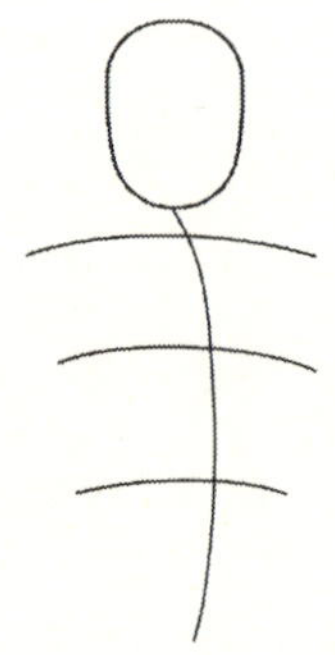

02

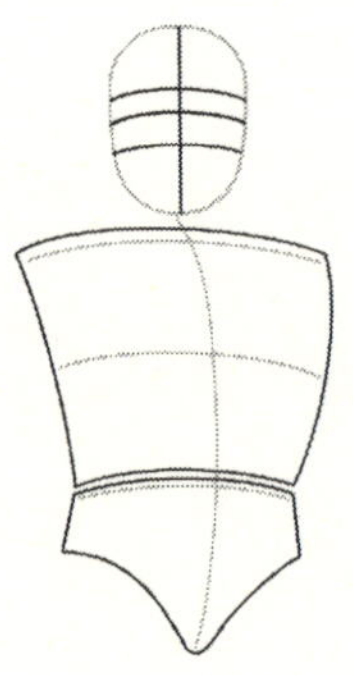

03

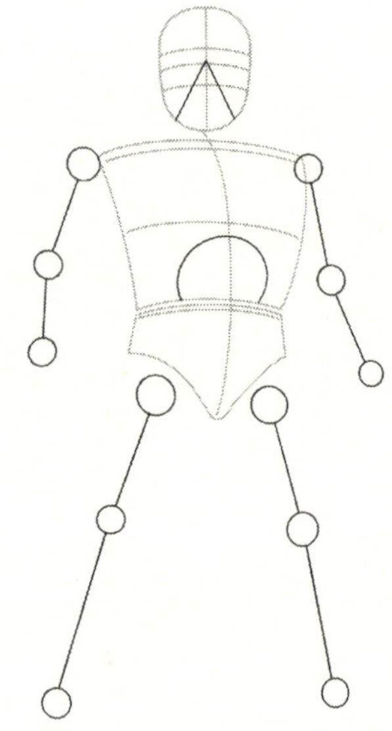

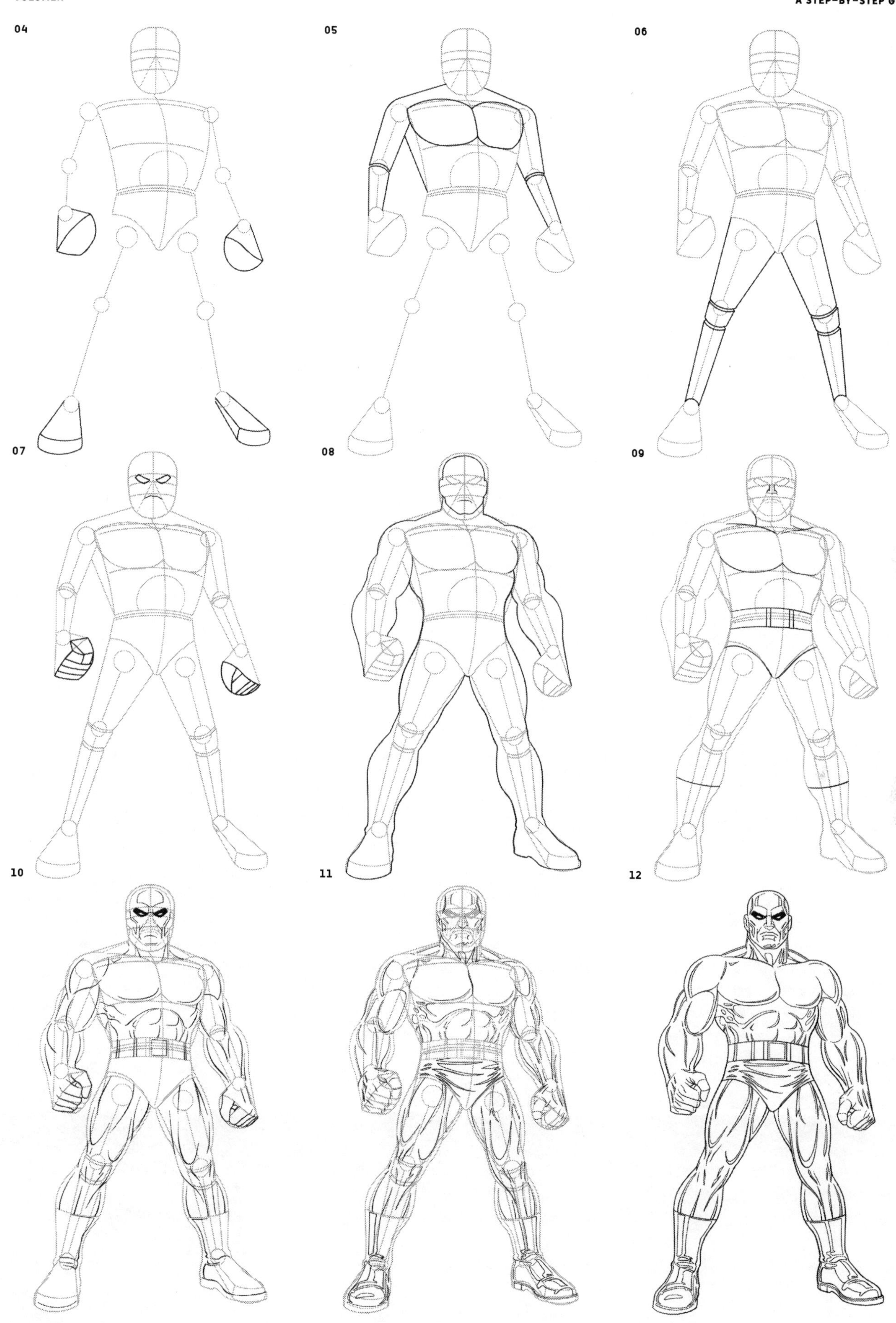
04
05
06
07
08
09
10
11
12

04| PULP, HORROR AND SCI-FI ICONS
DRAWING CLASSIC GENRE CHARACTERS

Every great comics universe stretches beyond the superhero. Lurking in the shadows, prowling the corridors of abandoned space stations, and stalking the foggy streets of the city are some of the most visually exciting characters you'll ever get to draw. This chapter is dedicated to them.

Pulp fiction, horror and science fiction have given us some of the most enduring and instantly recognisable archetypes in visual storytelling. These are the characters that have thrilled audiences for generations, appearing in the dog-eared pages of penny magazines, the flickering frames of black and white cinema, and the bold ink lines of comics dating back nearly a century. They are archetypes in the truest sense, figures so deeply embedded in our collective imagination that a reader needs only a silhouette, a shadow, a single visual cue to know exactly what they're looking at. That instant recognition is a gift to the comics artist, and in this chapter we're going to show you how to use it.

What makes these characters so compelling to draw is the sheer range of visual possibilities they offer. A zombie and a space agent could not be more different in appearance, in posture, in the story their design tells at a glance. Yet both belong to the same rich tradition of genre storytelling, and both reward the artist who takes the time to understand what makes them work visually. The shambling gait and decomposed form of the undead. The sleek, purposeful silhouette of an interstellar operative. The cold geometric mass of a robot built for something you probably don't want to think about too hard. Each of these characters has its own visual language, and learning to speak that language is what this chapter is all about.

The good news is that everything you've learned so far feeds directly into this chapter. Your understanding of the human figure, your grasp of dynamic poses, and your instinct for hybrid design will all come into play as we work through each character type step-by-step.

These aren't entirely new skills you need to acquire, they're the skills you already have, applied to a new and thrilling set of challenges. Whether you're drawing from scratch or putting your own spin on a classic, you'll find clear, guided steps to take you from blank page to finished character. The monsters, the machines, the masked and the macabre are waiting. Let's get to work.

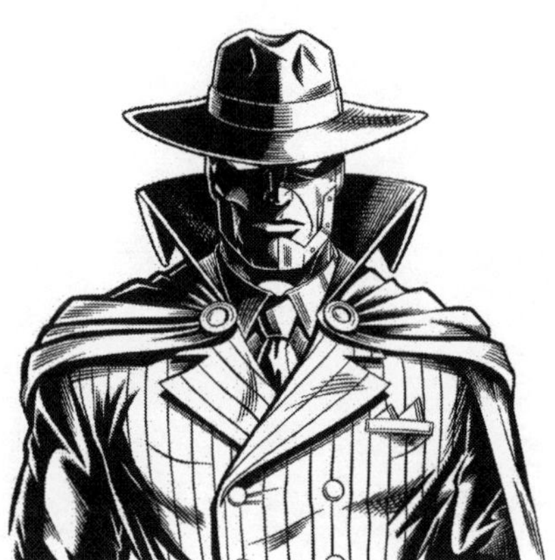

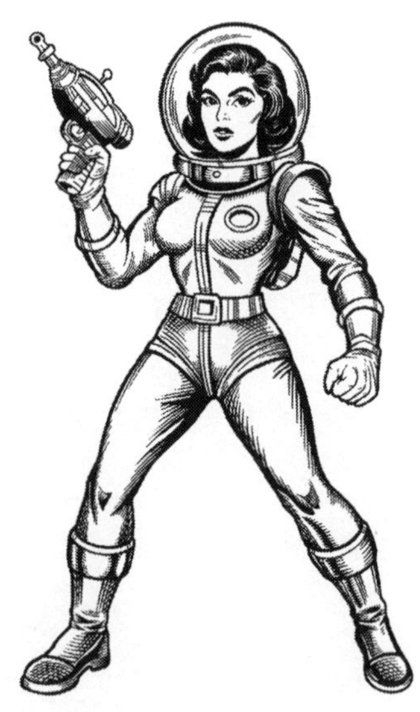

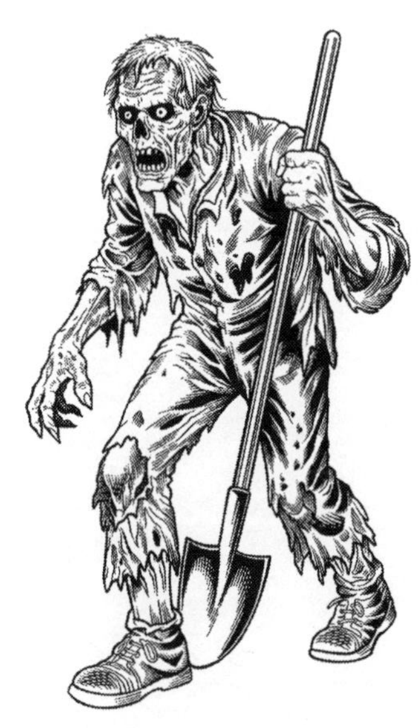

Pulp: The masked vigilante, the shadowy detective, the caped figure perched on a rain soaked rooftop. Pulp characters are defined by atmosphere, attitude and an iconic silhouette that is recognisable from across the room. There is a reason these archetypes have endured for nearly a century. They tap into something primal in the way we respond to mystery, danger and the romance of the night, and they do it almost entirely through visual language. A long coat, a wide brimmed hat, a mask that conceals as much as it reveals: these are the shorthand of pulp design, and learning to use them effectively is an art in itself. We'll explore what makes a pulp design enduring and guide you through building characters that feel mysterious, dangerous and compelling. From the cut of a costume to the set of a jaw, every detail contributes to the sense that this is someone who operates in the spaces between the law and the shadows, and we'll show you how to put that feeling on the page.

Sci-Fi: Sleek, sharp and built for a world that doesn't exist yet. Science fiction characters offer some of the most exciting design challenges in all of comics, from the streamlined authority of a space agent to the cold geometric power of a robot. What makes sci-fi design so rewarding is the balance it demands between the familiar and the fantastical. A character that is too alien risks losing the reader's connection entirely, while one that is too ordinary fails to sell the world they inhabit. The sweet spot lies in grounding your designs in recognisable human forms and then pushing them deliberately forward into the unknown. We'll show you how to blend futuristic elements with the human form in a way that feels visually compelling, internally consistent and utterly convincing.

Horror: This is where the rules get broken and the darkness gets to take the wheel. Horror characters occupy a unique space in comics, they are at once deeply human and disturbingly other, and that contradiction is precisely what makes them so compelling to draw. The genre has produced some of the most imaginative and visually arresting character designs in the history of visual storytelling, and the artists behind them understood something fundamental: fear is not about what you show, it's about what you imply. A shadow that falls at the wrong angle, a silhouette with too many joints, a face that is almost right but not quite. These are the tools of the horror artist, and they are far more powerful than any amount of graphic detail. We'll walk you through the design principles that make horror characters genuinely unsettling, showing you how to use distortion, proportion and the subtle subversion of the familiar to create characters that linger in the imagination long after the page has been turned.

PULP

THE LIQUIFYING MAN

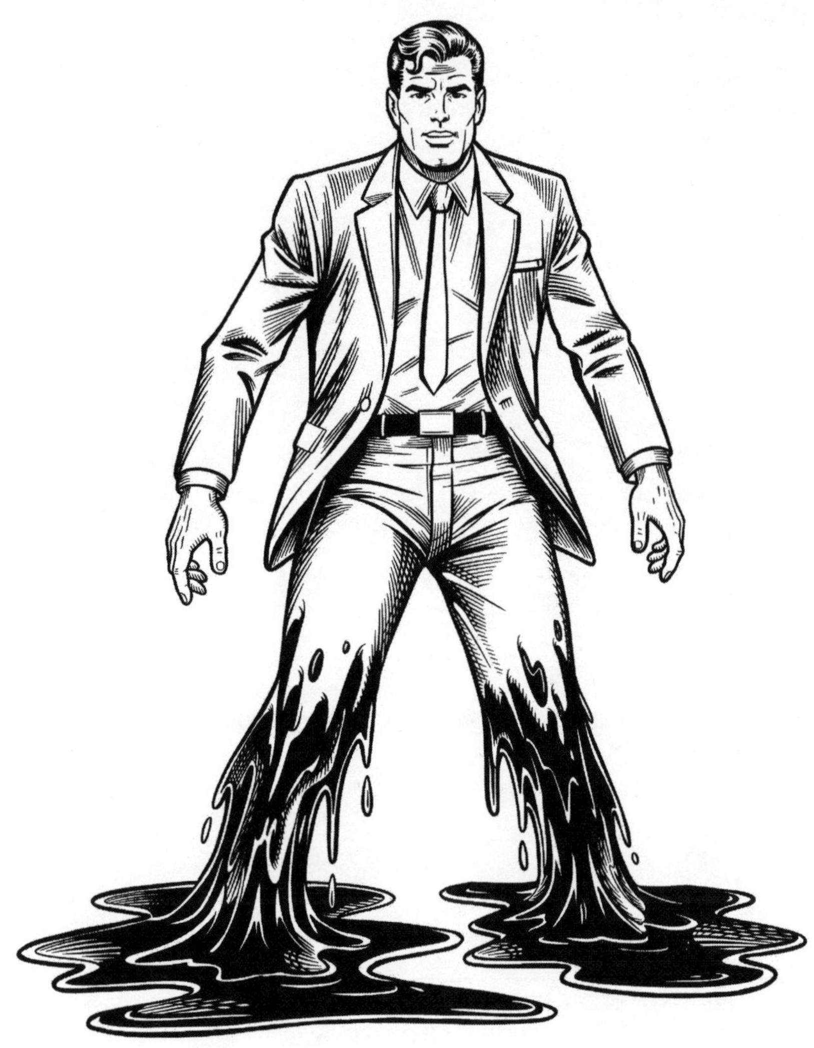

Pro Tip: The transition from solid to liquid starts just above the knees — keep the upper body crisp and defined while letting the edges break into irregular drips and puddles below. Vary the drip lengths to convey fluid irregularity.

01

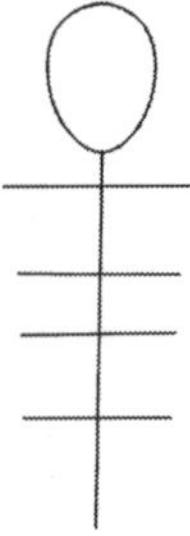

02

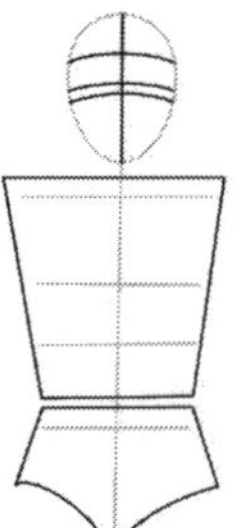

03

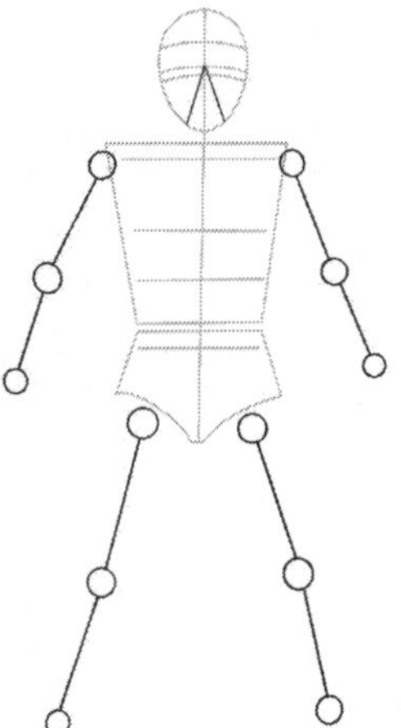

04

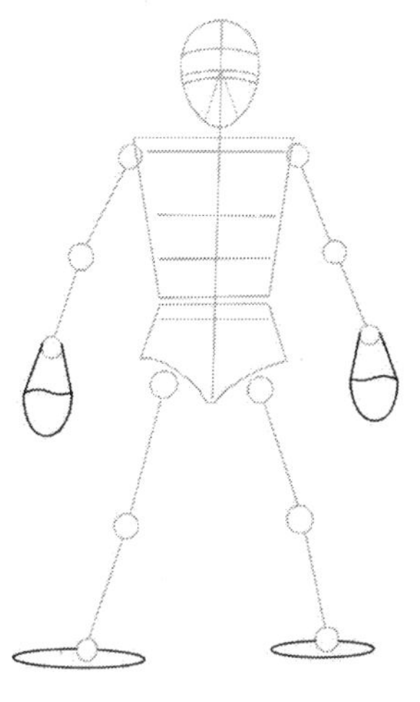

05

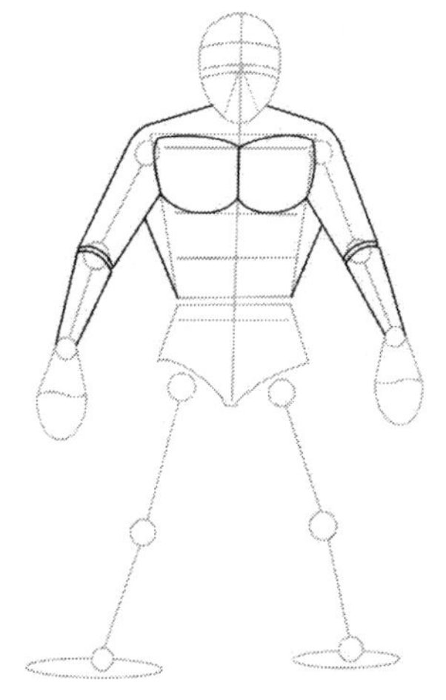

06

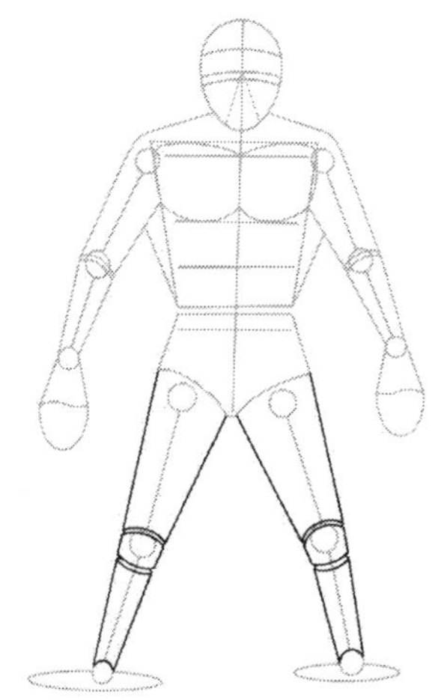

07

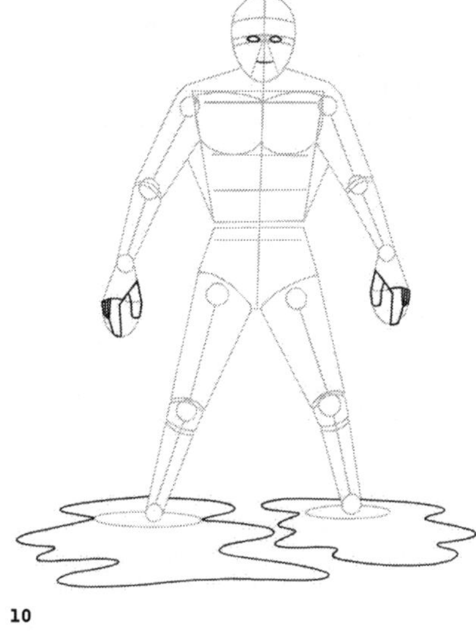

08

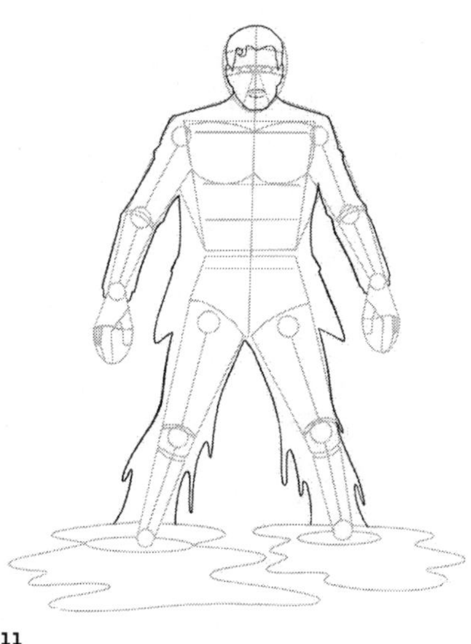

09

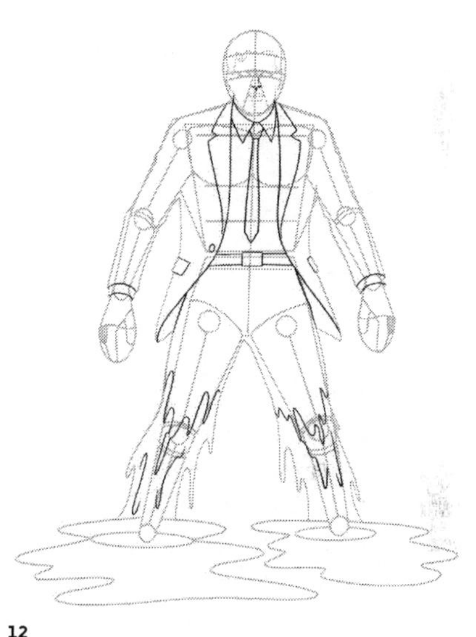

10

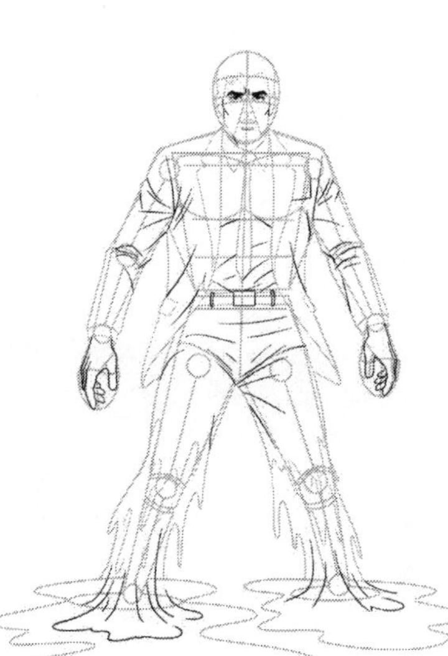

11

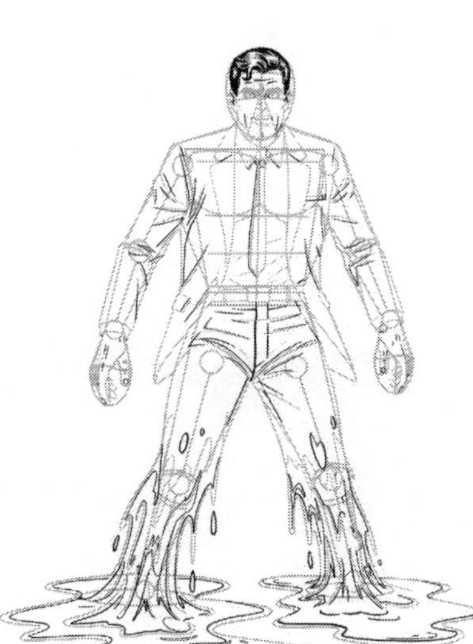

12

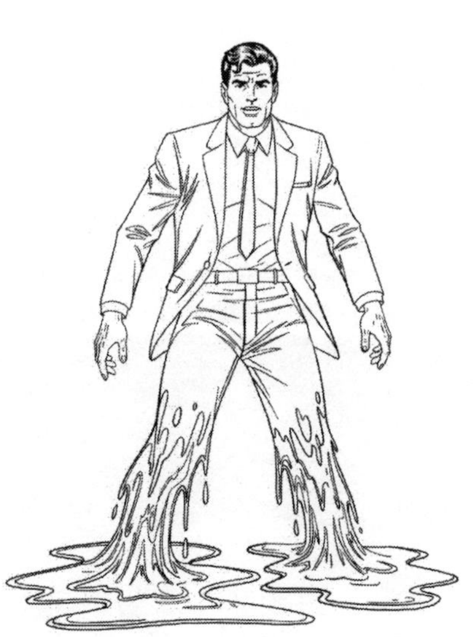

PULP

THE LASER-EYED HERO

Pro Tip: The laser beams should radiate from a single point at the eyes and splay outward in tight parallel lines to convey focused, devastating power. Angle the head slightly downward so the beams cut diagonally across the composition, adding drama and direction to the attack.

01

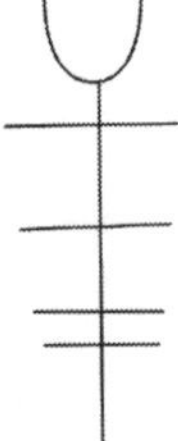

02

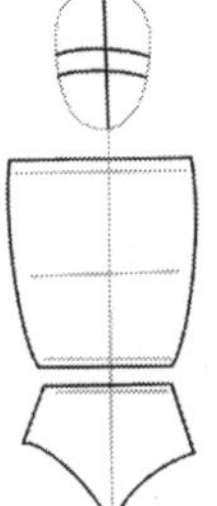

03

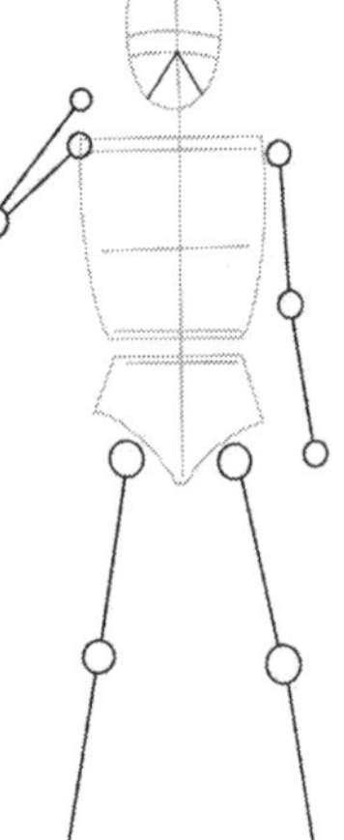

04

05

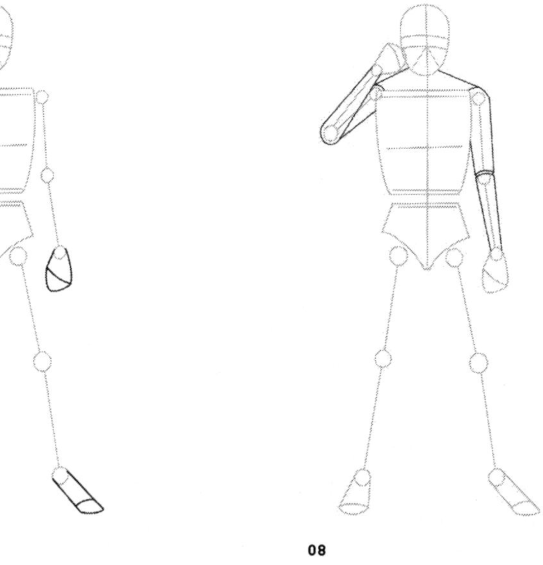

06

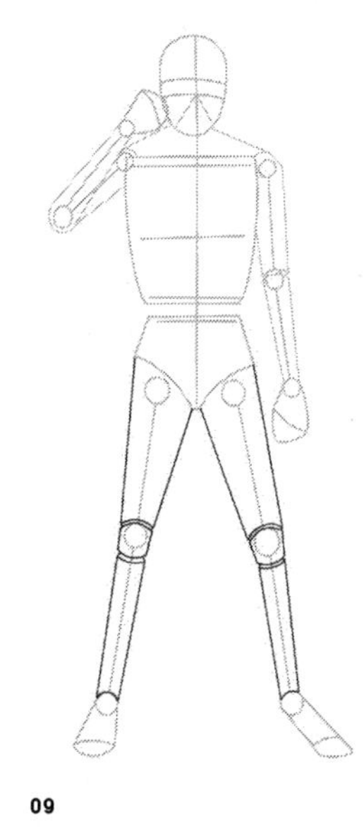

07

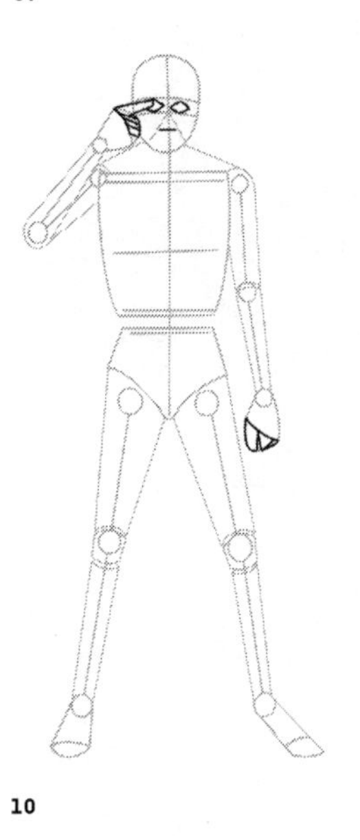

08

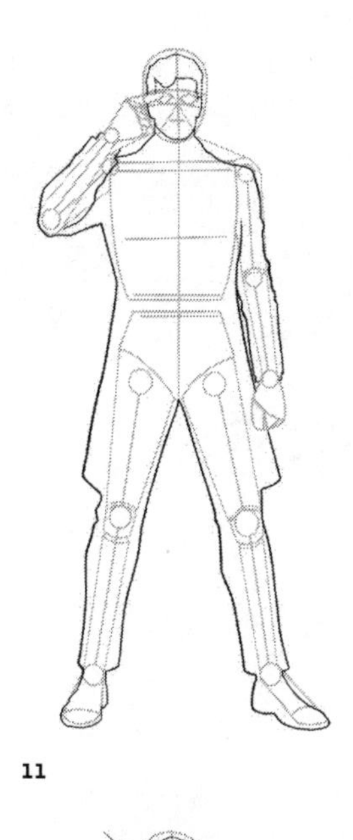

09

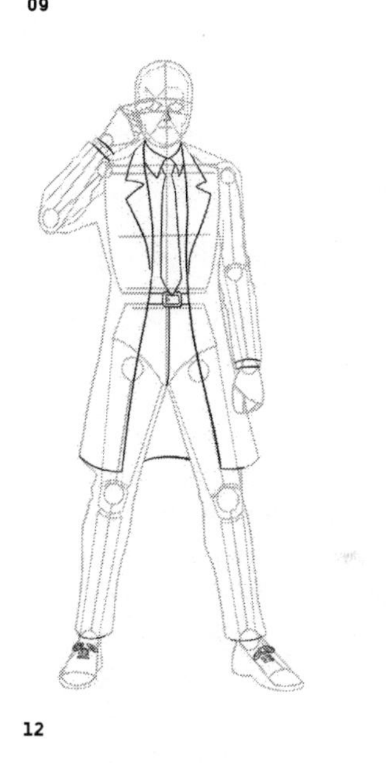

10

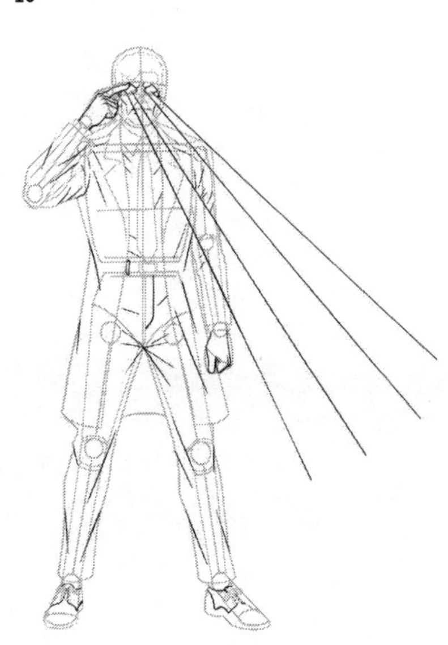

11

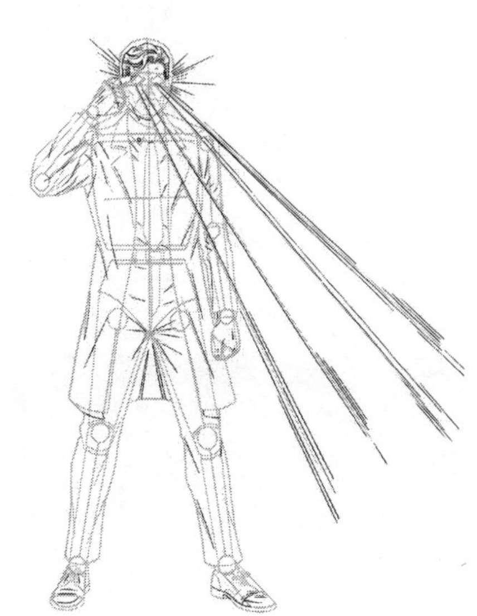

12

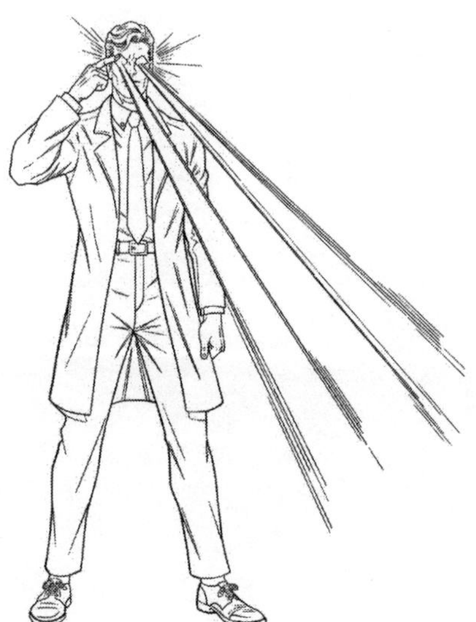

PULP

THE MASKED VIGILANTE

Pro Tip: The hat and sharp collar are the character's defining features — draw both with strong, pointed edges that frame the face dramatically. The hat brim should cast a shadow line across the upper face, leaving just enough visible to convey mystery and menace.

01

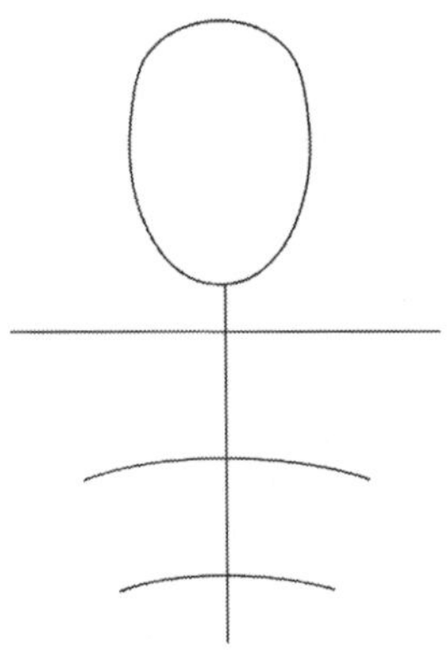

02

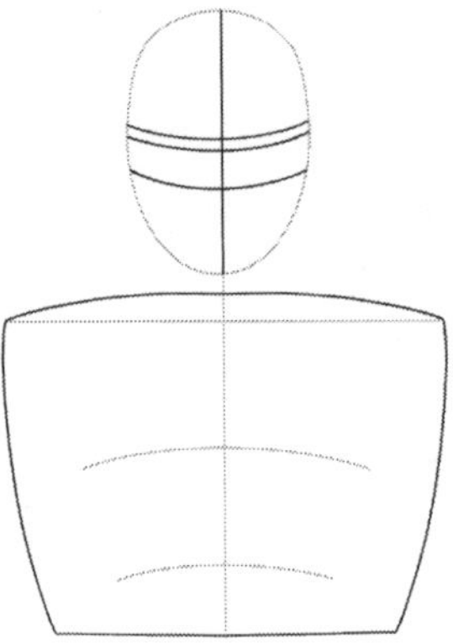

03

04

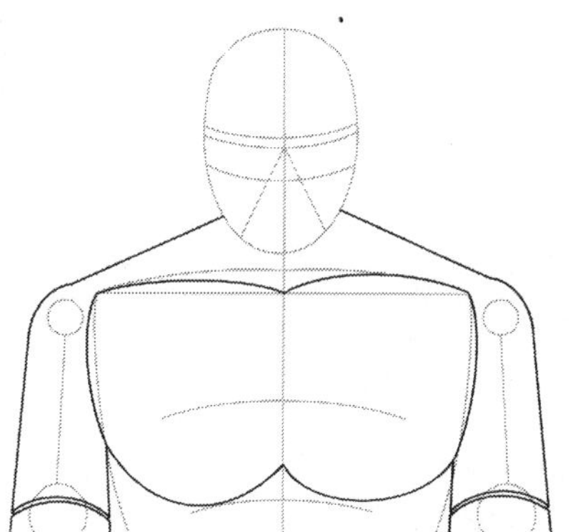

05

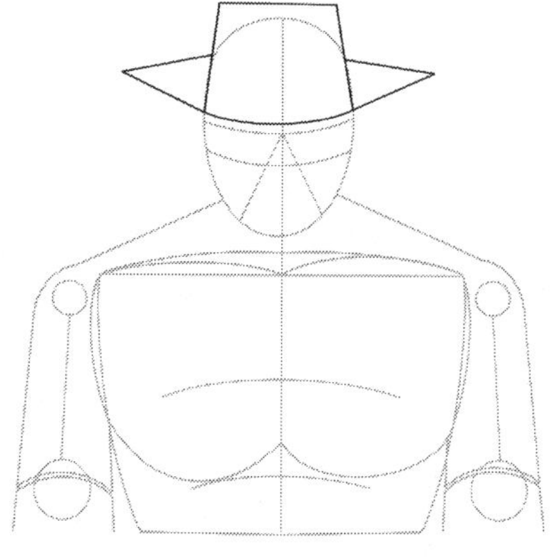

06

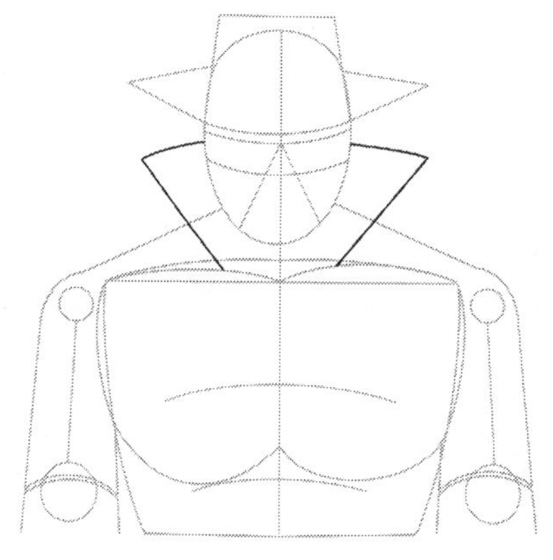

07

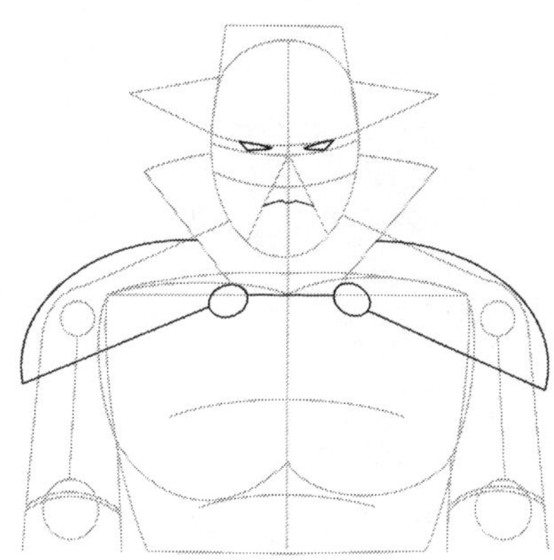

08

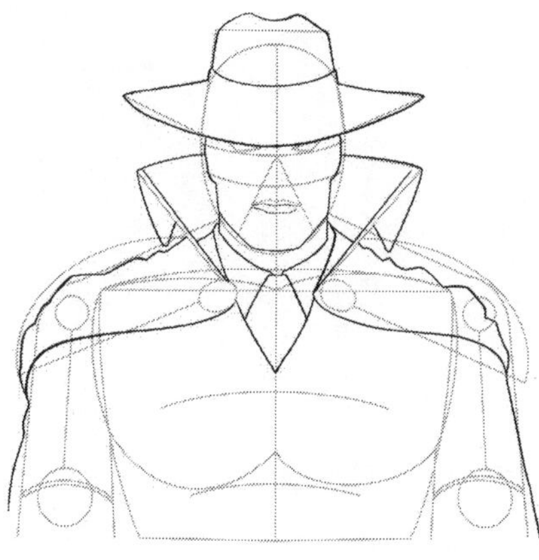

09

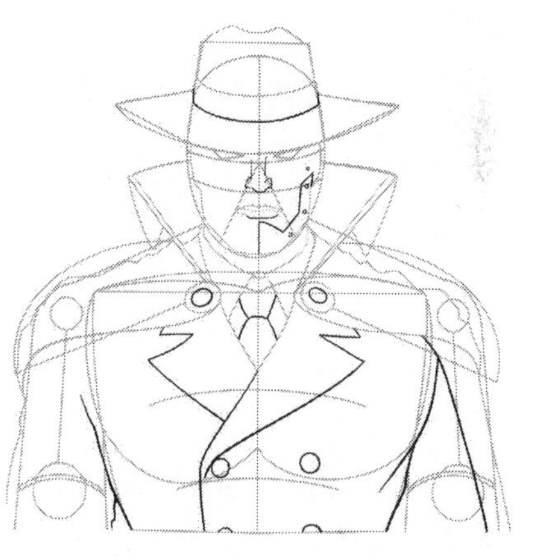

10

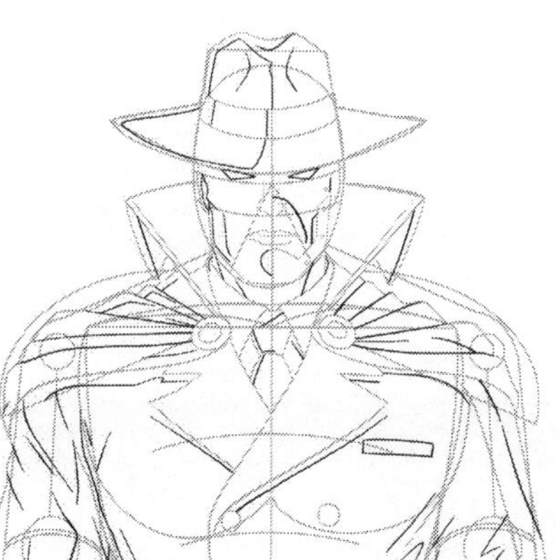

11

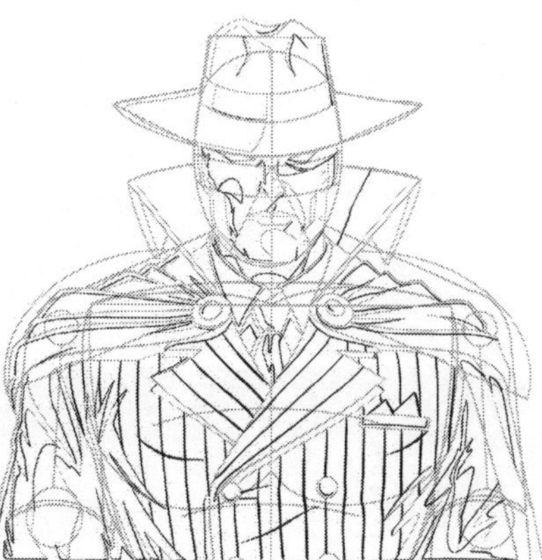

12

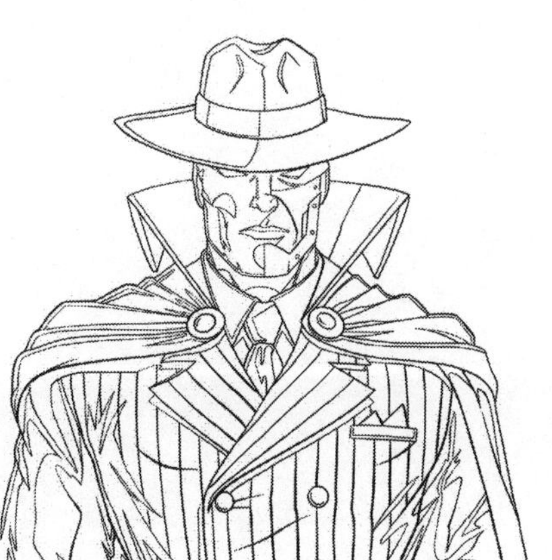

PULP

KILLER COMMANDO

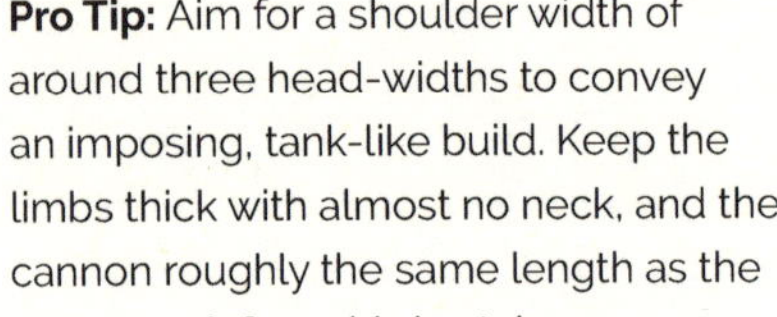

Pro Tip: Aim for a shoulder width of around three head-widths to convey an imposing, tank-like build. Keep the limbs thick with almost no neck, and the cannon roughly the same length as the torso to reinforce his brutal presence.

01

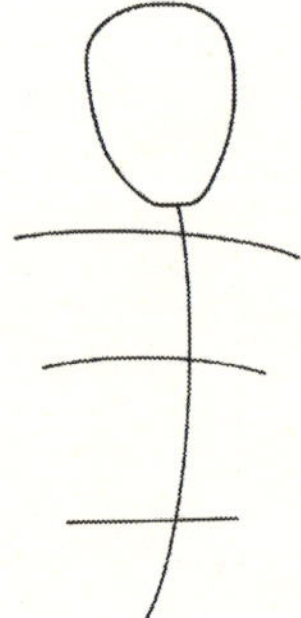

02

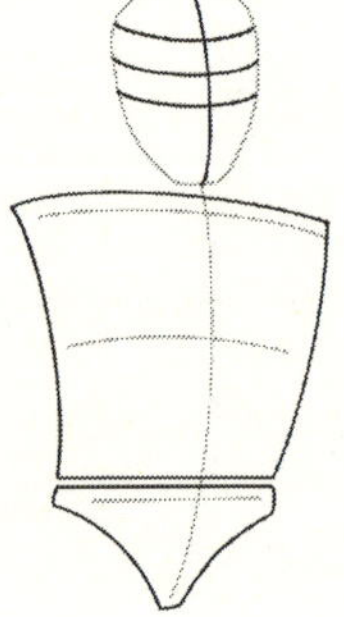

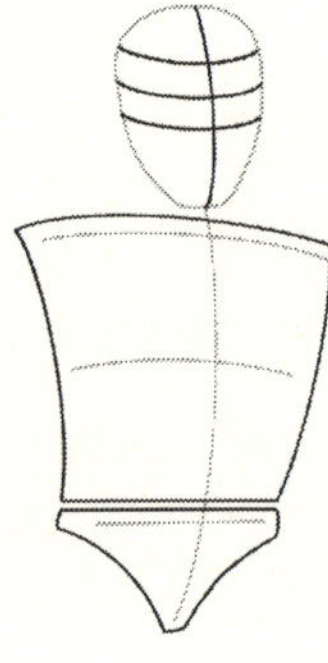

03

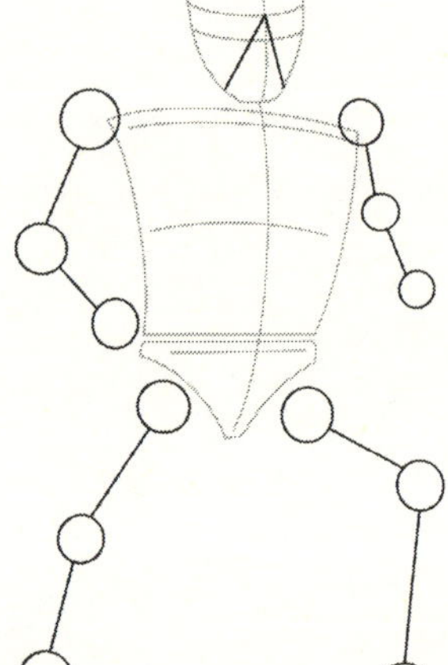

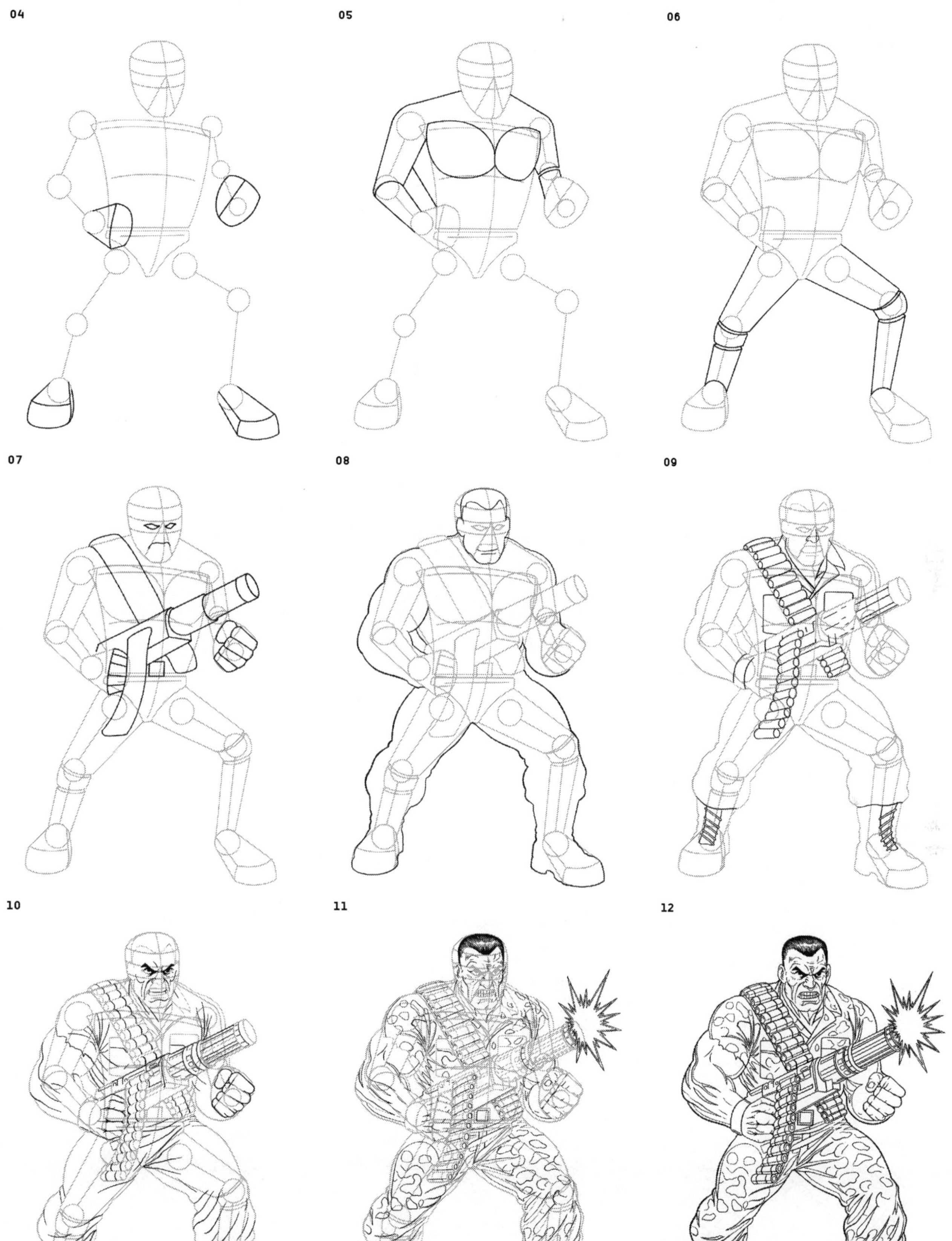
04
05
06
07
08
09
10
11
12

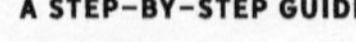

PULP

SEA-STATION SOLDIER

Pro Tip: Aim for a slender build of around seven heads tall to convey an athletic, streamlined physique built for cutting through water. The flippers should each measure roughly the length of the character's forearm.

01

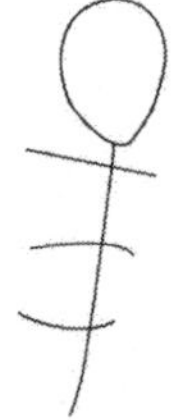

02

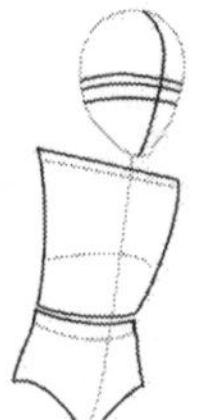

03

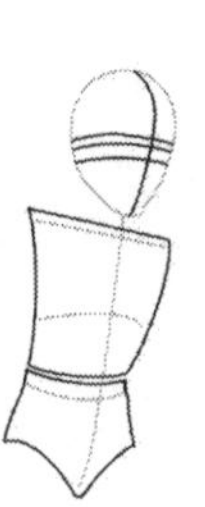

04

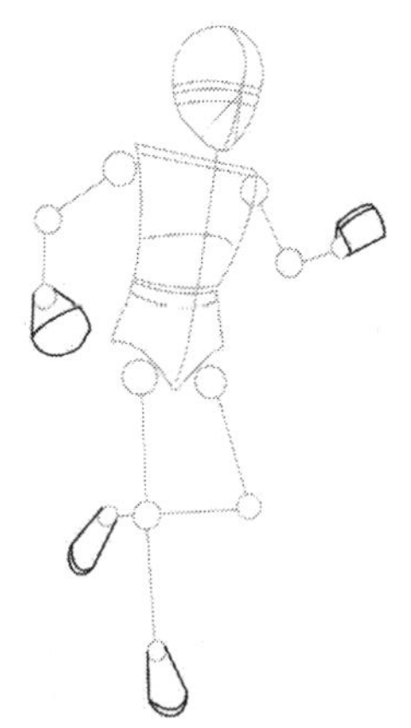

05

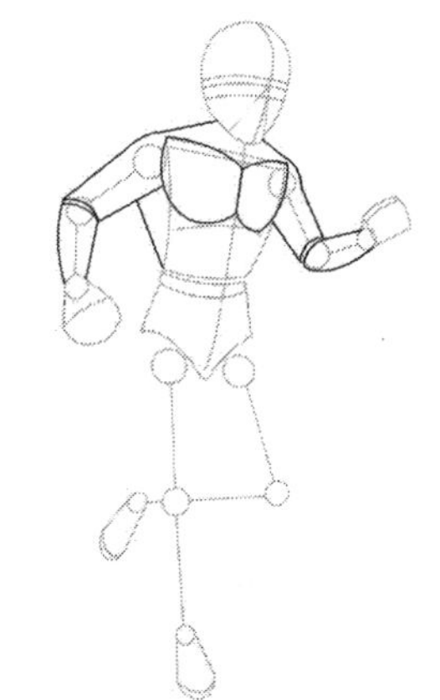

06

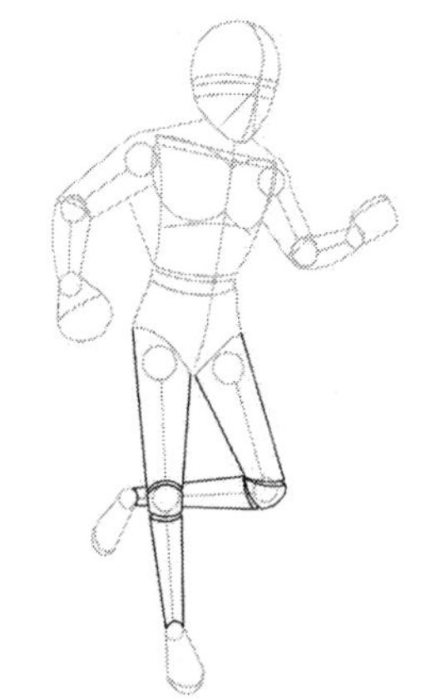

07

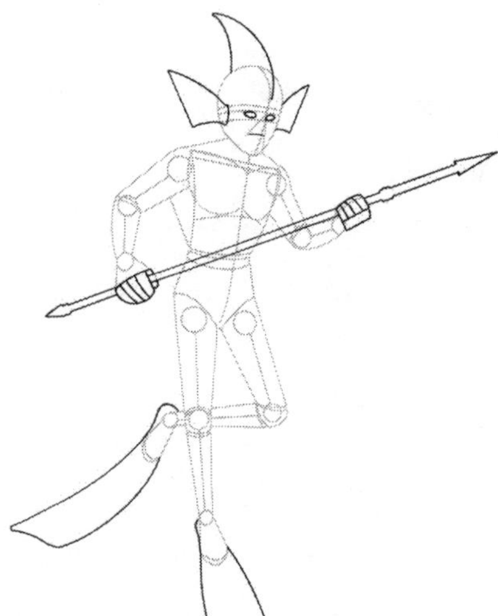

08

09

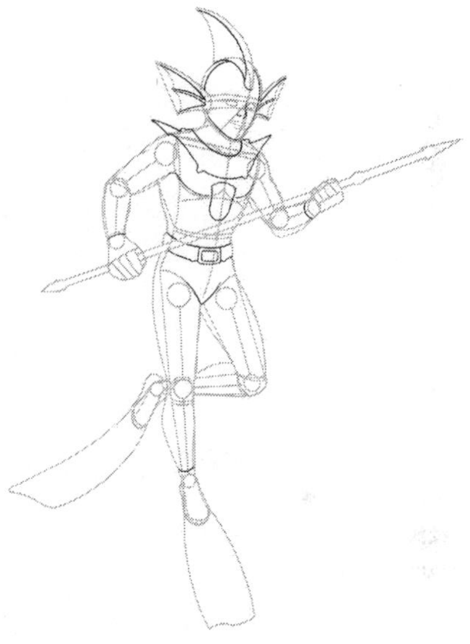

10

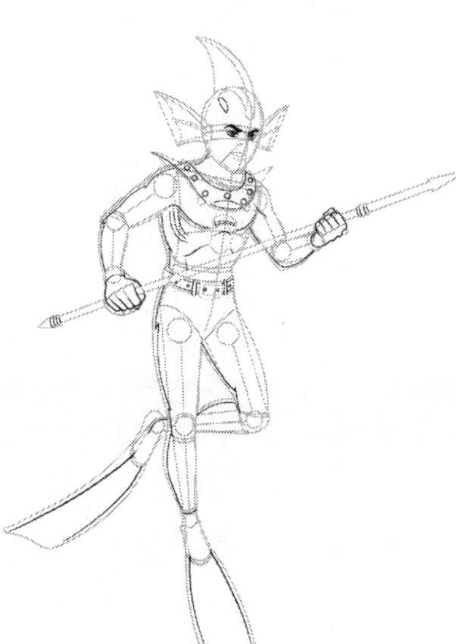

11

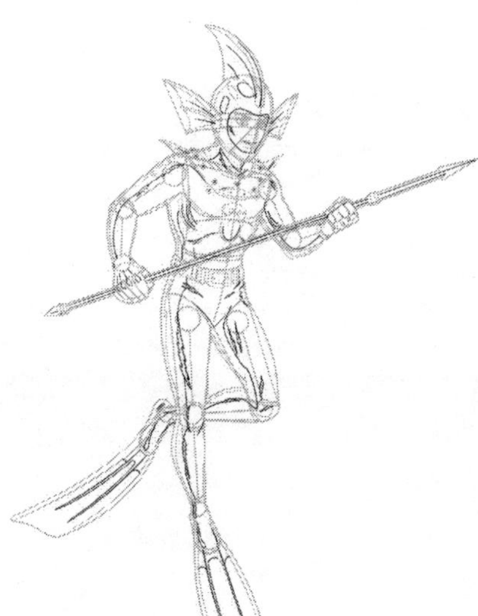

12

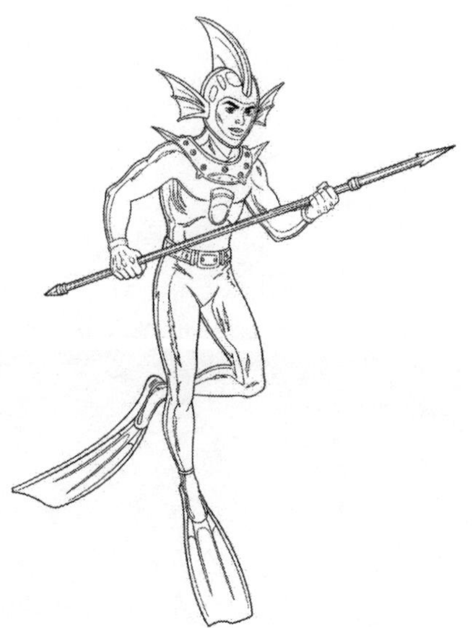

PULP

THE WHIZKID

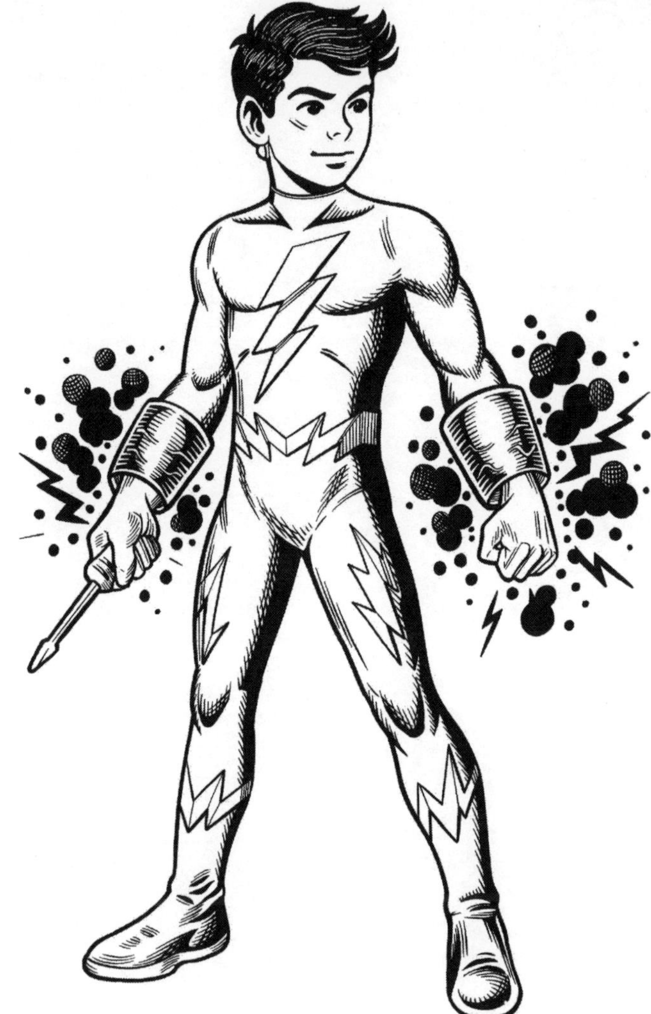

Pro Tip: For a teenage hero, aim for around six heads tall with a lean, lightly muscled build — powerful but not yet fully adult.

01

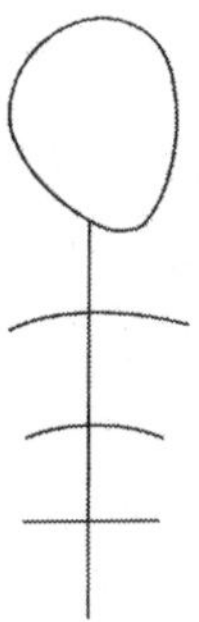

02

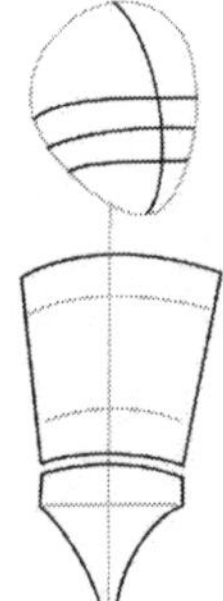

03

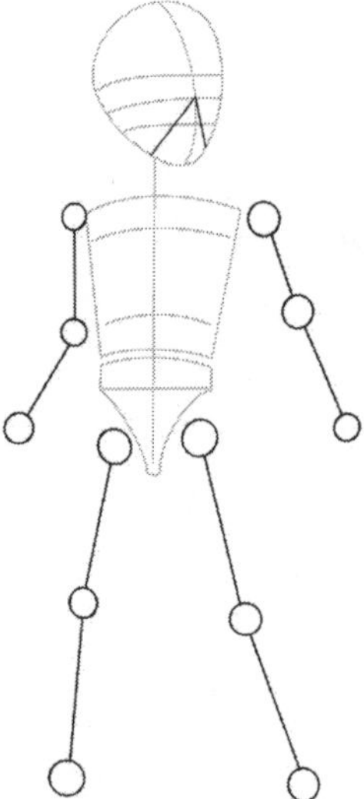

04

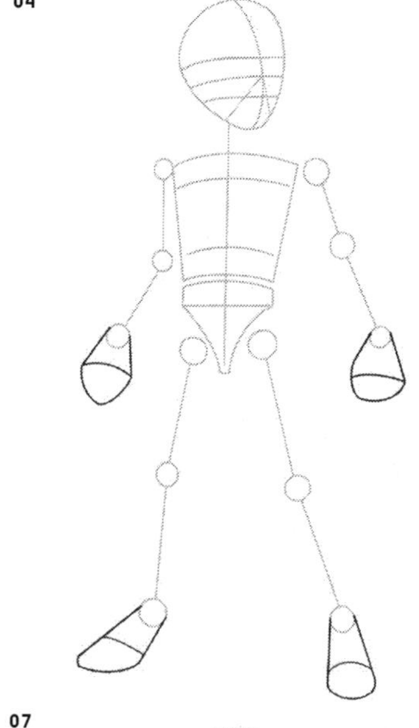

05

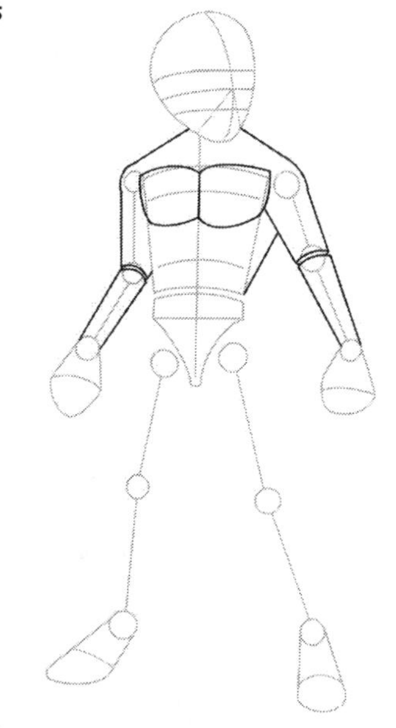

06

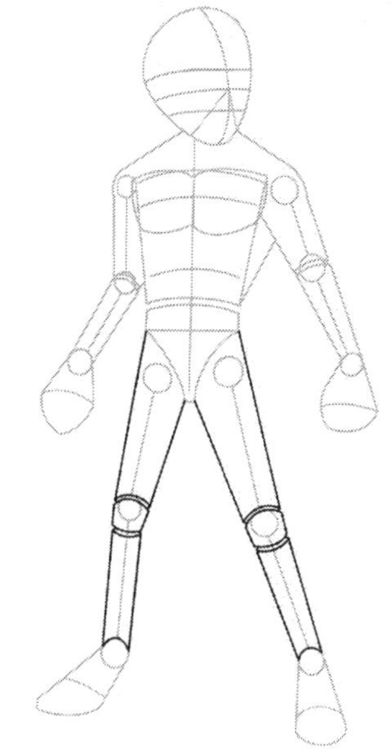

07

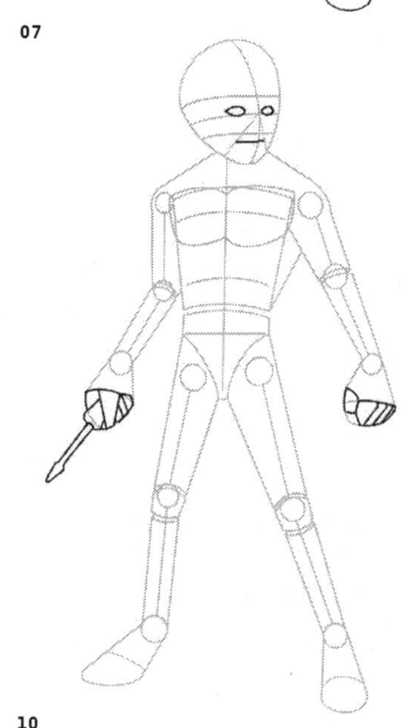

08

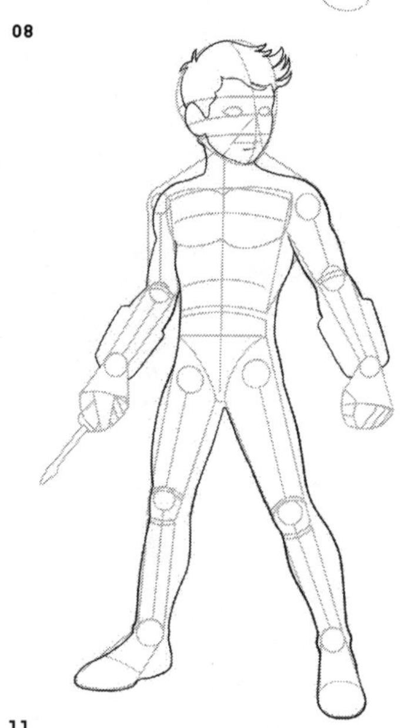

09

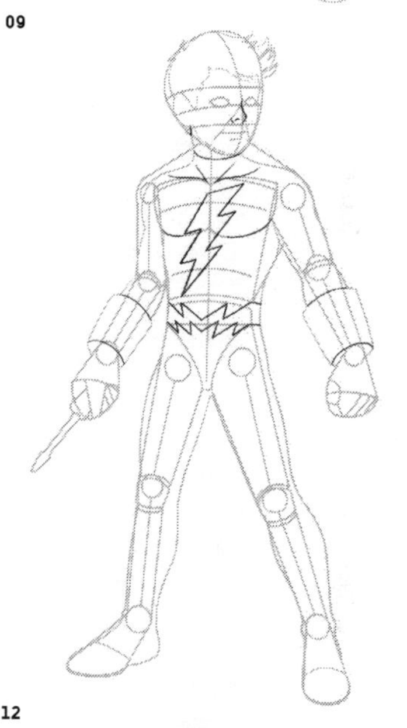

10

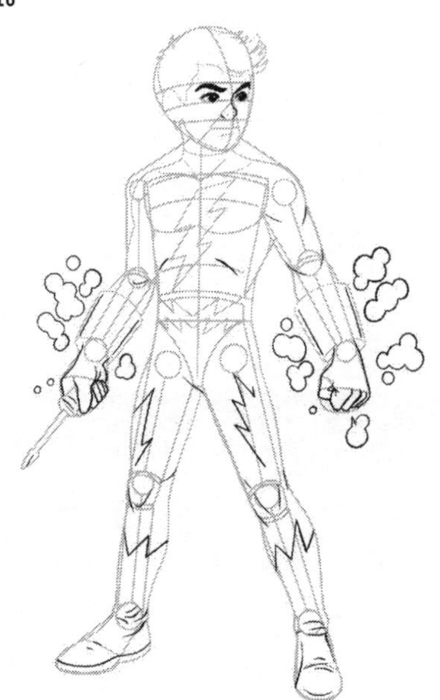

11

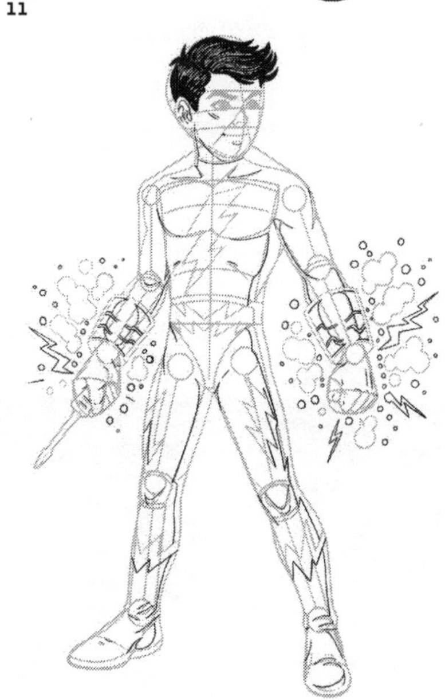

12

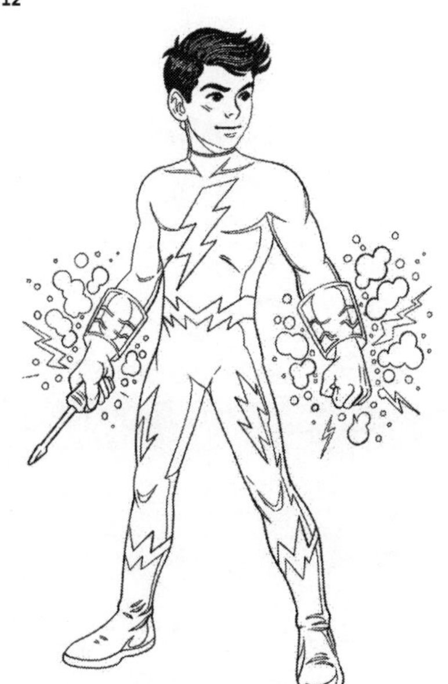

PULP

LAGOON WARRIOR

Pro Tip: The ragged, layered textures of fin, scale and feather are this character's defining feature — build them outward from the body in overlapping layers, growing wilder toward the edges.

01

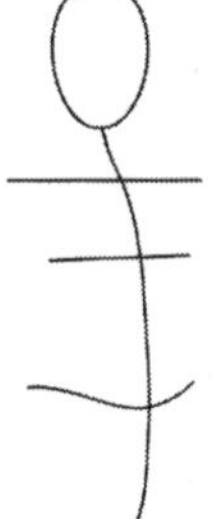

02

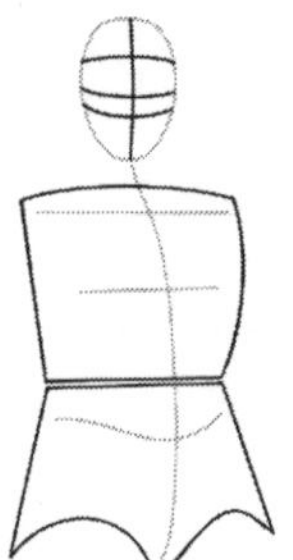

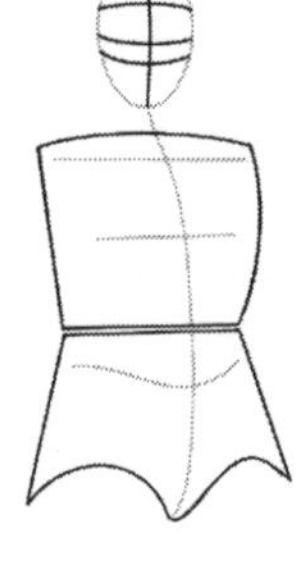

03

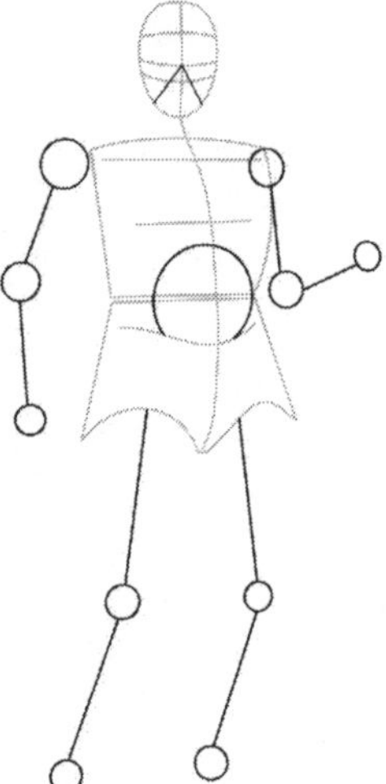

04

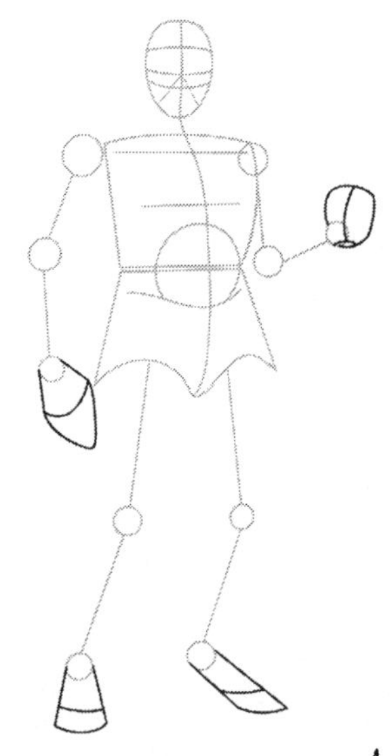

05

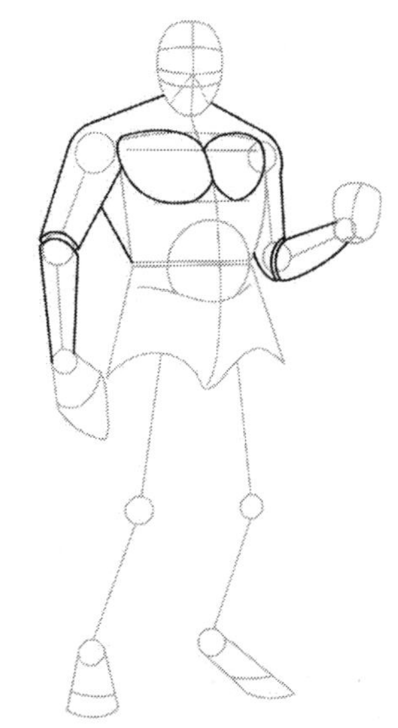

06

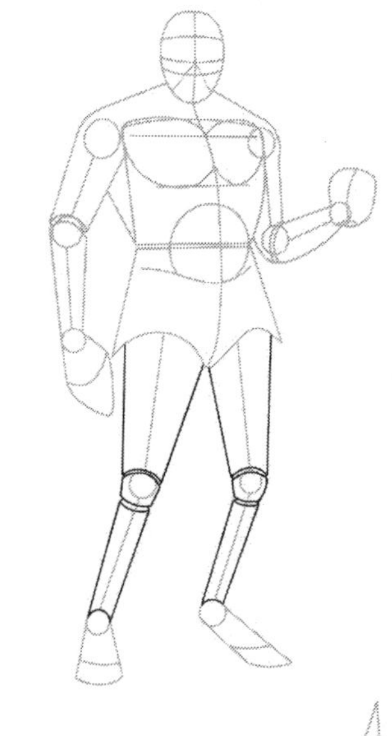

07

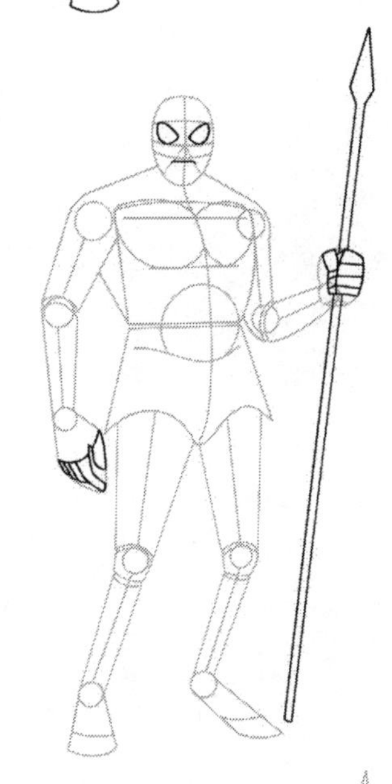

08

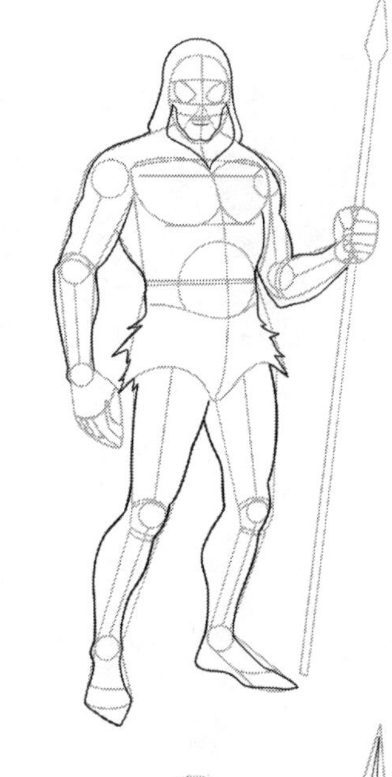

09

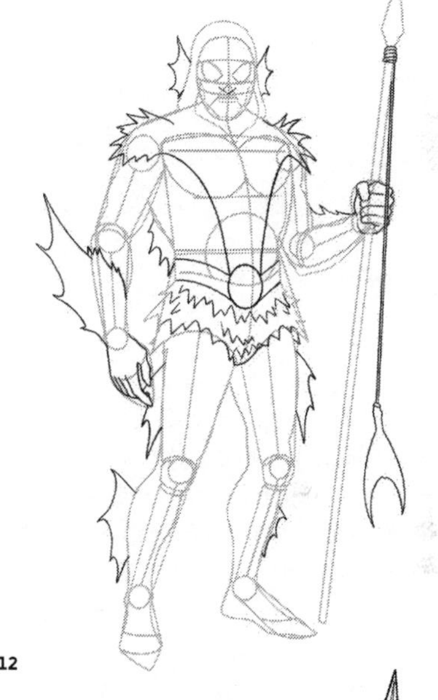

10

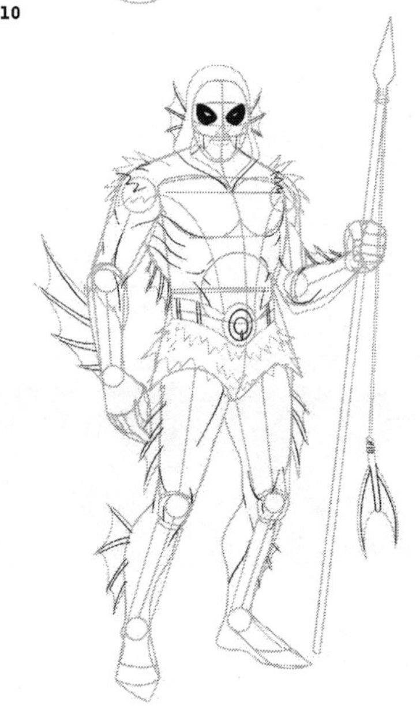

11

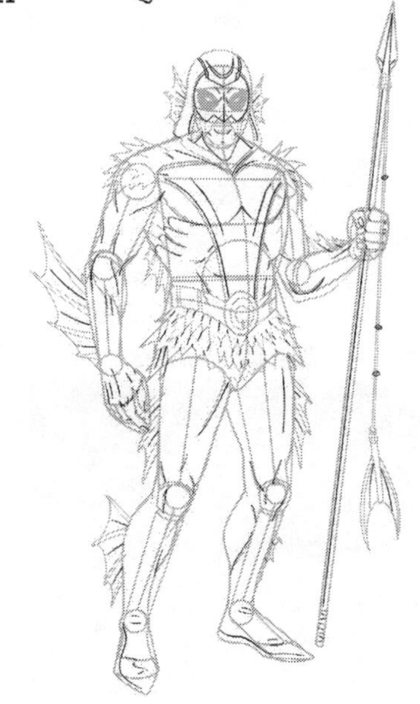

12

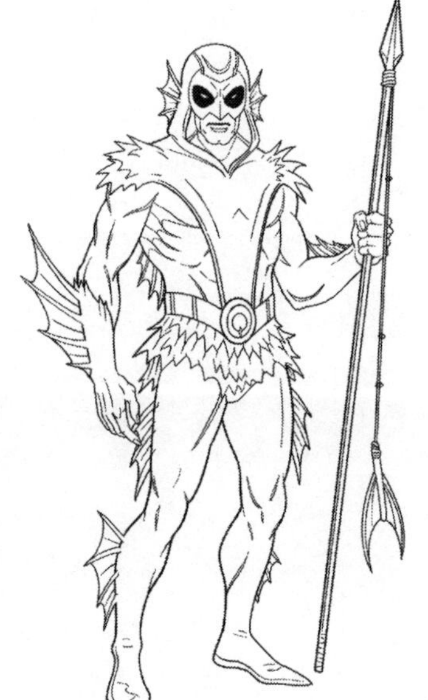

PULP

MERMAID WARRIOR

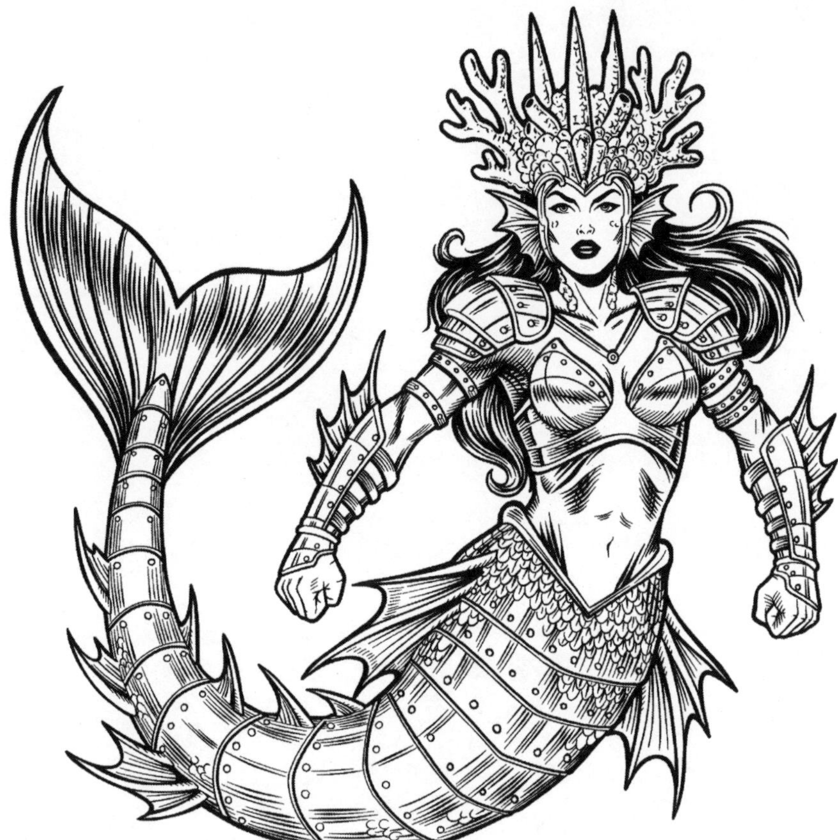

Pro Tip: The tail should be roughly the same length as the entire upper body from crown to hip. Start it broad at the hips, tapering gradually into a sweeping curve that fans out to a fin slightly wider than the shoulders.

01

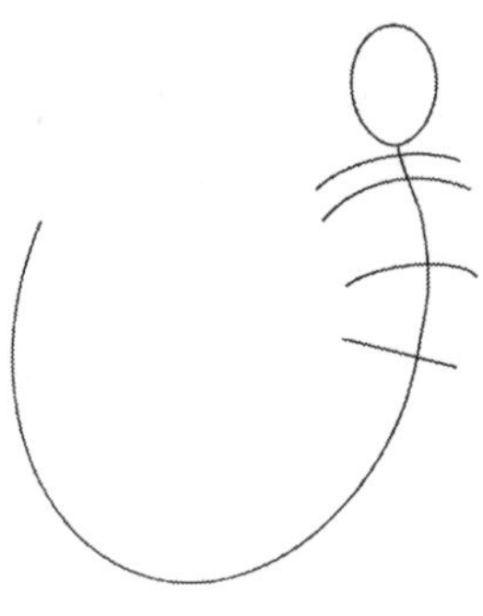

02

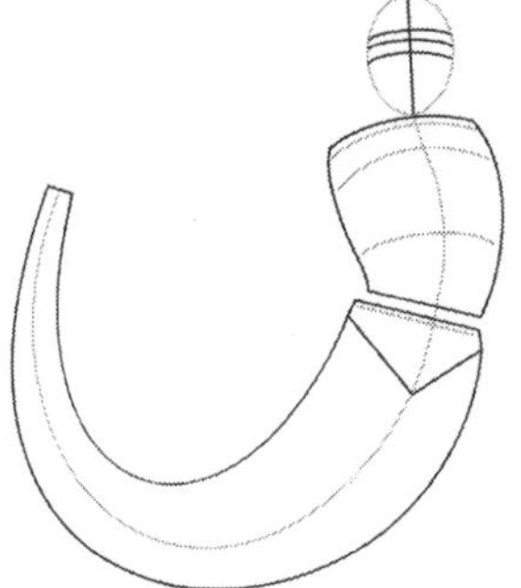

03

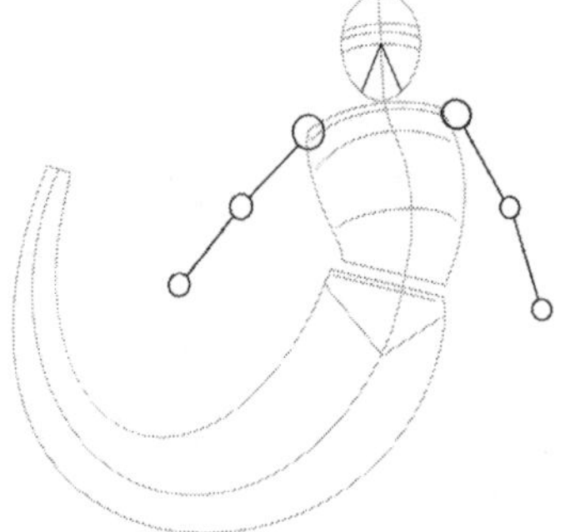

04

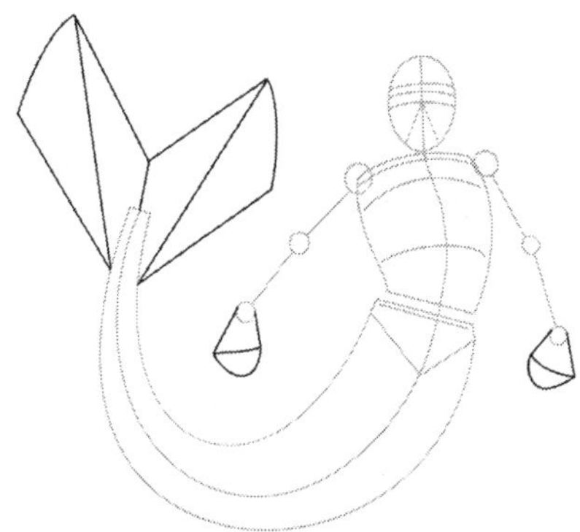

05

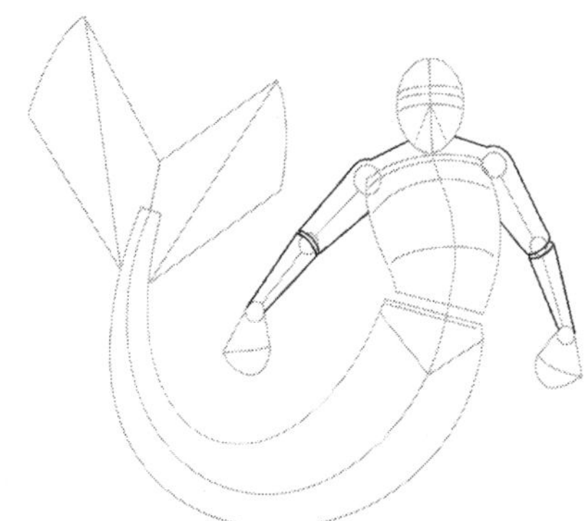

06

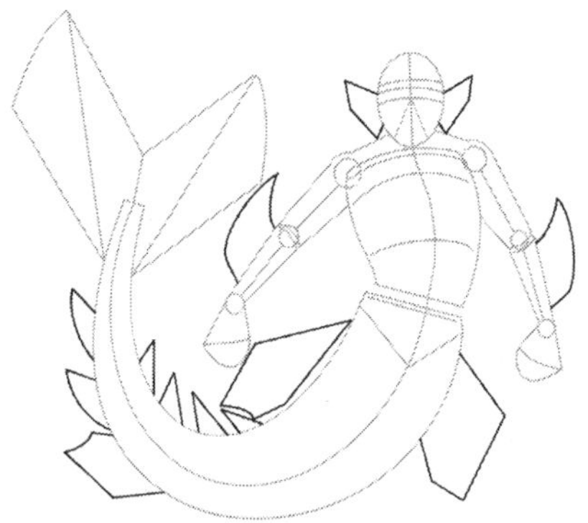

07

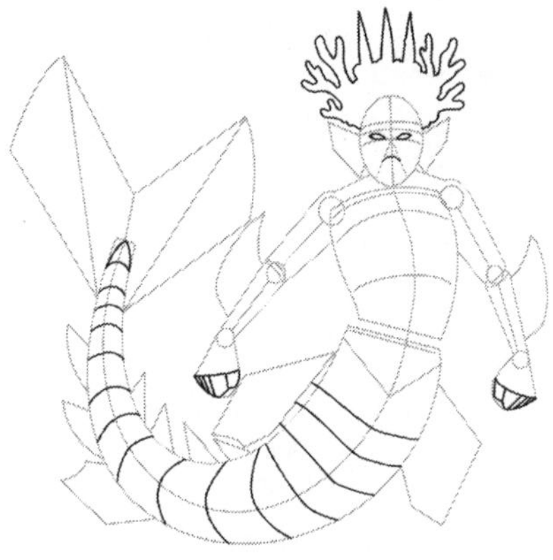

08

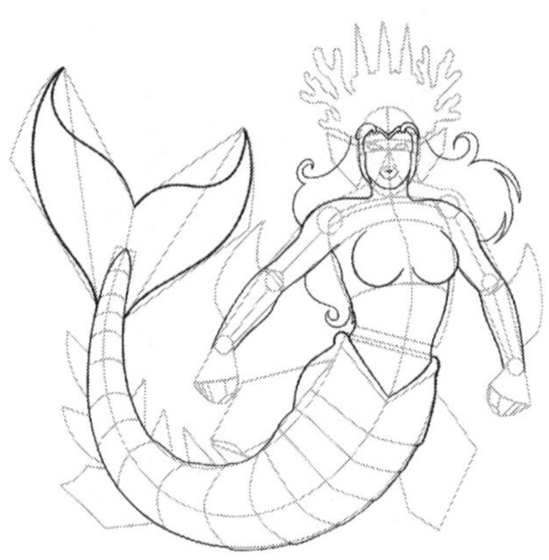

09

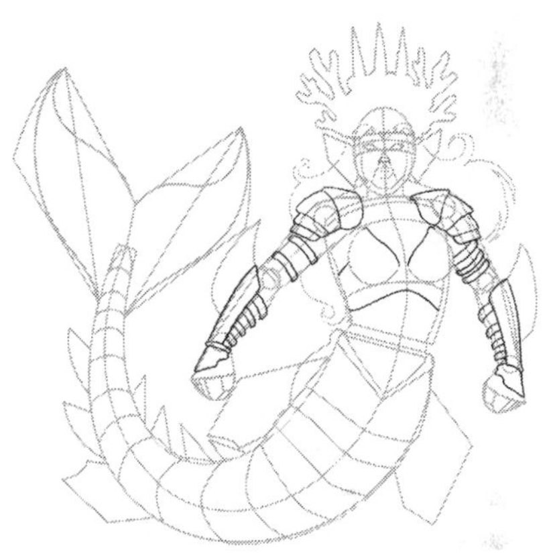

10

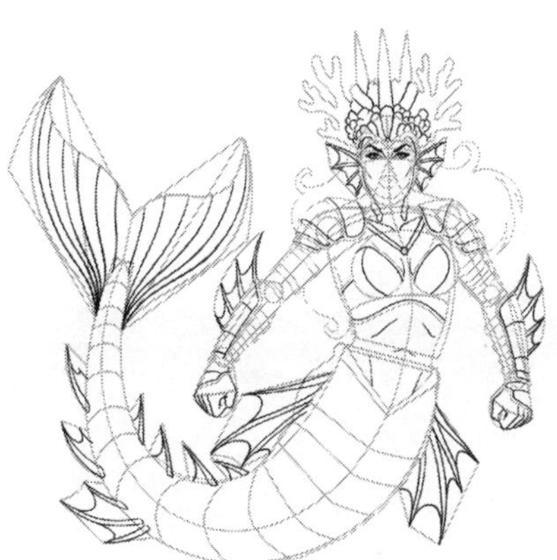

11

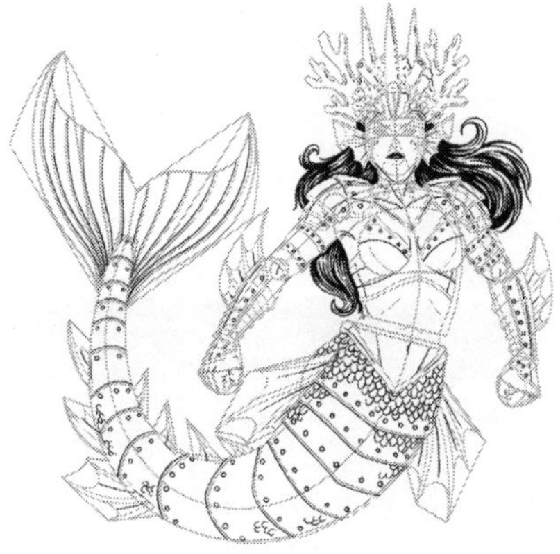

12

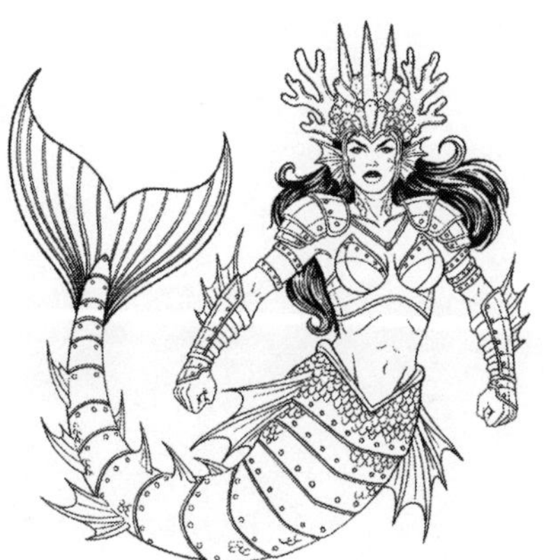

SCI-FI

KILLER ROBOT

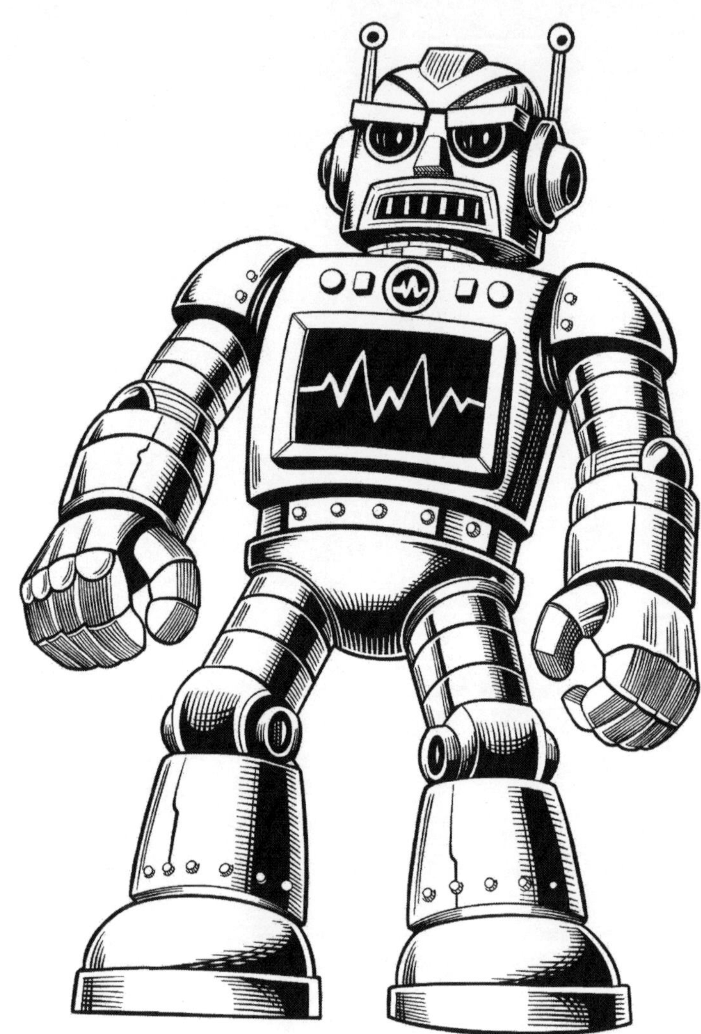

Pro Tip: The retro sci-fi robot is built entirely from geometric primitives — stack bold cylinders, rectangles and spheres with visible bolts and panel lines to convey clunky, mechanical menace.

01

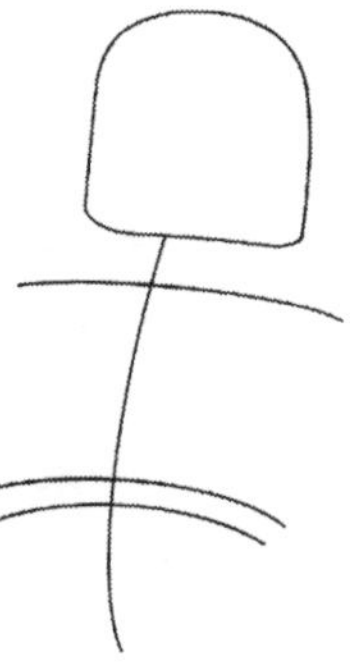

02

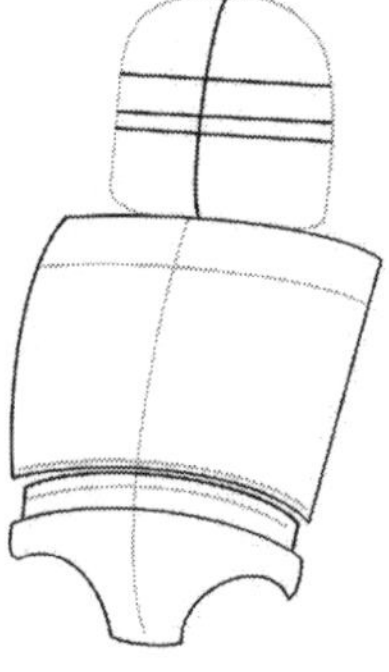

03

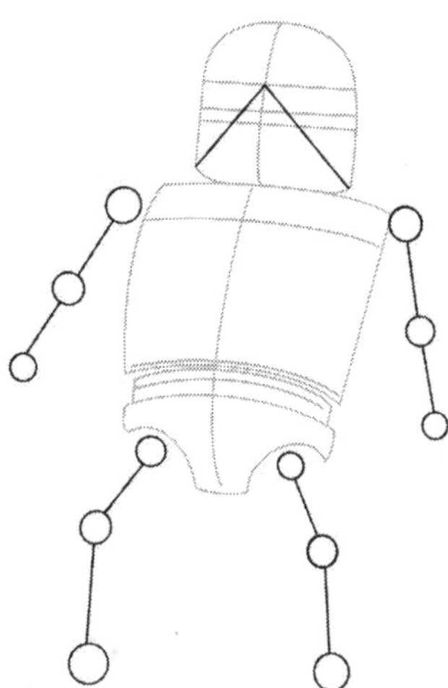

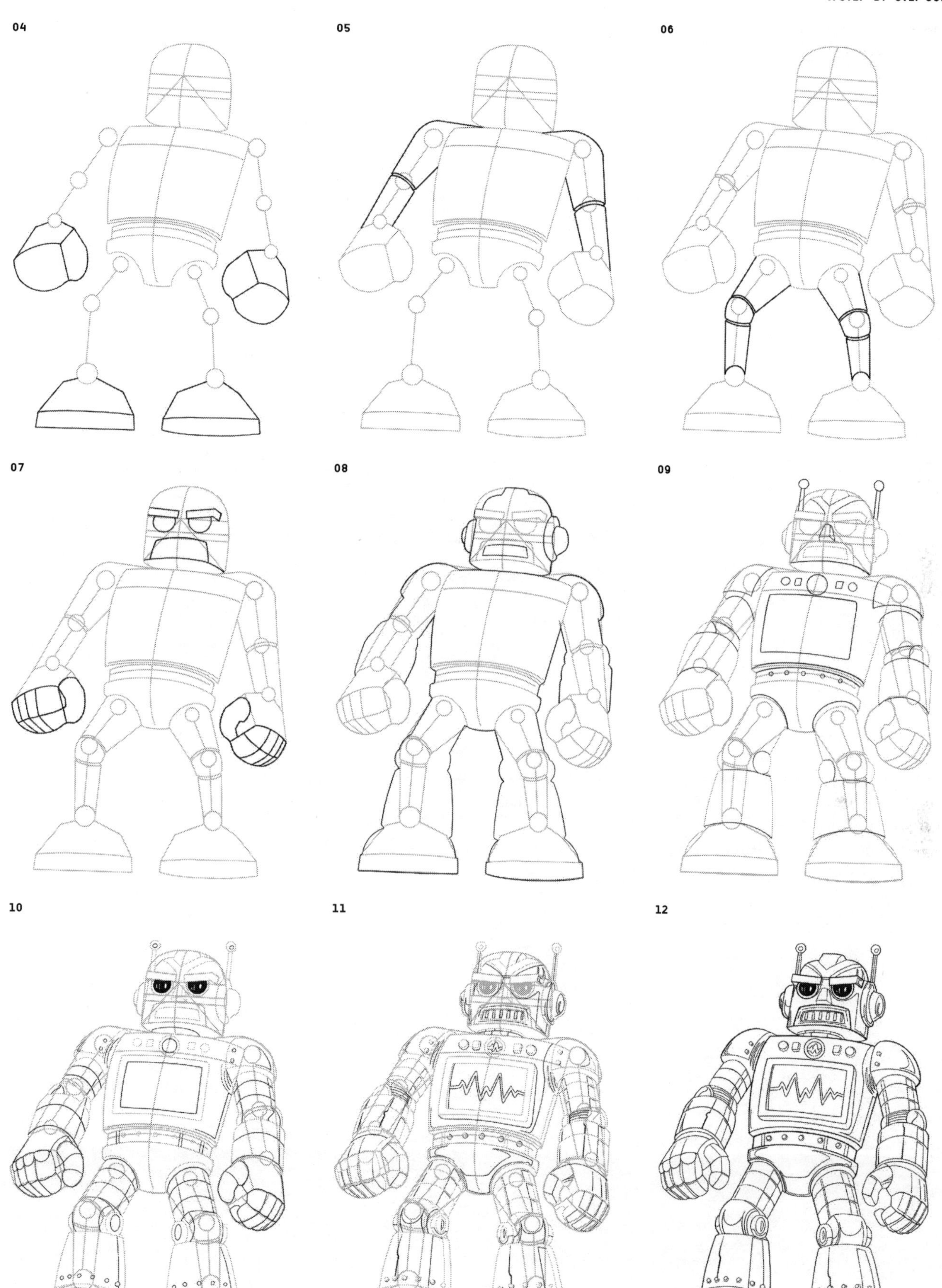
04
05
06
07
08
09
10
11
12

SCI-FI

SPACE AGENT

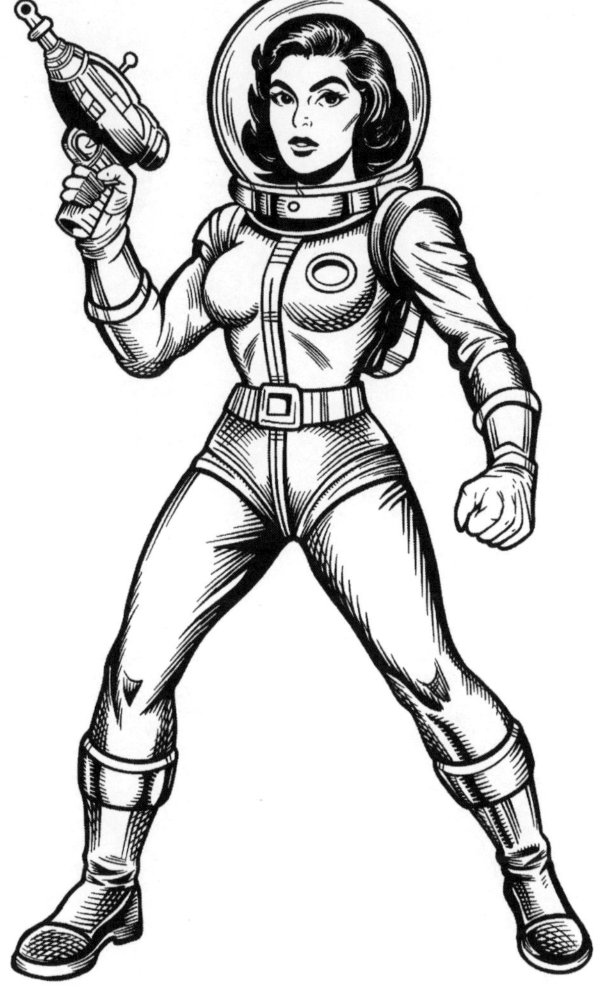

Pro Tip: Aim for around eight heads tall to convey a confident, heroic female figure. The helmet sphere should be roughly one and a half times the width of the head inside it, and the ray gun about the same length as the forearm to keep the retro-sci-fi proportions feeling authentic.

01

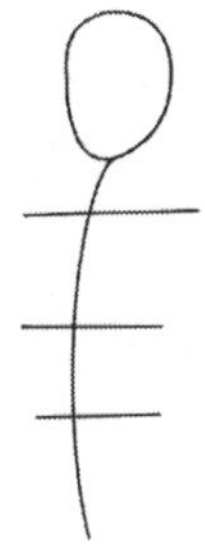

02

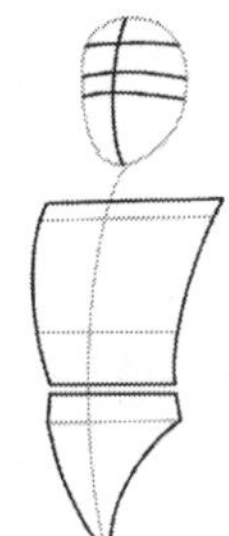

03

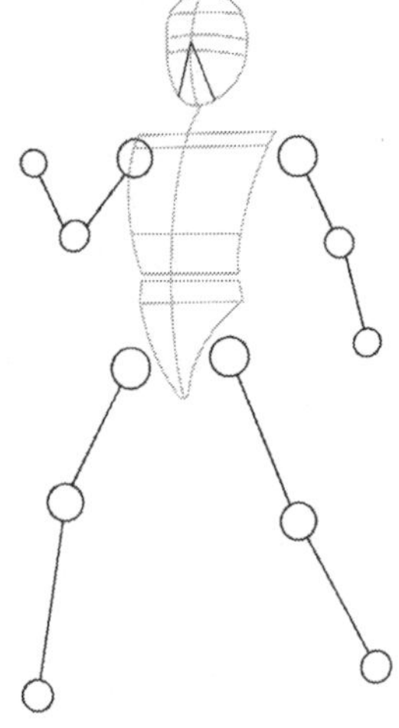

04

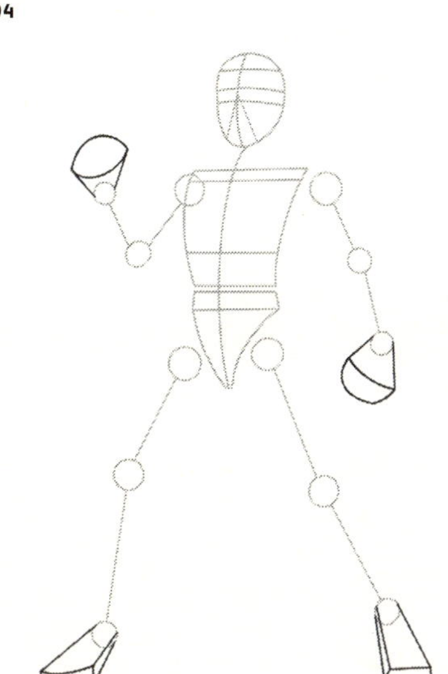

05

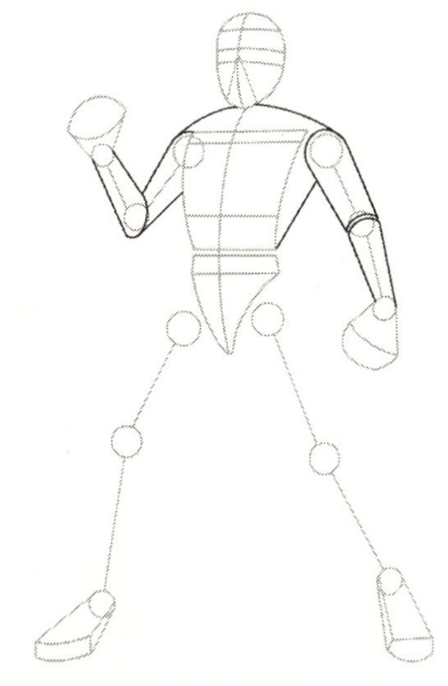

06

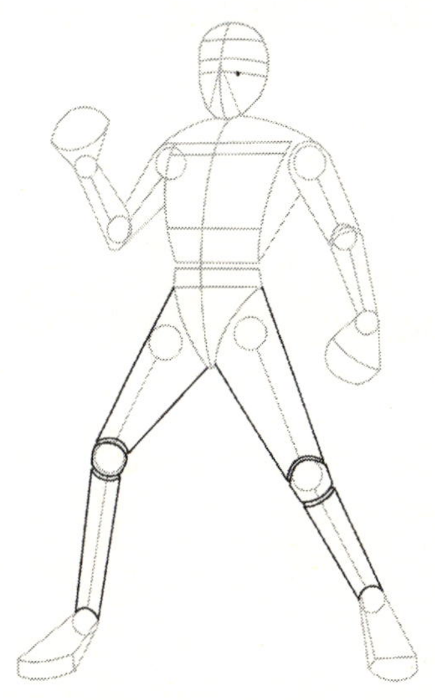

07

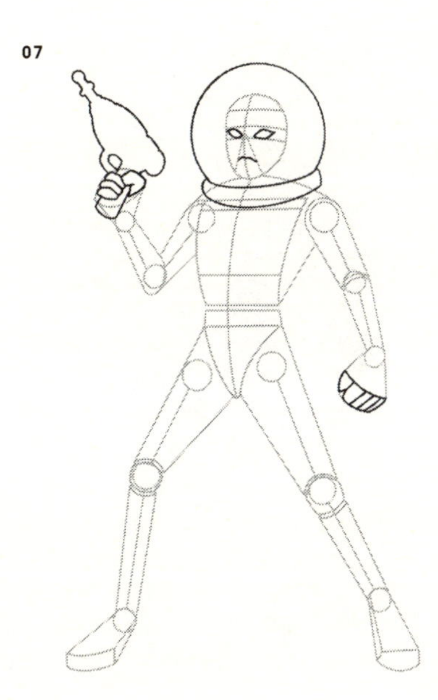

08

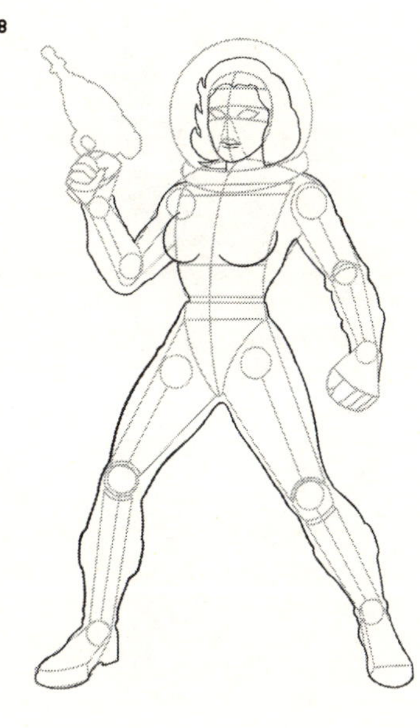

09

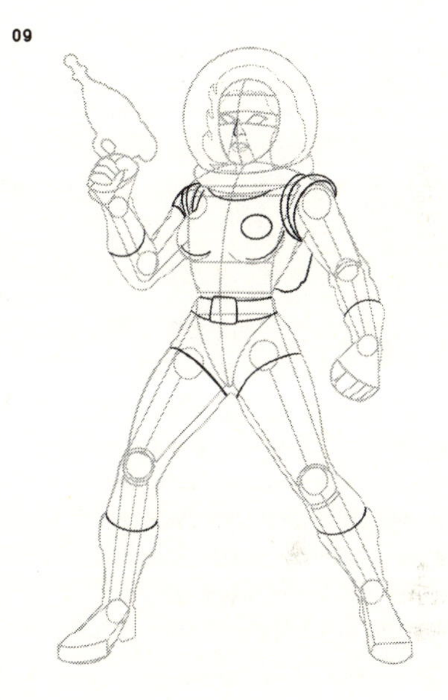

HOW TO DRAW SUPERHEROES

10

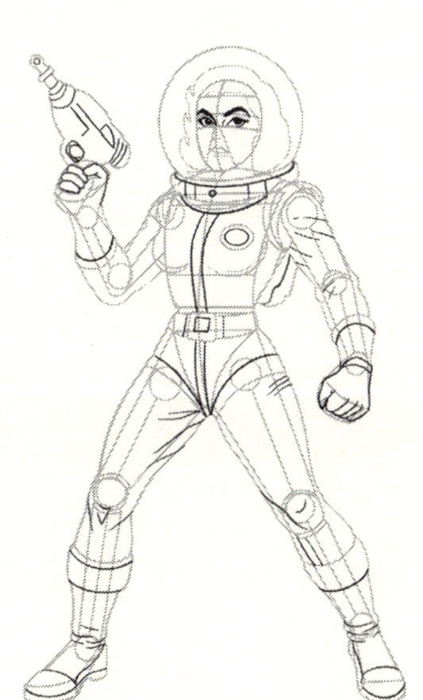

11

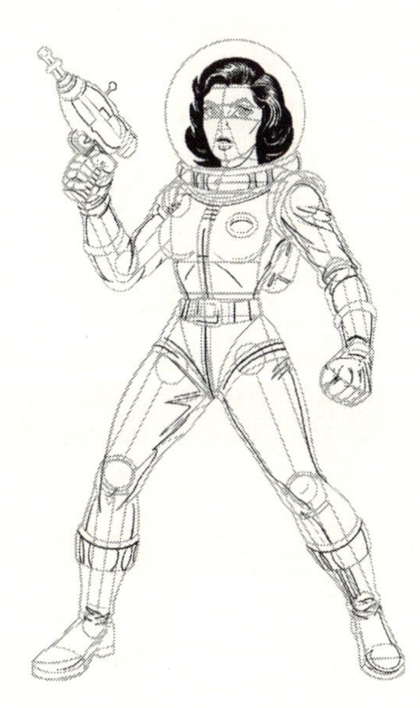

12

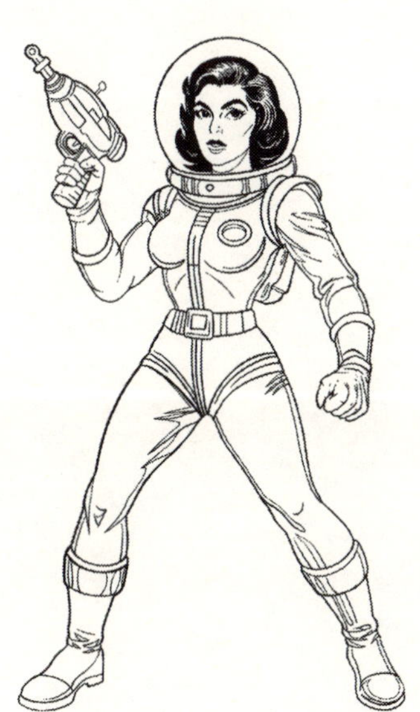

SCI-FI

EVIL SORCERER

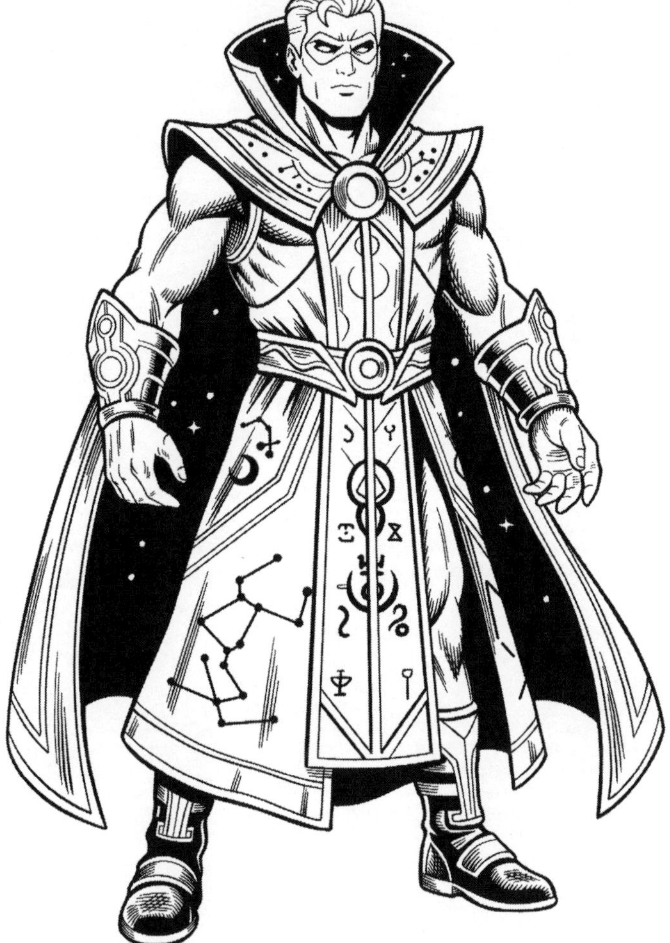

Pro Tip: The robes are the storytelling canvas — scatter arcane symbols and constellation glyphs across them to convey vast otherworldly knowledge. The high dramatic collar frames the face, drawing the eye to a character who commands absolute authority.

01

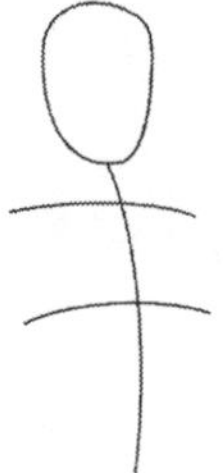

02

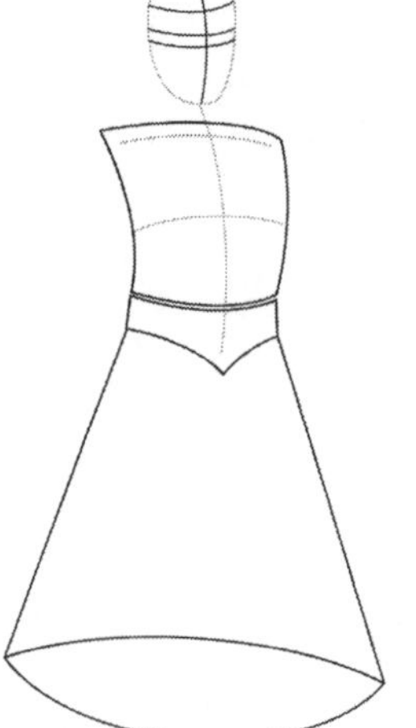

03

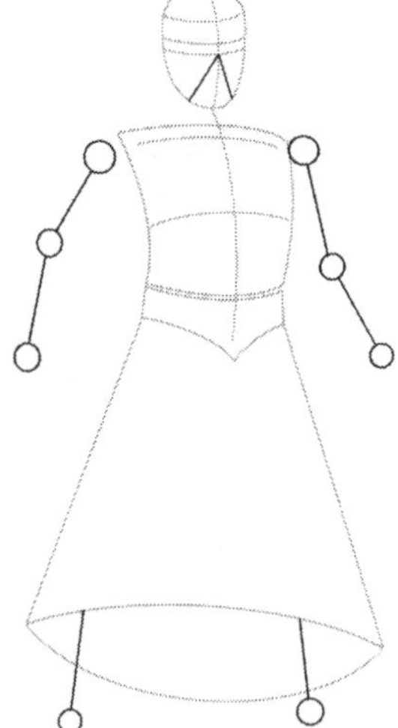

04

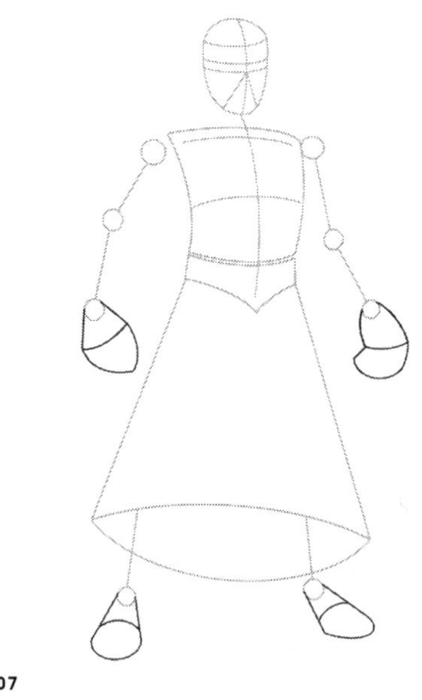

05

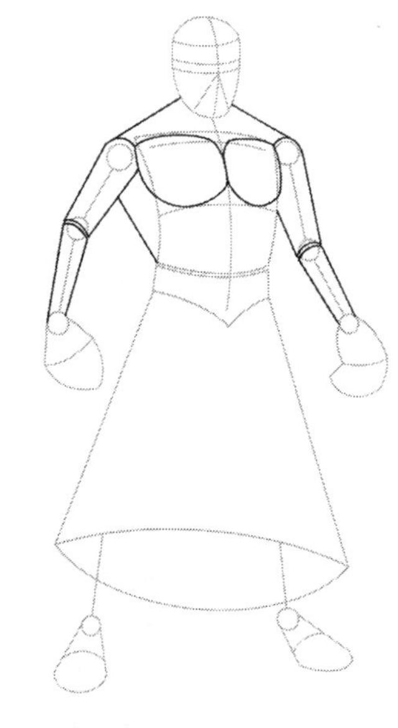

06

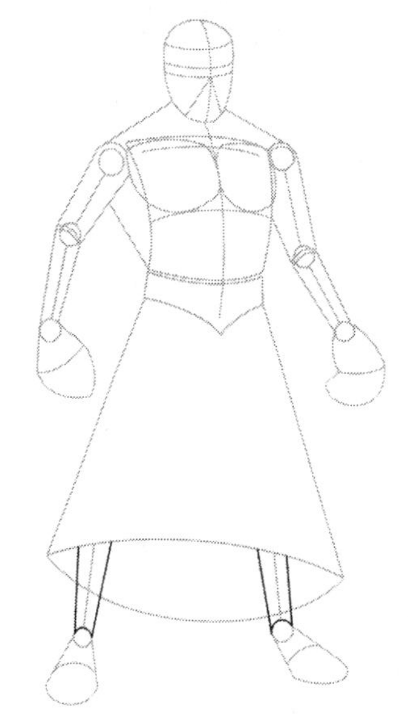

07

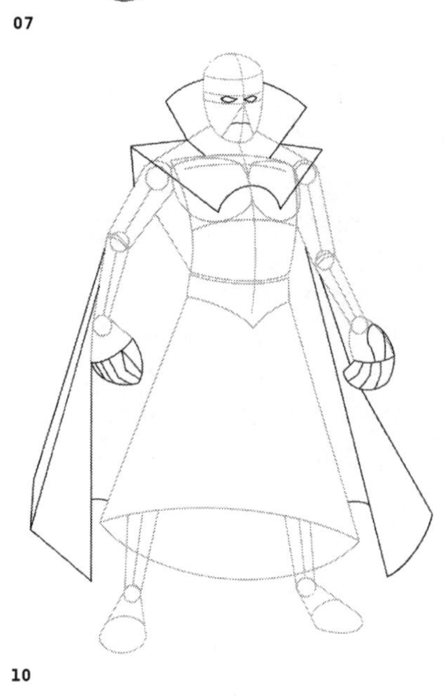

08

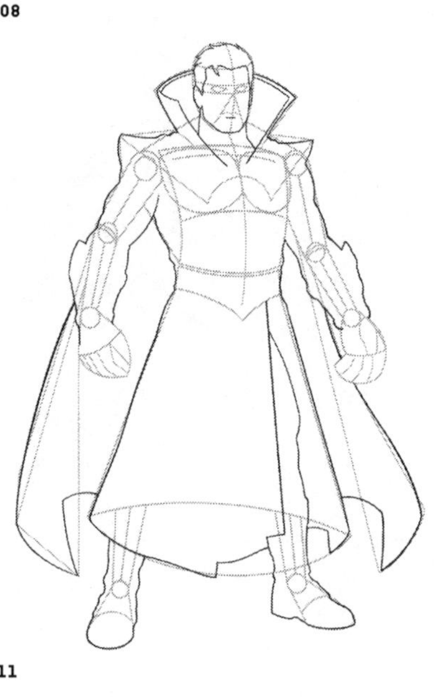

09

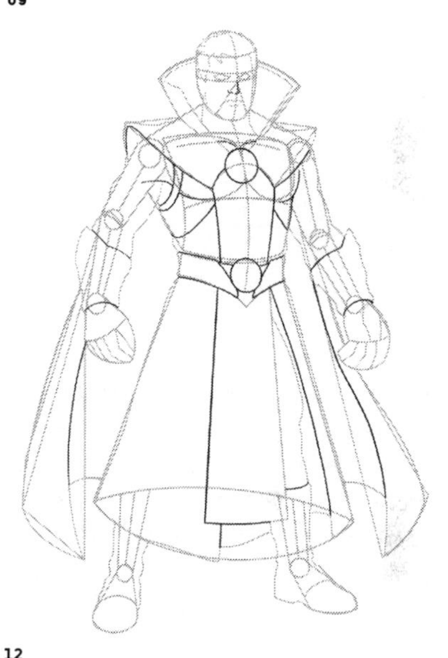

10

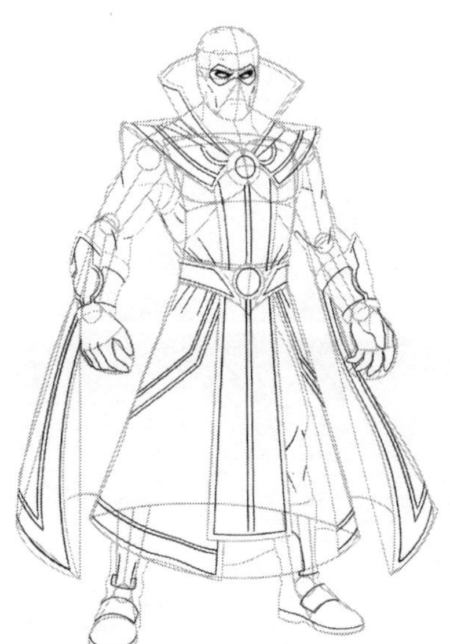

11

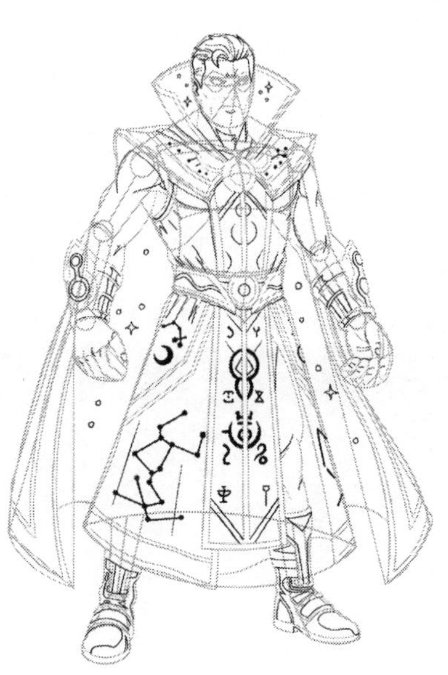

12

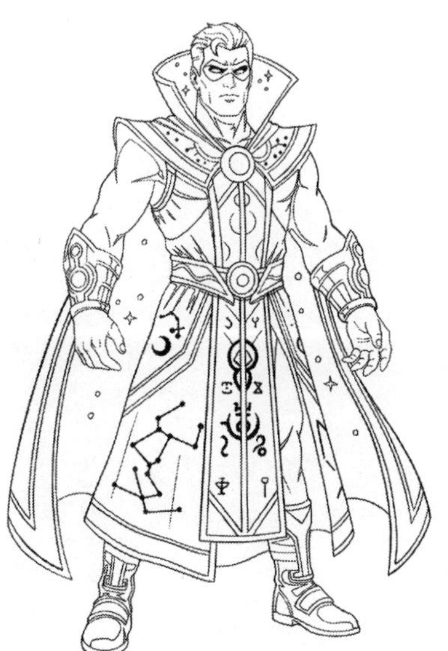

SCI-FI

CYBORG

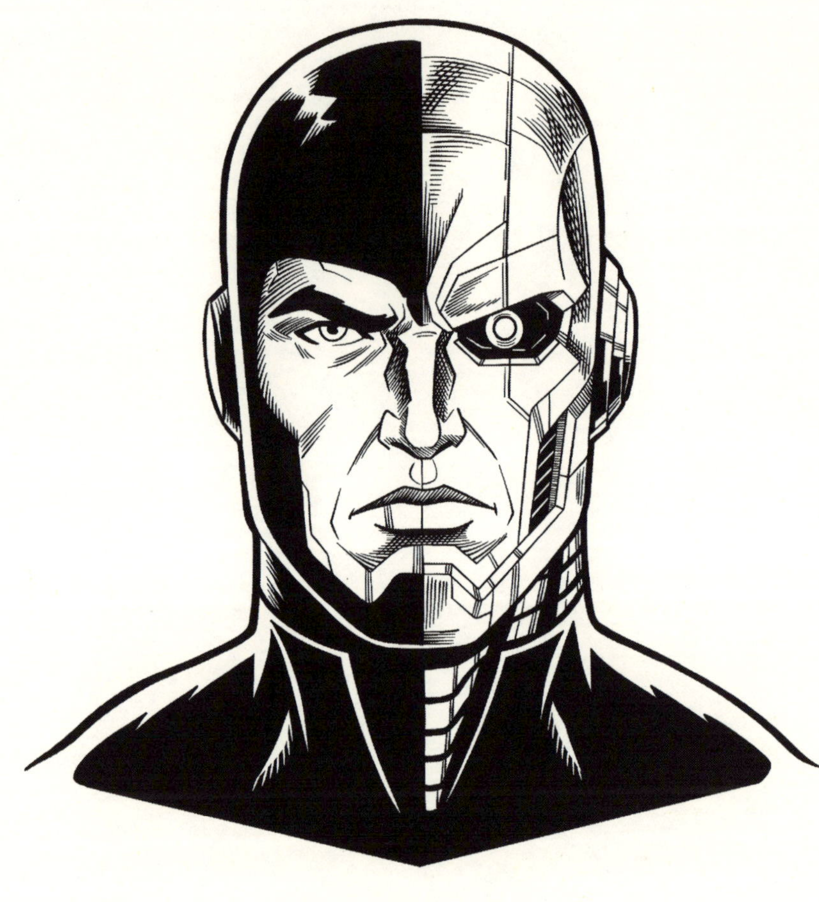

Pro Tip: The key is contrast — keep the organic side soft with subtle curves, while the cybernetic side uses hard, angular panel lines. Use the centre line of the face as your dividing guide to keep both halves balanced.

01

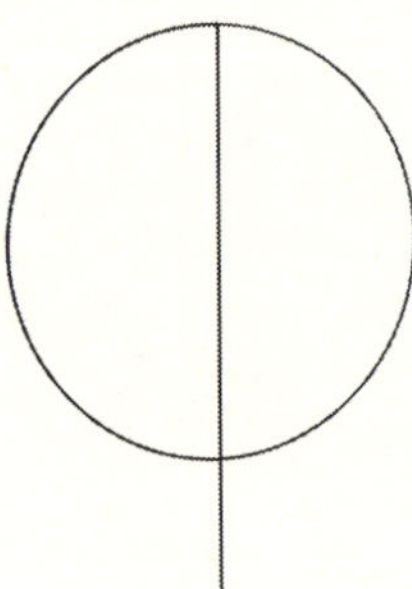

02

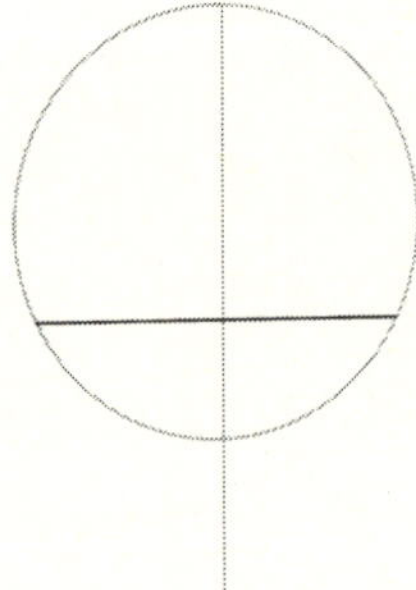

03

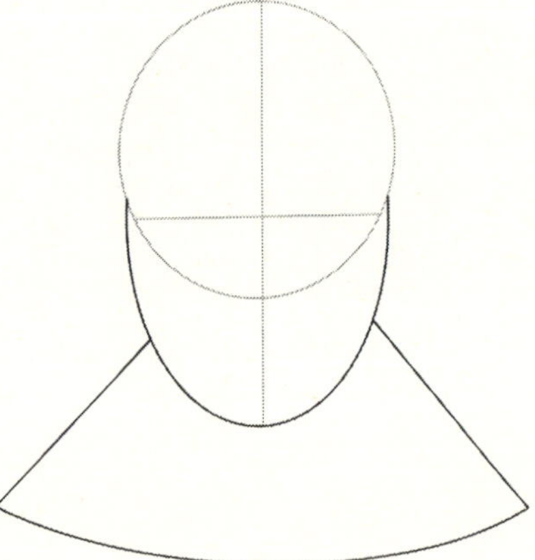

04

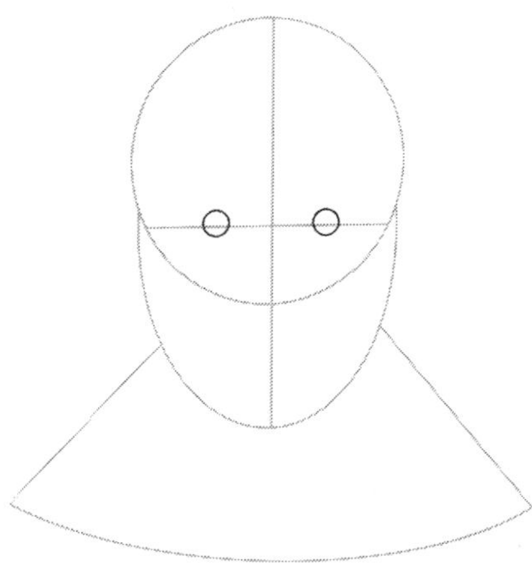

05

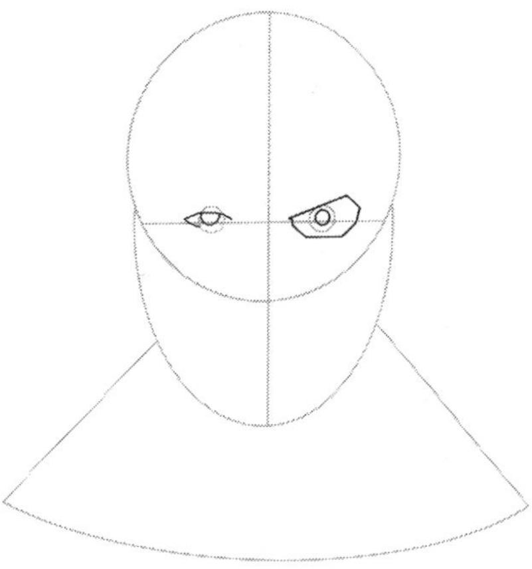

06

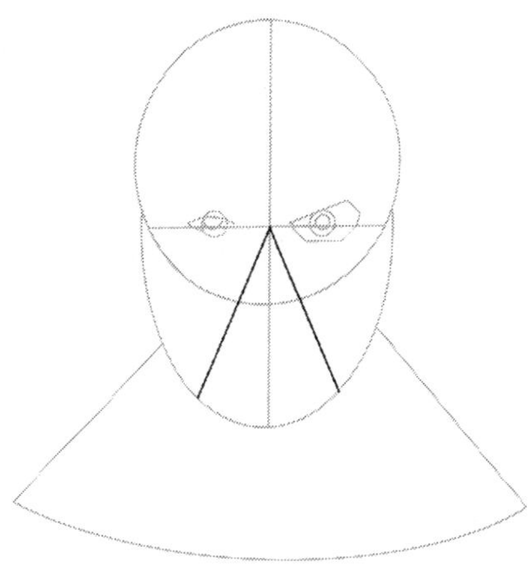

07

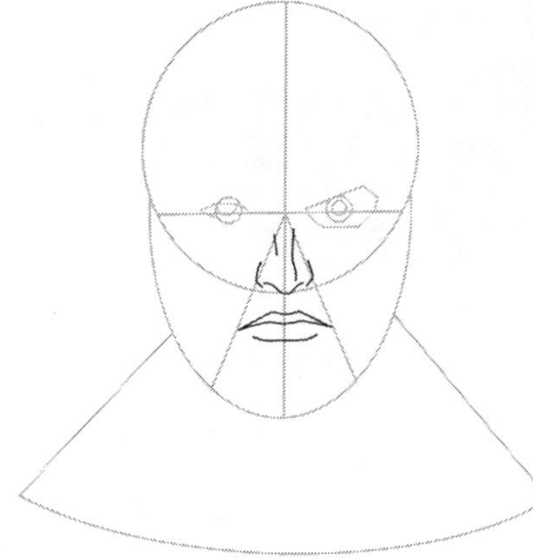

08

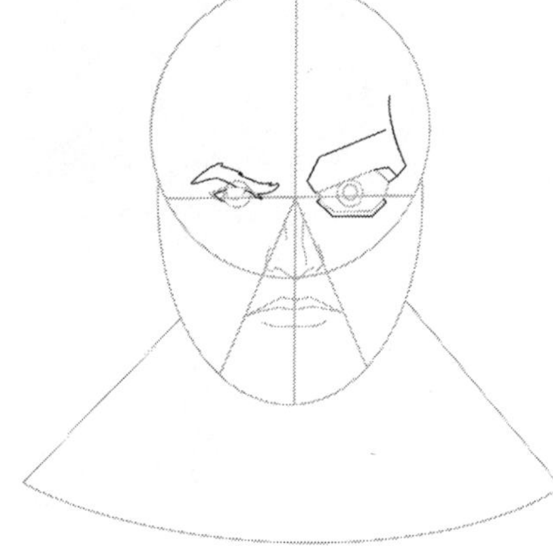

09

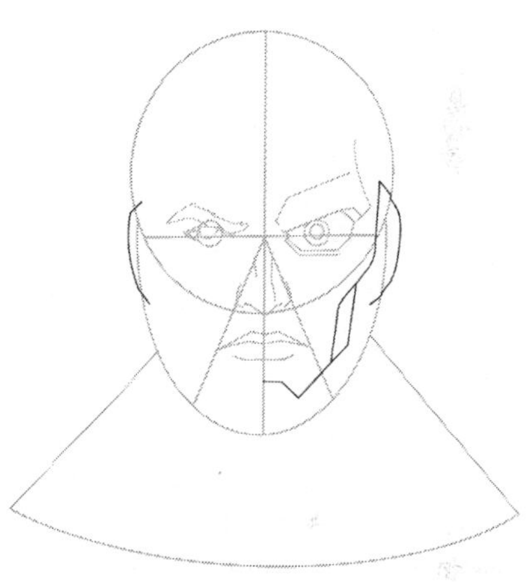

10

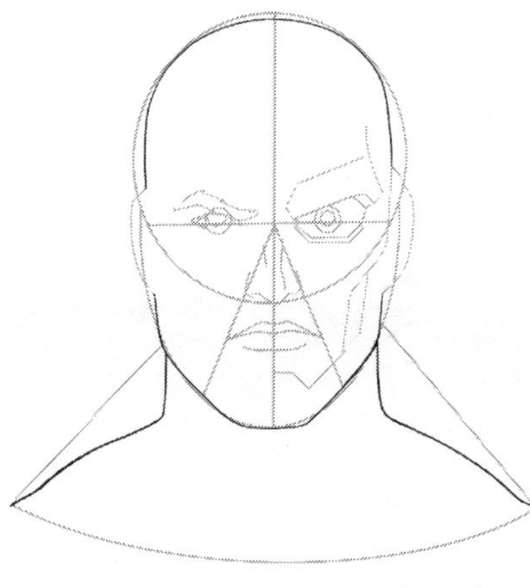

11

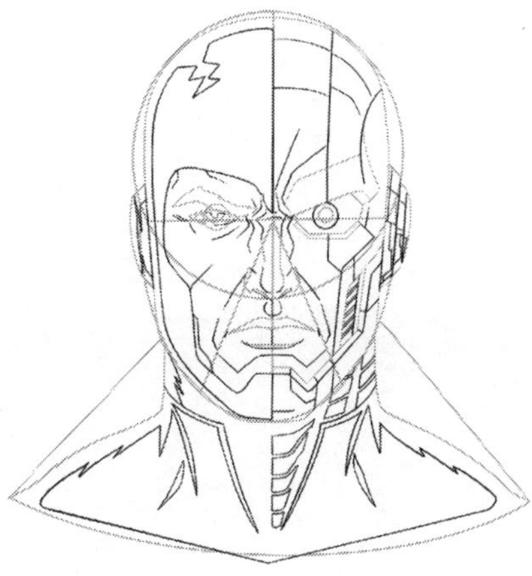

12

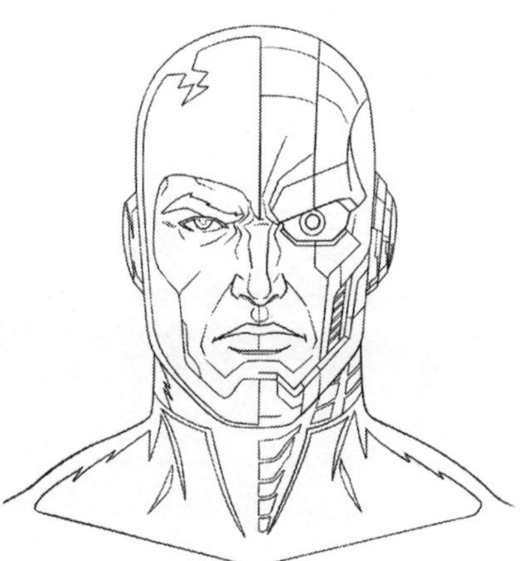

SCI-FI

ALIEN OVERLORD

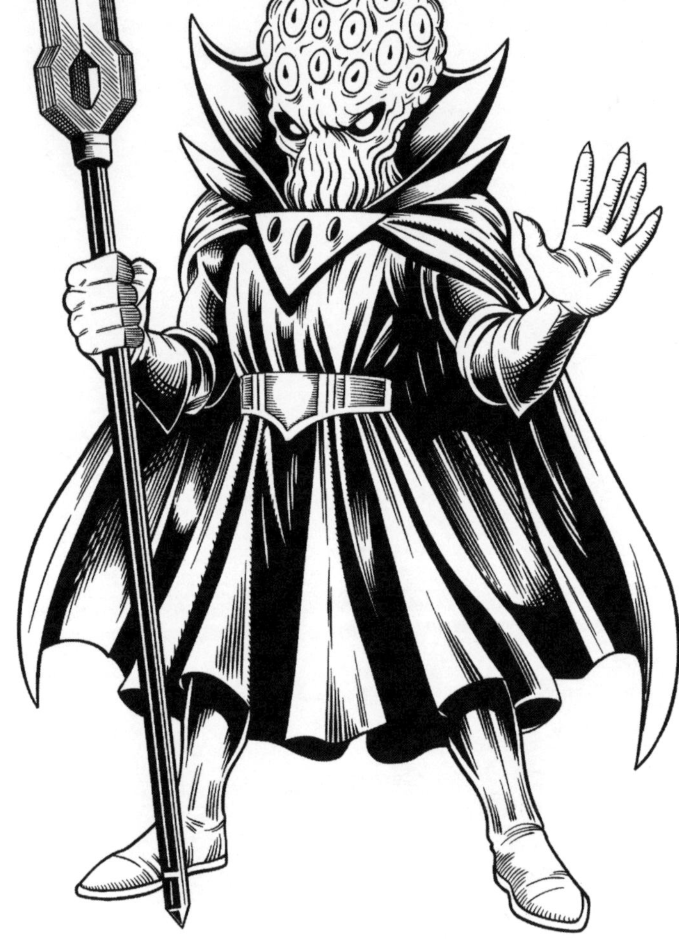

Pro Tip: Keep the body and robes broadly humanoid, then push the head into something otherworldly — clustered eyes and tentacle details that no human face should have, making the familiar deeply unsettling.

01

02

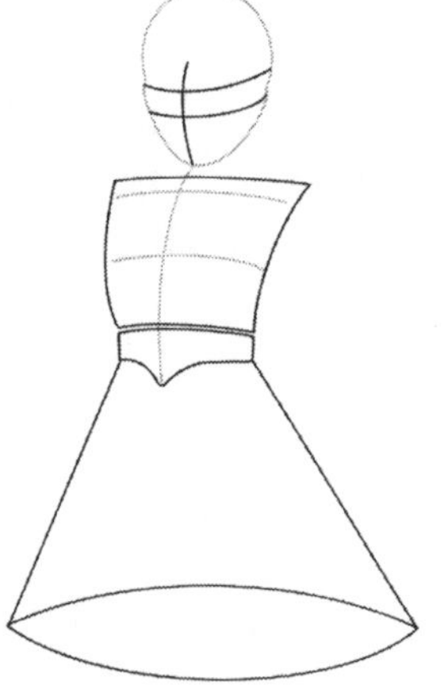

03

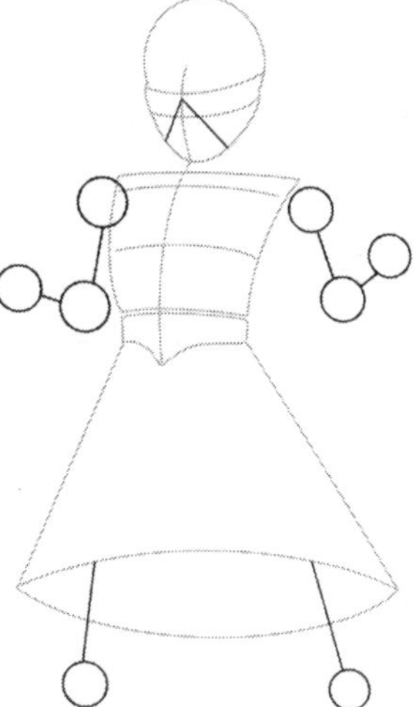

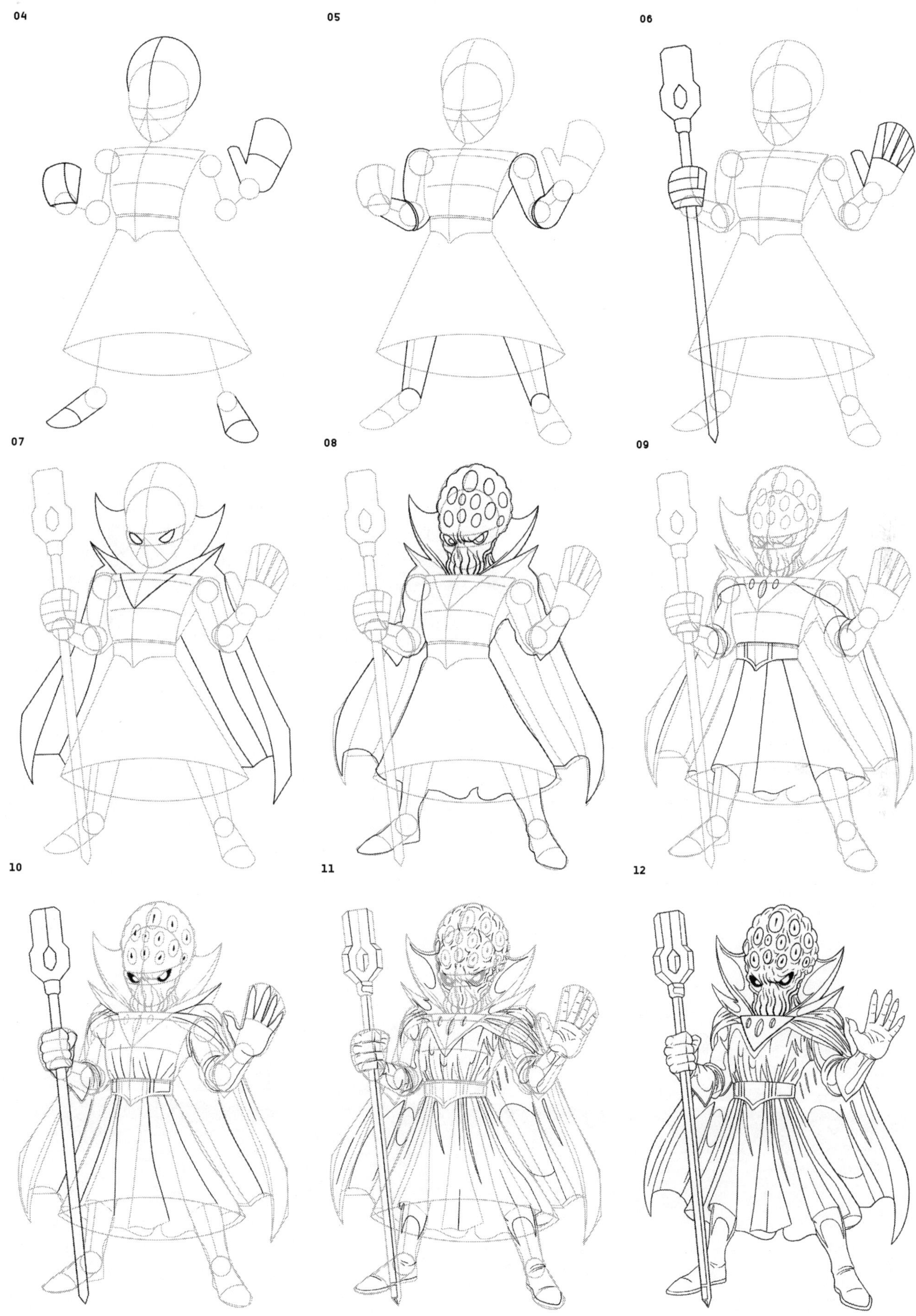
04
05
06
07
08
09
10
11
12

SCI-FI

BRAIN IN A MECHANICAL BODY

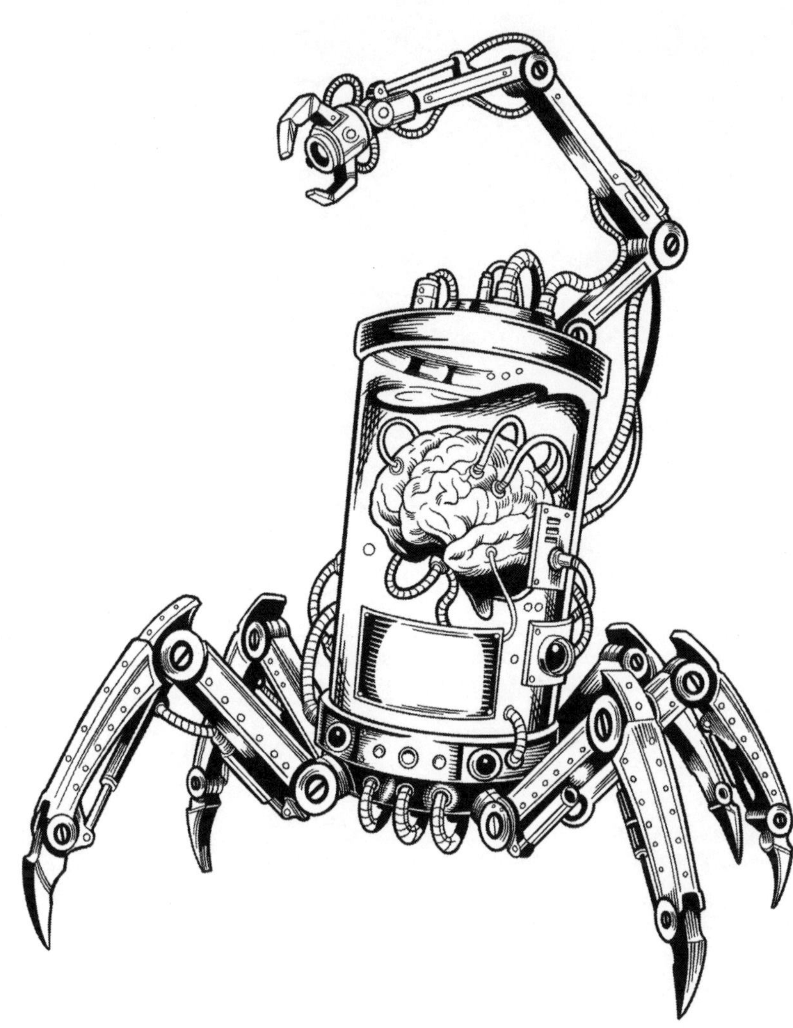

Pro Tip: The cylindrical jar body is the foundation — make it roughly twice as tall as it is wide. Space the legs evenly around the base, each extending outward to about the same width as the jar's height, to convey a mechanical stance.

01

02

03

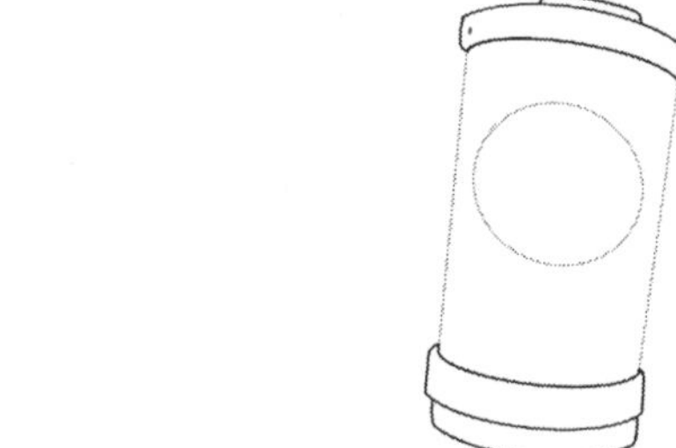

04

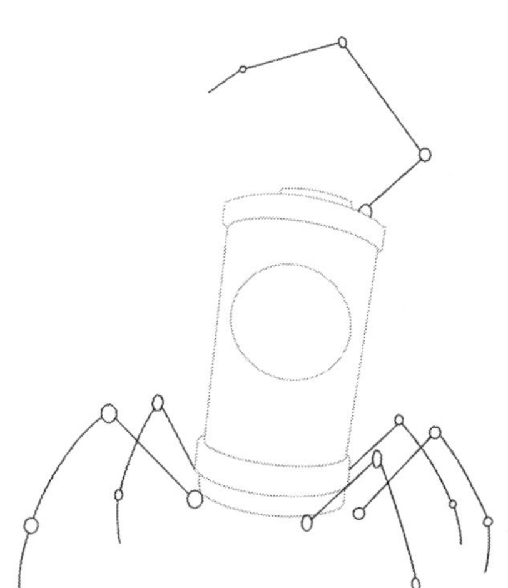

05

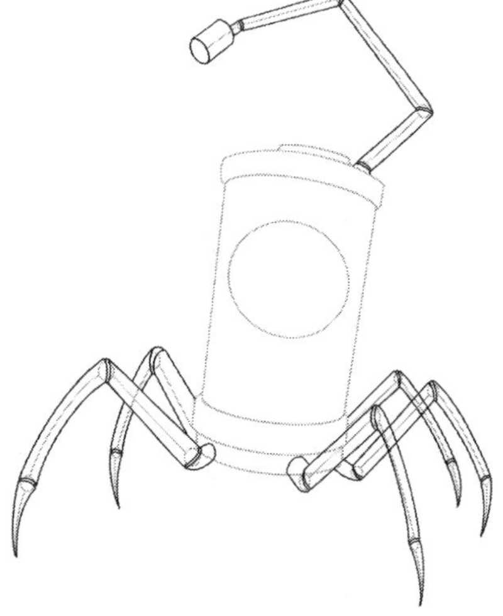

06

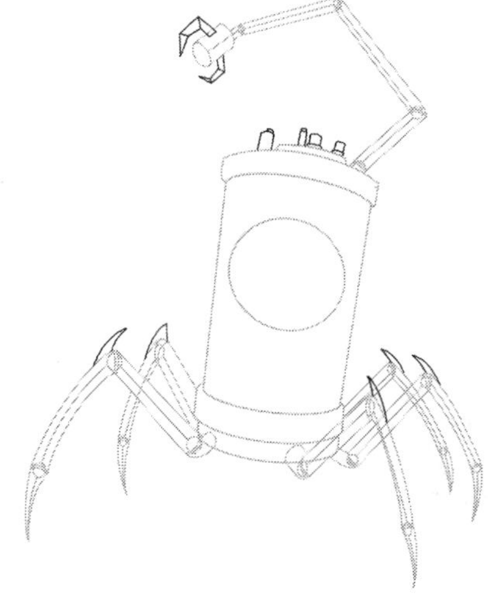

07

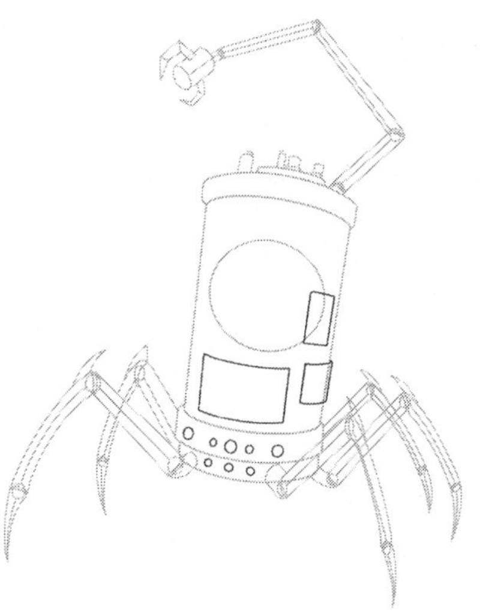

08

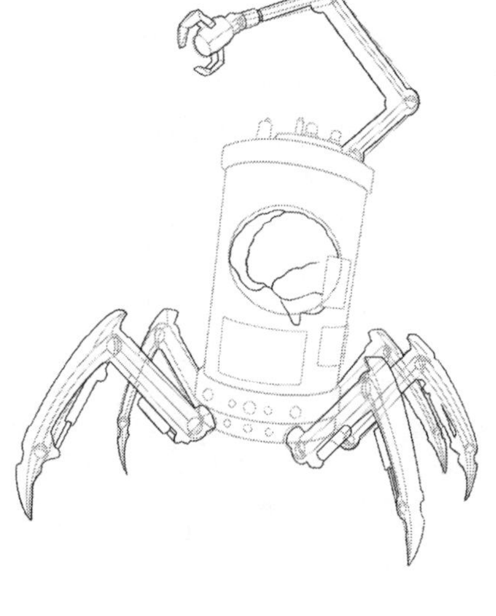

09

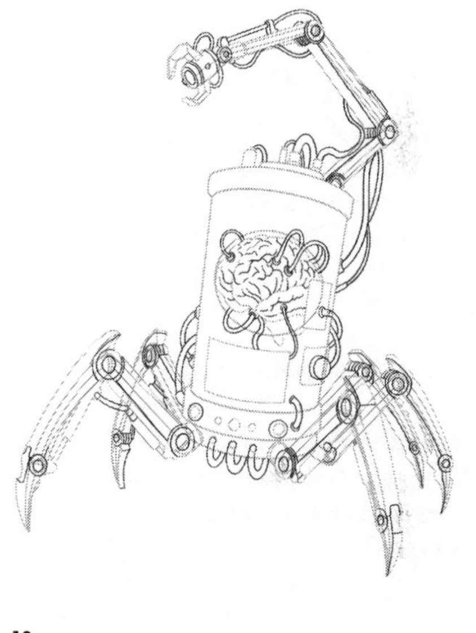

10

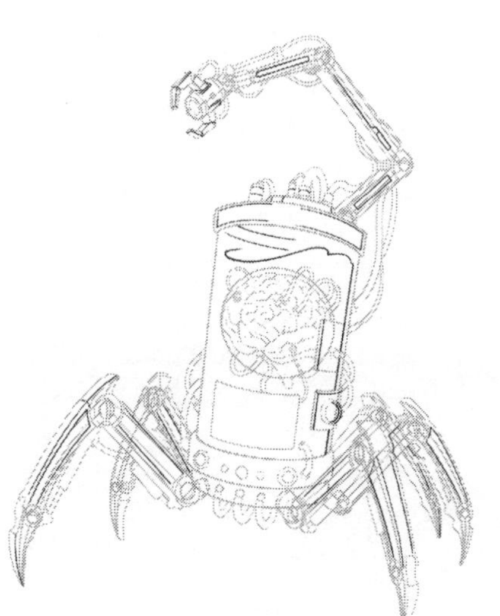

11

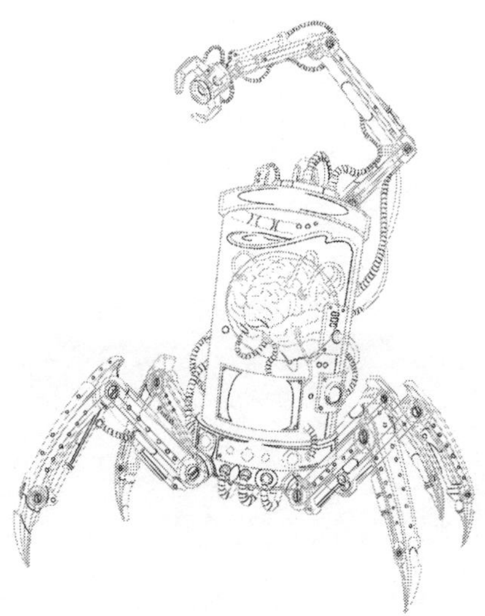

12

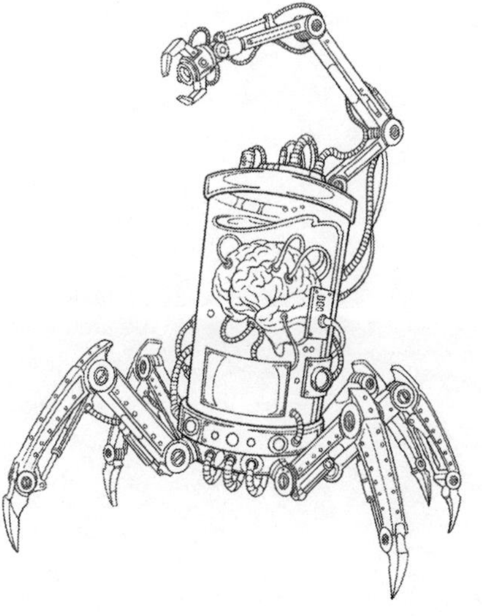

HORROR

ZOMBIE

Pro Tip: A zombie's shambling posture starts with a hunched spine and uneven weight distribution. No two limbs should look equally functional. Layer ragged, irregular edges over the clothing and skin to convey decay.

01

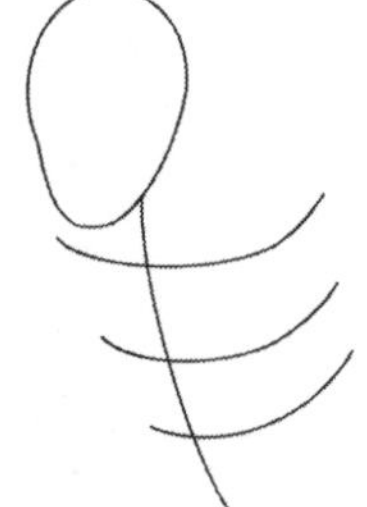

02

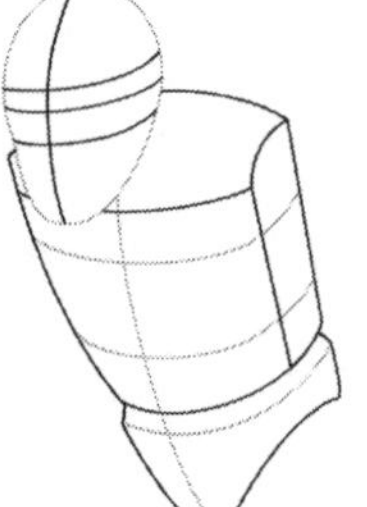

03

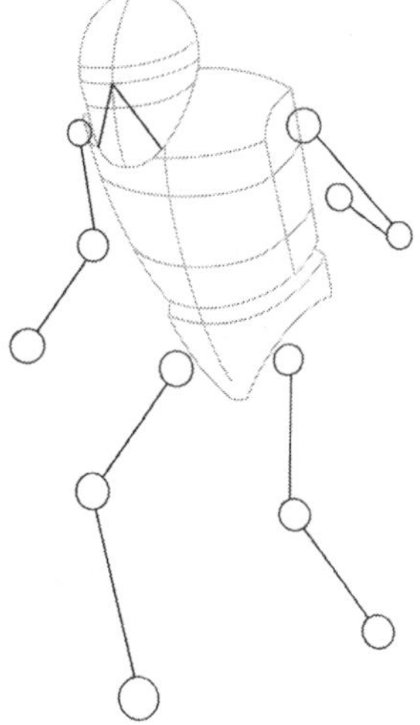

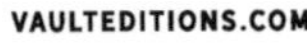

04

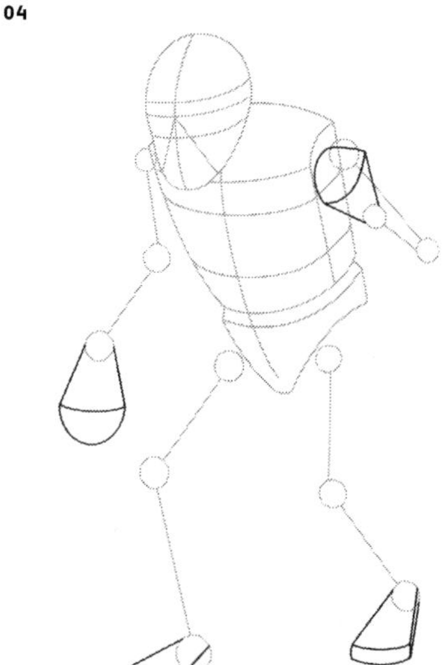

05

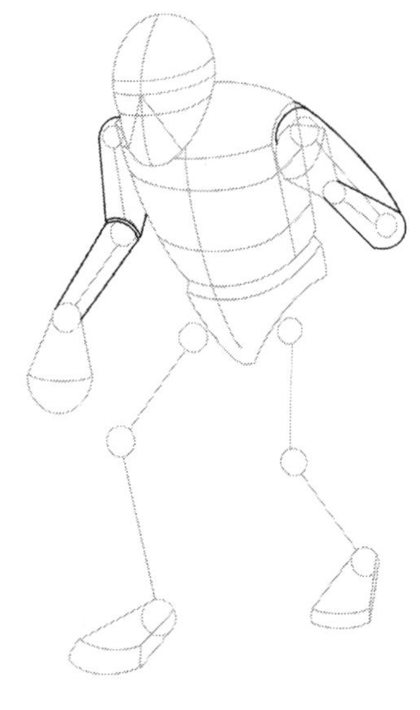

06

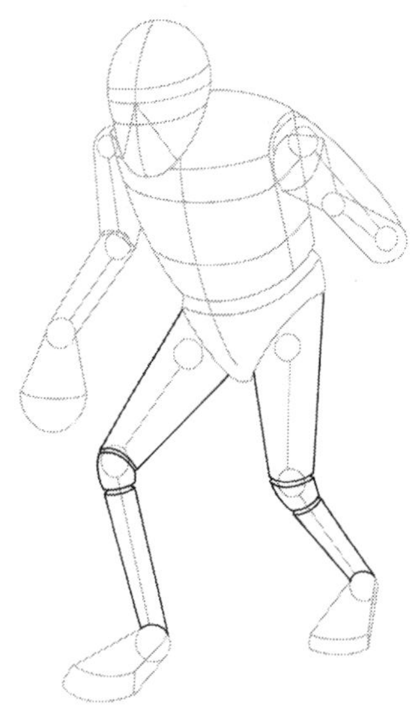

07

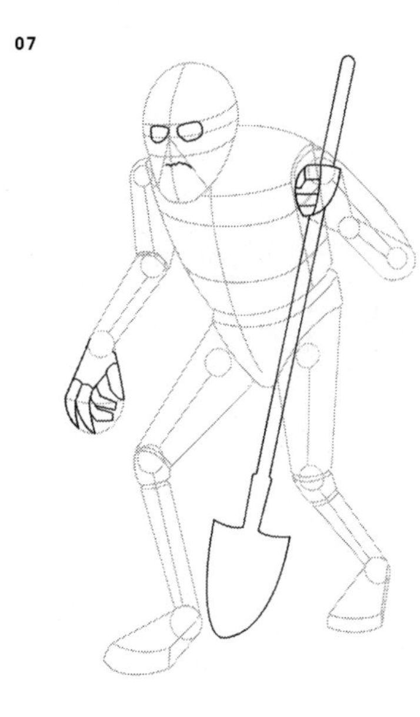

08

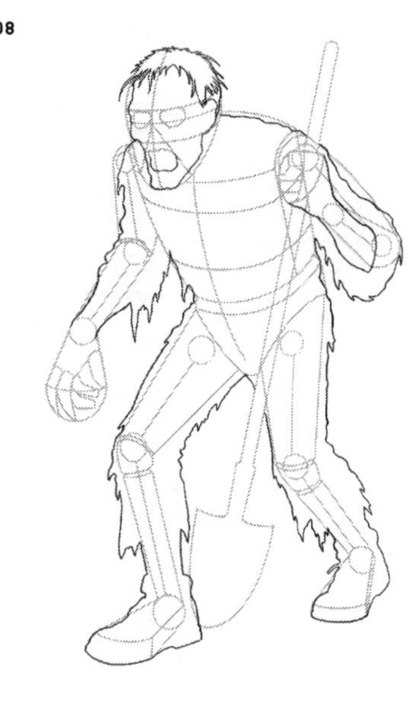

09

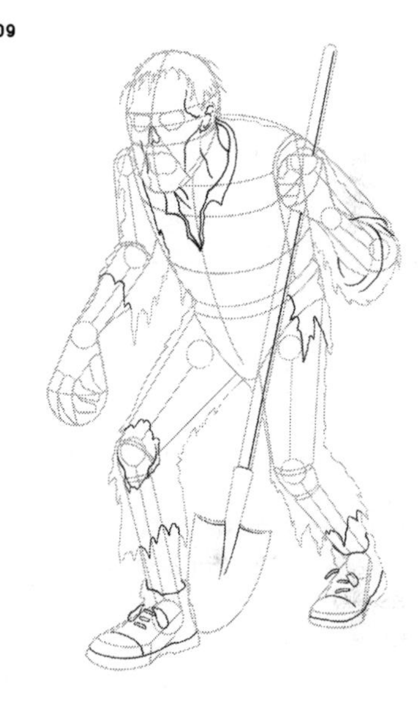

10

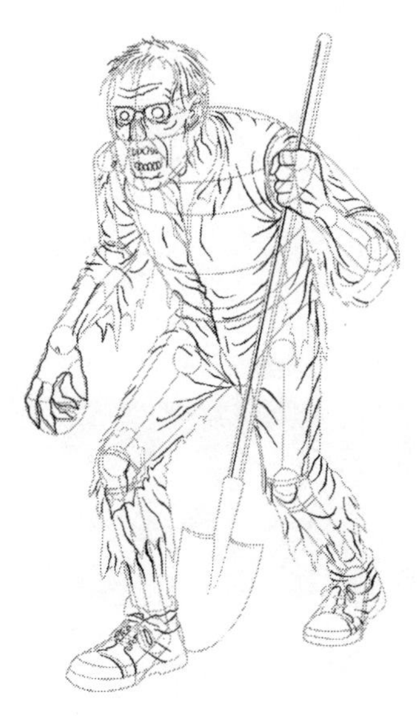

11

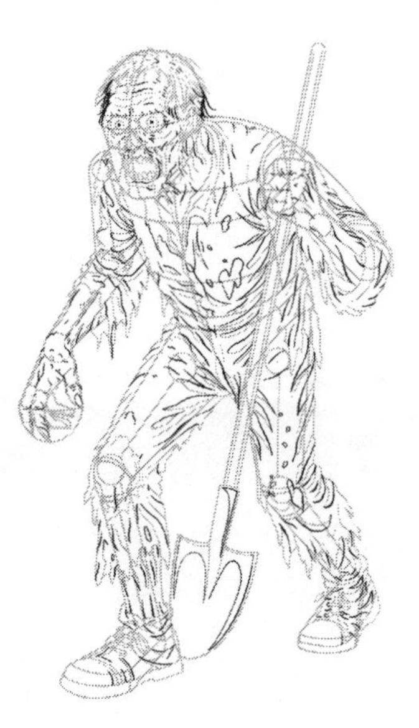

12

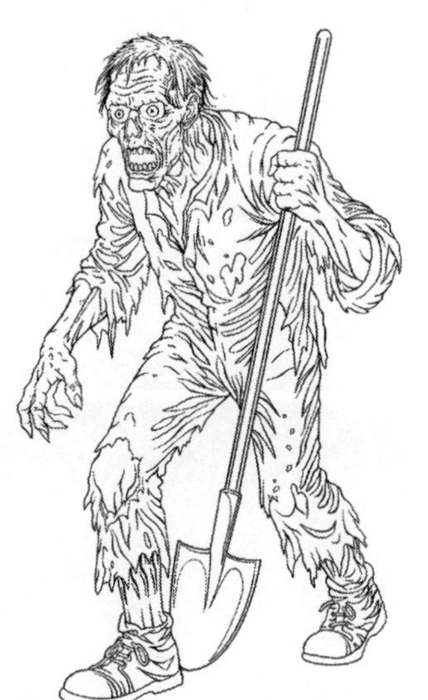

HORROR

SWAMP MONSTER

Pro Tip: Aim for a shoulder width of around three head-widths, then layer branches, roots and foliage outward to roughly double the arm width. Vary the texture between smooth bark-like surfaces and ragged, dripping edges to convey a living, overgrown mass.

01

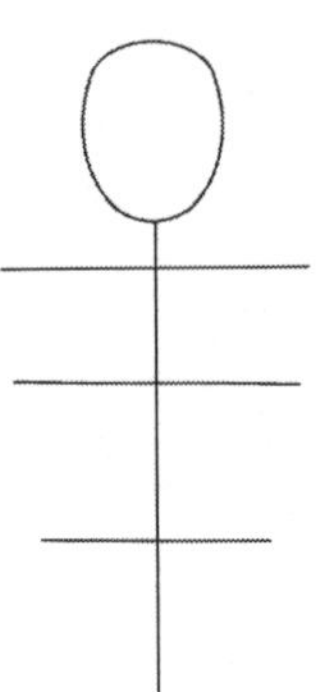

02

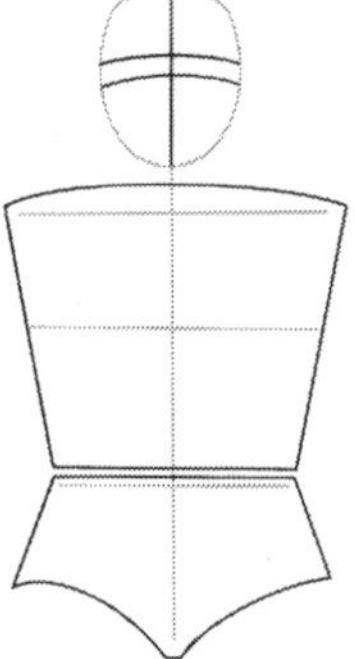

03

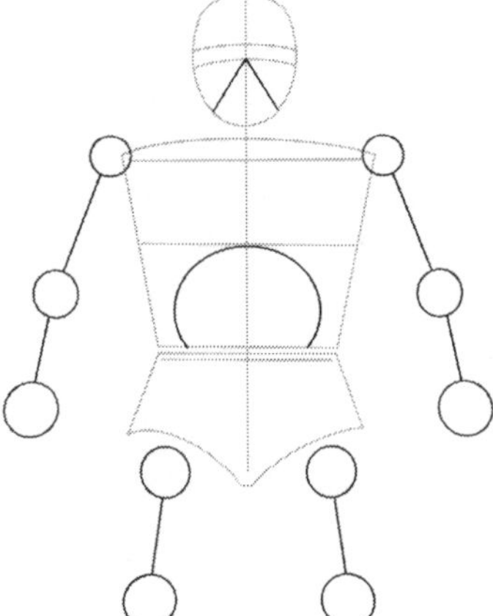

04

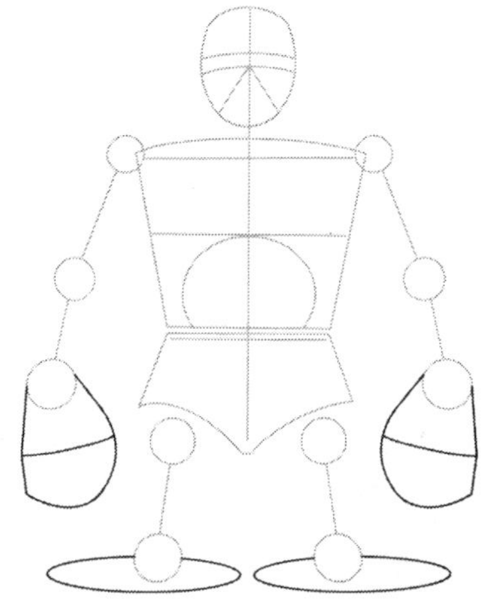

05

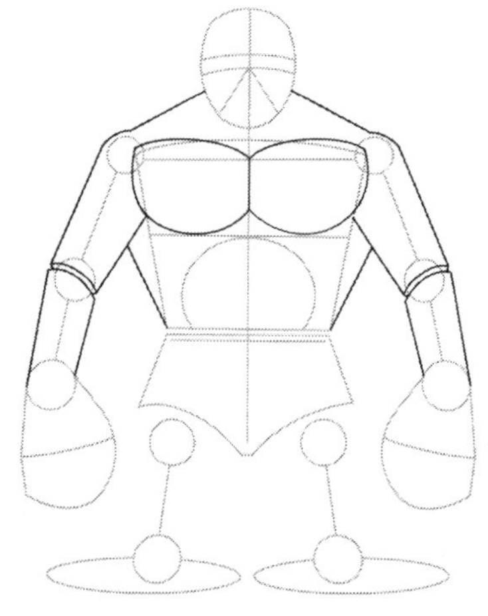

06

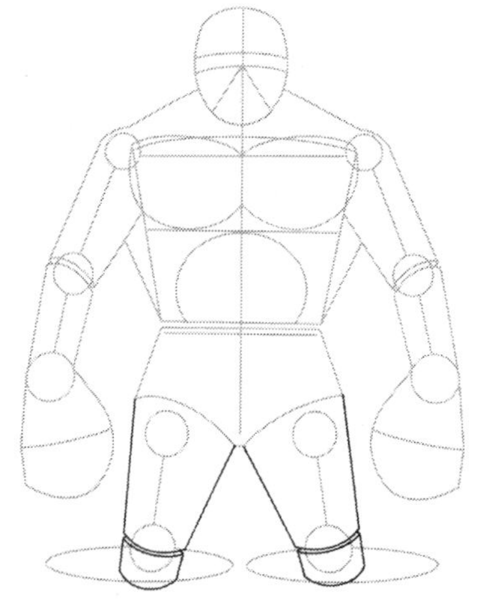

07

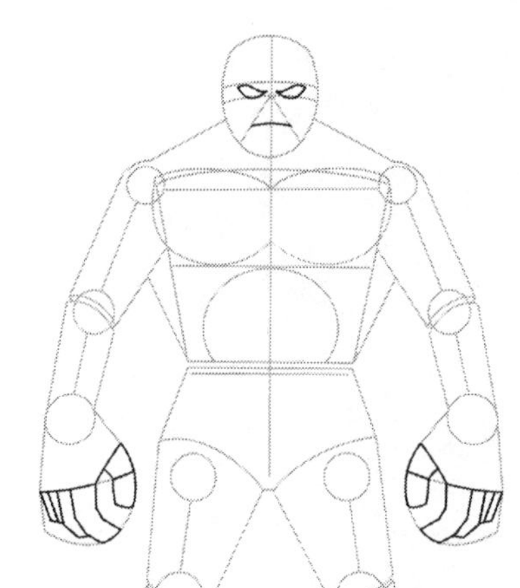

08

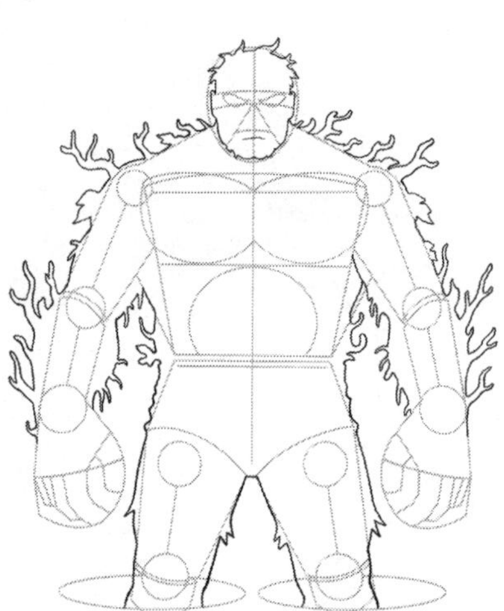

09

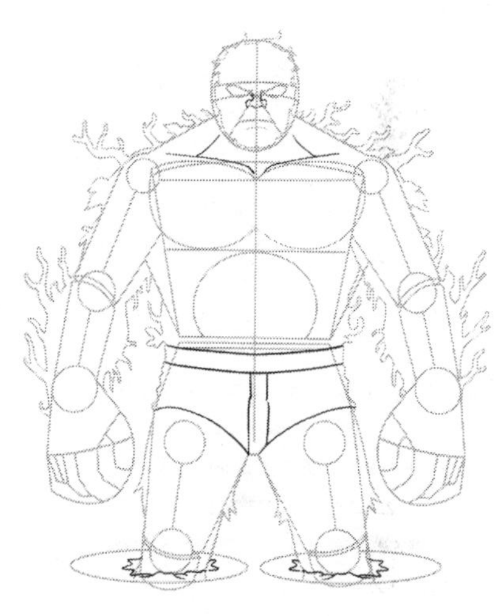

10

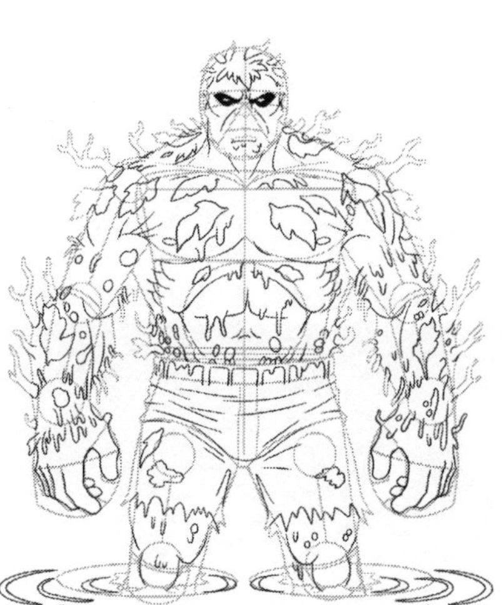

11

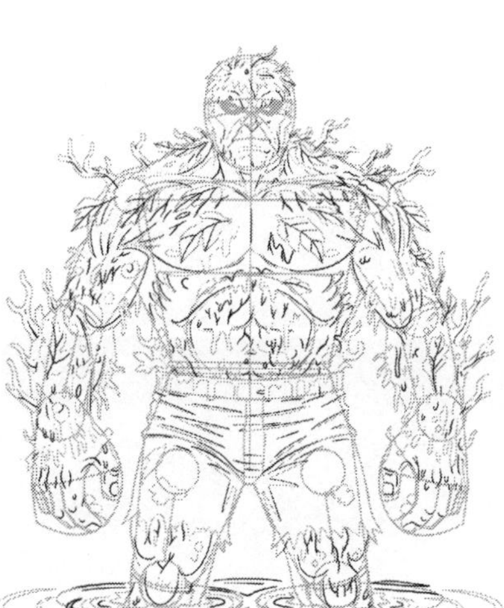

12

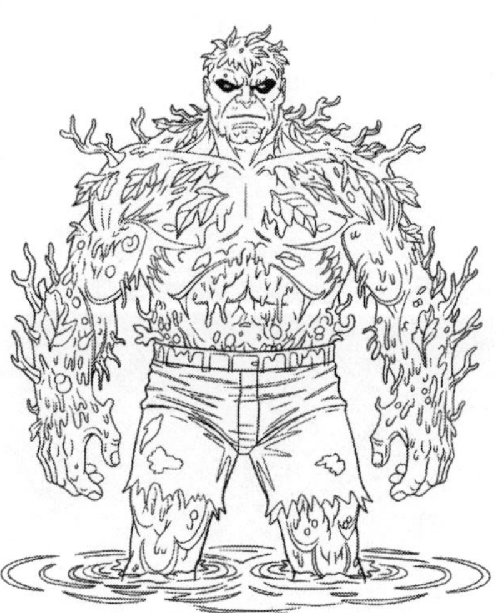

HORROR

THE UNDEAD KNIGHT

Pro Tip: Aim for a tall, imposing figure of around eight heads tall with a rigid, upright stance. The sword should measure roughly the same length as the legs to convey a sense of brutal, oversized weaponry.

01

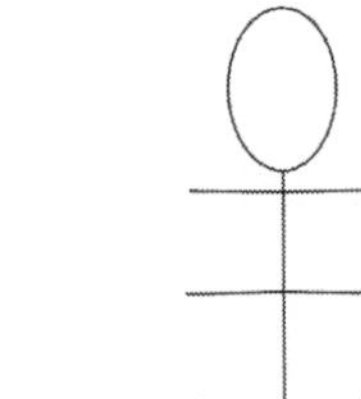

02

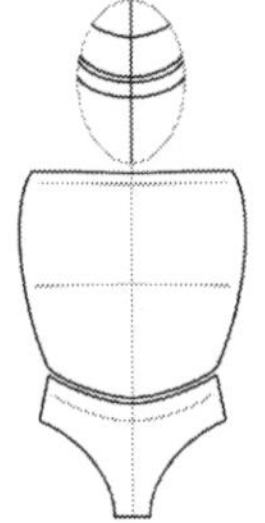

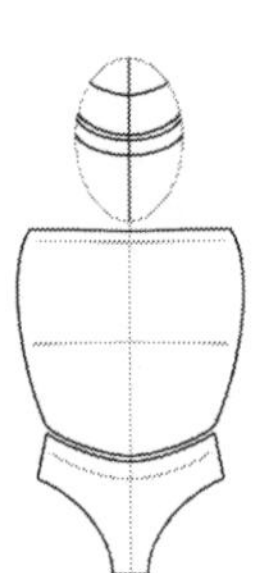

03

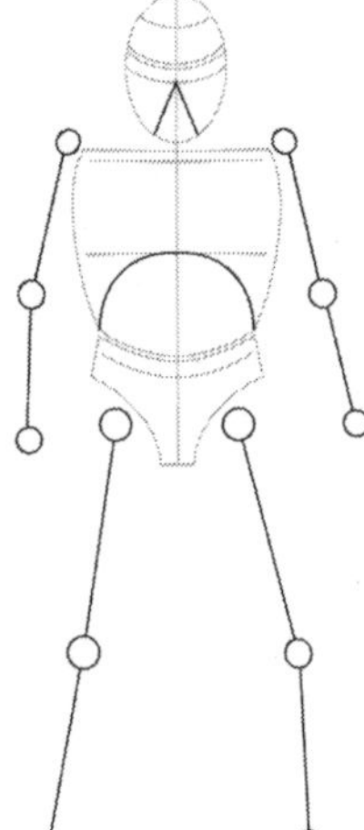

04

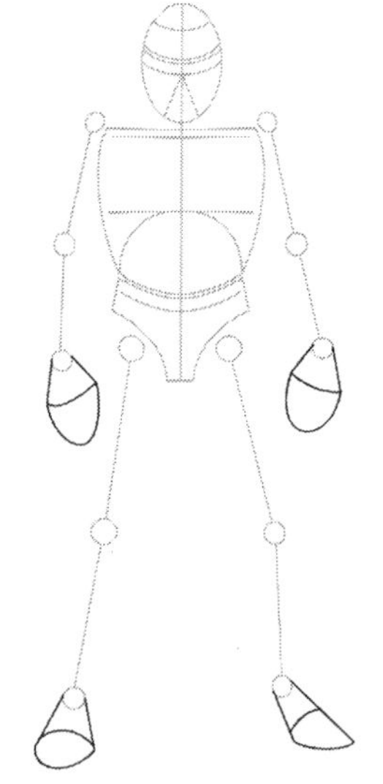

05

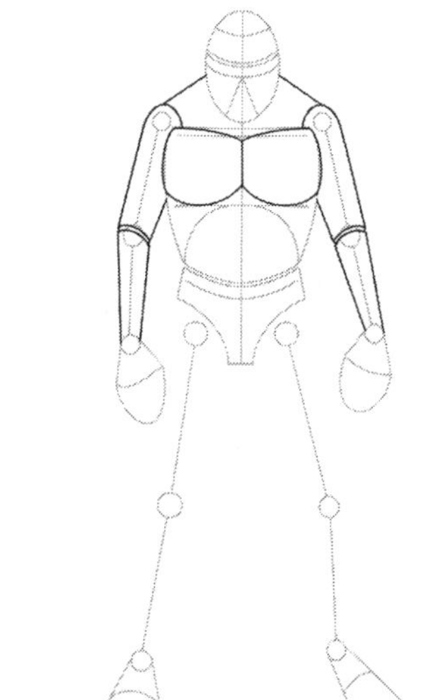

06

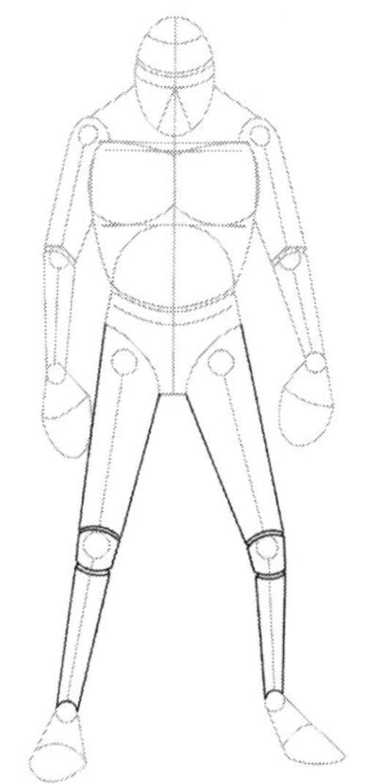

07

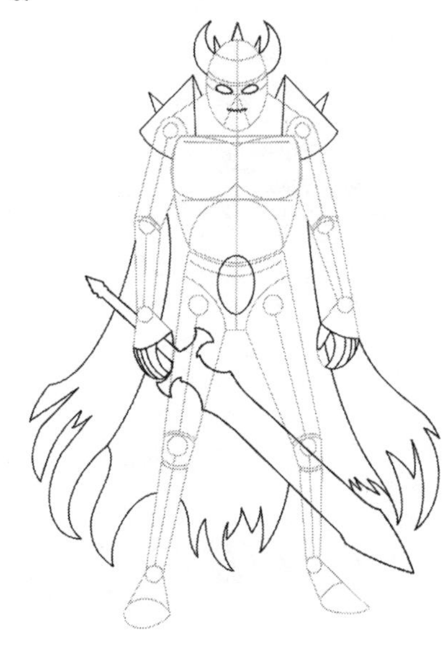

08

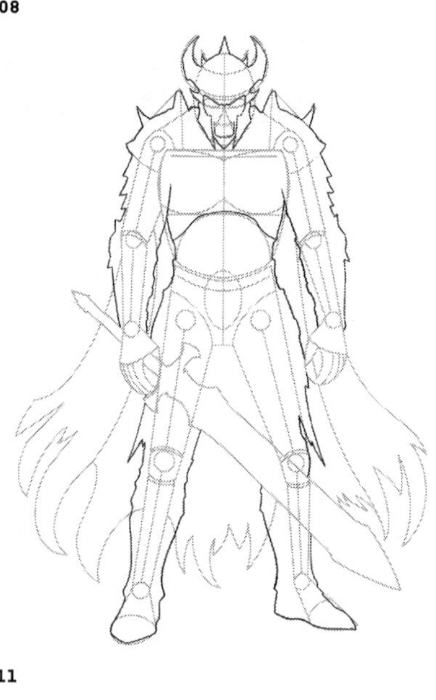

09

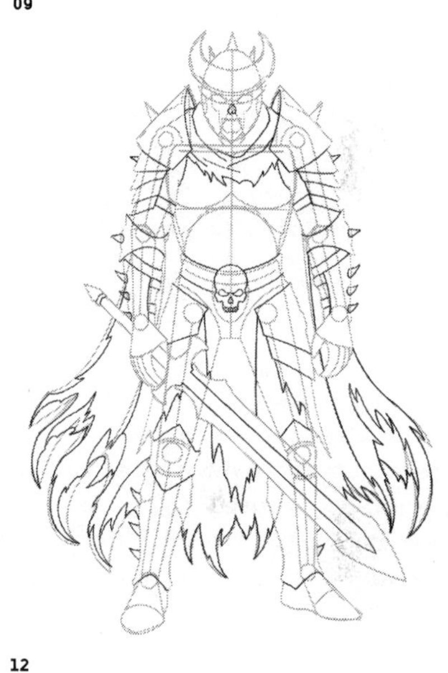

10

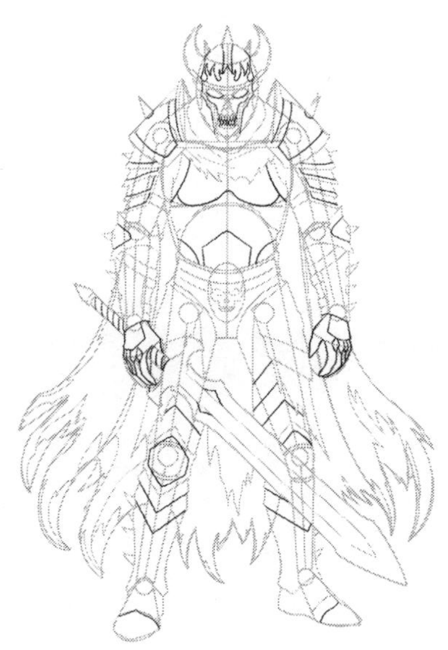

11

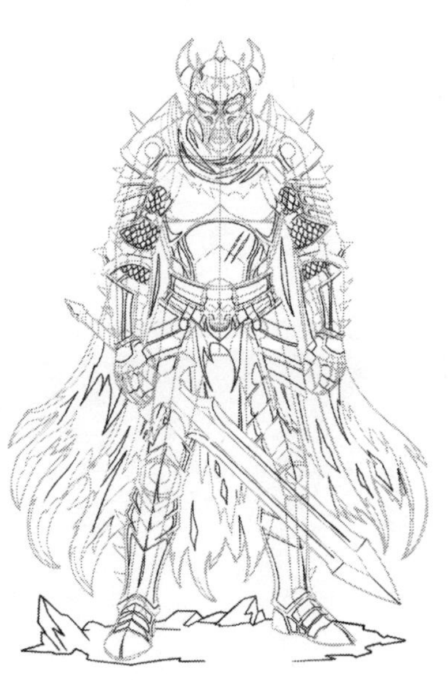

12

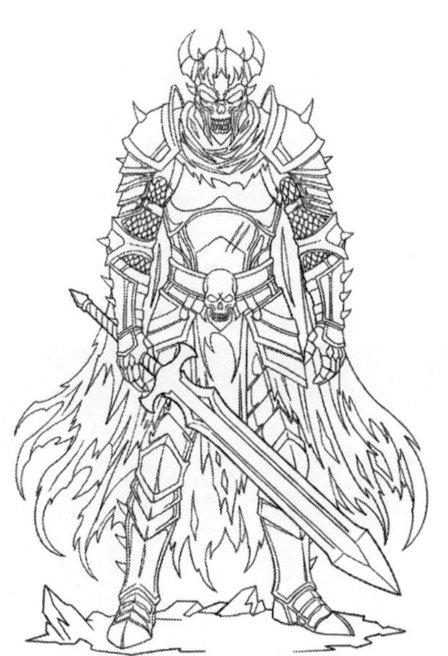

HORROR

WEREWOLF

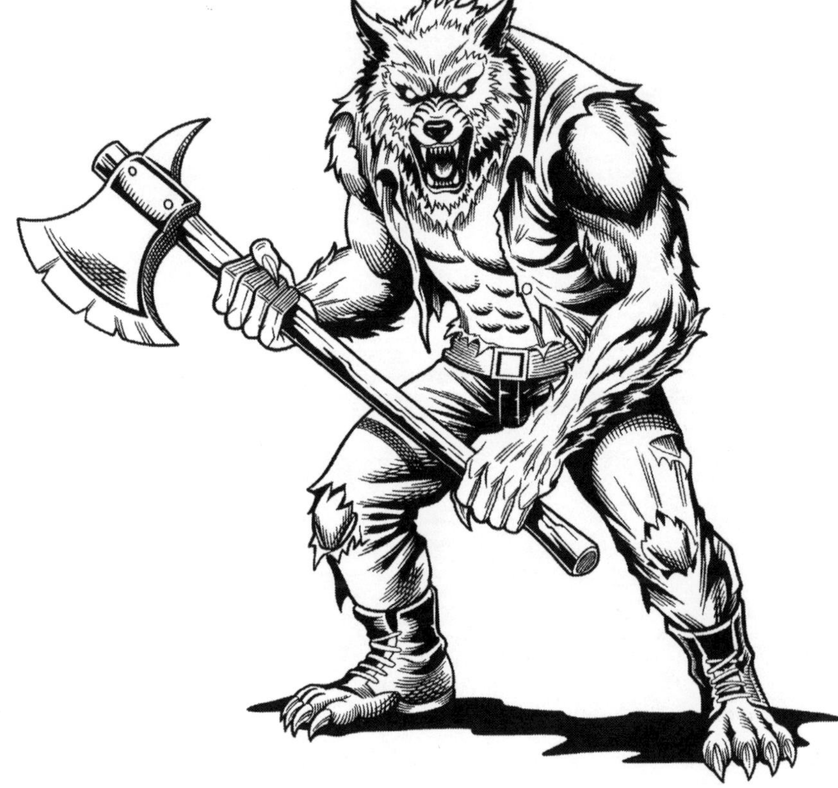

Pro Tip: A werewolf sits between human and beast — aim for around seven heads tall but with a hunched spine that reduces the standing height. The axe head should be roughly the same width as the shoulders to convey savage, oversized strength.

01

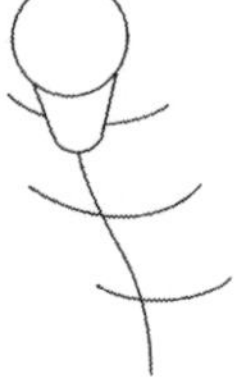

02

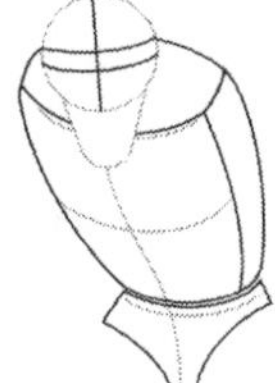

03

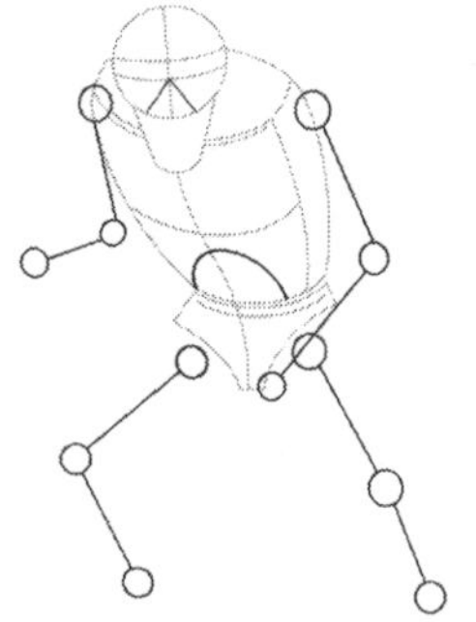

04

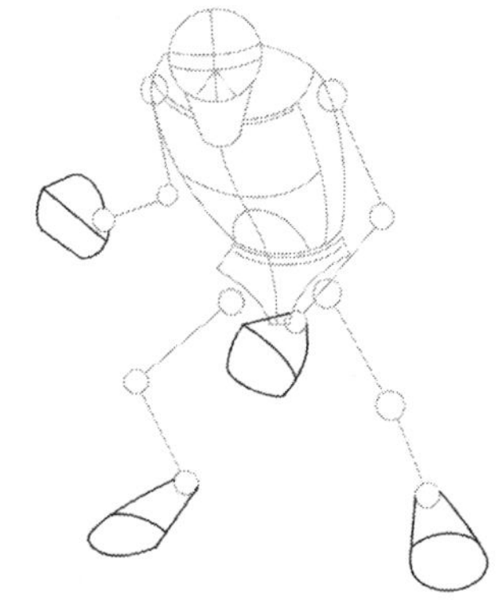

05

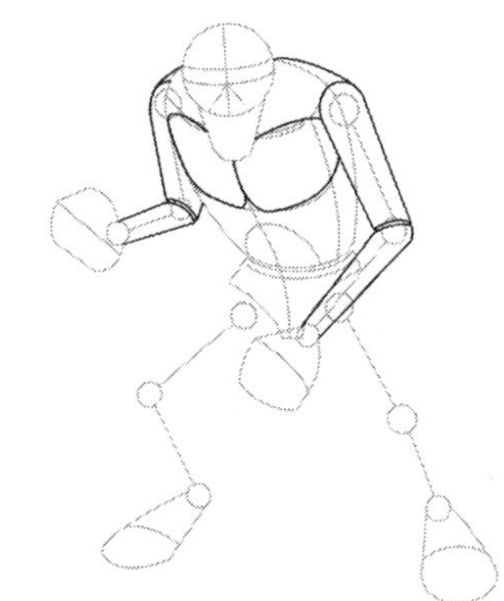

06

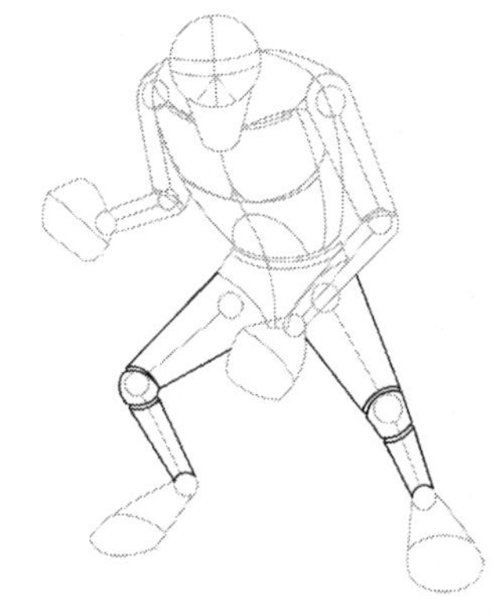

07

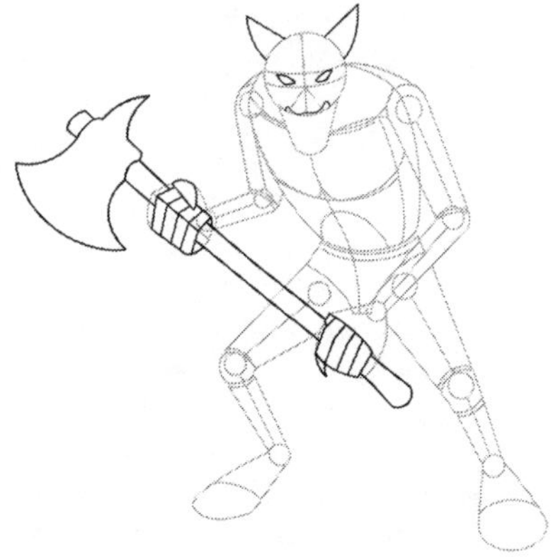

08

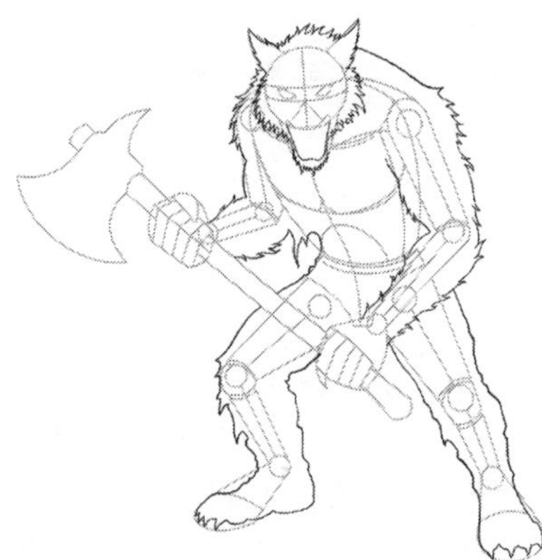

09

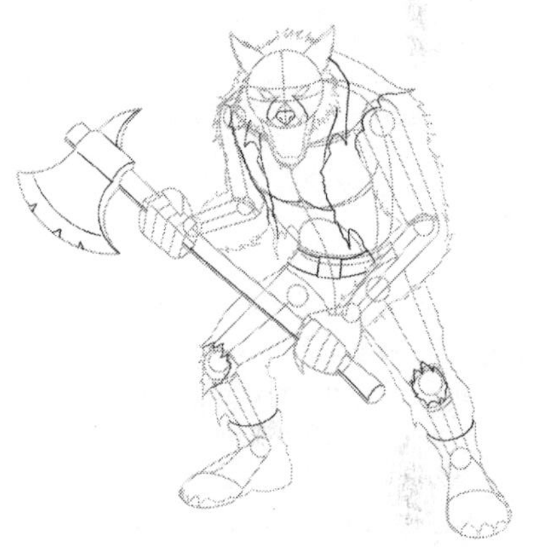

10

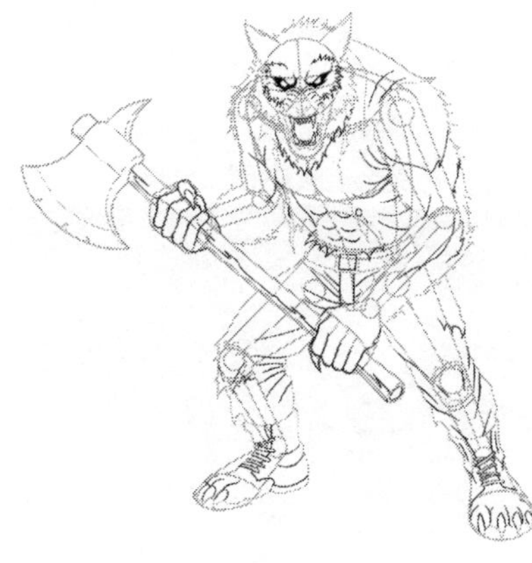

11

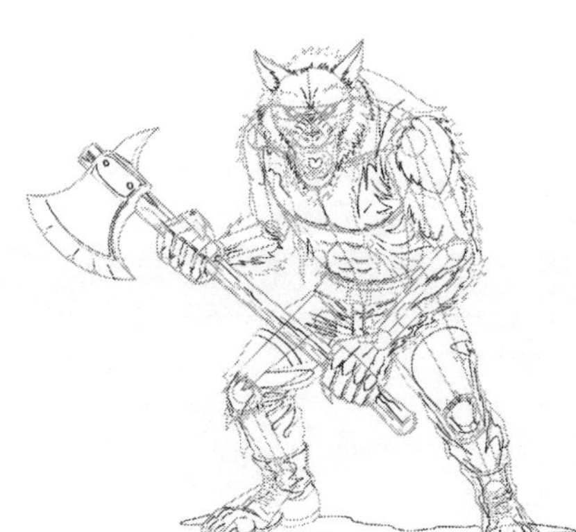

12

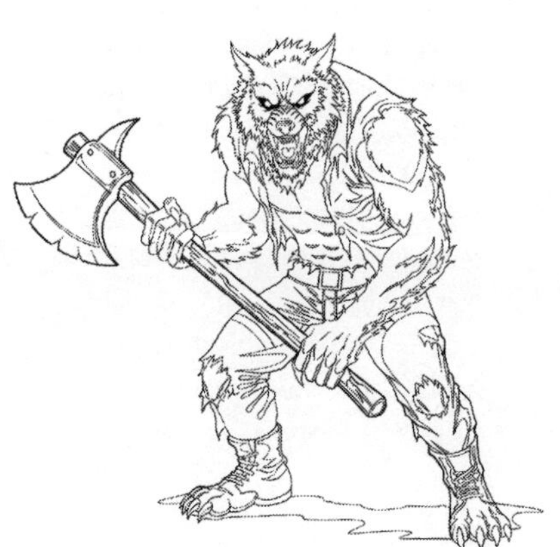

SPEECH BUBBLES

Speech bubbles are essential for guiding dialogue clearly and naturally through your comic. They show who is speaking, control the rhythm of the conversation and help lead the reader's eye through each panel. Keep your bubbles simple, with enough space around the text to stay readable, and place them so they follow the natural flow of the scene without covering important artwork. Tail the bubble toward the speaker's mouth and group bubbles in the order they should be read. Effective speech bubbles support the storytelling without drawing attention away from the action.

HOW TO DRAW VARIOUS PERSPECTIVES

One Point Perspective:
Start by drawing a horizon line across your page, then place a single vanishing point on it. Draw the front face of any object as a simple square or rectangle, and from each of its corners, lightly draw receding lines back to the vanishing point. Decide the depth of the object and add a parallel back edge between those receding lines. Use the same vanishing point for every object in the scene so they all share the same sense of depth, then tidy your construction lines and refine the final drawing.

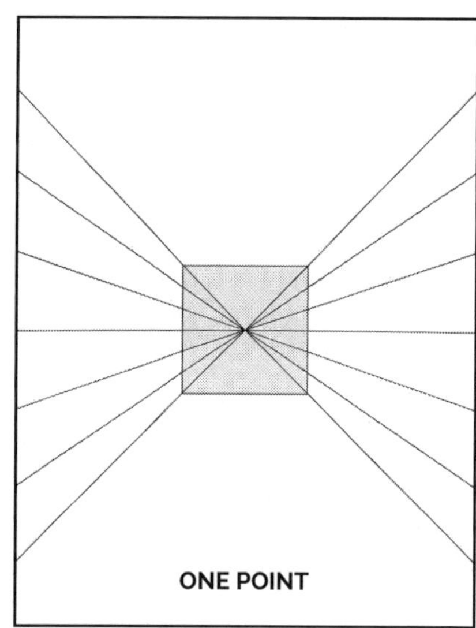

Two Point Perspective:
Draw a horizon line across your page and place two vanishing points at either end. Start by drawing the vertical edge of your object between them, then connect the top and bottom of this line to both vanishing points to form the receding sides. Decide the width of each side by adding two vertical lines between the receding edges. Every horizontal edge must angle back to one of the vanishing points, while all vertical edges stay straight and upright. Use the same two vanishing points for every object in the scene so everything shares the same sense of depth, then clean up your guidelines and refine the final drawing.

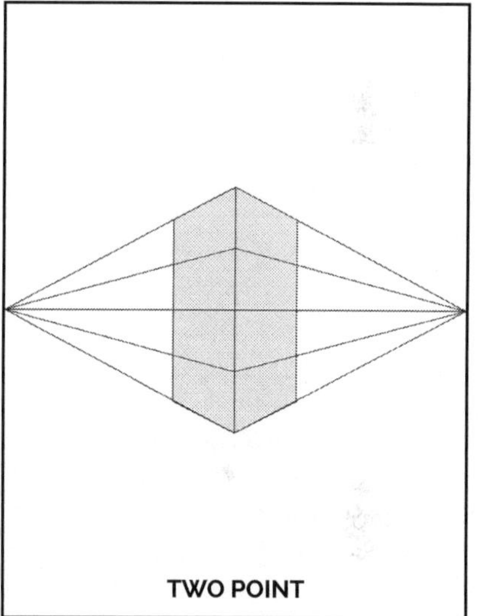

Three Point Perspective:
Draw a horizon line and place two vanishing points along it, then add a third vanishing point either high above or far below your object. Begin with a single vertical edge, but instead of keeping it straight, angle its top and bottom toward the top and bottom vanishing points. Connect the ends of this edge to the two vanishing points on the horizon to build the receding sides. All vertical edges now converge toward the third vanishing point, while all horizontal edges angle back to the left or right vanishing points. Use these same three points for every object so the entire scene shares the same dramatic sense of depth.

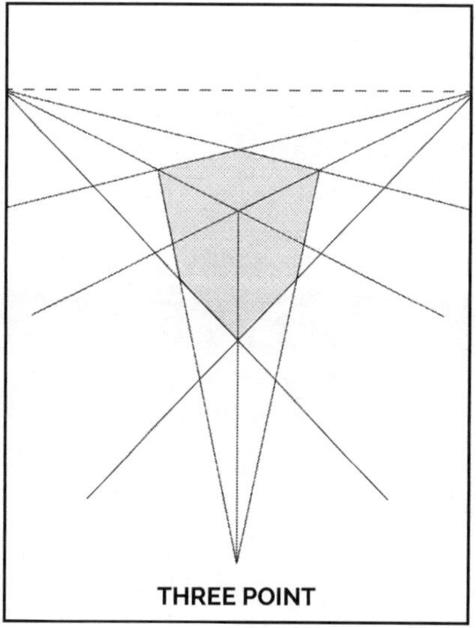

Pro Tip: Learning perspective is essential for creating believable spaces in your comics and gives your storytelling a stronger sense of scale, depth and drama. Mastering one, two and three point perspective allows you to place characters convincingly within rooms, streets, rooftops and entire cityscapes. It helps you control the viewer's eye, build tension and make action scenes feel grounded and dynamic. You'll use perspective constantly in backgrounds, interiors, alleyways, school corridors, urban skylines and dramatic low or high-angle shots. Even simple scenes become richer when the environment is drawn with accurate perspective, giving your world weight and making every moment feel more immersive.

COMIC PANELS

Comic panels are the building blocks of your page and control how your story unfolds. Start with simple rectangles, then vary their size, shape and placement to influence pacing and focus. Larger panels create breathing room for key moments, while smaller or angled panels add energy and urgency. Keep gutters consistent so the page feels intentional, and use changes in panel layout to guide the reader's eye smoothly from one moment to the next. Experiment with compositions, but always design panels in service of clarity and storytelling.

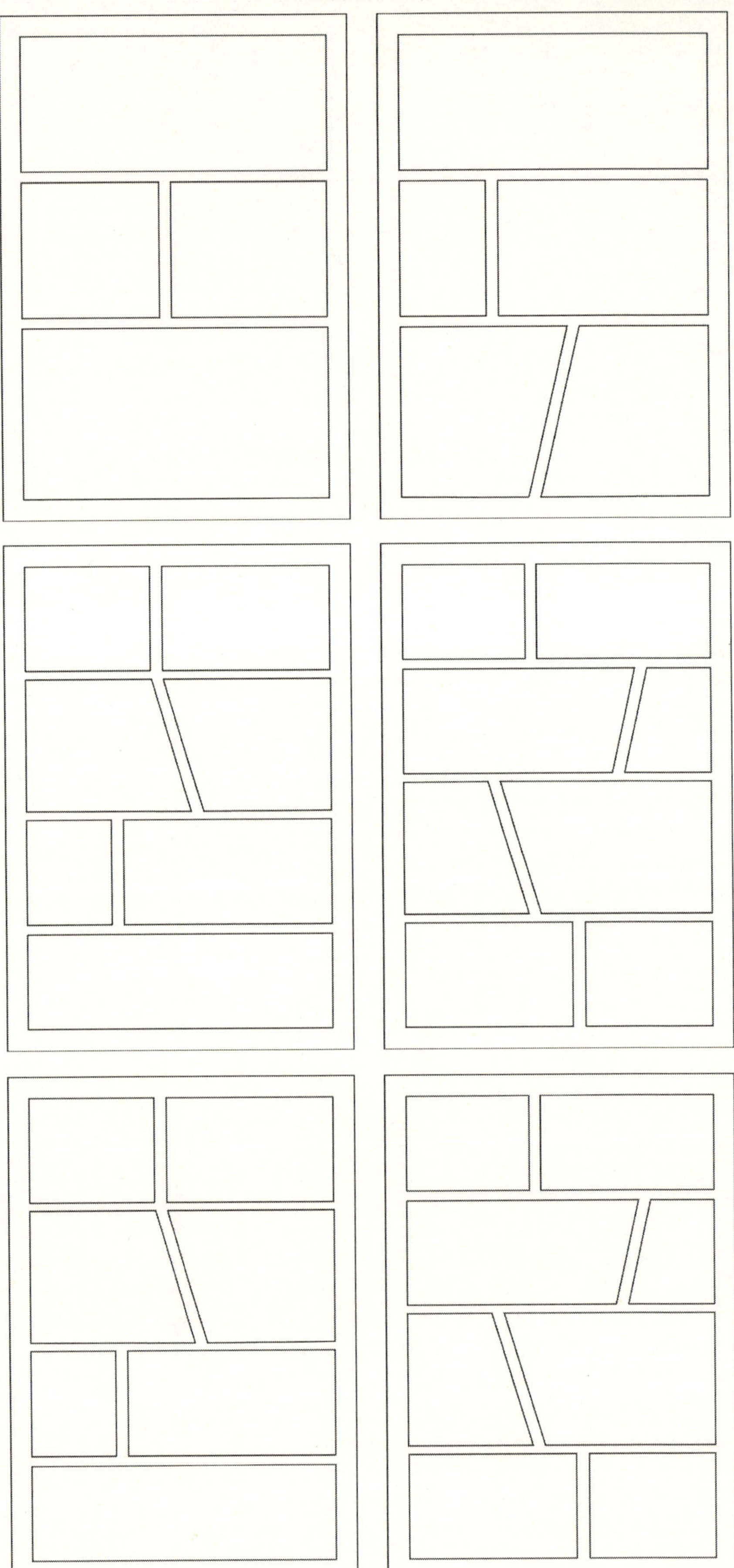

BREAKING THE FRAME

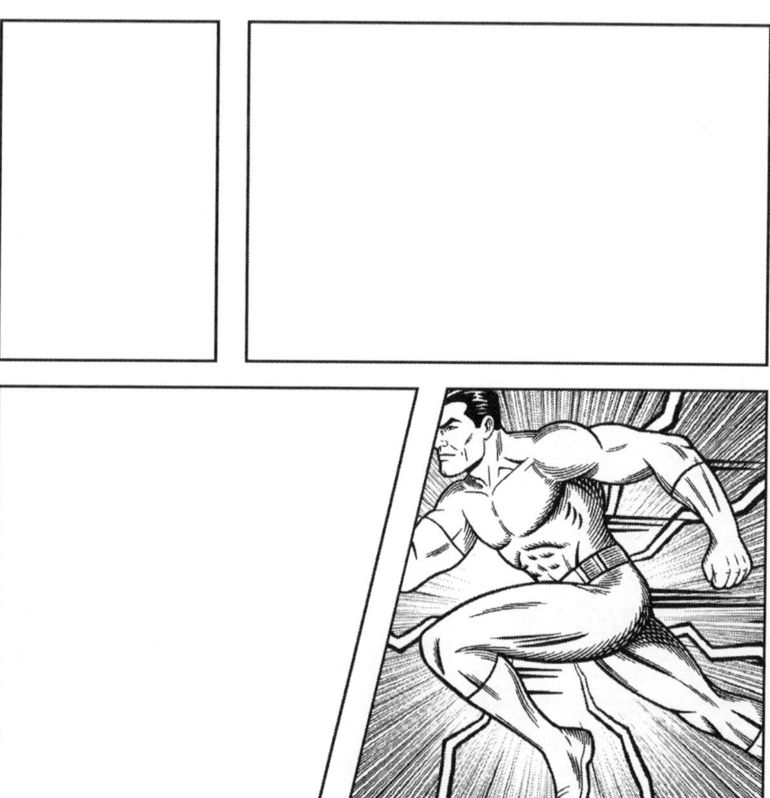

Trompe-l'œil, meaning "to deceive the eye," is an artistic technique that creates the illusion of three-dimensional elements emerging from a flat surface. In comics, you can use this effect by allowing parts of a character or object to break through or overlap the panel borders. A fist punching past the edge, a foot stepping out of the frame, or hair sweeping beyond the border instantly adds depth and motion. These controlled breaks make the scene feel more alive and draw the reader's attention to key actions. Used thoughtfully, trompe-l'œil effects create dynamic moments that feel immediate and cinematic while still keeping the overall page design clear and readable.

In the example at the bottom of the page, the character's head and hand appear to push past the panel edge, creating the illusion that he is bursting forward into the reader's space. By letting him break through the frame, the moment feels more immediate and energetic.

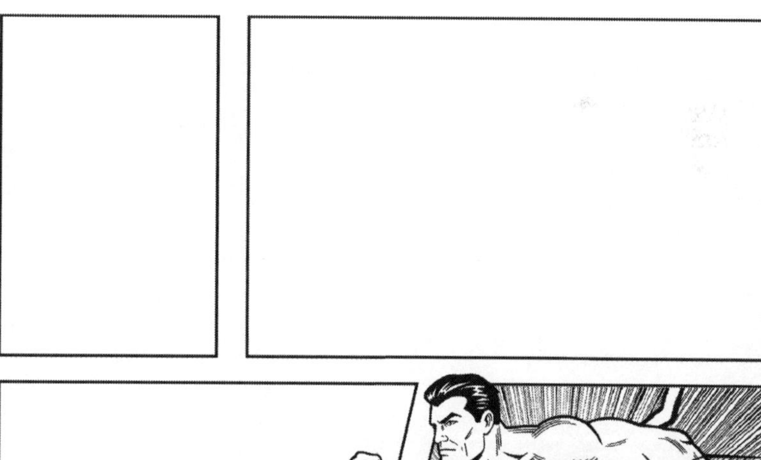

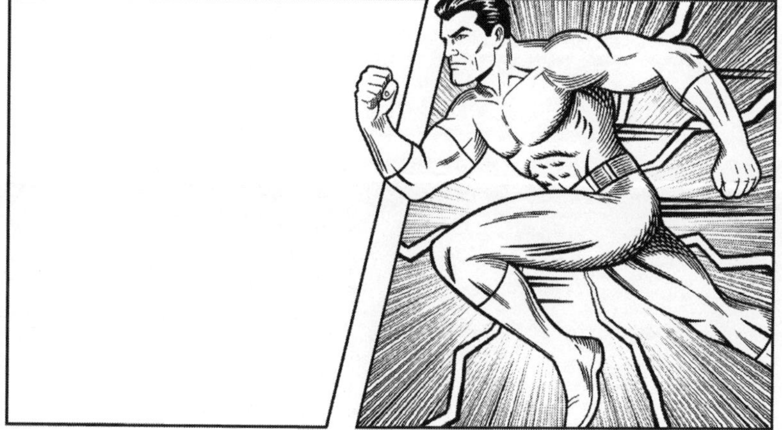

CONCLUSION

The hardest part of any creative journey isn't mastering the technique — it's beginning. And you've already done that.

Think about where you started. The proportions that confused you, the poses that felt stiff, the designs that didn't quite match what you saw in your head. Now think about where you are. You understand the figure. You can build a pose with energy and purpose. You can take a single idea and shape it into a character that feels alive on the page.

That didn't happen by accident. It happened because you put in the work. Every page you fill is a conversation with your own developing instincts. The gap between what you can imagine and what you can draw narrows every single time you pick up a pencil. So keep going. Draw every day. Push your characters further than feels comfortable. Make mistakes and learn from them without apology.

Your best work isn't behind you. It's in every drawing you haven't made yet.

Now go make them.

ABOUT THE ARTIST

Alfi Suvi, known professionally as Neizear Art, is an illustrator and character designer whose practice was forged in the heart of the metal music scene. This immersive foundation drew him toward the darker edges of visual art, shaping a distinctive aesthetic rooted in intensity, atmosphere, and raw expression.

With 13 years of experience, Alfi has built an extensive and impressive body of work spanning band merchandise, album covers, collaborations with clothing brands, and original character design — earning him a reputation as a trusted creative voice in underground and alternative culture.

Across both his illustration and character work, a deep commitment to experimentation sits at the core of his practice. Rather than following a fixed method, Alfi approaches each piece as an open exploration — believing that the willingness to try, reconsider, and evolve is what separates good art from truly powerful art. This philosophy carries through every mark he makes, from a single deliberate point to an expressive, commanding line.

LEARN MORE

At Vault Editions, our mission is to provide the highest-quality reference materials for artists and designers, offering meticulously curated resources that inspire and empower creativity. If you've found value in this book, we invite you to explore more of our expertly crafted titles at vaulteditions.com, where you'll discover a world of visual inspiration and practical tools designed to elevate your creative work.

REVIEW THIS BOOK

As a family-owned and operated independent publisher, reviews are essential to the success of our business. Please leave an honest review of this book wherever you purchased it.

JOIN OUR COMMUNITY

Are you the creative and curious type? If so, you will love our community on Instagram. Every day, we share bizarre and beautiful artwork ranging from 17th and 18th-century natural history and scientific illustrations to mythical beasts, ornamental designs, anatomical drawings and more; join our community of 300K+ people today by searching @vault_editions on Instagram.

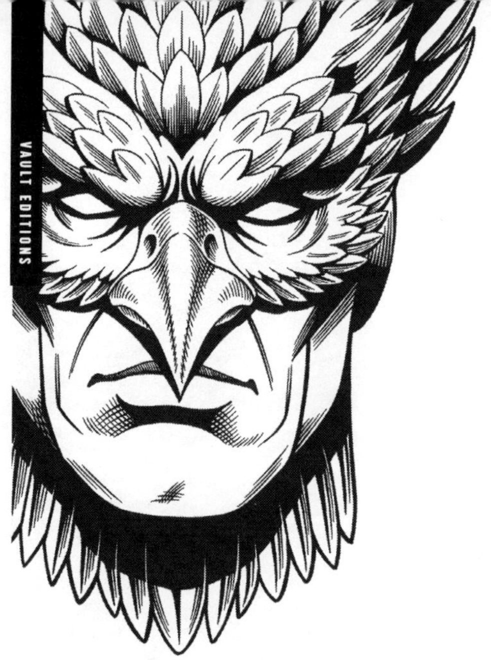

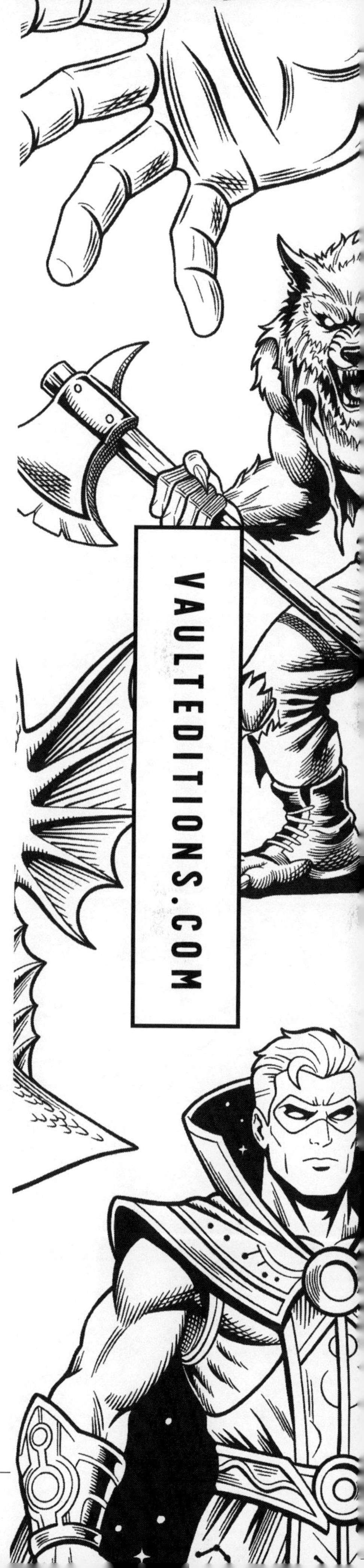

DOWNLOAD YOUR FILES

To enhance your comic drawing journey, this book comes with a digital PDF version of the book and a specially designed set of Procreate brushes. These resources are tailored to help you refine your skills and streamline your workflow, whether working traditionally or digitally.

The digital PDF provides easy access to the book's contents on any device, so you can reference the designs anytime, anywhere. It's perfect for artists on the go, allowing you to study and practice whenever inspiration strikes.

The custom Procreate brushes are designed to support the comic drawing process by helping you improve your draftsmanship and build stronger technical skills. They offer precision and flexibility as you sketch, refine, and finalise your artwork, making it easier to develop clean, confident lines and consistent forms.

Download yours now and get creating!

STEP ONE

Enter the following web address on a desktop or laptop computer in your web browser.

vaulteditions.com/pages/cas

STEP TWO

Enter the following password to access the download page:

cas736262sxda

STEP THREE

Follow the prompts to access your high-resolution files.

CONTACT

For technical support, please email: info@vaulteditions.com

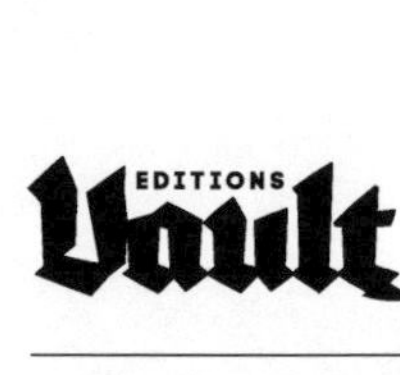

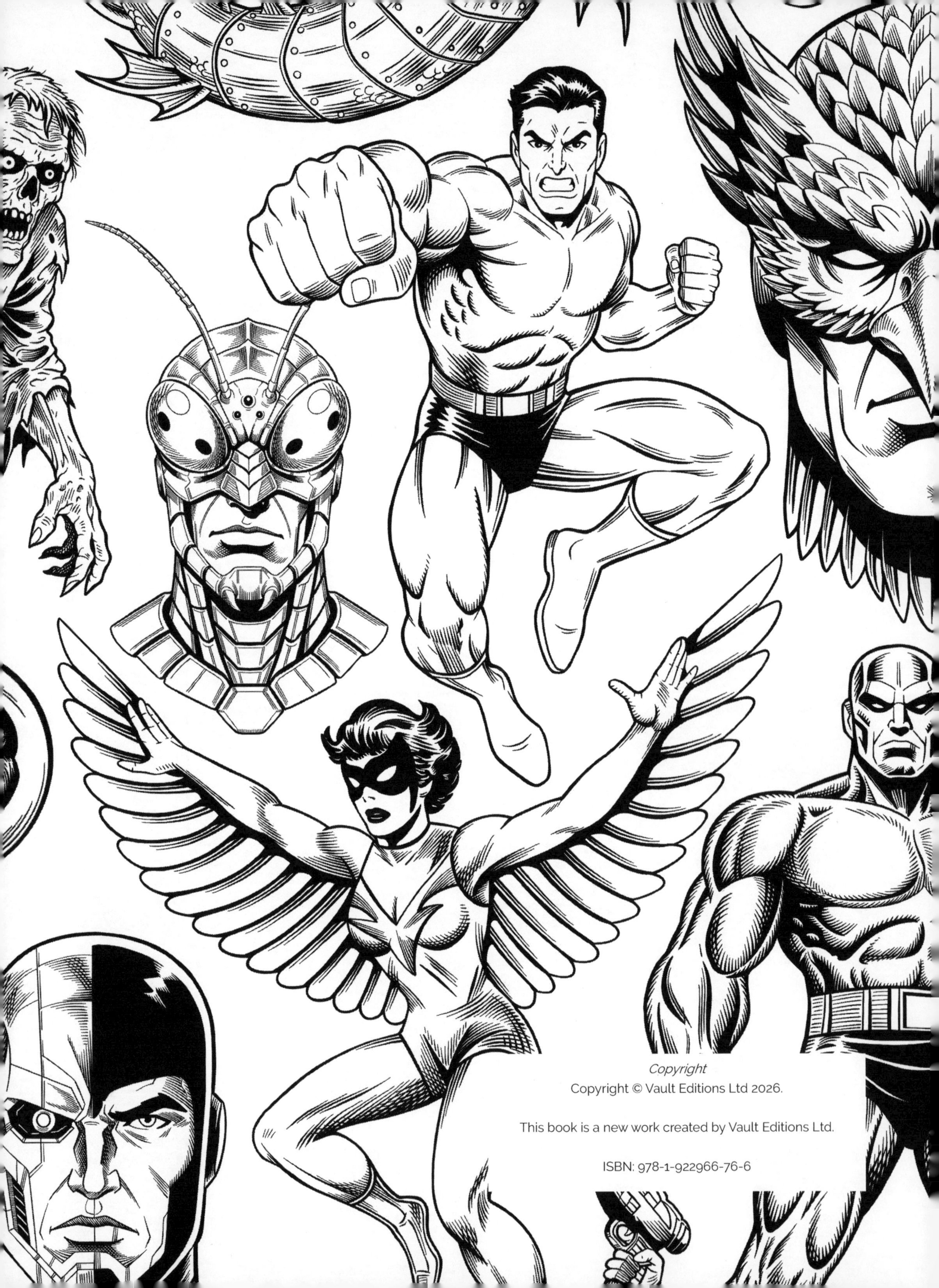

This book is a new work created by Vault Editions Ltd.

ISBN: 978-1-922966-76-6

Made in the USA
Monee, IL
07 July 2026

56662782R00076